The Philosophy and Economics
of Market Socialism

The Philosophy and Economics of Market Socialism

A Critical Study

N. SCOTT ARNOLD

New York   Oxford
OXFORD UNIVERSITY PRESS
1994

Oxford University Press

Oxford   New York   Toronto
Delhi   Bombay   Calcutta   Madras   Karachi
Petaling Jaya   Singapore   Hong Kong   Tokyo
Nairobi   Dar es Salaam   Cape Town
Melbourne   Auckland   Madrid

and associated companies in
Berlin   Ibadan

Copyright (c) 1994 by N. Scott Arnold

Published by Oxford University Press, Inc.,
200 Madison Avenue, New York, NY 10016

Oxford is a registered trademark of Oxford University Press

Library of Congress Cataloging-in-Publication Data
Arnold, N. Scott,
The philosophy and economics of market socialism : a critical study / N. Scott Arnold.
p.   cm.
Includes bibliographical references and index.
ISBN 0-19-508827-1
1. Mixed economy.   2. Marxian economics.   3. Socialism.   I. Title.
HB90.A77   1994
335—dc20   93-31714

2 4 6 8 9 7 5 3 1

Printed in the United States of America
on acid free paper

For Harrison and Andrew

Preface

There have been critics of capitalist society since its rise in the early nine-teenth century. Socialist critics locate its ills in the economic system, specifi-cally, in the system of private property rights in the means of production. In addition, socialists characteristically believe that a fundamental, that is, radi-cal, change in the economic system is at least a necessary condition for cur-ing these ills. When it comes to specifying an alternative economic system, however, socialists have been much less united, and indeed, many have not had much to say at all. On the other side of the ideological spectrum, the cap-italist economic system has had its defenders from the outset. They believe that its problems have been misperceived, misdiagnosed, or real but amenable only to amelioration and thus not solvable by radical change in the economic system. They further believe that socialist economic systems are invariably disasters from both a moral and a practical point of view.

The debate between those who favor socialism and those who favor cap-italism constitutes the framework for this book. Chapter 1 articulates that framework by attempting to determine the exact nature of the dispute and the burdens of proof that each side bears. It turns out to be a twofold debate about values, goals, or ideals—what I call a vision of the good society—and an empirical dispute about the role of economic systems in achieving or frus-trating the realization of such a vision. There is, therefore, a philosophy com-ponent to this dispute, which consists of an articulation and defense of the relevant values and ideals. There is also an economics component, which con-cerns itself with the empirical consequences of capitalist and socialist eco-nomic systems.

My main purpose in this book is to make some substantial progress in this dispute, perhaps to the point of coming close to resolving it. I seek to estab-lish that the most plausible models of a socialist economic system would not, in fact, be able to achieve or realize a widely shared socialist vision of the good society. Identifying those models has proved to be a difficult task. With the collapse of central planning and in light of a renewed appreciation for the market both in the real world and in the realm of ideas, it seems that the most defensible form of socialism would be some form of market socialism. But which form? In attempting to answer this question, I found myself hampered by the dearth of discussion among socialists about the system of property rights in the means of production that they favor. For obvious reasons, few want to defend full state ownership and control, and although many have spoken favorably of worker cooperatives, it has been difficult to get a clear picture of how ownership of these cooperatives and the capital they employ is to be understood.

I have dealt with this difficulty by starting with something socialists seem to agree on, namely, a certain critique of the capitalist system that has its roots in Marx but is not exclusively Marxist. This critique identifies five problems, or social vices, with the capitalist economic system, problems that a socialist economic system would presumably eliminate or dramatically reduce. According to this critique, the capitalist economic system is responsible for (1) various forms or manifestations of alienation, (2) systematic exploitation of the workers by those who own or control the means of production, (3) unplanned economic growth and development, (4) a wide range of social irrationalities, ranging from negative externalities (e.g., pollution) to mass cyclical unemployment to distorted economic priorities (e.g.., the production of too many luxury goods and not enough low-cost housing), and (5) substantial inequality in wealth and income, which is bad in and of itself and/or is responsible for other undesirable features of capitalist society. It is reasonable to suppose that socialists believe that a socialist system would prevent these problems from arising or at least would substantially reduce their incidence and severity. This constitutes a minimal socialist vision of the good society that all, or nearly all, socialists could agree on. Given that, the next step was to reconstruct a system of property rights in the means of production that could be called "socialist" and that could arguably be thought to prevent or substantially ameliorate these problems socialists have attributed to the capitalist system. All of this is done in the second and third sections of chapter 2. What emerges from this discussion is a system of self-managed worker cooperatives which lease their capital from society, or to be more precise, from a democratically controlled state, which is society's representative.

The primary purpose of the next five chapters is to argue that in point of fact, this system would not realize the socialist vision of the good society. In particular, the main problem with such a system would be exploitation. Not only would it not eliminate exploitation, it would be inherently more exploitative than a capitalist system (or, as I prefer to call it, a free enterprise system). If exploitation is a form of injustice, this is a serious charge, not only from the point of view of the socialist vision of the good society but absolutely. Chapter 3 contains a general theory of exploitative exchange; it is not the only possible theory of exploitation, but it has, I believe, considerable intuitive appeal and ironically enough, important connections with Marx's conception of exploitation. Chapters 4–7 apply this theory to both free enterprise and market socialist economic systems to evaluate the potential for exploitation in each type of system. These chapters make use of recent work in the economics of contracts and organizations. Chapters 4 and 5 give a nontechnical exposition of the relevant literature and explain its bearing on the topic of exploitation. Chapters 6 and 7 offer a comparative evaluation of market socialist and free enterprise systems on the question of exploitation. The general conclusion is that the economic organizations of a market socialist system—self-managed cooperatives and the state organizations from which they rent all of their capital—permit and encourage forms of exploitation that are prevented or discouraged by the characteristic organizations of a free enterprise system, namely, the classical capitalist (i.e., owner-operated) firm and the modern corporation.

Chapter 8 considers in a systematic way some alternative types of economic systems that look plausible or attractive from a socialist perspective. It is argued that these systems (1) are also inferior to a free enterprise system on the question of exploitation, (2) are not really forms of socialism, or (3) are unable to realize other elements of the socialist vision of the good society. This discussion is not meant to be exhaustive; but together with the arguments of chapters 6 and 7, it is intended to make the defense of any form of market socialism a daunting task.

Since the objects of discussion in this debate are systems of property rights, I found much of the literature on the economics of property rights, specifically on the economics of contracts and organizations (transactions cost analysis, as it sometimes called), to be directly relevant. That relevance is established in chapter 3, which argues for a conceptual connection between certain forms of inefficiency and exploitation. Much of transactions cost analysis is informed by a general evolutionary hypothesis to the effect that the policies, procedures, and organizational forms that are found in free enterprise systems exist or persist because they are efficient responses to various features of the economic environment. As a working hypothesis or methodological assumption this can hardly be objected to, but it cannot be taken as a complete and accurate description of economic reality. Fortunately for my purposes, the causal or explanatory claim to the effect that organizational forms (notably the classical capitalist firm and the corporation) persist because they are efficient is unnecessary. All that is needed are the claims that these organizations have the various transactions cost efficiencies that they do; they need not exist or persist because they have those efficiencies. This allows me to sidestep some of the more problematical aspects of this literature having to do with the explanatory significance of these efficiencies and the empirical confirmation or disconfirmation of more particular hypotheses derived from the general evolutionary hypothesis about the transactions cost efficiencies of what exists.

Although the general framework of this book is the capitalism/socialism dispute, that framework recedes into the background after the second chapter and does not reappear until the end of chapter 7. In chapter 6 and most of chapter 7, it seems that the worker cooperative, as an organizational form, is being subjected to relentless criticism. This appearance is misleading, however, since the object of criticism is not the worker cooperative per se, but the worker cooperative in the context of the type of market socialist system outlined and motivated in chapter 2. Many of the opportunities for exploitation that exist in the market socialist cooperative would not exist or would be minimized in an environment where a wide variety of economic organizations were permitted, something that market socialism cannot allow for reasons explained in chapter 2. In other words, I am not offering a comprehensive critique of worker cooperatives but a more limited comparison of market socialist worker cooperatives and the corresponding capitalist institutions. This, of course, is motivated by the larger purposes of this project.

This project exemplifies a certain way of conceiving of the relationship between social and political philosophy and the social sciences that may have applications beyond the capitalism/socialism dispute. Social and political philosophy traditionally concerns itself with the ideals, values, or fundamental principles to which social institutions should conform and what arguments might be offered in support of them. It considers such questions as what is equality and in what respects is it a desideratum? What is wrong with exploitation? What does justice require? On the other hand, the social sciences are supposed to explain the genesis and persistence of social institutions and how those institutions function. Typically, social scientists are insensitive to the variety and complexity of values, ideals, and fundamental principles that social institutions might realize or frustrate, as well as the arguments that might be offered in favor or against them. On the other side, philosophers are typically insensitive to the variety and complexity of actual existing social institutions. In particular and most importantly, they seem to know little of what social science can tell us about the likely effect of changes either in social institutions or in the social environment in which they operate. This apparent ignorance is part of what accounts for the air of unreality that surrounds much of contemporary social and political philosophy, a phenomenon that has been remarked on by philosophers and nonphilosophers alike.

Although I come to the capitalism/socialism dispute as a philosopher, I have found the empirical questions to be both more interesting and more tractable than the traditional philosophical questions raised by this debate (about, e.g., rights, justice, and equality). I have sought to articulate a set of values and ideals that most socialists subscribe to and then (without worrying about how one might justify them) to consider the empirical question of whether or not market socialist institutions could achieve or realize those goals. If, as I argue, those goals cannot be realized, there is no need to settle the thorny philosophical questions that surround those values and ideals, at least as far as the capitalism/socialism dispute goes. The philosophical questions remain, of course, but progress has been made on the most fundamental question of social and political philosophy, namely, What kind of institutions should we have?

In preparing to write this book, I have benefited considerably from the writings of many authors, among them, David Schweickart. His book, *Capitalism or Worker Control?*, defends a form of market socialism similar to the one outlined in chapter 2. Schweickart is one of the few philosophers who has made an effort to spell out a socialist system of property rights that is consistent with a market economy. Oliver Williamson's book, *The Economic Institutions of Capitalism,* proved to be invaluable; it provides a framework for thinking about exploitation in free enterprise systems (and, by implication, in other economic systems) toward which I had been groping for several years. Implicit in the perspective of that book—and, indeed, of transactions cost analysis in general—is a vision of an economic system in which exploitation can never be eliminated but where institutions, organizations, and contractual arrangements can preclude or minimize opportunities for exploitation that might otherwise exist. This coheres with my Churchillian vision of capitalism as an economic system with many vices but whose chief and decisive virtue is that it is better than all the alternatives.

Part of the argument of the second section of chapter 6 first appeared in "Equality and Exploitation in the Market Socialist Community," *Social Philosophy & Policy* 9 (Winter 1992): 1–28. A compressed and truncated version of the main argument of chapters 2–7 can be found in my "Market Socialism," *Critical Review* 6 (Fall 1993): 517–557.

There are many people and a number of (noncapitalist!) organizations that I have to thank for help on this book. This project was partially funded by the Discretionary Grant Program, Department of State, Soviet–Eastern European Research and Training Act of 1983, Public Law 98-164, Title VIII, 97 Stat. 1047–50. This grant was administered by the Hoover Institution at Stanford University. I would like to thank Richard Starr and the staff at the Hoover Institution for bringing me to Hoover and for the many kindnesses they showed me during the 1990–91 academic year. The facilities were outstanding, and the time I spent there was extraordinarily productive. I would also like to thank Paul Milgrom of Stanford's department of economics for allowing me to sit in on his graduate course on the economics of contracts and organizations.

Further support for this project came from the Social Philosophy and Policy Center at Bowling Green State University in Bowling Green, Ohio. I was able to complete the manuscript in my capacity as a visiting scholar there in the summer of 1992. Thanks are due to Fred Miller (executive director), Ellen Frankel Paul and Jeffrey Paul (associate directors), and the staff at the center. Many people read and commented on sections or chapters of the manuscript, and it is much improved as a result. They include Tom Bethell, Peter Cloyes, Gerald Cohen, Harold Kincaid, Eugene Fama, Terry Moe, Barry Weingast, and Justin Schwartz. Two people who helped me the most were Daniel Shapiro and David Miller. David Miller reviewed the manuscript at two different stages of the project and made penetrating criticisms and extremely valuable suggestions at both stages. Though he represents the other side in this dispute, I found his comments a model of judiciousness and fairness. Daniel Shapiro was also a visiting scholar at the Social Philosophy and Policy Center during the summer of 1992, and he provided me with immediate and useful feedback on the final chapters as they were written. I would also like to thank Angela Blackburn at Oxford University Press for her support.

Finally, I would like to express my gratitude to my wife, Theresa, for her support and for putting up with my absence during the many weekends I spent working on the book. I am also pleased to acknowledge her assistance in a more direct way: as a certified public accountant who has audited both small and large corporations, she was able to give me a perspective on how firms actually work in the real world that one cannot get from the writings of economists, not to mention philosophers.

Birmingham, Alabama   N.S.A.
June 1993

Contents

1. Capitalism versus Socialism: An Analytical Perspective, 3

Defining the Terms, 3
The Nature of the Dispute, 11
Criticizing Economic Systems, 16
Defending Economic Systems, 22
Resolution and Progress in the Dispute, 27

2. Why Market Socialism?, 34

Motivating the Market, 34
Social Ownership in a Market Economy, 43
The Motivations for Social Ownership, 56

3. Economic Exploitation, 65

Exploitation as the Failure of Reciprocity, 65
The Value of One's Contribution, 70
Fair Exchanges and the Value of One's Contribution, 74
The Question of Alternatives, 85

4. Exploitation and the Economics of Organizations, 93

Comparing Types of Economic Systems, 93
The Foundations of the Economics of Organizations, 100
An Illustration: The Classical Capitalist Firm, 106
The Empirical Preconditions for Exploitation, 111
Opportunism, Appropriable Quasi-Rents, and Exploitative
  Exchange, 117

5. Transactions Cost Efficiencies of Capitalist Organizations, 122

Some Methodological Considerations, 122
The Classical Capitalist Firm Revisited, 126
The Open Corporation, 136
The Employment Relation in a Free Enterprise System, 153

6. Exploitation in a Market Socialist Economy I, 165

More Methodological Considerations, 165

Exploitation among and by the Residual Claimants in the Cooperative, 175

Other Forms of Exploitation in the Small-to-Medium-sized Cooperative, 187

7. Exploitation in a Market Socialist Economy II, 206

Exploitation in and through the Large Cooperative, 206

Exploitation through State Organizations, 218

8. Other Options for Market Socialism?, 234

Equity Ownership and Market Socialism, 234

Other Forms of Ownership and Market Socialism, 246

The Socialist Vision of the Good Society, 255

Notes, 263

References, 283

Index, 293

The Philosophy and Economics
of Market Socialism

1

Capitalism versus Socialism:
An Analytical Perspective

Defining the Terms

Over the past 150 years, one of the most contentious intellectual and practical disputes has been between those who favor capitalism and those who favor socialism. An accurate historical chronicle of this dispute, either in the practical realm or in the realm of ideas, would be a monumental undertaking. An analytical account of the intellectual dispute is, however, a more manageable enterprise. Such an account seeks to identify the exact nature of the disagreement and the kinds of considerations that have been, and should be, brought to bear to resolve it. This analysis should be somewhat faithful to the historical record, but it will have a prescriptive component insofar as it distinguishes those facts, hypotheses, and modes of argumentation that are genuinely relevant from those which are spurious. After all, numerous thinkers have had something to say on these issues, and not every participant has advanced the discussion. In addition, contributors to this debate have had their say in widely varying contexts. Few have explicitly set out to vindicate one or the other system, even if much of what has been said is directly relevant to the main points in contention. An analytical account of the dispute provides a framework within which different contributions can be located and the criteria by which they should be judged. It will also provide guidance for those who seek to make a contribution in the future.

The purpose of this first chapter is to provide just such an account. This first section seeks an adequate definition of the key terms. The second section identifies the main points in contention. The main conclusions of these first two sections are that the objects of discussion are abstract types of economic systems and that the dispute is a twofold dispute about different and conflicting conceptions of the good society and conflicting empirical beliefs about the social consequences of the two types of economic systems. The third and fourth sections lay out the burdens of proof that both critics and defenders of the respective types of economic systems must shoulder. One of the conclusions of this discussion is that critics must defend and defenders must criticize. The last section seeks to identify what would count as progress in,

3

and a resolution of, the dispute. As might be expected, a resolution is difficult to achieve and not because of stubbornness on the part of participants. However, progress toward resolution is possible, and this section spells out what progress consists of. The aim of the remainder of this book is, quite simply, to make some progress in this dispute.

On the face of it, the dispute seems to be about economic systems. However, some writers have used the terms 'capitalism' more broadly to refer to a society in its entirety or even to a culture. 'Socialism' has sometimes been used in a similar way, and it has also been used to refer to a social movement. Using these terms in such broad ways serves to emphasize the interdependence of social institutions and the interconnectedness of social phenomena generally. Though these interrelations and interconnections can hardly be denied, one problem with understanding these terms so broadly is that the dispute becomes very difficult to evaluate, since the objects of discussion are entire societies, cultures, or social movements and not just economic systems.

The most natural alternative—and the one that will be adopted in this book—is to think of capitalism and socialism as economic systems. This way of understanding the subject matter of this dispute has a long and impressive historical pedigree and a high degree of contemporary relevance. On this understanding, the dispute between those who favor capitalism and those who favor socialism is a dispute about economic systems. Partisans of these alternative economic systems may or may not have significant disagreements about other matters; indeed, one of the questions to be investigated in an analytical account of this dispute is just how far these disagreements must extend, given a fundamental difference of opinion about economic systems.

However, it might be objected that to characterize this as a debate about economic systems is incomplete or misleading because economic systems are inextricably intertwined with other social systems and institutions, in particular, political systems. More precisely, even to describe an economic system, it is necessary to make some tacit or explicit suppositions about the accompanying political system. For example, in describing a capitalist economic system, one must presuppose the political recognition and enforcement of private property rights. On the other side, socialists typically envision a commanding presence in the economy for the state. Certainly, one cannot specify a socialist economic system without describing some elements of the state apparatus, at least at some level of abstraction.

Although political and economic systems cannot be completely separated, it is not necessary to specify the political system fully in order to discuss capitalist or socialist economic systems. After all, some aspects of the political system are not directly relevant to a given economic system and how it functions. In light of this, in what follows, capitalist and socialist economic systems will be conceived of as including whatever parts of the political system are presupposed in their respective descriptions.

To understand what capitalist and socialist economic systems are, let us begin with the general concept of an economic system. Economic systems are social institutions, and social institutions are rule-governed domains of human behavior that answer to some identifiable range of human needs. The economic system of a society is that social institution which regulates the production and exchange of exchangeable goods and services. (Not all goods are exchangeable—love and divine grace come to mind as examples.) Its function is to meet those human needs that can be met by exchangeable goods and services.

The specification of a social institution, for example, a society's economic system, requires a statement of the rules that govern behavior in the relevant domain. This governance has a descriptive and prescriptive dimension. As a matter of empirical fact, people do, in general, act in accordance with the rules that define the institution in question. However, these rules also have a prescriptive or normative dimension in that they say what behaviors are required, forbidden, and permissible. Sometimes this prescriptive component is backed by the coercive power of the state, as in the case of all current economic systems. But sometimes the rules of an institution are backed more informally. The social institution of language, for example, has rules that are prescriptive, but they are not backed by force (except in the case of some old-fashioned English teachers). On the other hand, the rules that regulate the production and exchange of goods and services—the rules of an economic system—are its property rights; their obedience is deemed important enough to warrant the coercive backing of the state. Historically important types of economic systems (e.g., feudalist, capitalist, and socialist) are individuated by the characteristic kinds of property rights that comprise them.

What, then, is meant by the terms 'capitalist economic system' and 'socialist economic system'? Let us begin by replacing the former term with the term 'free enterprise system.' There are a number of reasons to recommend this. First, it is arguable that someone or some group is going to have to play the role of capitalist in *any* economic system, in which case it is misleading to describe one economic system as "capitalist." Second, the term 'capitalist economic system' carries nineteenth-century Marxist connotations; in particular, it suggests that most firms are owned by one or a few individuals—capitalists—who do not labor. This is not, in general, the case today in so-called capitalist economies. More generally, it suggests that one who describes an economic system as capitalist subscribes to important elements of Marx's analysis of capitalist society, elements that are contentious and controversial. One is left wondering how much of that analysis one is required to accept as obvious and uncontroversial. The unbeliever feels rather like a Jew in a Baptist Bible study group.

On the other hand, though the term 'free enterprise system' is not without unwanted connotations, it is more descriptively accurate. To designate an economic system in this way is to suggest that firms are free to carry on production in whatever manner they see fit, subject only to specifically enumerated side constraints imposed by the state. It also puts the focus on the enterprises or organizations, which is especially appropriate for the purposes of this study; for as we shall see in later chapters, a crucial difference between the most defensible form of market socialism and a free enterprise system is that the former, but not the latter, mandates by law a certain type of economic organization, the self-managed cooperative. By contrast, in a free enterprise system, production can be and is in fact organized through a variety of different organizational forms.

What, then, does the term 'free enterprise system' mean exactly? The following seems to accord reasonably well with customary usage: a free enterprise economic system is any economic system in which (1) most of the means of production (raw materials, capital goods, etc.) are privately owned and (2) people are free to sell their labor on the market. As suggested, the first condition is to be understood as laissez-faire: subject to the constraints imposed by the rights of others and subject to other specifically enumerated restrictions imposed by the state, individuals and groups are formally free to acquire and dispose of means of production in whatever manner they see fit. Note that the definition says "most" of the means of production, since the state can and does own some means of production in existing free enterprise systems. Sometimes state involvement in the economy is so extensive and pervasive that it is not clear that private individuals and groups can be said to truly own the means of production. For example, in many Third World countries (e.g., the Philippines and at least until recently, Mexico), the state owns outright large segments of the economy and so extensively and arbitrarily intervenes in the rest of the economy that one is reluctant to describe the economic system as free enterprise. This is as it should be, since those on the Right are unwilling defend systems with these attributes. These observations call attention to some indeterminacy in the definition of a free enterprise system. There is some vagueness inherent in the concept itself.

The second condition about labor markets helps to distinguish a free enterprise system from systems of slavery and serfdom, as well as other primitive economic systems. Other systems have recognized private ownership of the means of production, at least for some individuals, but they have not countenanced the universal freedom to sell one's labor. Note that in existing free enterprise systems, the state does impose specifically enumerated restrictions on the sale of one's labor. For example, a wide range of occupations and professions require that individuals have state licenses to sell their labor. This includes not only doctors and airline pilots but also primary school teachers and plumbers. Curiously enough, although cosmetologists need a license, cosmologists do not. Nor do journalists, politicians, or clergy. In a highly regulated society, it is ironic that many of those who can most deeply affect a society and its citizens do not need a license to ply their trades.

Based on this definition of a free enterprise system, it is obvious that there can be significant variations within this general type. One dimension along which particular free enterprise systems can vary, at least up to a point, is the extent to which the production and exchange of goods and services is carried out through private enterprise as opposed to the state. States have removed the production and exchange of various goods and services from the domain of private enterprise in a variety of ways. Perhaps the most common is by awarding a legal monopoly on the production and distribution of some good or service to a nationalized or municipalized firm. States also exclude private enterprise through an outright ban on the production and/or distribution of some goods or services (e.g., recreational drugs, human organs).

Free enterprise systems can also vary in the nature and extent of side constraints imposed on the exercise of private property rights. Side constraints require or prohibit certain courses of action that an owner of private property must do or refrain from doing; the owner retains what might be called residual rights of control in the sense that he can do whatever is not expressly forbidden and can refrain from doing whatever is not expressly required. These side constraints go beyond the traditional prohibition on harmful use to include such restrictions as zoning laws, occupational licensing, and the imposition of various terms and conditions on the employer-employee contract. Over the past few decades, these constraints have grown more numerous and detailed in existing free enterprise systems. At some point, their proliferation so diminishes residual rights of control, and thus effective ownership, that such systems can no longer be accurately described as free enterprise. This is one reason why a state that is ever more intrusive in the economy is favored by opponents (and opposed by proponents) of a free enterprise system.

Finally, free enterprise systems also vary according to the extent to which the state tries to manage the economy. All modern states use tax and fiscal policy to affect the economy at both macro and micro levels, and some participate more actively through a variety of other instrumentalities, such as subsidies, public-private partnerships, and purely public investment in infrastructure. On the other hand, large-scale investment planning is not a function the state takes on in a free enterprise system. The definition of a free enterprise system employed here implies that it relies on private initiative for most new investment. All these variations are variations within a type. To reiterate, what makes an economic system a free enterprise system is that (1) most of the means of production are privately owned and (2) people are free to sell their labor on the market.

Let us consider now the term 'socialist economic system.' This term is harder to define, since socialists disagree among themselves about what socialism "really is." It would seem that everyone (socialists and nonsocialists alike) could at least agree that it is not a system in which there is widespread private ownership of the means of production. Thus, the terms 'socialist economic system' and 'free enterprise system' are logical contraries in that no system can be both, though a system may be neither. But what about Western European social democracies? Aren't they counterexamples?

It might be argued that the socialist character of these systems is to be found in the extensive social welfare programs provided by the state and perhaps in their relatively progressive tax systems. To some extent, the dispute here is merely terminological, to be settled by stipulation. On the other hand, it is, I think, more accurate and illuminating to say that these societies have free enterprise (or capitalist) economic systems and that their political systems contain structures that are intended to realize various goals or values that are commonly associated with socialism.[1] Furthermore, these political structures are from time to time run by people who call themselves "socialists." This way of thinking about what socialism involves forces one to distinguish institutional means from the ends one believes the institutions can or should achieve. To be a socialist is not just to believe in certain ends, goals, values, or ideals. It also requires a belief in certain institutional means to achieve those ends; whatever that may amount to in positive terms, it certainly presupposes, at a minimum, the belief that these ends and values cannot be achieved in an economic system in which there is widespread private ownership of the means of production.

In light of these considerations, it is fair to say that in a socialist economic system, private ownership of the means of production is, in general, prohibited. The "in general" qualifier is inserted to make room for some private ownership in a socialist economy, just as there is some public ownership in free enterprise systems. There is no need to be completely rigid in one's enthusiasm for any form of ownership. The only requirement is that private enterprise is the exception, not the rule, in a socialist system.

What else does a socialist economic system involve? Those who favor socialism generally speak of social ownership, social control, or socialization of the means of production as the distinctive positive feature of a socialist economic system. But what does this amount to? The main idea seems to be that an economic system is socialist only if control of the means of production is exercised in the interests of society at large or at least in the interests of the working class. The way this is usually explained is that just as private property serves private interests under capitalism, socialized property serves the public interest under socialism. On the Marxist variation, socialized property serves the interests of the working class, at least until all classes wither away, after which socialized property serves the public interest. To say that an economic system is socialist, then, is to say that in general, the means of production are not privately owned and that the ownership or control of same is social. As a definition, this is accurate as far as it goes, but it leaves quite a bit undetermined.

What is most sorely missing is a description of how this social control is to be institutionally realized. How are the means of production to be controlled "in the public interest"? The definition supplies no answer. This lacuna is not really a deficiency in the definition of a socialist economic system, however, because there are considerable differences of opinion among socialists about the institutional form that social control should take. In trying to formulate a general definition of a socialist economic system, it is important not to prejudge these internal disputes and rule out or *anathematize* (as grim socialists of earlier generations put it) any historically or philosophically significant strand of socialist thought. Nevertheless, it would be useful for illustrative purposes (and absolutely required for some important purposes later on) to describe some ways in which social control of the means of production could be institutionally realized.

One way is through complete state ownership. The state wholly owns most of the means of production within its borders. Historically, this is the form that the overwhelming majority of actually existing socialist systems have taken. Why might this be thought to be a form of social ownership or control? Many non-Marxists believe that the state (at least, if it is democratic) represents, albeit imperfectly, the public interest, that is, the interests of society at large. If the state owns the means of production, then it manages them in the public interest. That is why it is called social ownership. (The phrase "in the public interest" perhaps must be understood in terms of the stated intentions of those who are in control.)

On the other hand, a common Marxist view holds that whenever and wherever states exist, there is a ruling class whose interest states always represent. Thus, when the economic system is a free enterprise system, the (bourgeois) state represents the interests of the bourgeoisie. When the working class seizes state power, the proletarian state will manage the means of production in the interests of the working class. On the Leninist version of this story, at a crucial point in the class struggle, the Communist party comes in off the bench to substitute for the working class (and thereafter forgets to takes itself out of the game). After the revolution, it ultimately controls the means of production—still, however, in the interests of the working class. As noted, with the advent of a classless society, the means of production are to be managed in the interests of society as a whole. For these admittedly diverse reasons, many Marxist and non-Marxist socialists equate socializing the means of production with state ownership.

Notice that on either view, there is a contingent connection between state ownership and socialization of the means of production. It is logically possible for the state not to represent the public interest or the interests of the ruling class. Indeed, it is widely believed, even among socialists, that this sometimes happens. Thus, the debates within the socialist camp about whether certain economic systems are really socialist are, at one level, quite legitimate. However, these debates might be more usefully described as disputes about whether or not a *nominally* socialist economic system can or does realize various socialist goals or ideals.

State ownership is not the only way of understanding social ownership or control. Another way of conceiving of it is in terms of cooperatives, such as exist in what used to be Yugoslavia or, on a smaller scale, in the Mondragon experiment in Spain and the kibbutzim in Israel.[2] In systems like these, the workers themselves control the means of production with which they work; that is, most enterprises are self-managed. If an economic system consists primarily of self-managed firms, what makes that system socialist is that control of most of society's means of production is by—and thus presumably in the interests of—the workers. And, of course, in such a society most adults are workers. According to proponents of this form of socialism, social control of the means of production may be further augmented by democratic control of the state, which is to have a significant role in directing the economy.

There may be other ways in which the means of production can be socialized. In particular, the two modes of socialization just outlined need not be mutually exclusive. As we shall see in chapter 2, the concept of ownership is quite complex. It consists of a package of rights, terms, and conditions that may be distributed across worker cooperatives and the state in such a way that neither may be said to be "the owner." But even this may not exhaust all of the alternative ways of understanding social control of the means of production. Syndicalism, the view that entire industries should be owned or controlled by those who work in them, is one possibility, though no one has ever been able to explain how an entire system with only one firm per industry is supposed to function. There may be others. However, state ownership and worker cooperatives—or some combination of the two—have predominated in both the theory and practice of socialism. If a socialist economic system is defined as any system that prohibits most private ownership of the means of production and which mandates social control of same, then we have a definition of a socialist economic system that is indeterminate but determinable. That may be the best we can do, given the heterogeneity of socialist thought and the socialist movement.

There are two things absent from this definition that are worth pointing out. First, there is no mention of the ownership of labor. This is an issue that has not been clearly articulated in socialist thought and practice. Marxian socialists do not believe that workers in postcapitalist society would own their labor (labor power, in Marx's terminology), at least in the sense that implies the right to sell it or alienate it (Marx [1875] 1971, 16). On the other hand, they do envision worker control of the means of production and thus worker control of the conditions of labor. Additionally, in the centrally planned Marxist economies of the twentieth century (assuming they are socialist), the workers have had, at best, highly truncated ownership rights in their labor. Early Soviet thought and practice conceived of workers as soldiers in the struggle for socialism. Like soldiers everywhere, they were subordinated to the will of their commanders—in this case, the leadership of the Communist party. By contrast, as the next chapter shows, market socialists favor something like worker (self-) ownership of labor, subject to some restrictions. There are, of course, profound differences between workers' relationship to their firms in market socialist systems as compared to free enterprise systems. In particular, the workers have certain management and income rights in the market socialist firm that they lack in capitalist organizations. But in terms of control over their labor power, no proponent of market socialism believes that workers would or should have fewer rights than workers in a free enterprise system have.

A second thing to note about this definition of a socialist economic system is that it neither states nor implies that such a system is a market economy or a centrally planned economy or something in between. This is as it should be, since socialists, especially in recent years, have become more critical of central planning and more favorably disposed toward the market. Strictly speaking, either mode of socialization (state ownership or worker cooperatives) is consistent with reliance on central planning or the market, though those who favor state ownership have also generally favored central planning, and those who favor worker cooperatives have generally championed the market. Though there may be no logical connection between these modes of socialization and the respective ways of organizing production across enterprises, there may be empirical connections between a given mode of socialization and markets or central planning.

Before closing this section, one general objection to defining a socialist economic system in terms of property rights or ownership rights warrants brief notice. One of the most prominent figures associated with socialism, Marx, maintained that rights are not universal categories of social existence but are instead products of a particular historical epoch, namely, the capitalist era.[3] They are boundary markers between competing egoists that facilitate the pursuit of private interests. Any society that has a need for them and recognizes them is inherently defective. Postcapitalist society, at least in its higher phase, is not inherently defective and thus is a society that has gone "beyond rights." So, to define a socialist economic system in terms of ownership rights is incompatible with a leading socialist theoretician's conception of the ultimate alternative to the existing capitalist order.

The problem with this dismissive view of property rights is that it overlooks that fact that any society will have to have rules governing the disposition of means of production (and, indeed, labor)—rules with prescriptive content and backed by some important, though not necessarily coercive, sanctions. The reason for this is twofold: not all valuable productive ends can be achieved (i.e., there will always be scarcity in some form), and it is highly unlikely that there will ever be unanimous agreement about how to deal with that scarcity. Property rights in the means of production specify how these inevitable disagreements about the deployment of the elements of society's productive apparatus are to be resolved. In consequence, such rights—or some close functional analogue—will be part of any society's institutional structure for as far into the future as it makes sense to look.

If Marx did not think of a socialist economic system in terms of property rights or something like it, then so much the worse for Marx. Recall that an analytical account of the capitalism/socialism dispute does have a prescriptive component, so absolute fidelity to the historical record is neither necessary nor desirable. Indeed, a recurring weakness in socialist thought is that property rights in the means of production in a socialist economy have been incompletely specified beyond the rejection of private ownership. The diligent investigator must search carefully and rely on indirect evidence to ferret out socialist conceptions of property rights.

The Nature of the Dispute

What exactly is in dispute between those who favor a free enterprise system and those who favor a socialist economic system? As a first approximation, it might be said that the issue is about which type of economic system is best and why. But what does "best" mean in this context and for whom are the rival types of economic systems supposed to be the best? Let us consider the latter question first. It would not be accurate to say that either side necessarily believes that their favored type of economic system is best for any society at any time. Following Marx's theory of history, Marxian socialists have maintained that a free enterprise system is best for some societies at some times. And modest thinkers on both sides of the debate might be skeptical about what economic system is or would have been best for ancient or primitive societies about which little is known.

The dispute is most usefully conceived of as focused on complex industrial societies, either in the present or in the near-to-medium-term future. The debate has been going on since complex industrial societies came into existence around the time of the Industrial Revolution; it seems that most participants have thought in terms of a time frame that begins somewhere between the time at which they are writing and about a generation or so from then and extends indefinitely into the future. I suspect that the reason for this is that most parties to the dispute have intended, or at least hoped, that their cogitations would have some practical effect on existing institutions—either in conserving them or in bringing about fundamental (i.e., radical) institutional change. Of course, some authors have made more universal claims in both time and space for their favored systems, but the most plausible discussions include—or at least should include—restrictions of the sort just indicated.

The question about what "best" means in this context is more difficult to assay. It does suggest a comparative judgment of some sort. To say that an economic system is best is to say that it is better than all the others. But what are the others? And better in what respect or respects? Let us begin with the former question. One way to understand the comparison class is in terms of all logically possible types of economic systems or, more narrowly, all feasible types of economic systems. But either understanding presents a formidable difficulty, to wit, it is hard to see how one could formulate a useful list of all logically possible, or even all feasible, types of economic systems—at least in such a way that one could know that one had covered all the possibilities. If one is claiming a kind of global superiority for a favored type of economic system, it could well be exceedingly difficult to prove.

A more manageable comparison class would be any economic system of the type favored by the other side of the dispute under discussion. In other words, those who favor a free enterprise system believe that some such system is superior to any socialist economic system. The situation of those who favor socialism is similar, but it is complicated by the fact, noted in the last section, that there is a fundamental disagreement about what socialization of the means of production really means. Those who favor worker cooperatives, for example, maintain that an economic system that socializes the means of production in that way is superior to any free enterprise system, but they might not want to defend state ownership as superior to a free enterprise system.

Those on either side of this dispute may believe stronger claims on behalf of their favored system, but they would not have to establish anything more than what was just indicated to resolve the dispute in question.

Let us now turn to the question of the standard of comparison against which types of economic systems are to be judged. There are numerous social virtues and vices (as they might be called) for which economic systems have been held responsible. Efficiency, respect for basic rights, equality of one sort or another, and opportunities for self-determination are some of the social virtues an economic system might have. Social vices that have been blamed on economic systems include gross inefficiency, exploitation, alienation, and the denial of basic human rights.

These virtues and vices are diverse. This fact makes it difficult to give an overall comparative assessment of types of economic systems. This raises some difficult and important philosophical questions about whether a common metric (e.g., utility) is available to assess social institutions in general or economic systems in particular. A related problem, which will be discussed in more detail later in this chapter, is that there is disagreement even about what counts as a social vice (or virtue). For example, most advocates of socialism believe that a cardinal vice of free enterprise systems is that they permit and encourage substantial inequality of material condition. Those who favor a free enterprise system generally do not believe that this is a social vice or that relative equality of material condition is a social virtue.[4]

Since this chapter aims not to resolve the dispute but only to represent it accurately, it is not necessary to adjudicate these disagreements about the standard or standards of comparison. We only need some way to characterize the dispute which reflects all the issues involved. The social virtues and vices mentioned that have been attributed to economic systems are obviously of fundamental importance. The vices are alleged to be serious social ills, and the virtues are believed to be important desiderata that any society should satisfy. One way to capture what is at stake is to say that there is sharp disagreement between the two sides about the economic system of the good society. However the contending parties envision the good society, each participant in the debate believes that the economic system of the good society is a instance of one or the other of the two types. The two camps divide on the question of whether that type is socialist or free enterprise. But how is the concept of the good society to be understood? It might be most useful to think of it as a placeholder for something more definite—to be filled in differently by different theorists. Clearly, there are significant differences between, and even within, the two sides about the nature of the good society. But are there any general constraints on the concept of the good society that both sides should respect?

Some people might think of the good society as the best society imaginable (i.e., a kind of utopia) that may or may not be historically possible or realizable. On the other hand, others might think of it as the best society one can reasonably hope for. The former may best accord with how some participants in the debate have thought of it. There are, for example, significant strands of socialist thought that are utopian in the sense that they exhibit little or no sensitivity to the question of whether or not their vision of the good society could be realized in the foreseeable future or even as far into the future as it makes sense to look.[5] The same might be said of some libertarian defenders of the free enterprise system. However, this may not be the best way to think about the good society. At stake is the utility of different ways of thinking about social institutions generally and economic systems in particular. There are a number of reasons why it is useful to think of the good society in terms of the best society one can reasonably hope for, instead of in terms of an ideal society that might not be historically possible.[6]

The most important reason in favor of the former is that it imposes an epistemic constraint on one's speculations. Fourier's world of abundance in which the seas are made out of lemonade and lions lay down with lambs is ruled out, as it should be. Thinking about an economic system for a world like that is like thinking about a health care delivery system for a society in which no one ever gets sick. (People would still be hurt in accidents, so there would still be a need for such a system.) Since it is not reasonable to hope that all disease could disappear in the next three generations, there is no point in thinking about a health care delivery system for a society facing that eventuality. Analogously, one should not conceive of the good society as, for example, one in which human wants and needs are in such perfect harmony with each other and with what nature and a little labor can provide that there are no conflicts about how society's productive powers should be deployed; nor should one conceive of it as a society in which everyone values the common good so highly that any member of that society would sacrifice the most important of his or her own interests to make an insignificant contribution to some societal interest when the two interests conflict. There is, of course, a line-drawing problem here. One must be careful not to assume that some transitory aspect of contemporary social life is a permanent feature of the human condition. This is why speculation should only be restricted by what one can reasonably hope for, instead of by what one can reasonably believe. Our reasonable hopes outrun our reasonable beliefs but not our fondest dreams. Second, the types of economic systems that are being attacked or defended in this dispute are themselves realizable. What is ultimately at issue is what kind of economic system is to be preferred for the real world. It is not at all obvious that telling us about the economic system of a society that might be empirically impossible is contributing anything useful to this debate. This is true even if empirically impossible models of economic systems are of some use in economics proper.

To conceive of the good society in terms of what one can reasonably hope for is to impose a weak reality check on one's thinking. It suggests a role for the social sciences, especially economics conceived of as an empirical science. Only an empirically grounded social science can describe how social institutions function and what their effects are. The alternative is simply to ignore that reality check. If this debate is to have a salutary practical effect on existing institutions by helping to conserve them or to overthrow them in their essentials, then it seems most useful to think of the good society as a society that is at least arguably historically possible.

Each of the various participants in this dispute believes that a different type of economic systems is the economic system of the good society (employing, of course, different conceptions of the good society). What is the general nature of the relation between types of economic systems and conceptions of the good society? An answer to this question should tell us something the kinds of arguments that the participants have to make.

On the face of it, there seem to be two kinds of relations that could subsist between a type of economic system and a conception of the good society: instrumental and logical. An instrumental connection obtains when the functioning of a certain type of economic system causes, or at least is contingently responsible for, some necessary condition for the good society—what was earlier called a social virtue. On the other hand, a logical connection obtains when some defining feature of the type of economic system being defended is itself constitutive of the good society.[7]

Consider the following two examples of instrumental connections. Some defenders of a free enterprise system believe that a certain level of economic development, or even a certain rate of economic growth, is a necessary condition for a good society. They further believe that as a matter of empirical fact, only a free enterprise system (perhaps of a certain subtype) can achieve and sustain that level of development or growth. In a similar vein, a socialist might maintain that only a certain type of socialist economic system can achieve a relatively egalitarian distribution of wealth and income and that this sort of distribution is a social virtue; that is, that it has a relatively egalitarian distribution of wealth and income is part of what makes a society a good society, and only a society with a certain type of economic system can achieve that distribution.

In these two cases, the functioning of a certain type of economic system is claimed to be responsible for achieving something thought to be, in part, definitive of (i.e., a necessary condition for) a good society—in the former case, a certain level of economic development or growth, in the latter case, a relatively egalitarian distribution of wealth and income. (Why these social virtues are constitutive of a good society is a separate question.) Notice that the main claims being advanced in this context are empirical and are about how a type of economic system actually functions. This suggests a substantial role for economics, conceived of as an empirical science, in adjudicating some aspects of this dispute.[8]

The connection between an economic system and a conception of the good society may, however, be more intimate than merely factual or empirical. For example, according to some libertarian defenders of a free enterprise system, being free to buy and sell things, including means of production, to and from whomever one chooses is a basic human right. The freedom to exercise this basic human right is not merely an empirically necessary condition for something else that makes a society a good society (though it may be that, too). Rather, this freedom is itself a social virtue, that is, it is part of what makes a society a good society, perhaps because it is a requirement of justice.[9] In other words, on this libertarian vision, part of what makes a society a good society is that people have this freedom. Analogously, it may be that for some Marxists, social control of the means of production is constitutive of a good society. For them, it is a necessary truth that in a good society, people in their capacity as producers control the conditions of their interaction with the material world for the purposes of production. This state of affairs may have further good consequences, but control of these conditions may be held to be intrinsically valuable.[10]

Whether they are empirically or conceptually related to a conception of the good society, these conditions, constituents, or elements of a good society (i.e., these social virtues) derive from deeper views, such as theories of justice, theories of what sort of life is good for human beings, and views about the relation between the good life and the good society. These, in turn, depend on still deeper theories about the ultimate sources of political, moral, or practical obligation and theories of moral and nonmoral value. At this point, non-philosophers are likely to despair of ever reaching agreement and resolving the dispute. Philosophers, by contrast, hear the fire alarm go off, quit their card games, and don their gear. Disputes about the penultimate and ultimate sources of value and obligation are distinctively philosophical in nature.

The fact that there are both instrumental and logical connections between economic systems and conceptions of the good society indicates that the capitalism/socialism dispute has an economics component and a philosophy component. The line separating these two may not always be sharp, but the twofold nature of this dispute carries an implicit warning to participants from either discipline. Economists should realize that the philosophical aspects of this dispute are less straightforward and more complicated and difficult than they might have supposed but also that these issues are not wholly intractable. Philosophers, on the other hand, need to recognize that there are empirical constraints on conceptions of the good society and that questions about how economic systems actually function cannot be abstracted from or ignored and, indeed, must be systematically investigated. This distinction between the philosophy and economics components corresponds in a rough way to the distinction economists draw between normative and positive questions or issues. However, nothing should be made to depend on these distinctions; the lines between disciplines have become blurred in recent years, and (as most philosophers know and most economists do not know) the distinction between facts and values has been seriously questioned at least since the early part of this century in the writings of John Dewey.

Criticizing Economic Systems

If the dispute is conceived of as a dispute about the economic system of the good society, one may want to characterize it as follows: Those who favor a free enterprise system believe that in the economic system of the good society, most of the means of production are privately owned and people are free to sell their labor; those who favor socialism, on the other hand, maintain that most the means of production are socialized in the economic system of the good society.

This is correct as far as it goes, but it only represents half of the story. There is a more negative, critical edge to the debate that is absent from this characterization. It is not just that there is some nastiness in the dispute that has not been reflected. There is, after all, considerable nastiness in nearly any intellectual dispute. Rather, the point is that much of what each side has to say consists of bad things about the type of economic system favored by the other side. Socialists, especially, very often begin with a litany of complaints about the free enterprise system and/or criticisms of the arguments of its defenders (e.g., Miller 1989a, pt. 1). What unites each side—what constitutes the real basis for cognitive solidarity within each camp—is a belief in the wickedness of the type of economic system favored by the other side. Those who favor a socialist economic system spend much of their time arguing that a free enterprise system is by its very nature a disaster, and those who favor a free enterprise system say the same thing about socialist economic systems. Moreover, the chain of reasoning that leads from the offending type of economic system to what is wrong with it is usually fairly short. This is why many on each side believe that those on the other side are stupid, evil, or both.

To understand more clearly the nature of these critical claims, notice that the terms 'free enterprise system' and 'socialist economic system' refer to highly abstract types of economic systems. When a highly abstract type of economic system is the object of criticism, the claims being made are, logically speaking, quite strong. That is to say, because the types are so abstractly specified, there can be considerable variation among the particular economic systems (economic systems "on the ground" so to speak) that are instances of the types; and if the corresponding criticisms are well taken, they are more damaging than if the object of criticism is more narrowly specified.

The fact that criticisms of economic systems are usually pitched at a fairly high level of abstraction is what makes the critical side of this debate interesting. Socialist critics of the free enterprise system direct their complaints not against this or that version of the system but against any economy that meets the defining conditions of a free enterprise system (viz., private ownership of most of the means of production and the freedom to sell one's labor). The claim is that whatever the institutional details, any such system has the problem the critic has identified. For example, Marx's charges of exploitation and alienation against capitalism (i.e., free enterprise systems) have this generality, which is one of the things that makes Marx's critique of capitalism especially interesting.

Critics of socialism, on the other hand, pitch their criticisms of socialist economic systems at a somewhat lower level of abstraction, in part because there is such profound disagreement among socialists themselves about how to understand socialization of the means of production. (A big tent has many poles to knock down.) For example, a famous criticism by Ludwig von Mises and F. A. Hayek (discussed in chapter 2) about the inefficiencies of socialism is, strictly speaking, directed not against any socialist economic system but only those socialist systems in which the state owns the means of production and the economy is centrally planned. As such, these objections do not apply to a market socialist system dominated by worker cooperatives. To criticize effectively the latter type of system, different objections would be needed.

How these criticisms connect with the concept of the good society is straightforward: the defects attributed to the offending (and offensive) type of economic system are not minor or incidental; instead, they are sufficient to make any society that suffers from them not a good society. To put it another way, any society that has this type of economic system fails to meet some necessary condition for the good society. The key claims have to be so strong because what is at stake in this dispute are not minor problems around the edges of economic systems, but instead, profound problems that are rooted in the fundamental nature of the type of economic system in question. This explains the urgency of this debate in the minds of its participants. Whatever differences there are within each camp about the nature of the good society, all agree that some necessary condition(s) for a good society are not satisfied by a society which has the offending type of economic system. Admittedly, these conditions need not be the same for different theorists on the same side of the dispute. For example, one socialist might believe that X is a necessary condition for a society to be a good society and that any society with a free enterprise system lacks the attribute X. Another socialist may believe a comparable thing about attribute Y. Each may deny the proposition maintained by the other. In this way, they reach the same conclusion by different routes.

However, this possibility is more theoretical than actual. In point of fact, there seems to be a fair amount of agreement on each side about why the type of economic system favored by those on other side is not the economic system of the good society. Characteristic socialist complaints against free enterprise systems mention exploitation, material inequality, unemployment caused by the business cycle, alienation, and a lack of democratic control over one's economic life. Characteristic complaints against socialist economic systems are that they are grossly inefficient, gratuitously restrictive of personal freedom, and nonfortuitously associated with totalitarian political systems.[11] Implicit in these criticisms is the view that these defects are so serious that any society with the offending system is not a good society.

Is the foregoing just an observation about the psychology of the participants, or is there a substantive connection between each side's critical and positive views? This resolves itself into two questions: (1) do criticisms of one type of system presuppose any positive claims on behalf of the other type of system? and (2) does the positive case for one type of system require a critique of the other type of system? The former question is perhaps the more pressing of the two because it questions the legitimacy of a fairly common practice in this debate.

Let us begin with this question, relativized to one side of the debate. Can one be a critic of the free enterprise system without offering a positive defense of some version of a socialism? On the face of it, it would seem so. A Marxian socialist, for example, would presumably maintain that one reason why a free enterprise system is not the economic system of the good society is that its operation involves the systematic exploitation of the workers. To make this charge stick, it does not seem to be necessary to prove anything about a socialist economic system.

But as a matter of fact, the situation is a bit more complicated than that. First, any such criticism is going to presuppose at least a negative conception of the good society, that is, a conception of what the good society is *not*. As noted earlier, what truly unites the members of each camp in this debate is the belief that the type of economic system favored by the other side is fundamentally flawed, where the type is specified at a very high level of abstraction; that is, it has some social vice or vices (i.e., some sufficient condition for a society not to be a good society). To substantiate this belief, it is necessary to articulate and at least provisionally defend a minimalist, negative conception of the good society. Executing this task must be done in addition to making the (usually empirical) argument from the features of the disfavored type of economic system to the social vice in question.

The example about the Marxist charge of exploitation can be used to illustrate these points. Suppose someone maintains that any free enterprise system systematically exploits the workers. To substantiate this claim, it is not enough to produce an arbitrary definition of exploitation and then show that a free enterprise system is systematically exploitative because it fits that definition.[12] One must also be able to explain what is wrong with exploitation so defined. One way to do this would be to articulate a theory of justice according to which exploitation is a form of injustice. The reason for this is that presumably, a necessary condition for a society to be a good society is that it is not plagued by systematic injustice.

But the question remains: Does any of this require the critic to prove anything about socialism? As a matter of logic, the answer would seem to be, in general, no.[13] Criticisms of the free enterprise system do not appear to presuppose any substantive claims about a socialist economic system. However, if criticisms of this sort are conceived of in the larger context of the capitalism/socialism dispute, then the answer is different.

Pressing any such criticism does presuppose, at least pragmatically, that some socialist alternative would not face the problem the critic has called attention to—or at least would face a much reduced version of it. The reason for this is that criticisms of the free enterprise system are supposed to provide *reasons for* social change—change that moves a society in the direction of socialism. In lodging these charges, the critic at least tacitly supposes that some favored socialist alternative either will not face that problem or will face a much reduced version of it.[14]

There is something pragmatically self-refuting about denouncing a free enterprise system for its exploitation of the workers and then to add, "By the way, exploitation under socialism might be just as bad or even worse." Of course, no socialist has ever said this—not because they had available a decisive refutation of this charge against socialism but because this possibility simply has not been taken seriously. But it should be: socialism cannot be defined as whatever type of economic system is not responsible for the exploitation of the workers (or for any other social vice). One reason for this is that most of the claims against free enterprise systems are essentially empirical. Because of that, one cannot conclude that the elimination of (i.e., a revolutionary change in) an existing free enterprise system will preclude the recurrence of some social vice associated with that type of system. After all, the economic system that replaces it may also produce this defect. In light of this elementary observation, it is clearly intellectually dishonest to fail to investigate that possibility. Critics of existing economic systems bear an important burden of proof if they represent themselves as offering reasons for social change, as most of them do.

It is possible, of course, to maintain that one is not offering reasons for social change in criticizing a type of economic system. For example, a critic of a free enterprise system might claim to be simply making an assessment, taking a kind of moral inventory as it were, of that type of system. However, if this critic does not conceive of his task as, at least in part, providing reasons for social change, he is leaving open the possibility that genuinely beneficial change in the economic system in some particular respect cannot be achieved. This possibility reflects a pessimism or conservatism that few critics of the free enterprise system seem to endorse. Moreover, if one believes that this conservative diagnosis is at least a serious possibility, intellectual honesty would require that one call attention to it. Since critics of the free enterprise system have not called attention to this possibility (without exception, as far as I can tell) and are, we shall presume, intellectually honest, they must believe that there are potentially feasible alternatives to the way things are currently done that do not have the problem the critic has called attention to. For these reasons, failure to specify alternatives is not a live option for critics of the free enterprise system. Critics of socialism face similar burdens, though those burdens appear to be lighter, since these critics can point to existing free enterprise systems as embodying the main features of the economic system they favor.

These points can be illustrated by reference to Marx. Marx maintains that the two main evils directly attributable to a capitalist (i.e., free enterprise) economic system are exploitation and alienation. It is not enough for him to sustain these charges; he must also argue that the economic system of post-capitalist society will not be responsible for the continued existence of these problems. Unfortunately, Marx made no effort at all to provide these arguments.[15] On Marx's behalf, it might be objected that he did not do this because he did not think of himself as offering reasons for social change. His purpose was simply to describe the underlying forces and mechanisms by which social change takes place; social change takes place as the result of the clash of large-scale social forces, not merely because people have given reasons why society should change. Perhaps so. Or perhaps social forces operate through reasons, as those who favor rational choice explanations maintain. But however Marx conceived of his task, he is nevertheless committed to the belief that the systemic evils of capitalism are not permanent features of the human condition (or of industrial societies generally) but are, instead, transitory evils that attend one or more historically limited modes of production. And if these evils are transitory, then they will disappear in postcapitalist society. To hold that the evils of capitalist society are permanent or semipermanent features of the human condition is to hold a deeply conservative view, something of which neither Marx nor, indeed, nearly any other socialist, can be justly accused.

Moderate critics of existing systems, whether free enterprise or socialist, bear similar intellectual burdens. They believe that existing economic systems suffer a variety of defects, and they believe these problems can and should be cured by less drastic means than radical institutional change. Moderate critics of free enterprise systems (without any qualifying predicates) believe that private property rights in the means of production are responsible for some range of social ills; they propose a government program to ameliorate the problem they have attributed to the free enterprise system per se. Moderate critics of existing socialist systems favor the introduction of some market pricing of goods and services. Radicals on both sides regard these cures as homeopathic or worse; they may or may not be right. However, the general point remains that all intellectually responsible criticism requires the articulation and defense of an alternative or, at the very least, a frank acknowledgement of ignorance or skepticism about the possibility or prospects for improvement.

To sum up, explicitly or implicitly, one of the chief virtues claimed for each side's favored type of economic system is that it would prevent, preclude, or (at the very least) substantially ameliorate the evils that allegedly attach to the other type of system. In other words, they believe that the favored type of economic system has the virtue of not having the social vices associated with the other type. Not all social virtues can be construed as the absence of some social vice, but some of them are most naturally thought of in that way. If participants in this debate are to make real progress, they must not only substantiate a charge against an abstractly specified type of economic system; they must also make the associated case that a favored alternative does not suffer the same malady.

Let us turn now to my second question, namely, Does the positive case for one type of system require a critique of the other type of system? Once again, as a matter of logic the answer is, in general, no.[16] One could make a case in favor of a certain type of economic system without offering any criticism of an alternative type of system. On the other hand, in the context of this dispute, there does seem to be a pragmatic presupposition to the effect that at least some of the virtues of the good society attributable to the favored type of economic system are absent in the alternative type. If these virtues were present in the other type of system, then, in making their positive case, these theorists would not be giving us reasons to believe that one system ought, or ought not, to be replaced by the alternative. In point of fact, many participants in this debate begin with a systematic critique of the disfavored type of economic system and then move on to make the positive case for some favored type.[17] From a pragmatic point of view, this makes sense; the favored alternative is motivated by an attempt to avoid the social vices attributed to the other type of system.

Defending Economic Systems

Based on the discussion so far, the general form of the arguments against a type of economic system is reasonably clear:

1. Condition C is a necessary condition for a good society.
2. No society that has a free enterprise system (a certain type of socialist economic system) meets condition C. Therefore,
3. No society with a free enterprise system (a certain type of socialist economic system) is a good society.

What would be the form of argument in favor of some type of economic system? It would seem that one would begin with a premise to the effect that a certain set of conditions are jointly sufficient for a society to be a good society. The next premise would say that any society with the favored type of economic system meets all of these conditions. Therefore, any society with that type of economic system is a good society.

But this way of arguing will not work for two reasons. First, and most obviously, there is more to the good society than having the right sort of economic system. Economic systems are not society's only institutions; a fully formed conception of the good society (which only someone with a complete social philosophy has) would specify the other institutions of the good society, such as the political system insofar as it is independent of the economic system, the institution of the family or its analogue, and whatever other institutions a society must have. A second problem with this way of thinking about a defense of a free enterprise or socialist economic system is that there are considerable differences of opinion within each camp about what the economic system of the good society should look like. The discussions of the definitions of the terms 'free enterprise system' and 'socialist economic system' in the first section of this chapter make it evident that there can be significant variations among the different systems to which these terms respectively refer. These differences can be quite profound, especially in the case of socialist economic systems where the crucial notion of socialization of the means of production can be understood in fundamentally different ways.

Presumably, what most people have in mind when they are thinking about the economic system of the good society is something much less abstract than what is indicated by the term 'free enterprise system' or 'socialist economic system.' (By contrast, as noted in the last section, criticisms of types of economic systems tend to be pitched at a fairly high level of abstraction.) In sum, even within each camp, there are different conceptions of what the economic system should be. And yet there are points of agreement as well—points that go beyond the simple rejection of the type of economic system favored by the other side. In explaining what is involved in defending economic systems or types of economic systems, these commonalities and differences within each camp must be accurately represented.

How can this be done? This problem can be solved by distinguishing a more abstract from a less abstract type of economic system and a more limited from a less limited defense of a type of economic system. To understand these distinctions, let us begin with the following stipulative definition: A type of economic system, T_i, is defined by certain specifying features $F_1 \ldots F_n$. In other words, an economic system is of type T_i if and only if it meets conditions $F_1 \ldots F_n$. Particular economic systems—economic systems "on the ground"—are instances or tokens of many different types of systems, where the types are specified at higher or lower levels of abstraction. Type T_1 is more abstract than type T_2 if any system that satisfies the defining features (i.e., the F_i) of T_2 also satisfies the defining features of T_1 but not vice-versa. A highly abstract specification of an economic system would consist of merely the necessary and sufficient conditions given in the respective definitions for a system to be a free enterprise system or a socialist economic system. A less abstract (i.e., more concrete) specification of a type of economic system would mention those features but would also include other features. For example, one additional feature that might be mentioned in specifying a type of free enterprise system is something about a role for the state in providing public goods and/or goods and services for those unable to provide for themselves.

Now let us turn to the notion of a limited defense of a type of economic system. Such a defense links the specifying features, $F_1 \ldots F_n$, of that type (henceforth call these *type-defining features*) to some social virtues $V_1 \ldots V_n$. Recall that social virtues are necessary but not sufficient conditions for a society to be a good society. For example, one such virtue might be "the vast majority of people having a high standard of living," however that is defined. In other words, a necessary condition for a society's being a good society is that its economic system is responsible for a high standard of living for the vast majority of its people. In part, that is what makes a society a good society. Of course, this is not a sufficient condition for a society to be a good society, but it is arguably a necessary one.

Note that the conclusion of a limited defense is, in effect, saying that any society with an economic system that has the type-defining features (the F_i) also has some social virtue or other (the V_i). Claims of this sort are generally empirical and lawlike.[18] Their lawlike character suggests that they should be conceived of as containing an implicit ceteris paribus clause: All else being equal, any society that has this type of economic system will also have this social virtue.

Usually, a limited defense will consist of pointing out a causal connection, perhaps through mediating causes, between the type-defining features and some social virtue or virtues. The drawing of this connection will almost certainly require some additional assumptions about how human beings behave, subject to the institutional constraints (e.g., positive and negative incentives) implicit in the type-defining features. These assumptions may not hold in particular circumstances due to extraneous interfering factors. This means that statements linking the type-defining features and the virtue(s) in question cannot be proved outright. However, these statements can be well supported or confirmed.[19]

Defenses of types of economic systems can be more or less limited. A very limited defense would go from the type-defining features to a particular social virtue. A less limited defense would go from the same set of type-defining features to a number of different social virtues. Often, the main virtue or virtues that a theorist attributes to a specified type of economic system is that it precludes the vices attributed to the type of economic system favored by the other side. For instance, the chief virtue most socialists attribute to socialism is that it prevents the occurrence of social vices they have traced to the defining features of a free enterprise system. As indicated earlier, this is an empirical claim requiring empirical support. Indeed, a socialist who has criticized a free enterprise system in the manner indicated is (pragmatically) committed to the proposition that some type of socialist economic system lacks that vice or those vices — not fortuitously but in virtue of its type-defining features. The socialist who does not believe that some type of socialist economic system lacks those vices is committed to the proposition that the economic system of the good society (i.e., the best society one can reasonably hope for) is not socialist. Certainly, that would be enough to get her kicked out of the Socialist International.

To summarize, the preceding discussion calls attention to two important variables involved in a defense of a type of economic system. One is the abstractness of the type of system being defended. When one is defending a type of economic system, it is important to identify the defining features of that type and thus the level of abstraction at which the defense is being carried out. A second variable concerns how limited a defense is. A more limited defense argues from the defining features of the type to a particular social virtue (necessary condition for the good society). A less limited, that is, a more inclusive, defense argues from the same set of type-defining conditions to a number of different social virtues.

The main results of this section and the last are captured in the following schema, which represents the minimum that participants on each side of the debate agree on among themselves. It also provides a preliminary indication of what the burdens of proof are for each side. This issue will be explored in more detail in the next and final section of this chapter.

    A. Each party to the dispute who favors a socialist economic system maintains that

        1. Any society with a free enterprise system has social vices C_1 . . .

C_n (sufficient conditions for a society not to be a good society) because of its economic system.

2. Some type of socialist economic system, call it T, lacks all of the social vices $C_1 \ldots C_n$ because of the features $F_1 \ldots F_n$, which define type T.

3. These type-defining features are, or are responsible for, some social virtues $V_1 \ldots V_n$, that is, necessary conditions for a good society. (These social virtues include, but need not be limited to, the denials of the C_i.)

B. Each party to the dispute who favors a free enterprise system maintains that

1. Any society with a socialist economic system has social vices $C^*_1 \ldots C^*_n$ (sufficient conditions for a society not to be a good society) because of its economic system.

2. Some type of free enterprise system, call it T*, lacks all of the social vices $C^*_1 \ldots C^*_n$ in virtue of the features $F^*_1 \ldots F^*_n$, which define type T*.

3. These type-defining features are, or are responsible for, some social virtues $V^*_1 \ldots V^*_n$, that is, necessary conditions for a good society. (These social virtues include, but need not be limited to the denials of the C^*_i.)

For each side, schemata 1 and 2 entail that no society with the disfavored type of economic system is a good society, which accurately reflects how participants in this debate think about societies burdened with that type of economic system. Schema 3 entails schema 2; indeed, they may be logically equivalent if a theorist's defense of his favored type of economic system does not go beyond repudiating the vices of the other type of system. Note that this schema commits each participant to defending some version of the favored system against all the vices he has attributed to the other side; this does seem to be a positive duty for those who favor a socialist economic system or a free enterprise system. The reason is that the attribution of social vices to one or the other side is most naturally conceived of as the giving of reasons for social change in the direction of the favored side.

Conceiving of this dispute as a dispute about the economic system of the good society is not the only way to think about it. This approach is usefully pursued, however, insofar as it allows us to identify clearly the kinds of arguments and considerations that bear on it and to explain how progress might be made and, in the limit, how the dispute could be resolved. The purpose of the remainder of this section and the next is to argue for the utility of this approach along these lines. At the end of the next section, I shall explain how this book fits into the framework of the debate as it has been constructed here.

One important advantage of this approach is that it allows us to distinguish the philosophical from the economic issues. This dispute is partly a philosophical dispute about the kind of society that is ultimately desirable.

This is captured in the notion that different participants have different conceptions of the good society. However, another part of the dispute is about the consequences and the attending circumstances and conditions of different types of economic systems. This is a job for economists—at least insofar as economics is an empirical science and not a mathematical exercise.

Let us consider an example of each. Most socialists favor some egalitarian vision of the good society. Equality of material condition, or at least a much reduced range of inequality, is held to be a necessary condition for the good society.[20] Those who favor some version of the free enterprise system generally do not share this view. The socialist position raises two philosophical questions. The first is an analytical question about how one should understand equality of material condition. Does equality of material condition mean equality of welfare? of income? of resources? Clarifying the concepts has long been thought to be a primary philosophical task, at least in the Anglo-American philosophical community.[21]

The second question, sometimes not clearly separated from the first, is why the good society has to have this feature. One way to answer this is to develop a theory of justice that requires some version of equality of material condition. It is worth noting that this theory need not be completely a priori. It might be that the reason justice requires equality is that inequality has undesirable effects. In other words, there could be a substantial empirical component to this essentially philosophical dispute. In sum, the philosophical aspect of this dispute involves clarifying the concepts and developing a theory—or at least some justifying reasons—to provide support for some conception of the good society.

On the other hand, some aspects of this dispute fall squarely in the domain of economics. Disputants believe that economic systems of a certain type are contingently but nonfortuitously associated with various social vices and virtues; the economist's task is to develop the reasoning that leads from the type-defining features of the economic systems to the social virtues and vices. For example, those who favor some type of free enterprise system usually maintain that their favored type of system has important efficiency advantages over any socialist system (with the implication that having these advantages is a social virtue). The arguments for this come directly from economics.

Another advantage of conceiving of this dispute as a dispute about the nature of the economic system of the good society is that it allows us to clear up a persistent confusion that has clouded this debate for some time. Critics of socialism have frequently charged that socialists have simply assumed that a socialist society is a good society in some respect or other (by definition, as it were).[22] When existing systems fall short, they are simply dismissed as nonsocialist. What troubles these critics is that this seems to make the crucial claims about socialism empirically unfalsifiable. Interpreted in one way, there is some justice to this complaint, but interpreted in another way, socialists can successfully rebut the charge. We have seen how it is possible for a type-defining feature of a socialist economic system to be a necessary condition for a good society. Specifically, a socialist might believe that social control (or worker control) of the means of production is both a defining feature of a socialist economic system and a necessary condition for a society to be a good society. On this way of thinking, one can legitimately debate whether or not a system is really socialist; if the means of production are not controlled in the interests of society at large (however that is to be understood), or alternatively, if the workers do not really control the means of production, then the system is not, in fact, socialist. However, the critic can simply reformulate his objection as a query about whether or not a genuinely socialist economic system is empirically possible.

On the other hand, when the desirable feature is not part of the definition of a socialist economic system (e.g., it is some social goal, such as relative equality of material condition), the dispute must be conceived of as an empirical one that depends crucially on some facts about how the favored type of economic system would actually function. It distorts and trivializes the issues involved to think of these as definitional disputes about whether or not a system is really socialist.

The confusion, I suspect, ultimately lies in the word 'socialism', which is multiply ambiguous between an economic system, a conception of a good society, and the conjunction of the two. On the latter two understandings, it is necessarily and trivially true that socialism is a good society. In general, this book avoids the term 'socialism,' except where this systematic ambiguity does not threaten. The terms 'socialist economic system' and 'socialist conception of the good society' may be more ponderous, but they are also more precise. Separating the referents of these two terms is vital and sometimes more difficult than one might suppose.

Resolution and Progress in the Dispute

If the account of the dispute developed in this chapter is both accurate and illuminating, it should be possible to explain clearly what would count as a resolution of it, as well as what would count as progress short of resolution. Both of these can be done.

Would proving that the economic system of the good society is not a free enterprise (or socialist) system resolve this dispute? The answer is complex. Let us begin by recalling what this involves. First and foremost, it involves explaining some social vice or other by reference to the type-defining features of a free enterprise system (viz., private ownership of most of the means of production and the freedom to sell one's labor). This is more difficult than it might seem because one must establish a fairly direct empirical or logical connection between these very abstract defining features and some social vice or other.

What is at issue here goes right to the heart of the controversy between those on the Left, who believe that some social ills of existing capitalist societies can be blamed directly and entirely on the defining features of the free enterprise system, and those on the Right, who believe that these social ills, if they exist at all, are best explained by reference to exogenous factors, such as unrelated aspects of the political system, human nature (including original sin), historical accident, and especially the political activities of socialists and their fellow travelers. By contrast, those on the Left argue that any society with a free enterprise system would have this social problem because it is of the nature of such a system that it creates this problem. Let us call this kind of argument a *comprehensive critique*. The conclusion of such an argument has the following general form:

> (CC) Any economic system that meets the defining conditions for a free enterprise system (viz., private ownership of most of the means of production and freedom to sell one's labor) has some social vice V.

The argument for a statement of the form (CC) may or may not lead through mediating hypotheses of the form

> (MH) Any economic system that meets the defining conditions for a free enterprise system has property Q and any system with property Q has social vice V.

Though arguments of this form do bring in factors other than those cited in the definition of a free enterprise system, those factors are nonaccidentally related to these defining features, so such an argument would constitute a comprehensive critique of a free enterprise system.

A comprehensive critique can be achieved in another way. Suppose that one developed an exhaustive catalogue of subtypes of free enterprise systems and then gave different arguments running from the defining features of each subtype to some social vice or other (possibly not the same vice for each subtype). This would achieve the same result, because one would still be able to conclude that any society with a free enterprise system suffers some social vice (or other) and thus that a good society does not have a free enterprise economic system.

In offering either kind of comprehensive critique, a critic must also show that some type of socialist economic system avoids whatever vices have been attributed to a free enterprise system (or to all the subtypes of free enterprise systems). This positive task must be executed if the critique is to provide reasons for social change in the direction of socialism. This means that a successful attack on the free enterprise system requires at least a limited defense of some type of socialist economic system—limited to showing that the favored type of system has the virtue of not having the relevant social vice or vices. This can be done by showing that the relevant type-defining features prevent or preclude the vice(s) from emerging, or it can be shown that these type-defining features so significantly ameliorate the vices that they lose their status as social vices and become minor social defects (blemishes, so to speak).

An example will illustrate. Suppose a socialist shows that any free enterprise system will visit widespread alienation on the people who live in that society and that widespread alienation is a social vice. For the reasons indicated, this socialist must also show that some favored type of socialist economic system would prevent or preclude alienation altogether or at least would reduce it to insignificant levels.

Suppose that these arguments have been worked out. This would be at least a partial resolution of the debate—and would definitely constitute progress—because it would have ruled out one generic type of economic system as a candidate for the economic system of the good society.[23] Moreover, it would have been further shown that some type of socialist economic system suffers none of those vices. The question now becomes, Does proving that a type of economic system lacks a social vice or vices that can be justly blamed on the other type of system constitute a complete or total defense of that type of system? If so, then the dispute will have been completely resolved.

Unfortunately, the answer is no, and the reason is simple. In addition to proving that there are some virtues explainable in terms of the defining features of the favored type (beginning with the absence of the other side's vices), a complete defense also requires that one show that the favored type of economic system is not responsible for *any* social vice, not just the ones correctly attributable to the other side. The reason for this is that a complete defense proves that an economic system is, in virtue of its type-defining features, responsible for some of the things that make a society a good society and none of the things that are sufficient to make a society not a good society. In short, it does good deeds and sins not. Or, to be more precise, it commits no cardinal sins. The distinction is important. As was just suggested, there may be lesser social defects ("social blemishes") traceable to the type-defining features of the favored economic system. For an economic system to be the economic system of the good society, it need not be perfect. All that is required is that whatever defects it is responsible for are not sufficiently serious and avoidable to make the society in question not a good society; however a conception of the good society is articulated, it is, by definition, something that it is reasonable to hope could exist.

This is what a complete defense of a type of economic system establishes, and this is why such a defense must do more than show that a system of that type does not have some vice correctly attributable to the other generic type of economic system. A complete defense of a type of economic system would show that there are no social vices whatsoever traceable to those type-defining features. But how could one possibly do that? The burden of proof in a complete defense of a type of economic system appears overwhelming. Indeed, it seems that without some exhaustive catalogue of social vices, it would be an impossible task to execute. How could one know that some unspecified vice could not be traced to the type-defining features of the favored economic system, especially if, as seems reasonable to suppose, the favored type does not as yet exist anywhere?

The most obvious solution is to look to the theory of the good society for an exhaustive catalogue of all social vices. The problem with this suggestion is that a complete theory of the good society is probably something very few participants in this dispute have. (It would seem to require a fully formed social philosophy.) It is as if someone trying to figure out how to start an automobile company from scratch were advised to first get an unlimited line of credit from a consortium of the world's largest banks. The advice is sound but difficult to implement. The next question is, Is there any second-best solution?

One promising possibility is the following: suppose that in addition to showing that the favored type of system would not be responsible for the social vices associated with the other generic type of system, one could also show that this type of system would not be responsible for any of the social vices associated with existing economic systems of the same generic type as the favored one. For example, a socialist would show not only that the type-defining features of the socialist system she favors would prevent or preclude the social vices that she has successfully pinned on a free enterprise system. In addition, she would show that these type-defining features would prevent or preclude the social vices that have been attributed to existing (present or past) *socialist* economic systems.

Establishing all of that would still not prove that the type-defining features of the favored system would not be responsible for any social vice whatsoever. But accomplishing all of this would provide some—indeed, very good—reason to believe it would not. By hypothesis, one has shown that a certain type of socialist system has neither the serious problems attributable to free enterprise systems generally nor the serious problems that have been attributed to other types of socialist systems. That would seem to count for quite a bit, even if it is not an outright proof of the essential goodness of the favored type of economic system. Let us call this a *stout defense*. A stout defense is not a complete defense, but it does constitute a part—perhaps a large part—of one. If a type of economic system could be stoutly defended, it seems that one would be entitled to say that there is good reason to believe (though it is by no means certain) that the favored type of economic system is the best one can reasonably hope for. After all, it has none of the social vices attributable to existing socialist or free enterprise economic systems.

Consider the following hypothetical example of a stout defense. Suppose a socialist establishes that any free enterprise system suffers some social vices (e.g., systematic exploitation, objectionable inequality). He then defends a type of market socialism in which the predominant form of organization is the worker-owned cooperative. This defense consists of showing that such a system would have none of the vices of a free enterprise system and perhaps that it would have some additional virtues as well.

Suppose, further, that he provides good reason to believe that the very considerable social vices that have been attributed to existing socialist economic systems would not recur if this form of market socialism were instituted. One way to accomplish this would be to explain how the type-defining features of the favored system would prevent, preclude, or significantly ameliorate those vices. So, for example, if the vices of existing socialist systems are explainable by reference to the fact that these systems are centrally planned, the defender of market socialism would explain how reliance on the market mechanism would preclude or ameliorate these problems. In addition to doing all of this, suppose that the philosophical theory behind the virtues and vices is articulated and provisionally defended. (It is probably asking too much that this theory be proven to be true.) All this taken together would constitute a stout defense of this type of market socialist economic system.

By so elevating this type of socialist economic system above the ranks of the existing sinners of this world (both free enterprise and socialist), our socialist has not thereby proven that such a system could not itself be responsible for some social vice or other, but he has at least given a stout defense of this type of system. This would come close to resolving the dispute between those who favor capitalism and those who favor socialism—perhaps as close as one could reasonably hope for.

If a stout defense comes close to resolving the dispute, is there any way to make substantial progress short of a stout defense? I believe there is. Clearly, one of the most difficult prerequisites of a stout defense is a comprehensive critique of all economic systems of the other generic type. A more limited critique (and correlative defense of a version of the favored type) would target only a certain (sub-)type of free enterprise or socialist economic system, instead of all such systems. This is a more manageable project.

For example, some critics of socialism (Mises 1951; Hayek 1935) have targeted all and only those socialist economic systems that employ central planning. As in the case of a stout defense, if this critique is to have meaning in the context of the capitalism/socialism dispute, the critic must explain how a free enterprise system (perhaps of a certain type) avoids the social vice(s) attributed to centrally planned economies. In short, this critique would require a limited defense of some version of a free enterprise system. As the next chapter shows, these critics of socialism have discharged both parts of their task. Notice that this limited critique of one type of socialist economic system would leave untouched other types of socialist systems (e.g., market socialist systems) and so would not serve as a complete vindication of some version of the free enterprise system over all varieties of socialist economic systems—which should seem about right to those familiar with the Hayek-Mises critique of socialism.

The conclusion of a successful limited critique of a certain type of economic system is that the economic system of the good society is not of this type. In the example, this implies that if the economic system of the good society is to be socialist, it cannot be centrally planned. A critique of this sort narrows the range of systems still subject to debate and so represents real progress in the dispute. How much progress depends on the type-defining features that are called to account. If those features are widely instantiated in the real world or if they are prominent in socialist thought, then this critique represents significant progress.

There is at least one other way in which significant progress can be made. It is a fair observation that while participants in this dispute are willing to offer limited defenses of existing economic systems in virtue of certain features they have, few are willing to offer a stout defense of any existing economic system. This is so for the simple reason that most thinkers believe that substantial improvements in any existing system are genuinely possible. The type (or, to be more accurate, subtype) of economic system that someone is willing stoutly to defend has new and different attributes—attributes that are supposed to prevent various social vices and insure various social virtues. Let us call a type of system someone is willing to offer a stout defense of 'a well-motivated system.' To say that a type of system is well motivated is just to say that there is at least some reason to believe that it is responsible for none of the social vices that have been blamed on existing socialist or free enterprise systems. To put it another way, a well-motivated system is one for which a prima facie case can be made.

Suppose, now, that a well-motivated socialist economic system could be successfully criticized. This would involve showing that such a system would, in fact, be responsible for some social vice or vices and making a limited defense of some type of free enterprise system. This does not prove that no type of socialist system can be given a stout defense, but it does make the prospects look unpromising, if only because it is doubtful that there are very many well-motivated types of socialist systems out there in logical space. (Of course, the same considerations apply, mutatis mutandis, to free enterprise systems.) For these reasons, it seems that a critique of a well-motivated type of economic system would constitute real progress in this debate, though it still falls short of a comprehensive critique of socialist (or free enterprise) systems, that is, a critique of all forms of socialism.

The purpose of this book can now be stated quite simply: it is to give a critique of a well-motivated type of socialist economic system and a limited defense of a certain type of free enterprise system. Chapter 2 identifies a version of market socialism and provides the motivations for it. Motivating it involves identifying a minimal socialist vision of the good society that nearly all socialists subscribe to and sketching the reasoning that leads from the type-defining features of this form of market socialism to the social virtues that constitute this socialist vision of the good society. (One of those virtues is something nonmarket socialist systems have never realized, viz., achieving a decent standard of living in comparison to what has been achieved in free enterprise systems.)

Chapters 3–7 constitute a sustained critique of this model or version of a market socialist system and a limited defense of a free enterprise system. The main charge to be proved is that this type of system is responsible for widespread systematic exploitation of the sort that free enterprise systems preclude or minimize. Chapter 3 offers a general analysis or theory of exploitative exchange in a market economy. Chapter 4 discusses some recent work in the economics of organizations and provides a basis for identifying where, and explaining how, exploitation can take place in any market economy, whether it is free enterprise or socialist. Chapter 5 gives more details on the economics of organizations and explains how the predominant organizational forms of a free enterprise system (*capitalist organizations*) tend to preclude or minimize opportunities for exploitative exchange. Chapters 6 and 7 contain the heart of the argument against market socialism. These chapters consist of a comparative evaluation of capitalist organizations and market socialist organizations. It is argued that the latter permit—and, indeed, encourage —forms of exploitation that are prevented or discouraged by capitalist organizations and that therefore, on the basis of a widely shared socialist conception of the good society, this version of market socialism cannot be the economic system of the good society.

The larger significance of this conclusion depends on how well motivated this version of market socialism is and how important the elimination of exploitation is to the socialist conception of the good society. Chapter 8 addresses these issues. The first section considers other types of market systems that look attractive from a socialist perspective. It argues that these other systems are also more exploitative than free enterprise systems, are incompatible with other elements of the socialist vision of the good society, or are not really forms of socialism. Chapter 8 also explores the larger significance of exploitation for the socialist conception of the good society by discussing the philosophical significance of economic exploitation, in particular, its connection to distributive justice.

This chapter has tried to sort out the various possible positions in the capitalism/socialism dispute and the intellectual commitments that go with those positions. A recurring theme has been the essentially comparative nature of the case for or against any type of economic system. The virtues and vices attributable to economic systems may themselves be given a comparative formulation. But even if they are not, making the case for any type of system will require that the case be made against the other type of system, and vice-versa. The reason for this is that at least in this area of political philosophy, one's cogitations are supposed to issue in reasons for or against fundamental social change. These requirements give a philosophical expression to the general intellectual virtue of taking one's opponents seriously. A socialist's opponent believes that some version of the free enterprise system is a good system and that socialist economic systems are not good systems. It is incumbent upon those socialists to provide good reasons to maintain that both of these beliefs are in fact mistaken.[24] Similarly, a critic of socialism must provide some reasons for thinking that a socialist economic system is not the economic system of the good society and that those reasons are logically related to reasons why some form of a free enterprise is. The standards imposed on this debate are quite high, but they are not impossible to meet.

2

Why Market Socialism?

Motivating the Market

No discussion of the capitalism/socialism debate can ignore the dramatic changes that have taken place in the nations of the East in the late 1980s and beyond. Though much of this change has been in their respective political systems, there have been substantial changes in the economic systems as well. From the absorption of socialist East Germany by capitalist West Germany to privatization in Poland and Hungary, to the floundering reforms in the former Soviet Union, a common theme has been the repudiation of central planning. The term 'repudiation' accurately describes the current attitude toward central planning; even where it is extant, no one defends it. To the extent that it persists, it does so only because the political leadership does not know how to create a market economy or some third alternative. When public figures defending central planning are limited to the likes of Fidel Castro, Kim Il Sung, and that late, great Albanian, Enver Hoxha, central planning has lost all credibility.

Why this has happened when it did is something of a mystery. Every economic system has its problems, and in the abstract, there seems to be no way to know how high a standard of living an economic system ought to be able to deliver. However, it may be that growing and glaring comparative deficiencies have finally undermined faith in central planning, even and especially among the elites. Over the past twenty years or so, market economies have initiated, assimilated, and exploited dramatic new technologies so effectively that the gap between the standard of living in the socialist East and the capitalist West (which now includes a number of countries in the Western Pacific) has once again begun to grow. Furthermore, this fact has become increasingly well known as the East has become more accessible to Western travelers and journalists and as many people in the East have learned more about the standard of living in the West. In this harsh comparative light and in the absence of any plausible exogenous factors (e.g., war) to explain away these salient differences in living standards, no one any longer believes that centrally planned economies would or could come close to, much less surpass, the standard of living enjoyed in the West.

Paralleling these changes in public attitudes have been changes in the intellectual climate. Up until about the middle 1980s, it was possible to find respectable thinkers, including some economists, who had some praise for and were optimistic about centrally planned economies. For example, Robert Heilbroner and Lester Thurow have said, "Can economic command [i.e., central planning] significantly compress and accelerate the growth process? The remarkable performance of the Soviet Union suggests that it can. In 1920 Russia was but a minor figure in the economic councils of the world. Today it is a country whose economic achievements bear comparison with those of the United States" (1984, 629). Now Heilbroner and Thurow do not say what kind of comparison these achievements bear, but the tone is clearly one of restrained admiration. Up until the end of the 1980s, a significant segment of mainstream opinion had it that just as Western capitalist economies had their problems, so, too, did centrally planned socialist economies. The problems were different, and the general standard of living in the East was lower for a variety of (mostly historical) reasons, but the basic difficulties were not categorically different in their extent or severity, though they might be in their etiology.[1]

This view is no longer intellectually respectable. This is not a simple consequence of the repudiation of central planning in Eastern Europe and the former Soviet Union. Sometime in the middle-to-late 1980s, something approaching a limited consensus began to emerge among the intelligentsia in the West.[2] This consensus holds that the inefficiencies endemic to any centrally planned economy are serious to the point of being catastrophic and that the only reforms that have any chance of success are those which are part of a process of fundamental change that replaces central planning with the market. The view that central planning must be *replaced* by some form of market economy and not just augmented by the market in some way or other seems to be the distinctive feature of the new consensus.

In retrospect, the publication in 1983 of Alec Nove's *The Economics of Feasible Socialism* may have been a turning point, at least among socialists in the anglophone community. Most of the book is really about the economics of infeasible socialism, that is, central planning. Nove offers a systematic structural critique of centrally planned economies. Only in the last chapter does he get around to talking about feasible socialism, and it involves a substantial reliance on the market. Perhaps because Nove is himself a socialist (and a specialist on the Soviet economy), this book was not dismissed out of hand by those on the Left and was in fact well received.[3] The basic message seemed to be that these systems do not work very well—for deep structural reasons— and that recognition of this fact does not require giving up on socialism.

To say that a view is no longer intellectually respectable is not to say that no one holds it anymore. Nor does saying so have much probative value: truth is not discovered by a show of hands. However, this consensus is, in fact, well founded; it is not surprising that the best arguments in support of it come from the Right. This is not because those on the Right have a monopoly on high-level critical skills. It is just that the opponents of a position are most likely to see clearly its most serious weaknesses. By contrast, it would be surprising if a position's most fervent supporters were to discover its main draw-back. It is a testament to the intellectual integrity of many Eastern European socialists that they have come to see (often at the end of a protracted and painful period of soul-searching) that central planning has been at the root of the problems facing their economic systems and that nonradical reforms have no chance of success.[4]

Let us turn from the history of ideas to the arguments. The Austrian economist Ludwig von Mises (1919) published a paper in which he claimed that rational economic calculation in a socialist community was impossible. At the time, socialism was identified with central planning, and the real object of Mises's attack was central planning. This paper inaugurated what came to be known as the socialist calculation debate. In the course of this debate there was some wasted effort on both sides, owing in part to Mises's peculiar a prioristic methodology and in part to his critics' inability to get the simple point that he was not talking about some abstract model of an economy but instead about a real-world economic system. Mises's argument was restated and elaborated by F. A. Hayek (1937, 1945) in two important papers in the 1930s and 1940s.[5] The details of the debate need not detain us here. The main contention Mises and Hayek advanced is that in the absence of market prices, there would be no way to arrive at an accurate valuation of the true costs (i.e., the opportunity costs) of producer and consumer goods. Since central planning does away with market pricing, it cannot properly value economic inputs and outputs. This makes it profoundly and inherently inefficient.

The argument for the necessity of market prices starts from the fact that production in the modern world is enormously complicated. A wide range of producer goods and different kinds of labor go into the production of even the simplest consumer good. Think of what is involved in getting a pencil from unimproved raw materials to the consumer. For production to proceed efficiently, there must be coordination between and among suppliers of raw materials and labor, producer goods firms, and consumer goods firms. Otherwise, shortages and surpluses will develop and inappropriate goods (e.g., parts that don't fit, shoddy products) will be produced. To effect coordination in a centrally planned economy, planners assign firms production targets, expressed in physical terms, such as so many tons of nails or so many automobiles. They also grant firms the authority to requisition inputs— authorizations that are also expressed in physical terms. All production coordination is, therefore, ex ante.

Because so much depends on the particulars of both what is supplied and what is demanded, the planning system must assimilate and process enormous amounts of information if the plan itself is to be well informed and ultimately successful. For example, if there is a need to transport tomatoes from Tbilisi to Minsk, it is not enough to know that there are trucks available in Tbilisi. One must also know that these trucks are not used to haul manure, that they are actually running, that there is adequate fuel along the way, and so on. Highly specific or particular information is required for effective planning, yet the only manageable way to gather and process the huge quantities of information needed to plan a large economy is to put that information in statistical form. The problem with using statistical information for planning was clearly recognized by Hayek.

> The statistics which such a central authority would have to use would have to be arrived at precisely by abstracting from minor differences between things, by lumping together as resources of one kind, items which differ as regards location, quality, and other particulars, in a way which may be very significant for the specific decision. It follows from this that central planning based on statistical information by its very nature cannot take direct account of these circumstances of time and place. (1945, 524)

The central planners, then, are faced with an intractable informational problem in that the information they have access to is not very helpful, and the information they need is largely unavailable.[6] What enormously complicates this basic problem is that the relevant information is constantly changing. Mises called attention to five broad categories of change: (1) change in the physical world, (2) demographic change, (3) changes in the means of production (e.g., tools and machinery wear out), (4) technological change, and (5) changes in consumer preferences (1951, 196–208). These categories cover all of the fundamental determinants of scarcity value. Since these determinants are in a constant state of flux and since they interact in unimaginably complex ways, the planners cannot achieve successful coordination of production by groping toward something that works tolerably well and then simply repeating it (i.e., letting the economy "reproduce" itself, as Marxists sometimes say). At the micro level—the level at which production decisions are actually made—future conditions are rarely the same as existing conditions, and predicating decision-making on the supposition that they are would be plainly irrational. In point of fact, however, that is exactly the supposition that centrally planned economies have made; this is what accounts for their sclerotic and irrational performance in a changing world (Rutland 1985, 115–24).

In addition to these informational difficulties, there are several serious motivational problems involved in formulating the plan and getting it executed. It is not just that people will not work very hard in a centrally planned economy (although that has been a genuine and chronic problem). An equally serious difficulty is that key individuals have a strong incentive to prevent the efficient utilization of resources. For example, since managers are evaluated by the success of their units at meeting production targets, they have an incentive to underestimate plant capacity, to hoard means of production and labor, and to overstate actual production. All of these activities impede the timely convocation of producer goods and labor services required for efficient production. A third motivational problem is that there is little incentive to produce high-quality goods or goods that are actually needed. This is in part an echo of the problems involved in knowing what is actually needed and what trade-offs between quality and cost are acceptable in both producer goods and consumer goods. But it is also in part a motivational problem stemming from the fact that what actually drives production are the planning directives from the center and not the needs of downstream producers and consumers. Finally, the attempt to plan comprehensively all production discourages innovation in both production techniques and final products. Because innovation upsets existing ways of doing things, there is no place in the system for new ideas.

The true significance of these motivational and informational problems is evident only by a comparison with an alternative way of organizing production, namely, the market. In a market system, both consumers and firms transmit their needs and wants to supplier firms by their acts of buying and abstentions from buying. The retailer, the wholesaler, the manufacturer, the supplier of capital goods, and the owners of original factors of production (natural resources and labor) all get information from the market by way of prices for their outputs and costs for inputs and outputs. Hayek's (1945) central insight is that market prices are fraught with epistemological significance. The prices at which goods and services exchange tend to reflect and amalgamate both the plans of market participants and their beliefs about the alternatives open to them.

Moreover, changes in prices reflect changes in those plans or changed beliefs about alternatives. For example, suppose that the Florida citrus crop is repeatedly decimated by frost. When the frost hits, the price of citrus will be raised by those with product to sell. This serves as a signal to others on both the supply and the demand side that less of this crop will be available than was previously thought, and people adjust their plans accordingly. Other suppliers who are not affected (e.g., the Brazilians) may move to increase production; buyers will turn to substitutes, which will drive up those prices, which, in turn, will lead to an increase the production of substitutes for substitutes, and so on.

In short, production will have been recoordinated to be brought better into line with the new economic realities. No one person or committee had to make all of these decisions about production. Prices transmit the necessary information from those who have the knowledge to those who need to know. Entrepreneurial profit or pure profit (as it is sometimes called) comes from being among the first to notice, either through luck or foresight, that people's plans are not as well adjusted as they might be relative to the changing underlying economic realities. The constant changes in the five broad categories listed means that there will always be profit opportunities "out there" for firms and individuals with foresight or luck or both. The hope of making positive profits and the fear of suffering negative profits (i.e., losses) comprise the main incentives for firms and individuals to act in ways that improve the coordination of production.

Of course, these processes do not always operate without impediments—some thrown up by entrepreneurs themselves and some by their friends in the state. This story abstracts from monopolies, externalities, artificial barriers to entry, public goods problems, and so forth. The system is not perfect. However, these are complications or wrinkles on a more fundamental story about how a market economy works. According to that story, resource allocation, and thus the coordination of production, is fundamentally achieved by entrepreneurial decisions based on prices and motivated by the desire for profits. The contrast with how production is coordinated in a centrally planned economy could hardly be more stark and dramatic.

The preceding is a fairly compressed statement of the Mises-Hayek argument for the superior efficiency of a market system relative to central planning. The notes to this chapter direct the reader to more elaborate discussions of these points. The main ideas, however, should be clear enough. This argument and the surrounding discussions over the years constitute a clear instance of progress in the capitalism/socialism debate. Mises and Hayek have offered a comprehensive critique (see chapter 1) of a significant (sub-)type of socialist economic systems, namely, those with a centrally planned economy. Nearly all existing socialist systems have had this type of economic system; until recently, many people believed that central planning is, in many respects, comparable to a market system.[7] However, Mises and Hayek argued that the economic system of the good society could not be a centrally planned economy because, by its very nature, such a system is grossly inefficient relative to what a market system can achieve. The main problem with these economies was not capitalist encirclement, political despotism, a poor natural resource base, or any of the other excuses that have been trotted out over the decades. Instead, it is—and always has been—central planning itself.

Notice that this critique of central planning includes a limited defense of a free enterprise system. Mises and Hayek explain not only the informational and motivational deformities of central planning but also the corresponding excellences of a free enterprise system. This is as it should be, since they conceived of themselves as giving reasons against a certain kind of social change that was high on the socialist agenda in the early part of this century: the abolition of the market.

This argument also spurred socialist theoreticians to think about how a socialist economic system might employ markets. Mises's first and most important opponent in the calculation debate, Oskar Lange, even suggested that a statue of Mises be erected in at the Ministry of Socialization in every socialist country in recognition of Mises's contribution to socialist thought (1938, 57–58).[8] On Lange's view, Mises had called attention to a heretofore unrecognized problem that socialists needed to solve. As a result, the capitalism/socialism debate has narrowed to the point that the dispute can now fairly be characterized as between different types of market systems.

It is beyond the scope of this book to give a history of attempts to combine markets and socialism beyond noting the origins of the idea in the calculation debate. There are, however, two related terminological points that warrant brief mention. Sometimes in discussions of attempts to reform or change existing socialist economies, the term 'market reform' is used to refer to any change which tries to take scarcity values into account in a more systematic way than central planning does. This seems to be what many journalists (East and West) and government spokesmen in Eastern Europe and the former Soviet Union have meant when they talked about market reforms, at least before the events of 1989–91. For example, it has been reported that in the former Soviet Union, a plane ticket for a five-hundred-mile trip cost less than a blank video cassette and that until Poland dismantled its centrally planned economy, subsidies on bread made it economical to feed it to hogs. Market reforms, as the term was used, involved repricing these goods and services to diminish these apparent irrationalities.

In a similar vein, the term 'market socialism' has been used to refer to any centrally planned socialist system that tries to take scarcity value into account in a more systematic way than they have previously done, with, however, no commitment to decentralized market pricing, that is, to letting firms charge whatever they think the traffic will bear. These ways of using the term 'market' may be appropriate for discussions of gradual reforms in centrally planned economies, but the 'market' part of market socialism must be defined more narrowly for the purposes of this book.

A market socialist system must, by definition, be one in which the market pricing mechanism, as it was just described prevails. The reason for this is simple: the preceding discussion indicates that the efficiency of the market is to be found in the process by which market pricing coordinates production. If a market socialist system is to be about as efficient as a free enterprise system, it must employ a market pricing mechanism. Accordingly, let us say that an economic system is a market economy if and only if most production is coordinated through market pricing. This implies that firms in a market socialist economy are free to raise and lower the prices of both producer and consumer goods as they see fit. This definition allows for exceptions to, and restrictions on, the basic market process along the lines discussed in Chapter 1, provided that they do not individually or collectively overwhelm the market pricing mechanism.

The primary motivation for wanting a socialist economic system to be a market economy in the sense just defined is not far to seek: it permits the economy to approximate the efficiency of a free enterprise system. An appreciation of the efficiency of market pricing is now widespread among socialists (Nove 1983, 180–82; Miller 1989b, 30–32; Schweickart 1980, 67–68; Horvat 1982, 501; Estrin and Winter 1989, 106–7). The term 'approximate' is carefully chosen, but it has some misleading connotations.

First, the misleading connotations. Socialist respect for the market is hedged, qualified, and highly conditional; in short, it is grudging. In light of this, it is a little misleading to suggest an attitude of emulation toward free enterprise systems among those who favor market socialism. No such suggestion is intended here. Moreover, this way of talking suggests a comparison with free enterprise systems (or aspects thereof) as they exist "on the ground." For socialists who think in pictures, this conjures up images of Wall Street, the Chicago Board of Trade, and even Las Vegas. Nothing like these institutions finds its way into the socialist vision of the good society. However, as the terms of the debate have been defined in chapter 1, the objects of comparison are never economic systems as they exist "on the ground" but are, instead, *types* of economic systems, which are abstractly specified by their type-defining features. When comparing types of economic systems, one abstracts from all other properties of existing economic systems except those that are relevant for the purposes at hand. Whatever market socialists find objectionable about existing free enterprise systems, it is not their basic pricing mechanism; it is primarily this feature (and perhaps only this feature) that market socialists find admirable and worthy of emulation, however reluctant they are to put it in those terms.

The misleading connotations neutralized, or at least noted, it does seem to fair to say that market socialists believe that the efficiency of a market socialist economic system is at least in vicinity of what one finds in a free enterprise system. Certainly, they do not believe it would be significantly less efficient. And because the basic method of coordinating production is the same, it is doubtful that they believe such a system would be dramatically and categorically more efficient. It is difficult to be more precise than this, in part because it is difficult to find clear pronouncements on this question in the writings of contemporary market socialists. The usual view seems to be that a favored type of market socialist system would be about as efficient as a free enterprise system. In support of this, some authors simply point to the efficiency advantages of the market in such a way that there is no apparent presupposition of private ownership of the means of production. The implication is that social ownership would be equally efficient. (See Selucky 1979, 208–9; Horvat 1982, 205–8; Miller 1989a, 9; Miller 1989b, 31.)

Other authors recognize that their favored system may be subject to some inefficiencies that do not face free enterprise systems (e.g., Vanek 1970; Schweickart 1980, 73; Cohen and Rogers 1983, 164; Bonin and Putterman 1987; Estrin 1989, 175–76). On the other hand, they believe that a market socialist system would not have some of the inefficiencies facing free enterprise systems. The reasons given are various, but a common (if not universal) thread is the enhanced role of the state in the economy. On their view, the state in a market socialist system is better able to handle externalities and public goods problems; through its control of new investment, it can dampen or eliminate the inefficiencies associated with the business cycle.[9]

However the finer points of this issue are decided, a free enterprise system can and should serve as at least an implicit standard of comparison for market socialist economic systems for at least two reasons. First, to the extent that socialists' acceptance of the market is motivated by a rejection of central planning, that rejection is based on a comparative judgment between centrally planned economies and free enterprise systems. Although the Mises-Hayek argument is cast in terms of private ownership of the means of production, market socialists are clearly committed to the view that their favored type of system would compare about as favorably with central planning as free enterprise systems do.

Second, for reasons that need not detain us here, noncomparative efficiency assessments of economic systems of any sort seem to be deeply problematic.[10] In consequence, it may be that only comparative judgments of the efficiency of economic systems are possible. If that is true, market socialists are faced with saying that their favored type of system is much less efficient, about as efficient, or much more efficient than free enterprise systems. The first alternative is plainly unacceptable, and there is no justification for the third option. Only the middle alternative is one that both has some prima facie plausibility and supports the market socialist view that the economic evils associated with central planning are not endemic to socialism.

But why does efficiency (comparative or otherwise) matter at all? It is not simply a question of keeping up with the Joneses, that is, the capitalist West. Rather, this efficiency is important because, at the very least, it makes it possible for everyone's basic material needs to be satisfactorily met. Material needs are those that can be met through the economic system (e.g., needs for food, clothing, and health care). In other words, they are needs that can be met by exchangeable goods and services. 'Satisfactorily' and 'basic' probably must be understood historically and relatively. Every society that persists for any period of time meets most people's basic material needs at some level. Clearly, however, not every existing society (today or in the past) is a good society when it comes to meeting people's basic material needs. When most of a society's population regularly waits in line for food and other basics, when that food (including staples) is of poor quality and often unavailable, when a duplex for two families is two adjoining rooms instead of two adjoining houses, when medical care for all but an elite falls far below what widely available technology and a little skilled application can offer, then people's basic needs are simply not being satisfactorily met. By contrast, most people in the West do not face these problems. To be sure, the West has its homeless and hungry, but these comprise a tiny fraction of the total population. The vast majority do have their basic needs satisfactorily met, something that simply cannot be said of those who have lived under a regime of central planning.

It seems to be the case (though it is hard to document directly) that market socialists believe that people's basic material needs would be satisfactorily met by whatever version of a market socialist economic system they favor and however 'basic' and 'satisfactorily' are understood. Its proponents believe that their favored type of system would at least do what centrally planned economies in the East have been unable to do and what existing free enterprise systems in the West have been able to do for most of their citizens, namely, satisfactorily meet those basic material needs. The standard of living that market socialists believe is achievable by their favored type of system might be higher, say, at the level of the middle class in advanced Western countries. It would probably have to be at least that high if market socialism is to garner democratic support in the West in the absence of a total economic collapse. To the question, Why this standard of living? or, more cautiously, Why must an economic system satisfactorily meet people's basic material needs?, the most obvious answer is that it is a necessary condition for any society—now or in the foreseeable future—to be a good society.

Though economic efficiency is perhaps the primary reason for market socialists to favor the market, it is not the only one. Another desideratum that the market can achieve (and that is part of most socialists' conception of the good society) is freedom of occupational choice (Miller 1989b, 33). There may be others. However, in light of the catastrophic failure of central planning—the main form that actually existing socialist economic systems have taken in the twentieth century—the most important motivation for the 'market' part of market socialism is that it can approximate the efficiency of a free enterprise system. That level of efficiency is itself necessary for satisfactorily meeting people's basic material needs, which, in turn, is a necessary condition for a society to be a good society. Market socialists may well believe that their favored type of system would do much better, but they at least are committed to satisfactorily meeting people's basic material needs. They believe, quite plausibly, that a market economy is adequate to that task.[11]

Social Ownership in a Market Economy

The first section of this chapter concerned the 'market' part of market socialism; the present section is about the 'socialism' part. It begins with a discussion of ownership of the means of production in a free enterprise system. The reason for this is twofold. First, social ownership is best understood by way of contrast with the characteristic form of ownership in free enterprise systems, namely, full liberal ownership. Second, and perhaps more important, the social vices attributed to existing free enterprise systems are traced to the ownership rights that define that type of system. A large part of the motivation for market socialism is to be found in these critiques of free enterprise systems. After a brief discussion of full liberal ownership, the plan for the rest of this section is to articulate one conception of social ownership, a combination of worker cooperatives and partial state ownership of the means of production. Along the way, I shall suggest why socialists should eschew another primary mode of socialization of the means of production, namely, full state ownership. These considerations are not offered as decisive objections to full state ownership but, instead, as part of the motivation for the type of market socialist system to be discussed in the rest of this book. The next section further elaborates the motivations for this type of system, primarily in terms of the perceived or alleged social vices of free enterprise systems that it promises to avoid. Implicit in this discussion is a minimal socialist vision of the good society.

Private ownership, or full liberal ownership, is actually a complex of rights, terms and conditions. These "incidents of ownership" as A. M. Honoré calls them in his classic study, "Ownership" are

1. the right to possess, that is, the right to exclusive physical control
2. the right to use, that is, the right to personal use and enjoyment of the thing owned, as distinct from incidents 3 and 4
3. the right to manage, that is, the right to decide who shall use the thing owned and for what purpose(s) it shall be used
4. the right to the income from the thing
5. the right to the capital, which consists of the power to alienate and the freedom to consume, waste, modify, or destroy all or part of the thing
6. the right to security, that is, immunity from expropriation by others
7. transmissibility, that is, the power to bequeath
8. absence of term, that is, the fact that the other incidents are held indefinitely
9. prohibition of harmful use, which is usually defined in terms of the nonviolation of the rights of others
10. liability to execution, that is, liability to judgment debt, insolvency, or taxation
11. residuary character, that is, rules governing the disposition of the thing when the other rights lapse. (1961, 112–28)

Any system of ownership is going to have to specify these rights, terms, and conditions. What is distinctive about private ownership is that all of these can be held by one individual, or they can be distributed among any number of individuals in whatever constellation they find mutually agreeable.[12] Clearly, the most important of these for economic purposes are incidents 3–5. (Incidents 1 and 6 are tacitly assumed to be assigned to whomever has 3 and 4.) It is primarily through these incidents of ownership that private individuals control the means of production to further their private interests. And it is the concentration of these rights in private hands that defenders of a free enterprise celebrate and their socialist opponents abhor.

By definition, a socialist economic system prohibits widespread private ownership of the means of production, which means that in most cases it prohibits persons from individually holding the rights identified in incidents 3–5. The definition of a socialist economic system also requires the socialization or social ownership of the means of production. How is this to be understood? As was suggested in chapter 1, there are fundamentally two positive conceptions of what socialization of the means of production amounts to that are compatible with a fully functioning market economy.[13] One conception holds that the means of production should be owned by society (or possibly the working class) as a whole. By itself, this idea has no clear meaning; some institutional stand-in for society has to be found. For a variety of practical and philosophical reasons touched on in chapter 1, the most obvious candidate in modern societies for that role has been the state. In the past, this led socialists to favor nationalization as the primary way of socializing the means of production.[14] In this socialist vision of the good society, the state has full liberal ownership rights in most of the means of production. The idea is that just as private ownership serves private interests, public or state ownership would serve the public interest.

Although societies in which the state owns the means of production historically have had centrally planned economies, this form of ownership is in principle compatible with a market economy.[15] In such a system, state-owned enterprises would be ultimately controlled by political authorities, who may or may not be democratically elected. These firms would buy inputs from each other and sell outputs to each other and to consumers. To approximate the efficiency of capitalist firms, managers appointed by the state would seek to maximize profits, possibly subject to various side constraints; these profits would be plowed back into the firm or go to the national treasury, or both.

However, many, if not most, contemporary proponents of market socialism do not favor full state ownership as the primary way to socialize the means of production. Historical experience with nationalized firms in both state socialist and capitalist economies has given little cause for optimism about state ownership of the means of production. The underlying reason for this aversion to nationalization seems to be that both the state and the nationalized firms that the state controls have, or come to develop, their own separate interests—interests that do not necessarily coincide with the interests of those who work in the firm or of society at large.[16] More exactly, the interests of the politicians and the ministers who are supposed to oversee the nationalized industries and the interests of the managerial elites who actually control these firms very often do not coincide with the public interest or the interests of the workers. This has led to repeated interference by political authorities with the workings of market mechanisms for reasons that have nothing to do with traditional justifications for state intervention (e.g., market failure) and have everything to do with furthering the private interests of the parties involved.

In addition, the widespread nationalization of the means of production does not sit easily with another characteristic feature of a socialist economic system: the abolition of wage labor. One of the defining features of a free enterprise system is that people are free to sell their labor (labor power) to those who control the means of production. This sale implies a separation of the worker from control of the means of production. The problem with nationalization as a mode of social ownership is that it certainly seems that employees of nationalized firms are selling their labor to the state in exchange for a wage. The only difference between this system and a free enterprise system in this respect is who is doing the buying—in this case, the state. It might be argued that workers in nationalized firms are, qua citizens, part owners of these firms, so they cannot really be wage laborers. But this conclusion does not follow and seems specious on its face. Workers in a capitalist system can be part owners of their firms (through, e.g., the holdings of their pension funds) without thereby ceasing to be wage laborers.

More important, a market socialist economic system in which the state fully owns the means of production may well suffer many of the problems attributed to a capitalist (free enterprise) system in general and wage labor in particular. The crucial difference between this type of system and capitalism is that the former precludes private ownership of the means of production. However, this difference may not come to very much beyond the elimination of interest income to nonworkers in an economic system in which most enterprises have been nationalized. Even if the ownership of firms is public, actual control of the means of production would be by state-appointed managers and not the workers.

In addition, in a society in which most of the means of production have been nationalized, the workers would likely be forced to deal with the bureaucrat-managers just as they are forced to deal with capitalists under capitalism. This, coupled with management's directive to maximize profits, creates the structural conditions for the exploitation of the workers by bureaucratic elites, and it bodes ill for ameliorating alienation.

These observations are not meant to be decisive objections to complete ownership of the means of production by the state, since it may be possible to fashion institutional devices to preempt these potential problems. And these considerations are certainly not telling against all forms of state ownership. However, they do constitute a prima facie case against full state ownership that many thoughtful socialists have found, or should find, persuasive, especially in light of the historical record of socialism (as well as state ownership under capitalism) as it has been realized in the twentieth century. Though most people—and virtually all socialists—believe that the government should have a significant role in the economy, few believe anymore that it would be a good idea to turn over complete ownership of most of society's means of production to the state.

The second way of socializing the means of production (currently the preferred mode of socialization for most proponents of market socialism) is through the establishment of worker cooperatives (Vanek 1970, 1977a; Selucky 1979; Schweickart 1980; Horvat 1982; Cohen and Rogers, 1983; Dahl 1985; Bowles and Gintis, 1986; J. Cohen 1989; Estrin 1989; Miller 1989a).[17] This means, first and foremost, that enterprises are self-managed. All and only workers in the cooperative collectively decide (1) how work relations are to be structured, (2) what pay differentials should be for different jobs, (3) what working conditions should be (e.g. coffee breaks), (4) who will exercise day-to-day managerial tasks and what the scope of their responsibilities will be. In short, they have ultimate decision-making authority about what happens in the firm.

In this type of system, firms buy their nonlabor inputs and sell their output in the market—a market in which prices are free to seek their own level. Workers' income is determined by the total income of the firm, net of nonlabor expenses. Because of the way their income is determined, the workers are said to be the residual claimants. Do workers have full liberal ownership rights in the firm? The answer to this question must be no for two reasons: (1) if they had full liberal ownership rights, they could sell their management and income rights to non-members, which would violate the general prohibition on private ownership; and (2) if the workers were to have the kind of income rights in their cooperatives that owners of capitalist firms have, they would receive all of the returns on the cooperative's capital. The reason this is problematic from a socialist perspective is that for technical reasons, capital-to-labor ratios vary enormously from one firm to another. Workers in highly capital-intensive firms, such as petrochemical refineries, would realize a much greater per capita share of society's total return on its capital investment than those who happen to work in less capital-intensive firms, such as truck farming operations. This would result in income inequalities too large for any socialist to accept.

The first problem can be precluded by prohibiting workers from selling their management rights in their firms to anyone who is not a member of the firm, or indeed possibly to anyone at all. The second problem could be solved by socializing the returns to capital. The simplest and most obvious way to do this is to require cooperatives to pay a capital usage fee to the state.[18] The returns to capital must be taken into account in some manner for the simple reason that capital is scarce, so that decision makers must economize on its use. Payment of a capital usage fee forces a recognition of this fact.

The rationale for paying this fee to the state is that it is the most natural way of giving expression to the idea that society as a whole should have an ownership stake in its means of production. Of course, under this system the state does not have complete ownership of those resources, since the workers have the corresponding management rights. However, by receiving the returns to capital, society as a whole, as represented by the state, retains a real ownership stake in its productive apparatus. This ownership stake is further enhanced by requiring the cooperatives to maintain properly the means of production they are entrusted with and to maintain a capital reserve fund (sometimes called a "depreciation fund") to replace capital goods when they are used up or wear out (Vanek 1977a, 171–85; Horvat 1982, 237; Schweickart 1980, 50). As Schweickart says, "Societal ownership manifests itself in an insistence (backed by law) that the capital stock of a firm be kept intact. Depreciation reserves must be maintained; workers are not permitted to allow the assets in their trust to deteriorate in value or to sell them off for personal gain" (1980, 50).

In this way, firms can be thought of as renting all of their capital (except perhaps that which is formed from internally financed new investment) from society at large. If a firm in a capitalist system rents a capital good such as a compressor or a backhoe, it must maintain the good in proper working order, and it must pay a rental fee. Part of that rental fee goes to replace the piece of equipment when its useful life has expired and part of that fee is the owner's return on his investment. In like manner, the cooperative must properly maintain all of its assets; it must pay a rental fee, part of which goes into a capital reserve fund to replace "their" capital goods as they are used up and part of which goes to the owner of these assets—society at large—in the form of a capital usage fee. The capital usage fee can also be conceived of as comparable to interest paid to a lender of financial capital (e.g., a bondholder) in a free enterprise system. The state, like a bondholder, would have no management rights or residual income rights in the firm, but the firm would be contractually obligated to pay a certain rate of return to the lender. In this scenario, the workers' income rights in the firm, as distinct from the capital that it uses, would represent a claim on the returns to labor plus any residuals (roughly, the returns to entrepreneurship).

The conception of the state as a stand-in or representative of society as whole is, of course, potentially problematic. Following Marx's lead,[19] most socialist theoreticians are aware of the fact that states can develop an unhealthy autonomy from society, which is why many contemporary socialists do not favor concentrating all economic power in the hands of the state and why nearly all of them strongly favor a highly democratic, participatory state, which thereby has a legitimate claim to reflect the public interest (e.g., Selucky 1979, chap. 6; Schweickart 1980, 138–40, 150–58; Horvat 1982, chap. 11; Nove 1983, 197–98, 208; Cohen and Rogers 1983, chap. 6; Dahl 1985; Miller 1989a, chap. 12).

Another advantage of this arrangement is that it facilitates one of the goals of social ownership in market economy favored by most socialists: it subjects the rate and direction of economic growth and development to collective choice. Nearly all market socialists include a substantial role for the state in directing the economy, primarily through the control of new investment (Vanek 1977b, 183; Selucky 1979, 179; Schweickart 1980, 49–53; Cohen and Rogers 1983, 161–62; Nove 1983, 207–8; Horvat 1982, 230; Levine 1984, 9–10). These theorists usually envision firms financing some expansion or even some new projects from undistributed earnings, but they also believe that the state should control most new investment.[20] This could be done in any number of ways. For example, the proceeds from the capital usage fee could be funneled through state-owned banks, which would be given a list of investment priorities (so much for biotechnology projects, so much for tourism, etc.). It would then be up to the banks to choose which new investment projects to fund, so long as they stay within the guidelines for new investment determined through the political process.

Just as in free enterprise systems, new investment would be largely financed by the returns to capital if the capital usage fee were used to fund new investment. However, unlike in a free enterprise system, both the level of that fee (i.e., the rate of return on society's investment) and the direction of economic development would be a matter of social choice. In other words, the overall rate and direction of economic growth would be a matter of collective social choice that a society makes and not something that just happens, as is the case in a free enterprise system.[21] In the latter, the economy is characterized by a swarm of individuals and groups pursuing their own private interests. There is no economic institution concerned with new investment that represents the interests of society as a whole. The same would be true of a market socialist system, if the state did not have the kind of presence in the economy just described.

To summarize, in a system of worker cooperatives, the levying of a capital usage fee, payable to the state and used to finance most new investment, is a natural and obvious way to give expression to the socialist principle that society as a whole should retain some form of ownership in its productive apparatus and that society itself is ultimately responsible for its own economic destiny. This account of social ownership is not fully determinate. Some of the rights, terms, and conditions have been only incompletely specified. For example, the institutional mechanisms by which the state controls new investment have not been specified. The account of the rights of self-management does not require or prohibit a one person–one vote rule. Usually that is implied, but it might be reasonable to advocate something different in some circumstances. Other rights, such as (personal) use rights, have been left entirely unspecified. Nevertheless, the core of this type of market socialist economic system consists of the following four elements:

1. It is a market economy, which means that most production is coordinated by market pricing.
2. The predominant type of enterprise is the self-managed cooperative. All and only workers have management rights in the firm.
3. Workers' income is the total income of the firm, net of nonlabor expenses; the latter includes a capital usage fee paid to the state. The workers' income rights make them the firm's residual claimants, and only they have this status.
4. Most new investment is financed by the capital usage fee, which is controlled by the state. There is an important sense in which the state owns the firm's capital, namely, the workers effectively lease the capital they use from the state; this means that in addition to paying a capital usage fee, they must maintain it properly and put enough aside to replace the capital goods they control as those goods are used up.

Element 1 constitutes the 'market' part of this form of market socialism. Elements 2–4 define social ownership of the means of production and thus constitute the 'socialism' part of this system. Finally, as noted in chapter 1, a market socialist economic system can allow for some private ownership and some state ownership of the means of production, provided that these forms of ownership do not individually or collectively dominate the economy.

This is the type of market socialist economic system to be discussed in most of the rest of this book.[22] Or perhaps it would be more illuminating to refer to it as a family of types, since there are different ways to fill in some of the rights mentioned. Its specification is relatively abstract in that many different systems could instantiate this general type. This makes for logically stronger conclusions in the end. It also tries to capture many of the common elements in contemporary market socialist thought. But most importantly, it is a well-motivated type of economic system. The motivation for element 1, the market, was discussed in detail in the first section of this chapter. The task of the next section is to motivate elements 2–4. This involves explaining why it might be thought that an economic system that has these general features would avoid the social vices that socialists have attributed to free enterprise systems and why, by implication, it would realize some of the social virtues that constitute a widely shared socialist vision of the good society.

The Motivations for Social Ownership

The motivations for social ownership are to be found primarily in the social vices that socialist critics have attributed to a free enterprise system. Indeed, the best place to find widespread, if not unanimous, agreement among socialists about the good society is in their critiques of the free enterprise system. A widely shared socialist vision of the good society is in part negatively defined by the systemic evils socialists have attributed to free enterprise systems. And perhaps the best place to begin a discussion of those evils is Marx's radical critique of capitalist society. Though socialists have disagreed with Marx about how to conceptualize the notion of class, about the dynamics of class societies, and indeed about a whole host of other matters, most socialists seem to be broadly sympathetic to his views about what is wrong with the capitalist (free enterprise) economic system and, by implication, capitalist society.

Marx's critique attributes basically two systemic evils to capitalism's economic system: alienation and exploitation. In another work, I have reconstructed and critically evaluated Marx's arguments for attributing these evils to that type of economic system (Arnold 1990, chaps. 2–5). The purpose of the first three parts of this section is not to summarize and assess these arguments. Rather, it is to identify those elements of his critique of capitalist economic systems for which a plausible prima facie case can still be made. This is done as a way of motivating the features of market socialism identified above in elements 2–4. To that end, this section also explains in each instance how or why it might be thought that market socialism would eliminate or significantly ameliorate these problems. The larger purpose of this section is to sketch or outline a stout defense (in the sense defined in chapter 1) of this type of economic system. To put it more simply, the purpose of this section is to explain why this type of economic system looks intellectually attractive from a socialist perspective.[23]

The End of Alienation in the Workplace

According to Marx, two types of alienation that are endemic to capitalist society are the alienation of the worker from his or her labor and the alienation of the worker from his or her product. The latter manifests itself in the phenomenon of commodity fetishism and a variety of so-called market failures; it will be discussed in the next subsection. The former, which is the subject of this subsection, most prominently manifests itself in worker dissatisfaction with—and on—the job. As Saul Estrin has said,

> Workers have no say in the major decisions affecting their working lives: the production processes used, the pace of manufacture, the noise levels, manning arrangements, the layout of the plant, the decision to increase or reduce the labour force or even to close the factory. Their dissatisfaction

comes out in a number of ways: their attitude toward work, . . . to management in general, and to the owners is often highly negative—the "them versus us" mentality. If the labour force is not unionized, this often leads to uncooperative attitudes, inflexibility with regard to work practices, high rates of absenteeism, shirking, and labour turnover. If it is unionized, [it leads to] unions' militancy, industrial action, and strikes. (1989, 170–71)

These manifestations of alienation are explained by the fact that management rights (in particular, ultimate decision-making authority) and income rights (rights to the residuals) are not held by the workers themselves.[24] The residual claimants, who also control the means of production, seek to maximize their profits, so they drive the workers as hard as they can. They only show concern for what the workers think and want to the extent that maintaining their profits demands it.

Not coincidentally, the reason why these problems would be ameliorated in market socialism is to be found in the structure of management and income rights that characterizes the cooperatives. Since self-management is self-management by all of the workers, and not just some, management rights are to be held collectively. This means that important decisions about matters of the sort mentioned will be made via participatory and democratic procedures. Though workers may delegate some day-to-day managerial tasks to specialists, they cannot delegate too much decision-making authority without losing control of their productive lives.

Moreover, since the workers have income rights, as well as management rights, in the firm, it will be up to them to decide what trade-offs between income and other values are acceptable. Suppose there is a drop in demand for the product a firm produces. Under market socialism, workers may respond by collectively deciding to take a pay cut, to work longer hours, to reorganize production in less intrinsically satisfying but more productively efficient ways, or to defer new investment—or some combination of these options. Capitalist firms have all of these options as well, but in a capitalist system, unlike a market socialist system, those most directly affected—the workers—do not decide which of these strategies will be adopted. Instead, these decisions are made by others, namely, the bosses. Finally, because of their income rights in the firm, workers have a bigger stake in the firm's health and survival. This eliminates (or at least significantly dampens) the "them versus us" mentality noted by Estrin.

A dealienated or unalienated workforce and what that implies is clearly part of the socialist conception of the good society. Strikes and industrial actions would be rare or nonexistent, and job redesign would ensure more meaningful work—or at least, the workers would have consciously chosen the greater income that goes with more alienating labor. Absenteeism, shirking, and job turnover would be minimized. Estrin and others who favor market socialism do not explicitly promise that workers' control over their own productive lives, ensured by the management and income rights they hold in the firm, would eliminate all of these problems (see, e.g., Horvat 1982, 190). Some of them may never go away entirely. But they do hold out prospects for significant amelioration of these manifestations of alienation.

The Elimination of Commodity Fetishism and the Attenuation of the Irrationalities of the Market

Another form of alienation in a capitalist economy that Marx discusses is the alienation of the worker from the product of his labor. Not only does the worker not own the product of his labor, but when it is sold in the marketplace, it becomes part of a larger alien system, what Marx calls a system of commodity production. What he means by this can be best understood by way of his most fundamental distinction among types of economic systems: the distinction between systems of commodity production (i.e., production for exchange) and systems of production for use.

In precapitalist nonexchange economies, the producer either is the consumer or is part of the same relatively small social group to which the consumer belongs (e.g., the family, the feudal manor). Production decisions are guided by the need for particular producer or consumer goods (what Marx calls 'use-values'), though, of course, not always for use-values that meet the needs of the direct producers. By contrast, capitalism is a system of commodity production, or production for exchange, in which the purpose of production is to get exchange value in the marketplace. The need for use-values only contingently and indirectly determines production.

Characteristic of a regime of commodity production is the phenomenon of commodity fetishism in which relations among producers masquerade as relations among the products of labor. What Marx means by this can be explained as follows: since the overriding purpose of production in a system of commodity production is to get exchange value, relative exchange values determine how social labor gets apportioned among the various lines and branches of production. To put this point in the fetishistic language of economists and businessmen, productive resources go where there are profits to be made. This deployment of productive resources happens automatically and behind the backs of the direct producers, so to speak. No one decides that there will be X number of steel mills or Y number of automobile manufacturers; that is just the way it works out. The market serves as an automatic and impersonal device for the coordination and allocation of social labor, which entails that the large-scale social organization of production is not determined by, or subject to, the conscious control of anyone, most especially the direct producers.

By contrast, in systems of production for use, production is directly determined by the need for particular use-values and is not mediated and mystified by the market. Of course, production under, say, feudalism is not the realization of a harmony of interests between serf and lord; the serf, after all, is being exploited. But this fact is completely clear in such a system (in contrast to capitalism, where exploitation is obscured by the wage contract). The social division of labor in systems of production for use has a kind of transparency and permits a kind of social self-understanding that is lacking in a regime of commodity production.

Marx seems to have regarded the lack of social self-understanding and control that this involves as an intrinsically bad thing. However, he also believed that it had bad consequences. A system of commodity production unleashes forces that have a devastating and unpredictable impact on people's lives and livelihoods. For example, as Marx points out in *The German Ideology*, a machine can be invented in England that deprives countless workers of their livelihood in India and China and completely overturns these societies ([1848]1976, 51). This happens even though it was no part of the intention of the inventor to cause this disruption. Technological developments, shifts in demand, discoveries of new sources of supply, and so on and so forth, whipsaw firms and workers alike, enriching some and dispossessing others. Commodities are, in effect, loose cannons on society's deck. In a related vein, since a regime of commodity production is guided by no overall plan, coordination among independent producers can and does break down, leading to recession or depression with associated massive unemployment. The tremendous dislocations and suffering this involves are what Marxists have in mind when they speak of the "anarchy of the market."

For all these reasons, Marx maintains that the worker's product confronts him as a hostile force in a regime of commodity production. And what makes that hostile force an alien force is the fact that the producers are linked together in ways that they neither understand nor control.

On the face of it, it would seem that all of these problems would face a market socialism, since it is a regime of commodity production in the sense that production decisions are based on market signals. However, its proponents would argue that certain features of this system prevent commodity fetishism and the other unfortunate consequences of the alienation of the worker from his or her product. They would maintain that Marx's blanket condemnation of commodity production is unwarranted.

One of the crucial differences between a capitalist system and a market socialist system is that market socialism involves state planning of most new investment. Under capitalism, there is no economywide plan for new investment. Marx's radicalism led him to believe that only the abolition of the market as a coordinating mechanism could solve the problems to which he called attention. For reasons discussed in the first section of this chapter, market socialists believe that would be unwise. They believe that market forces should be harnessed, not abolished; just as engineers harness the power of a river by building a dam, a market socialist society harnesses the power of the market by controlling the rate and direction of economic development through its control of new investment, funded by the capital usage fee (Schweickart 1980, 108–10, 114–15; Horvat 1982, 230).

As noted in the last section, the level at which the capital usage fee is set determines the overall rate of growth because it is the primary generator of funds for new investment. The direction of development is determined by the details of the investment plan. This can be done in a variety of ways. One way, which respects the complexity of a market economy, is to direct different percentages of the social investment fund to various sectors of the economy or to various geographical areas. Political representatives at the national level need not determine which firms get what funds; that can be left to the banks or investment firms through which the funds are channeled. They simply set the broad priorities with the advice and assistance of planners. Since this is accomplished by and through the democratic state, it represents a collective choice that society makes and not something that just happens, as in the case of free enterprise systems. As Schweickart says, "Governmental control here does give, in an important sense, control over the whole economy. That is precisely what we want. We want political control over investment to head off the anarchy of the market, to subject the growth of the economy to human direction, to eliminate the boom-bust cycles of capitalism. The appeal here is to efficiency, material well-being and autonomy" (1980, 143).

In this way, a market socialist system dispels the fog of commodity fetishism. This quotation from Schweickart hints at some related advantages that a market socialist economic system is supposed to enjoy in comparison to a free enterprise system. Despite their appreciation for the virtues of the market, market socialists are characteristically quick to point out the vices of the market as it is found in free enterprise systems. Commonly cited defects and problems include positive and negative externalities, monopolistic and oligopolistic pricing, and irrationalities in the structure of production caused by the grossly unequal distribution of income.[25]

Three examples will illustrate. First, the pollution problems of capitalist society stem from the fact that pollution is a negative externality; that is, it is a negative effect on third parties, which is not taken into account by the owners of the polluting factory or their customers. Second, it is often maintained that oil companies make extraordinary profits in times of international crises because they comprise an oligopoly or at least have considerable market power. Third, a great many urgent needs, such as health care for the poor, go unmet while significant resources are devoted to the production of luxury goods.

These and other systemic defects of the market in a capitalist system could be elaborated in much greater detail, but the basic problem, as many socialists see it, is that the commitment to the market as it is found in societies with a free enterprise system is a commitment to procedures at the expense of outcomes.[26] According to market socialist critics of the free enterprise system, this means accepting the "social irrationalities" (as they might be called) that emerge from the blind operation of market forces. The willingness to accept these irrationalities might be called "market fetishism."

Defenders of a free enterprise system can often be talked into qualifying their defense by allowing for some government intervention to correct or otherwise compensate for some of these social irrationalities. However, these interventions are hard to defend in a principled way, so they usually feel badly about it afterward. No such regrets cloud the socialist mind. If the market produces some social irrationality, that irrationality can and should be corrected by state intervention in the economy. For example, it may happen for some exogenous reason (e.g., historical circumstance) that there is not enough low-cost housing or decent medical care in a certain geographical area. Or perhaps there are too many luxury goods being produced, given that some urgent needs are unmet. Society must have an ultimate recourse available to correct these fortuitous imbalances thrown up by the market. For the market socialist, that recourse is the state. The state can correct these imbalances by providing the goods or services to those who need them, either free or at subsidized prices; it can tax companies that make windfall profits or impose price controls on them; it can prohibit pollution; or it can use its control of new investment or interest rates to nudge the market in the right direction.

All of these things are done by the state in a existing free enterprise systems, but they are often done in a half-hearted way and only after the problems have become particularly egregious or pervasive. From a socialist perspective, much of the explanation for the state's lackluster performance is to be found in the society's ideological commitment to respecting private property rights and thus the irrational outcomes that result from permitting market forces to work themselves out.

By contrast, though there is some presumption in favor of the market in a market socialist system, there is no principled opposition to bypassing it when some social irrationality demands it. Indeed, there is a principled commitment to do just that. Market socialists are not thereby committed to the belief that the state is infallible in discerning or dealing with these irrationalities. But there is a readiness to use the state as an instrumentality for dealing with the various failures of the market that is just not in the hearts and minds of those who favor a free enterprise system. These social irrationalities are consequences or manifestations of the alienation of the worker from his or her product in a free enterprise system. Market socialism promises the elimination or significant amelioration of these irrationalities—these social vices of the free enterprise system.

Another reason why a market socialist system might be expected to do better on these social irrationalities than societies with free enterprise systems is that the market socialist state would have proportionately more resources at its disposal to address these problems. States in free enterprise systems cannot tap the funds used for new investment in the way that a market socialist state could, since all that the former has at its disposal are revenues raised through (ordinary) taxation. The market socialist state has this source of revenue, but it can also use its control of funds for new investment to deal with these problems. This is a vast store of social wealth to which the state in a free enterprise system has no direct or easy access.

Finally, in a market socialist system, just as new investment is not something that just happens, so too the market is not the way production just happens to be organized. Instead, it is something that is consciously, collectively, and democratically chosen. As David Miller has said, "The market must appear as an expression of collective will. People must both understand the reasons for having markets and act on those reasons when they legislate for their existence through a democratic assembly. Moreover, this decision must always be open to reversal. . . . Only in this way can we conceive of overcoming alienation" (1989a, 223). Clearly, this is not how people in capitalist society view the market; nor is it how the market is viewed by those who defend the free enterprise system, however limited or qualified that defense is. In capitalist society, people are the playthings of market forces they neither control nor understand. By contrast, Miller's conception of how people in a market socialist society conceive of the market implies a social self-understanding incompatible with commodity fetishism and the blind acceptance of the market that entails. An analogy would be the contrast between the immigrant who consciously chooses to become a citizen of another country and the native who is born into the society and citizenship. The immigrant is much more likely than the native to be aware of the country's strengths and weaknesses and to have made the choice in light of this knowledge. On the other hand, the choice has already been made for the native. In a similar manner, in a market socialist system, since people collectively choose the market and understand the reasons for doing so, they are not subject to forces they neither understand nor control. This is another reason why the fetishism of commodities that afflicts capitalist society would not afflict market socialist society.

To summarize in the language of chapter 1, commodity fetishism and a whole range of social irrationalities are social vices attributable to free enterprise systems. Although a market socialism is a market economy, it does not suffer these vices. Commodity fetishism is suppressed for two reasons: First, the market is collectively and consciously chosen as the basic method of coordinating production; it is not a system under which people just happen to find themselves living. Second, because the state controls new investment, the rate and direction of economic development (and ultimately the entire structure of production) is a matter of social choice and not something that just happens to a society. In addition, the social irrationalities that would otherwise emerge from the unfettered market are also suppressed (eliminated or attenuated) by state action in a market socialist system. The verdict of the market is not sacrosanct; rather, it is subject to appeal in a way in which it is not in a free enterprise system. For all of these reasons, this type of market socialist system does not suffer the social vices of the free enterprise system that arise from the separation of the worker from his or her product.

The Elimination of Exploitation

Another generic defect of capitalist society that Marx traces to its economic system and that market socialism is supposed to eliminate is exploitation. It is a standard socialist criticism of capitalism that the workers are systematically exploited by the capitalists. Historically, the most important argument for this comes from volume 1 of Marx's *Capital* ([1863] 1977, chap. 1). Although this argument has at least one serious problem, contemporary socialists have tried to reformulate it so as to avoid this difficulty.[27] It will prove instructive to take a brief look at Marx's argument if only because it has the general form that most socialists think an argument of this sort should have. Moreover, this argument also provides some insights into the concept of exploitation that will prove useful in chapter 3, which develops an independent account of exploitative exchange.

Early in volume 1 of *Capital*, Marx establishes to his satisfaction that the value of a commodity is just the quantity of socially necessary labor required to produce it. This is the labor theory of value. This implies that the surplus value the capitalist realizes as profit comes from the worker. Despite the fact that the capitalist in his role as capitalist does not labor, he is nonetheless able to capture this surplus value on a regular basis. What explains this phenomenon is a complex set of facts. In the wage bargain, what the capitalist buys from the worker is not his labor but his labor power. Labor power is a commodity like any other commodity, so its value is just the quantity of socially necessary labor required to produce it. This is represented by the subsistence wage. However, when this labor power is discharged, the value (i.e., embodied socially necessary labor) that goes into the product is greater than the value of his labor power. In effect, then, for part of the working day the worker works for free. This fact is obscured by the wage contract, which represents the wage as payment for labor instead of for labor power. Marx's theory of surplus value states that the surplus value that accrues to the capitalist as profit represents the difference between the value added by the worker when he works for the capitalist and the value of the labor power that the capitalist purchases. Because capitalists own nearly all the means of production, the worker is effectively forced to participate in this arrangement. The exploitation of the worker by the capitalist consists in this systematic appropriation of surplus value by means of this coercive or quasi-coercive relationship.

The fatal flaw in this account is that the labor theory of value is not true.[28] The value of a commodity is not just so much "congealed" or "ossified" (socially necessary) labor, to use Marx's terms. Given that, one cannot conclude that the surplus value that accrues to the capitalist comes out of the hide of the laborer, so to speak. Suppose for a moment, however, that the labor theory of value is true and that Marx's account of exploitation under capitalism is basically correct. In what exactly does the exploitation consist?

Part of the answer seems to be that there has been a breakdown or failure of reciprocity in the relationship between the capitalist and the worker. Reciprocity requires that one return "good for good," proportionately.[29] In a joint undertaking, what this means is that the benefits each person receives from the undertaking must be proportional to that person's contribution. In a commercial venture, where benefits and contributions are conceived of primarily in economic terms, this means that the value each person realizes must be proportional to the value of that person's contribution. If that proportionality does not hold, then the failure of reciprocity requisite for exploitation exists.

On Marx's account, the capitalist in his role as capitalist contributes no value at all. He simply buys labor power, sets it to work on the means of production that he owns, and reaps the profits. It is true that the means of production that the capitalist provides are wholly or in part used up in the process of production. Some of the value received when the product is sold goes to replace that. But the capitalist gets something over and above that replacement value—a positive return on his investment. And that, according to Marx, is the something that he gets for nothing.

There is, therefore, a massive and systematic failure of reciprocity. (Comparable failures of reciprocity can also be found in the master-slave and lord-serf relationships, which are also exploitative.) Capitalists are able to do this because of their monopoly control of the means of production; consequently, the worker has no choice but to sell his labor power to the capitalist. One way of understanding this charge of exploitation, then, is that the worker is compelled to be a party to a relationship that systematically fails to be reciprocal. As was pointed out, contemporary socialists have tried to argue, without presupposing the labor theory of value, that these two conditions are, in fact, met in contemporary capitalist society. As for the failure of reciprocity condition, somehow, the crucial fact is the existence of interest income (the returns to capital) that goes to the capitalist—a nonworker—simply in virtue of his ownership of the means of production. A number of thinkers have maintained that this fact indicates that the worker is working more hours than it takes for her to earn the goods she buys with her wage and that this is what makes reciprocity fail.[30]

G. A. Cohen (1979) has taken a similar line in what he calls the Plain Argument. According to the Plain Argument, the failure of reciprocity in the worker-capitalist relationship consists in the fact that the worker creates the product—the thing that has value—while the capitalist (in his role as capitalist) creates nothing; he simply allows "his" capital to be used. The worker is the producer, and the capitalist is not. However, the latter receives some of the value of the product in the form of interest income. Once again, it is a classic case of getting something for nothing, and so there is a breakdown or failure of reciprocity between the worker and the capitalist. On Cohen's Plain Argument, there is no need to suppose that all value is created by the worker. Maybe value is not created at all, as the subjective theory of value holds; maybe it is created in some other way. The charm of this argument is that it is independent of what the source of (exchange) value is.

Most writers have maintained that the "forcing condition" for exploitation also holds; that is, the workers are forced to work for the capitalists.[31] However, there has been some dispute about this or about how best to understand this forcing condition (Cohen 1983; Brenkert 1985; Gray 1988). Cohen (1983), for example, maintains that the workers are individually free but collectively unfree to leave the ranks of the proletariat. Nevertheless, there seems to be agreement among socialists at least on the proposition that for the vast majority of workers, there is no feasible alternative to participation in the capitalist system. This fact, however it is described, coupled with the failure of reciprocity, is what makes the workers exploited in the capitalist economic system.

The point of this rather compressed discussion of the charge of exploitation is to make it clear that the failure of reciprocity is central to the concept of exploitation employed by all of these authors. This is not the only way to understand exploitation, but some variation on this theme seems to be the dominant view in contemporary writings on exploitation.[32]

Given this account of exploitation under capitalism, it is easy to see how it could be argued that exploitation would be abolished in the market socialist community. Recall that the workers—and only the workers—have both income rights and management rights in their firms and that the returns to capital go to the state. This means that there is no class of nonworkers with a claim on either the net income of the firm or on the returns to capital. Furthermore, the returns to capital (in the form of the capital usage fee) go to the state, which represents society as a whole. These monies are used to finance new investment, which ultimately benefits society as a whole. To some extent, this represents an intergenerational transfer of wealth from the present to the future, but such transfers could be defended as payment for the benefits of capital accumulation by previous generations. (Somewhere in here might be an argument for not increasing dramatically the rate of capital accumulation.)

In light of these considerations, one can see why the systematic failure of reciprocity alleged against capitalist society would not exist in a regime of market socialism. And since the firms are self-managed, workers would not be forced to deal with others who control the means of production. As members of the cooperative, they are full partners in the firm. On this basis, it could be argued that the workers are not exploited under market socialism.

The Achievement of Relative Equality of Material Condition

Perhaps the most widely shared aspect of the socialist vision of the good society is that it achieves some measure of real equality of material condition. One's material condition is determined by what the economic system provides. This includes not only material goods in the narrow sense of the term but also services such as medical care and education. What makes something material, in this sense of the term, is that it is something of value that can be provided by the economic system. In short, it is an exchangeable good or service.

There are many interesting theoretical and conceptual problems about equality that have been discussed by philosophers in recent years. For example, there has been a dispute about whether the appropriate ideal is equality of wealth, of income, of opportunity, of resources, of needs satisfaction, or of well-being.[33] For the purposes of this section, these disputes can be sidestepped, however. Whatever disagreements there are among contemporary socialists, there does seem to be substantial agreement on at least two matters. First, one of the social vices of societies with a free enterprise system is substantial inequality of material condition (see, e.g., Plant 1989, 54; Miller 1989b, 31–32; Roemer 1988, 152; Levine 1984, 133–34; Schweickart 1980, 93–94). Second, and not coincidentally, whatever their ultimate goals or values, most socialists believe that reducing the range of inequality of material condition (possibly, but not necessarily, to zero) is a desideratum for a socialist society (Selucky 1979, 139, 180–82; Horvat 1982, 190; Le Grand and Estrin 1989b, 4, 7; Nove 1983, 215–16; Nielsen 1985; Bowles and Gintis 1986, 206–7; Bonin and Putterman 1987, 6; Miller 1989a, 327–30; Estrin and Winter 1989, 115; Winter 1989, 162). More precisely, it is a necessary condition for most socialist conceptions of the good society.

The explanation for this vice of existing free enterprise systems is to be found in the blind operation of market forces. There are no effective limitations on either the amount of income a person can make or the amount of wealth that can be accumulated. Beginning with Marx's insights about the close connection between production and distribution in a market system ([1875] 1971, 18), socialist critics of the free enterprise system have argued that the distribution of wealth and income cannot be significantly affected without fundamental change in the relations of production. Whether the state is viewed as the executive committee of the ruling class or as a semiautonomous entity constrained by the fundamental interests of the ruling class,[34] socialists have long argued that relative equality of material condition cannot be achieved by state-mandated redistribution of wealth or income so long as there is private ownership of the means of production. Those who have great wealth and the power that accompanies it have both the will and the means to block measures that would significantly redistribute wealth and income in the direction of greater equality. This is one of the main motivations for the kind of fundamental social change socialists advocate.[35]

How is the social vice of material inequality, as it is found in existing free enterprise systems, to be avoided, and how is relative equality of material condition to be achieved under market socialism? Or, to put it another way, how are inequalities of material condition to be held within a tolerable range (however 'tolerable' is defined) in the market socialist community? The primary way this is supposed to happen is through the mechanisms by which workers' income is determined, mechanisms that are built into the structure of the market socialist economy. Recall that workers' income is the income of the firm net of nonlabor expenses, including the cost of capital. The fact that there is no nonlaboring class receiving the returns to capital removes one major source of material inequality found in free enterprise systems. The returns to capital go to the state. Because the workers collectively receive the residual income of the firms, these residuals would be spread much more widely throughout society than under a free enterprise system where they go exclusively to the owners of capital. Additionally, it is envisioned that the net income of each firm would be divided up relatively equally among the membership. As Saul Estrin has said,

> The distribution of income between people of different skills within each enterprise becomes a matter for internal debate and vote under self-management. . . . While the outcome will still reflect to some extent the market position of those with special skills, it is likely to be more egalitarian than pertains in capitalist firms. In particular, it seems unlikely that the very high salaries and other perks accorded to themselves by top managers would survive open scrutiny and democratic vote by other employees. (1989, 171)

What Estrin and others envision is a democratic determination of the division of the firm's income (e.g., Horvat 1982, 270). It is not necessary that each worker receive the same income. As the quotation from Estrin indicates, it may well happen that those with especially valuable skills or abilities will make more because of their recognized value to the firm. However, for the reasons cited by Estrin, the range of inequality in incomes would likely be much reduced relative to what one finds under existing free enterprise systems.

The collective structure of management and income rights also prevents workers' cooperatives from making extensive use of hired (i.e., wage) labor on a permanent or even temporary basis. That would create a group of second-class workers (proletarians, if you like) who, as wage laborers, would not be entitled to a share in the firm's net income and whose productive lives would be controlled by others. No genuinely socialist society can tolerate that phenomenon except at nonsignificant levels.

There is one final source of inequality in income that has to be taken into consideration. In any market economy, some firms will be more successful than others, which means that there will be interfirm variations in income. How would a market socialist society deal with these variations? Proponents of this version of market socialism favor (or at least do not oppose) inequalities that arise in this manner, but only up to a point. After all, the possibility of making these profits and the larger income that entails is supposed to be an incentive for cooperatives to produce efficiently. However, no socialist society can remain indifferent to income inequalities that fall outside a certain range. How are these to be dealt with? One obvious solution is for the state to levy a progressive income tax on individuals or on firms; the steepness of the progressivity of this tax could be determined by whatever range of income inequality is deemed to be socially acceptable (Miller 1989a, 153). This would be much easier to do in a society not antecedently committed to whatever outcome emerges from the operation of the market.

Recall that a social vice is any feature of a society that is a sufficient condition for that society not to be a good society. Since a good society is, by definition, something that it is reasonable to hope could exist, social evils must be eliminable or at least capable of being attenuated to the status of social blemishes. It was fashionable in the 1960s to blame every social ill on "the capitalist system." Taken with its original Marxist connotations, this would mean that all social vices are ultimately traceable to the economic system of Western society. Not a very plausible view, then or now. However, it is a plausible view that a society's economic system, in virtue of the type of system that it is, is responsible for some social vices (sufficient conditions for a society not to be a good society) or social virtues (necessary conditions for a good society).

The main purpose of this last section has been to identify the social vices that socialists have attributed to a free enterprise system, qua free enterprise system, and to sketch some of the reasoning or explanations that connect that type of economic system to these social vices. This section also contains a prima facie case linking the absence of these vices, and/or the presence of various virtues, to the structure of the type of market socialist economic system that has been outlined in the preceding two sections.

The story of this section and the first section can be summed up as follows. An economic system composed of worker cooperatives characterized by collectively held management and income rights, together with an activist state that controls most new investment, would realize the following social virtues:

1. the achievement of a reasonable standard of living, which is to be understood in terms of satisfactorily meeting people's basic material needs[36]
2. the end of alienation in the workplace
3. the elimination of commodity fetishism through control of the rate and direction of economic growth and development
4. the prevention or correction of the social irrationalities that would otherwise emerge from the operation of the market
5. the prevention of economic exploitation of the workers
6. the reduction of inequalities of material condition to a tolerable range.

The realization of these elements of the socialist vision of the good society would be ensured by the following four features of a market socialist economy:

a. The market is used to determine the price of and to allocate both factors of production and consumer goods.
b. The firms are worker-controlled cooperatives, which means that all and only the workers in the cooperatives have management rights and income rights (rights to the firm's net income) in the cooperatives.
c. The state owns society's capital and rents it to the cooperatives. This requires the cooperatives to pay a capital usage fee to the state; they must also properly maintain the capital goods they are entrusted with, and they must pay into a capital reserve fund, which is used to replace capital goods as the latter are used up.
d. The state controls most new investment.

The causal, or at least the explanatory, connections between institutional means a–d and socialist ends 1–6 are schematically indicated in Figure 2.1.

INSTITUTIONAL MEANS

A. Market pricing of factors of production and consumer goods

B. Worker-controlled cooperatives

  (i) All and only workers have management rights in their firms

  (ii) All and only workers are entitled to the net income of their firms

C. Social (i.e., state) ownership of capital

  (i) Capital usage fee paid to the state

  (ii) Capital maintenance and replacement requirements (workers as stewards of society's capital)

D. State control of most new investment

SOCIALIST ENDS

1. The achievement of a reasonable standard of living

2. The end of alienation in the workplace

3. The collective control of the rate and direction of economic growth and development

4. The prevention or correction of the social irrationalities that would otherwise arise from the operation of the market

5. The elimination of exploitation

6. The achievement of (relative) equality of material condition

Figure 2.1 Relationships between Institutional Means and Socialist Ends

1 is explained by A
2 is explained by B (i)
3 is explained by C (i) and D
4 is explained by C (i) and D
5 is explained by B and C (i)
6 is explained by B and C

The discussion of this section appeals to widely shared elements of the socialist vision of the good society. To be sure, this vision as it has been revealed here is incomplete in at least two important respects. First, there are social virtues and vices that either have nothing to do with a society's economic system or are only partially rooted in it. The consumerist mentality found in contemporary societies with a free enterprise system might be an example of a vice only partially rooted in the economic system. The latter may be partly responsible for this; but the available evidence suggests that this mentality is quite widespread and is probably due as much to technology and its perceived benefits as it is to the free enterprise system. Second, there are undoubtedly social vices in existing societies with free enterprise systems that are traceable to other, noneconomic social institutions such as the political system (insofar as it can be distinguished from the economic system) or even possibly the modern family. A discussion of these vices and how they might be dealt with in a socialist society would take us far afield.

Even in a limited and partial way, however, it is perhaps misleading to speak of "the" socialist vision of the good society, since there are clear and serious differences among socialists about what makes a society a good society. Yet there are some elements that while perhaps not universal, are at least widely shared among those who have advocated socialism, both today and in the past. These elements of the socialist vision of the good society come out of a socialist critique of free enterprise (capitalist) economic systems and a recognition of the main failing of existing socialist economic systems. The main purpose of this section has been to identify these elements and tell some plausible stories about how they might be connected to a certain type of market socialist economic system.

It would be a philosophically interesting task to elucidate these elements of the socialist vision of the good society more clearly and to provide some philosophical argumentation in support of them by reference to some fundamental values or moral/political principles. Why, for example, is equality of material condition a social desideratum? Philosophers characteristically leap to this task, ignoring most of the details of the economic institutions that are supposed to realize these values and principles.[37] By contrast, the emphasis of this book has been and will be on the empirical arguments and explanations that link institutions (specifically, an economic system conceived of as a system of property rights) and elements of a socialist vision of the good society.

However, a substantive discussion of these arguments requires an appreciation of some of the complex conceptual issues that most interest philosophers. Consequently, the next chapter concerns philosophical questions about exploitation. It aims to elucidate a philosophically defensible conception of exploitative exchange. This is a necessary preliminary step toward developing both a critique of the type of market socialist economic system discussed in this chapter and a limited defense of a free enterprise system, two closely connected tasks that will be executed in chapters 4–7.

3

Economic Exploitation

Exploitation as the Failure of Reciprocity

What distinguishes economic exploitation from other types of exploitation is that it involves the distribution of wealth and/or income in a society; at a minimum, the exploited person is not getting some wealth or income that he or she would get in the absence of exploitation. This does not mean that exploitation can be prevented or remedied by a simple redistribution of wealth or income; for economic exploitation might be embedded in the structure of an economic system in such a way as to make its elimination impossible without a fundamental change in the type of economic system. This is a claim that radical critics of capitalist or free enterprise systems have been making at least since the time of Marx. A considerable literature on economic exploitation has developed in recent years in support of this contention. Almost without exception, contributors have been sympathetic to Marx's conclusion that the workers are systematically exploited by the capitalists in a capitalist economic system. The challenge has been to restate or reargue Marx's position in such a way that it does not rely on the labor theory of value, though this contrast with Marx's reasoning is often not made explicit.

It is worth considering why so many thinkers have devoted so much effort to this. What would success in their endeavors accomplish? One natural answer is that by proving that there is systematic exploitation in capitalist society, one could conclude that capitalist societies are inherently unjust. This would be an interesting conclusion on its own merits; on most plausible conceptions of what constitutes the good society, it would warrant the further conclusion that capitalist societies are not good societies. Proving this, in conjunction with a parallel defense of some form of socialism on this point, would count as significant progress in the capitalism/socialism debate.

However, the purpose of this chapter is not to investigate this charge against capitalism as it has been made by those sympathetic to Marx.[1] Rather, it is to develop a theory of economic exploitation that is potentially applicable to all economic transactions that take place in a market economy, whatever type of market economy it is. This contrast with the traditional focus of discussions of economic exploitation warrants some elaboration. One of the peculiarities of this literature is that nearly all of these authors focus almost

65

exclusively on the relationship between the capitalist and the worker.[2] The accounts that are developed are general only to the extent that they can also be applied to the master-slave and lord-serf relations, which, following Marx, are brought in for contrast and for comparison. However, within the confines of the capitalist economic system, these writers have never cast their gaze beyond the relationship between the capitalist and the worker.

What is peculiar about this is that the contemporary world of free enterprise systems seems to be far too complicated to be analyzed solely in terms of capitalists and proletarians, even on the subject of exploitation. It is not just that some workers own means of production (e.g., through their pension plans) and that most of those who own means of production also labor (e.g., as managers and as professionals who own stock in corporations). If that were the only problem, it would be possible to get around it by speaking of the capitalist in his or her role as capitalist and the worker as worker. (Implicitly, that has been the way the discussion has been carried on in the literature.) Rather, the problem with restricting the discussion to capitalists and workers is that there is no reason to think that it is only in his or her role as capitalist that one person might economically exploit someone else. For example, firms—or those in charge of them—deal with suppliers, customers, stockholders, and bondholders. One would think that there are, or at least that there might be, opportunities for economic exploitation in all of these exchange relationships. In addition, it seems at least possible that individuals and groups might be able to engage in economic exploitation through political institutions. A theory of economic exploitation should have something to say about whether and how economic exploitation can take place through the state. The purpose of this chapter is to develop a theory that is general enough to address these other relations in a society with a market economy.

The strategy is to begin with another look at the various Marxist accounts of exploitation sketched in chapter 2. Despite the limitations of the Marxist approach just noted and despite the problems that the relevant arguments face (problems that will be spelled out in more detail this time), these Marxist accounts of exploitation are worth a brief second look. The reason is that they provide some insights into the concept of economic exploitation that will prove useful in developing the more general theory of economic exploitation that is the principal purpose of this chapter. In other words, the Marxist accounts of exploitation have the right general form, even if they are wrong or inadequate in substance.

Recall that one of the things that makes the relationship between the capitalist and the worker exploitative, according to Marx's account, is that there is a failure of reciprocity between the capitalist and the worker. The capitalist gets interest income, that is, income over and above replacement costs for used-up capital, while contributing no value himself, since only laboring creates value, and the capitalist *qua* capitalist does not labor. Marx also maintains that the worker is forced to participate in these arrangements. This forcing, coupled with this failure of reciprocity, is what makes the capitalist-worker relationship exploitative.

Central to Marx's argument is the claim that the capitalist, in his role as capitalist, contributes no value at all in the production of the product. However, Marx does not say that the capitalist makes no contribution at all. Quite to the contrary. In various writings, including *The Communist Manifesto*, Marx and Engels call attention to, and indeed celebrate, the fact that the capitalist forces the accumulation of surplus value necessary for developing the forces of production ([1848] 1976, 482–96). This development ultimately leads to the self-destruction of the capitalist system. They never say whether they think the capitalist deserves the profits he appropriates as a reward for fulfilling his world historical mission. (I suspect that their gratitude toward capitalists did not extend quite that far.) However, when he is not an actor on the stage of world history, when he is back at the factory, the capitalist is doing what he does best and likes most: squeezing surplus value from the workers, that is, exploiting them. But this argument works only if the labor theory of value is true, which it is not. The value of something is not just so much socially necessary labor that the worker pours into the product, as it were. The falsity of the labor theory does not imply that the worker is not exploited by the capitalist, but it does show that Marx's argument for this claim fails.

The other arguments adverted to in chapter 2 proceed along similar lines, though ostensibly without making use of the labor theory. In these arguments, the failure of reciprocity consists in the fact that the capitalist is getting a return on his investment (i.e., interest income) over and above replacement costs simply in virtue of his ownership of the means of production, which means that the worker is working more hours than it takes to earn the goods she buys with her wage. This means that the worker is doing at least some unpaid labor for the capitalist. Or, on G. A. Cohen's version of the argument, reciprocity fails because only the worker is a producer, yet some of the value of the product she makes goes to the capitalist who, qua capitalist, is not a producer. The capitalist, who receives this interest income and yet does not create the product, is getting something for nothing. Since the worker is in some manner forced to participate in the arrangements that make all this possible, the worker is exploited by the capitalist.

Central to Marx's argument and these other arguments is the supposition that the capitalist, in his role as capitalist, contributes no value, or nothing of value, to production.[3] As David Schweickart has said, "The basic problem in trying to justify capitalism by an appeal to contribution is the impossibility of identifying an activity (or set of activities) engaged in by all and only capitalists which can be called (preserving the ethical connotations of the word) 'contribution'" (1980, 20).

However, as I have argued elsewhere, this is mistaken.[4] Think of the capitalist as someone who lends a sum of money to an entrepreneur, who then marshals various factors of production and puts them to work. This capital is then used to purchase raw materials and semi-finished products, to rent equipment, and to pay laborers. The owners of these various factors of production all receive payment at the time when they provide their goods or services. By contrast, the capitalist must wait until production has taken place and the product is actually sold until he gets his money—both the principal and the interest. The service the capitalist has rendered—the contribution that he makes—is to allow those who provide other factors of production to get paid "up front." (This account can be generalized to cover the provision of capital goods other than money). All production takes time, and time is both scarce and valuable. In effect, what the capitalist contributes is *time* in the form of command over present goods, in exchange for which he receives an interest payment.

Does this contribution "justify" his return on investment? Does this make morally legitimate all of those interest and dividend payments that go out to the leisure class year in and year out? Well, 'justify' is a strong word, and this question really needs to be approached in a much more global and systematic way. Indeed, that much is suggested by the framework for the capitalism/socialism debate advocated in chapter 1. Certainly, this argument does not establish the legitimacy of most capitalists' initial holdings. However, the dispute about exploitation is supposed to be logically independent of that. In other words, critics of capitalism intend to show that even if the capitalist came to acquire his holdings in a wholly unobjectionable way, he would inevitably turn into an exploiter by the mere fact of his participation as a capitalist in the capitalist system. Unfortunately, the above considerations show that this charge cannot be sustained on the basis of arguments like Marx's and the others sketched earlier. The capitalist does contribute, however easy it is for him to make that contribution. This fact, however, does not rule out the possibility that some other argument might establish the conclusion that the capitalist exploits the workers. It just means that the kinds of arguments usually offered for this conclusion will not do.

Despite the fact that these arguments all fail, they have in common something that is profoundly right, namely, that a failure of reciprocity is the root idea in the concept of exploitation. If their arguments had been successful, they would have established that in the capitalist-worker relationship, someone is benefiting without contributing, and others are contributing in a way that is systematically out of proportion to the benefits they receive. This disproportionality between the two parties constitutes a failure of reciprocity, and that is a necessary condition for exploitation.

The contention that exploitation presupposes a failure of reciprocity is further supported by considering exploitation in non-economic contexts. In ordinary parlance, when one says that A is exploiting B, it means at the very least that A is taking unfair advantage of B, that unfairness consists of a failure of reciprocity. Consider the Hollywood director who gets a child actor to cry by telling him his mother has died—gross exploitation. What is exploitative about the situation is that the director has benefited substantially (in getting the kind of scene he wants) by imposing terrible costs on the child.

Reciprocity consists of giving "good for good," proportionately (Becker 1986, 143), something that is clearly not in evidence here. The failure of reciprocity consists in the fact that in this joint undertaking, one party has ben-efited considerably at the expense of the other party. 'At the expense of' car-ries causal connotations; in this example, the exploiter has caused the exploited person harm. In general, it seems that the failure of reciprocity implies a causal connection of some sort between the action(s) of the exploiter and the condition of the exploited. 'Exploits' is an active verb; ordinary usage suggests that it is something that someone does to someone else. The action of the exploiter is at least a causal factor in, if not the cause of, the condition of the exploited. This, of course, is exactly what happens in an exploitative exchange.[5]

Failure of reciprocity need not be limited to cases where there is harm on one side and benefit on the other. There can be failures of reciprocity in which both sides benefit, but disproportionately relative to their respective contributions. Suppose, for example, that a graduate student, Smith, per-forms a series of experiments and writes them up. Jones, a senior professor, recognizes this work as path-breaking. She makes some minor suggestions of the sort a journal editor would make and then tells Smith they should submit it as a coauthored paper. It gets published in a blind-reviewed journal, which means that Jones's reputation had no bearing on its acceptance. Smith and Jones are later coawarded the Nobel Prize, but Jones never acknowledges how modest her contribution was. Whether or not there has been exploita-tion (Smith might have freely shared the honors and the award out of a mis-placed sense of gratitude or a faulty assessment of the extent of Jones's con-tribution), there has certainly been a failure of reciprocity in the sense that two people have benefited from a joint activity about equally although their contributions were vastly different. In other words, there is a significant dis-proportionality between the benefits received and the contribution made or, to be more exact, the *value* of the contribution made.

This distinction between the contribution someone makes to a project or social activity and the value of that contribution merits some attention.[6] Some-times when we speak of someone's contribution to something, we are speak-ing in a wholly neutral way, making no judgments at all about the value of that contribution. In principle, someone could make a contribution which has no value at all. Indeed, the scholarly journals in most fields are filled with such contributions. And then there are the contributions with negative value. In this value-neutral sense, the contribution someone makes to a project or social activity is simply whatever one brings to and leaves with that project or activity. It is the difference that person makes and it may or may not have any positive value. The stuff of contributions, so to speak, can be quite heteroge-neous. It could be a quantity of labor, a speech act, some ideas, or a physical object or process.

What, then, is the value of a person's contribution? A complete answer to this question would seem to require a completely general theory of value, something few philosophers (including the present author) have. Fortunately, the concerns of this book do not require an answer to this general question. Since this chapter is concerned with economic exploitation and not exploitation in general, attention can be restricted to the economic value of a person's contribution. (Hereafter, in speaking of value, the qualifier 'economic' will be suppressed unless confusion threatens.)

The question of what constitutes or determines the value of someone's contribution is perhaps the central question that a theory of economic exploitation must answer and is the subject of the next section. Before passing on to that question, however, it might prove helpful to summarize the main points of the theory as it has been developed thus far.

A theory of economic exploitation appropriate for evaluating market economies must potentially apply to any and all economic exchanges or transactions, not just the transaction between the worker and the capitalist.[7] Moreover, although it may turn out that all capitalists exploit workers, that must be an implication of the theory—a result of applying the theory to one general type of exchange in a market economy—and not a fixed intuition around which the theory is constructed. Economically exploitative exchanges or transactions may be in the consumer goods markets, producer goods markets, or markets for original factors of production. A necessary, though not sufficient, condition for exploitation is a failure of reciprocity in those transactions. That failure consists in a disproportionality between the value that the exploiter receives relative to the value of his or her other contribution (i.e., the value of what the exploiter offers in an exchange), as compared to the value of what the exploited person receives relative to the value of his or her contribution (i.e., what the exploited offers in an exchange). However, this partial account of exploitation is satisfactory only if it is possible to give some meaning to the notion of the value of someone's contribution. In other words, it is necessary to identify, determine, or define the economic value of what someone brings to an exchange. It is to this question that we now turn.

The Value of One's Contribution

In asking this question, one could be asking what Marxists call the qualitative question or the quantitative question. The former is really an ontological question: What is the nature of economic value? or What sort of thing is economic value? For present purposes, this question need not be answered; whatever economic value is, the important question for a theory of economic exploitation is what determines the *magnitude* of economic value of an exchangeable good or service. It is the misalignment of magnitudes between the value of someone's contribution and what that person receives relative to the situation of the other party to the exchange that constitutes the failure of reciprocity that is a necessary condition for an exploitative exchange.

The standard answer to this quantitative question given by contemporary subjective value theory is that the value of something is determined by whatever someone would be willing to pay (exchange) for it. Notice that this presupposes an exchange economy. In a centrally planned economy with no market prices (a least in producer goods), it is hard to make sense out of the willingness to pay, except on the black market or in terms of bribes. In such economies, those who use producer goods are simply authorized to requisition them. Thus, the transactions between suppliers and the production units (firms) they supply are not exchanges. Without exchanges, there can be no markets in these producer goods; without markets, it is difficult to determine the values of these goods, according to subjective value theory. Indeed, this very point is central to Mises's critique of central planning, which was discussed in chapter 2. However, the question of how to determine the economic value of something in a centrally planned economy need not detain us here because the systems to be compared in this book are market socialist and free enterprise systems, both of which are types of market economies. Nevertheless, it is worth noting in passing that the account of exploitation to be developed in this chapter may be difficult to apply to nonexchange economies. If there are exploitative transactions is such economies, identifying them may not be a straightforward matter—if for no other reason than that the value of what is being traded is so hard to ascertain.

That complication to one side, there are nonetheless some difficulties in understanding the value of someone's contribution in a market economy as simply whatever someone would be willing to pay for it. One is a kind of indeterminacy. Who is the someone? For any particular item offered for sale, there might be numerous buyers willing to pay widely different prices. Which buyer's price is the relevant one? Two alternative answers immediately come to mind: one is that the item has as many different values as there are offers or potential offers; the other is that the value of the thing is determined by whoever ends up buying it. Each of these alternatives is plagued by essentially the same problem: aside from the fact that some items with economic value are never actually purchased, each of these alternatives imply that in no market system does someone ever get more or less than the value of what he is exchanging. Not only does this seem to be an intrinsically implausible and indeed an odd thing to say, but it also implies that no one is ever economically exploited in a market economy, even a little. The reasoning for this is straightforward: in an exploitative exchange, the exploiter receives more than the value of his or her contribution (i.e., what the exploiter is giving up in the exchange) and the exploited receives less than the value of his or her contribution (i.e., what the exploited is giving up). If the economic value of a person's contribution is whatever he or she actually receives in an exchange, then no one ever gets more or less than the value of the contribution; thus reciprocity always holds. Consequently, it would be impossible for anyone to be economically exploited by anyone else in a voluntary exchange.

This is implausible on its face and is something almost no one wants to accept. Even those who favor a free enterprise system do not maintain—or, at least, should not maintain—that it is literally impossible for people not to get the economic value of what they contribute in a voluntary exchange and, by implication, that it is impossible for people to be economically exploited. When the subject is real-world economic systems, claims of perfection should always be viewed with the highest degree of suspicion. More realistically, those who favor a free enterprise system want to say that it is something about how markets actually function in such a system that it usually or almost always works out that people get the value of what they contribute. On the other view, nothing about how markets actually function is brought in to explain how or why people always get the economic value of what they contribute. The issue is effectively decided by the definition of value.

Intuitively, the problem with these proposals is that they do not take into account the various defects and limitations—in a word the imperfections—of real-world markets for the goods and services that are the objects of exchange. To solve this problem, perhaps the value of what someone is exchanging should be understood as what he or she would get if the market were an ideal market in the sense defined by standard neoclassical welfare economics. An ideal market is defined by the following very strong assumptions: all participants in that market are rational and fully informed as to prices and the characteristics of the good in question, goods from different suppliers are qualitatively homogeneous, the costs of enforcing property rights (contracts) is zero, all firms are price takers (i.e., no firm can raise or lower prices without lowering net revenue), and there are no barriers to entry into the market. Any market that satisfies these last two conditions is said to be perfectly competitive. A perfectly competitive market that satisfies all of the other conditions is called an ideal market.[8]

The value of something, according to this proposal, is what it would fetch in an ideal market. The advantage of this way of understanding the value of someone's contribution is that it connects economic value to the judgments that people would make about the relative importance of that person's contribution to their well-being *in ideal circumstances*. In particular, these value judgments are as well informed as they could be in that (1) the buyer of the good or service knows everything there is to know about the product and (2) there is no better price for either the buyer or the seller. In a perfectly competitive market, if a buyer lowers his offer, he finds no sellers, and if a seller raises her price, she finds no buyers. That is a consequence of each firm or individual's being a price taker. Given the current state of natural resources, technology, and human and nonhuman capital—in short, given the current state of the rest of the economy—there is no way for either participant in this exchange to do better. The exchange rate that would be found in an ideal market, on this proposal, is the "true" value of the object in question.

As attractive as this proposal is, it nevertheless faces a problem. This problem stems from the very strong conditions of the model of the ideal market. Though some real-world markets may be so close to being ideal that the difference between the ideal and the reality is insignificant, that is simply not the way it is in most cases. Most markets do not have indefinitely many suppliers of a homogeneous good; instead, there are usually just a few suppliers of a good, and goods of that general type are, or at least appear to be, highly differentiated. Most market participants are neither completely rational nor perfectly knowledgeable about prices and quality; very often, entry into a market is restricted; and so on.

But why is this a problem? Indeed, critics might use these observations to make the following objection to free enterprise systems: "In the theory of the free enterprise system (i.e., in the models), people generally get the value of what they contribute. However, because reality diverges from the theory so dramatically, in the real world, people do not get the value of their contributions. This gap between theory and reality supports a negative judgment about real-world free enterprise systems on this score. This divergence shows how inefficient free enterprise systems really are; it suggests—though it does not by itself imply—that such systems are plagued with widespread economic exploitation." Critics might also point out that neoclassical economics has an ideological role to play in diverting attention from reality to a much more satisfactory ideal, but that is another story.

This criticism proceeds too quickly, however. The fact that very few markets closely approximate the ideal in their structure does not imply that actual prices (i.e., real-world prices) differ significantly from what they would be if those markets did bear a close structural resemblance to the ideal. In the real-world markets that do not closely resemble the ideal market, there may be offsetting imperfections that cancel each other out, so that the real price and the ideal price are, in fact, approximately the same. More importantly, the competitive process may have worked itself out to the point where the price of an item in a given market is about what it would be if that market had the ideal structure even if, in point of fact, that market bears no structural resemblance whatever to the ideal market. This last point warrants some elaboration.

The story told at the beginning of chapter 2 explains how the competitive process coordinates production in a market economy. It describes the operation of an adjustment process by which supply and demand are brought into balance in a given market by the successful entrepreneurial actions of firms and/or individuals. They raise or lower bids to buy and offers to sell and combine factors of production in new and different ways in an attempt to produce existing products more cheaply—all this in response to perceived profit opportunities. If these perceived opportunities are real, entrepreneurs have correctly perceived that there are inefficiencies in existing ways of doing things or that there have been changes in the underlying economic conditions with the result that existing prices are less consonant with those conditions than before. This competitive process results in factor prices being bid up and product prices being driven down. One can think of the entrepreneurs who animate this process as buying a bundle of factors of production (e.g., raw materials, semifinished products, and the labor to put it all together) in the factor markets and selling that bundle, in the form of the final product, in the product market. When the total price of the bundle in the factor markets equals the price in the product markets, entrepreneurial profits, or "pure profits" (as they are sometimes called), have been squeezed out and reduced to zero. Equilibrium in this market—a local and perhaps temporary equilibrium—has been achieved. Under these circumstances, the price of the product is about what it would be if the market were ideal in terms of its structure, since in both the real case and the ideal case, there are no pure profits. All income from sales goes to those who provide factors of production approximately in accordance with the marginal value of what they are selling.[9] The structure of this market, however, may differ considerably from the structure of an ideal market.

What has been described in the preceding paragraph is not a process that occurs in a model, that is, in an ideal market. Instead, it describes what can and does actually happen in the real world. Let us say that a market in some good or service in which there are no opportunities for pure profit on either the supply or the demand side is a *competitively efficient market*, and let us call exchanges in such markets *F-exchanges*. In an F-exchange, both parties are price takers; that is, no competitor is in a position to undersell the seller or outbid the buyer.[10] If the seller or one of his competitors were to lower the price of the good being sold, he would have to pay one of his suppliers (including himself if he were a supplier of labor or capital) less than the going rate for that factor of production. Similarly, if a buyer were to raise his bid, he would have to charge his customers more than the going rate for his product.

The terms of an F-exchange can be used as the standard to determine the value of someone's contribution. In an F-exchange, those who are selling something are getting the value of what they are selling (i.e., what the good or service is really worth, so to speak) and those who are buying are getting their money's worth. In a nutshell, F-exchanges are *fair*. These exchanges can be rechristened *fair exchanges*.[11] The proposal, then, is that the value of someone's contribution is what she would get in a fair exchange. Sometimes, people get the value of what they offer in an exchange, and sometimes they do not. It all depends on whether or not the market is competitively efficient—or so it is claimed. Actually, at this point all that is on the table is a proposal about how to understand or conceive of the value of someone's contribution and a stipulative definition of a fair exchange. Why is it appropriate to say that these so-called fair exchanges determine—or more aptly, *reveal*—the value of someone's contribution? A related question concerns the criteria by which these exchanges can be identified. In other words, how are competitively efficient markets to be identified? The next section addresses both of these questions and considers some additional complications.

Fair Exchanges and the Value of One's Contribution

To begin with the first question, the reason it is appropriate to say that these fair exchanges are reflective of the value of what parties have to contribute in an exchange is to be found in Hayek's insight into the informational significance of market prices remarked on in the first section of chapter 2.

Hayek (1945) claims that the price that emerges through the competitive process both reflects and amalgamates the beliefs of market participants (buyers and sellers) about how that good and/or its inputs contribute to their well-being.[12] Suppliers and demanders learn the quantities of what others are willing to exchange at various prices. Suppliers are learning not only about demanders' offers but also about other suppliers' responses, which in turn reflect the latter's beliefs and desires. The analog holds true of demanders. In this way, the competitively efficient price provides an accurate indicator of the relative scarcity of the product in question, given the current state of society's productive apparatus and given people's beliefs and desires (values). In a competitively efficient market, there are no profit opportunities, so no one would be able to give either party to the exchange a better offer. The competitive process, insofar as it has worked itself out in the way just described, reveals or reflects the true social significance of what someone has to offer or contribute to society.

By contrast, if an exchange is not fair, then the terms of the exchange do not accurately reflect the relative scarcity of one or the other party's contribution to the well-being of others. Two examples illustrate. Suppose that Mary pays $15,000 for an automobile that (unbeknownst to her) is sold in many places around town for considerably less. Suppose that this market is not competitively efficient—perhaps because of some market failure, such as imperfect information due to insufficient advertising on local television. Further suppose that a price between $11,000 and $12,000 would emerge if this market were competitively efficient. In this case, the value of what she is giving up (the $15,000) is significantly more than the value of what she is getting (the automobile), which is "really" worth between $11,000 and $12,000. Thus, her exchange is not a fair one (which does not by itself imply that it is exploitative). If that market were competitively efficient, she would have paid about $11,500 from that dealer or perhaps $12,500 from a dealer who offered superior sales advice and service.

To take another example, suppose that the purveyor of a good has a state-guaranteed monopoly, which he uses to make monopoly profits on the sale of this good. In this case, the price on the factor markets of the bundle of goods and services that make up the product is significantly less than the price of that bundle on the product market. In buying that bundle on the product market from the monopolist, purchasers of the product have been systematically misled about the true relative scarcity of that bundle of inputs.

This account of what constitutes a fair exchange and the value of someone's contribution works reasonably well when the markets in question are stable, whether or not they are competitively efficient. If the cost and the price of an item are fairly close, sellers are getting the value of what they are selling and buyers are getting their money's worth. On the other hand, if the price markedly exceeds the cost, then the seller is able to appropriate some value that he would not be able to get if markets were competitively efficient. An analogous situation arises if the cost exceeds the price.

However, there is a difficulty with this account of fair exchange and the value of one's contribution, which becomes apparent when one tries to understand the value of the entrepreneur's contribution. When the market for a firm's product is competitively efficient, the residuals are zero, and the entrepreneur receives nothing—which seems appropriate, since no entrepreneurship is exercised. Of course, the entrepreneur may receive income for other services (e.g., providing capital, performing ordinary managerial labor), but qua entrepreneur, he receives nothing at all. However, if the value of someone's contribution is defined in terms of what that person would receive in a competitively efficient market, then the value of an entrepreneur's contribution will always be zero, since that is what he gets in a competitively efficient market.

Clearly, however, entrepreneurs make a contribution—indeed, a very valuable one when markets are not in equilibrium (i.e., not competitively efficient). Consider a case in which an entrepreneur institutes a technological innovation that lowers a firm's costs and allows it to pass some of the savings on to its customers. If the market had been competitively efficient, it no longer is so, because of this change in the cost of producing the product. By his action, the entrepreneur is moving the market toward competitive efficiency, both directly by changing the price he charges and indirectly by informing the rest of the market that prices are not properly coordinated relative to underlying economic conditions. Other purveyors of the product will have to find a way to lower their prices if they are to remain competitive. Call this a *market in transition*. The terms of exchange offered by this entrepreneur are on the *leading edge* of this market; that is, these terms are closer than any existing alternative to the new competitive equilibrium price that will emerge, a price that may be unknown to anyone at that time.[13] The primary contribution of the entrepreneur is the signal he sends to the market by changing his price. That is the difference he makes, and that signal provides more accurate information (by hypothesis, the best currently available information) about the true relative scarcity of the product.

In a market in transition, that is the entrepreneur's contribution. What is its value? An obvious suggestion is to identify the value of that contribution with the pure profits that the firm earns as a result of the entrepreneur's action. Those profits represent the difference his decision makes to the firm. However, if the pure profits that the firm makes on the leading edge of a market in transition constitute the value of the entrepreneur's contribution, this creates a problem for our account of the value of a good or service and the associated definition of a fair exchange. In contrast to what is implied by this account, it now looks as if the person buying a product on the leading edge of a market in transition is not paying more than the value of what she is getting. Rather, it seems that she is getting her money's worth and that some of the value she gives up is payment for the service that the entrepreneur provides. However, the market is not—at least not yet—competitively efficient. In other words, if the value of the entrepreneur's contribution on the leading edge of a market in transition is to be taken into account, the value of a firm's product cannot be identified with what it would fetch in a competitively efficient market, because in the latter, the value of the entrepreneur's contribution is zero.

This problem can be easily fixed by altering the definition of a fair exchange and the associated account of the value of one's contribution to take these considerations into account. The definition of 'fair exchange' can be restated as follows:

> DEFINITION. An exchange e is fair if and only if either (i) the market in which e takes place is a competitively efficient market or (ii) e is on the leading edge of a market in transition.

As indicated, a market in transition is defined as one in which the terms of exchange are moving toward what will emerge when the market is competitively efficient; an exchange on the leading edge of such a market is defined as one for which there is none closer to the new equilibrium exchange rate. Suppose, for example, that the competitively efficient price of a copy machine had been $5,000. Because of a new technological development that drives down production costs, the new competitively efficient price that will eventually emerge is $4,000, whether anyone knows that at the time or not. There are five sellers of the product. During the transition, firm A sells it for $4,500, firm B sells it for $4,750, and three other firms sell it for $5,000. Transactions at $4,500 are on the leading edge of this market. These are fair exchanges.

The $500 in pure profit that firm A makes represents the value of the entrepreneur's contribution. He is signaling to both customers and competitors that there have been changes in the underlying determinants of the competitively efficient price. As Adam Smith might say, this signaling is done out of self-interest and not the goodness of his heart, but it is a vital service that must be performed in any market economy. Indeed, it is no exaggeration to say that the efficiency of a market economy depends on this signaling. Nothing in this story assumes that this entrepreneur knows where the new equilibrium price will be; indeed, that is what the market process discovers. But under the assumption that this exchange is in fact on the leading edge of a market in transition, this entrepreneur is pointing the market in the right direction.

Notice that exchanges that take place with the other sellers are not fair exchanges according to the definition—which is as it should be. In the case of those continuing to sell at $5,000, their price tells the market nothing about the changes that have taken place. In the case of sales at $4,750, the fact that the seller earns $250 more than firm A makes no additional contribution to informing the market about changes in underlying conditions, so the seller is receiving more than the value of his product, which is now $4,500.[14] This is true even if his cost structure is higher, and he has not been able to figure out how his rival sells the product for less.

The same considerations apply if a market is moving in the other direction. Consider, for example, changes in the price of heating oil. Suppose an especially harsh winter is setting in, and the firms that own the heating oil refineries raise the price of their product to distributors. They are informing people about the changing relative scarcity of heating oil. The higher prices tell those who need to know that the situation has changed or is changing, which will have the result that all participants in the market will make adjustments in their plans. Those who need to know are primarily their customers and competitors, but these price changes will also send shock waves up the distribution-production chain. Of course, the market process does not operate without mistakes and false starts, but by hypothesis, the cases under consideration are those in which the process is working properly, namely, a situation in which the entrepreneur guesses correctly about which way the market is heading. It is often said that these speculators do nothing to earn these profits, but that is just not true. They pass along vital information that the market needs to know, and they do so in a way that is effective in getting people to adjust their behavior to the new realities. The information they transmit by changing their prices is sometimes not good news, which leads some people to want to shoot the messenger, but it is the essence of the market process to transmit information in this way.[15]

On the other hand, it is important to call attention to the fact that not all pure profits pocketed by firms and individuals are captured on the leading edge of these transitional markets. Not only are there exchanges in transitional markets that are not on the leading edge, but there are also markets that are neither competitively efficient nor in transition. Some of these might be called 'stagnant markets.' In a stagnant market, prices are stable but some participants are making persistent pure profits or suffering persistent pure losses. Of course, firms suffering persistent losses will soon disappear from the scene, unless they are subsidized by someone (usually the state). The explanations for persistent profits are various. Firms might have a government-guaranteed monopoly or a state subsidy, or they might be facing different cost structures even though those with the lowest costs have not lowered their price. The pure profits that this company appropriates serve no signaling function at all and thus are not a return to any positive contribution. They are like monopoly profits, which are imputable to the monopolist's status as sole supplier and serve no efficiency function. In a competitive environment, however, companies will usually not sit on cost savings for long, since they can often increase net revenues and market share by lowering their price, and they may face losing both if a competitor makes the same discovery and lowers her price.

Thus far, competitively efficient markets, markets in transition, and stagnant markets have been discussed. There is one final possibility to consider. Sometimes market conditions are so chaotic that prices are very widely dispersed or are highly volatile and not trending in any direction. Any of these circumstances may hold for an extended period of time, even if the competitive process usually eliminates either condition in relatively short order. Causes of these phenomena include exogenous shocks such as war, political upheaval, or unforeseen changes in the regulatory or legal environment. There may be endogenous causes, too, though an examination of this possibility would lead us further into macroeconomics than this book can go. Whatever the cause, it is relevant to ask what the value of something is in a chaotic market. Although various hypothetical equilibria can be defined, perhaps the most natural answer to this question is that the value of something under these circumstances is simply undefined; that is, there is no such thing as *the* value of a good or service in a chaotic market; there are only different prices at which people are making exchanges, and those prices do not bear any very close relationship to any of the usual underlying determinants of price.

Consider, for example, a highly volatile stock whose price fluctuates dramatically on the most insubstantial rumors. If someone buys this stock, is it really worth what she is paying for it? The question seems to evaporate. If this is correct, no meaning can be assigned to the question, Are people getting the value of their contributions in chaotic markets? Although chaotic markets do exist, the belief that price theory (perhaps the best-established part of economics) tells us a fair amount about the real world presupposes that these chaotic markets are the exception and not the rule.

To summarize, the notion of a fair exchange can be defined in terms of what one receives in a competitively efficient market or on the leading edge of a market in transition. If the market is stagnant or if the exchange is not on the leading edge of a market in transition, then one of the parties is not getting the value of his or her contribution. This is the account of a fair price and the value of someone's contribution that will be used in the rest of this book.[16] It is a necessary but not sufficient condition for exploitation that someone is not getting the value of his contribution. Before passing on to consider the criteria for identifying competitively efficient markets and markets in transition, there is an objection to this account of value that merits some discussion.

It starts from the observation that in any market system it is inevitable that some consumers have more "dollar votes" than others. In existing free enterprise systems, this means that considerable resources are devoted to the production of luxury goods that would otherwise find other employment. This fact influences the entire structure of production and, indirectly, the terms of exchange for all goods and services. Can it really be that people are getting the "true value" of their contributions in a society that, for example, pays athletes millions of dollars a year; manufactures and sells perfumes, Rolls Royces, and fur coats; allows huge disparities of income and wealth; supports even half the number lawyers that American society supports; and so on? The various social irrationalities, as they were called in chapter 2, distort the structure of production in ways that defeat any attempt to identify some rate of exchange for any good or service in this type of economy as "fair."

The problem with this objection is that it takes the terms 'true value' and 'fair exchange' too literally and in too moralistic a fashion. It is possible to distinguish two senses of these terms. One sense describes the terms of exchange that would exist in the good society, or at least in someone's vision of the good society. For example, on some socialist's conception of the good society, the exchange value of the writings of Milton Friedman would be about the same as the exchange value of the writings of Marx and Lenin in the former Soviet Union, namely, slightly above the value of scrap paper. That would be a fair exchange in the market for Milton Friedman's writings in the good society, according to this socialist's vision. Although it might be easy, one can suppose, to assess the 'true value,' in this sense, of Friedman's writings, it would much more difficult to assess the 'true value' of many other goods in the good society (according to this vision of it), assuming that no existing society is too close to the theorist's vision. This is especially true of producer goods, such as oil drilling equipment and road grading machines, since existing exchange rates reflect factors and forces that would not exist in that society. So, it might be argued, there is a sense in which one cannot know the true value of many things—or possibly even anything.

However, according to the other sense of the terms 'fair exchange' and 'true value'—the sense being employed here—what one is talking about is the rate of exchange that would be found in existing society if the relevant markets were functioning properly. Prices in competitively efficient markets reflect how people do value things, not how they ought to value things.

Indeed, one has to make a distinction like this to criticize the values that a society happens to hold—values made manifest by where and how productive resources are deployed. In speaking of the value of someone's contribution (or the terms of a fair exchange), one is speaking of the value of that contribution in the society as it actually exists. This means that the point of reference is the set of actual values people have and express through their purchases, whatever those values are and whatever the distribution of that purchasing power is. One can acknowledge that people are getting (or not getting) the value of what they have to offer and yet still criticize the values that ultimately determine those exchange rates, or the distribution of wealth or income in that society that determines people's "dollar votes," or both. There is a sense in which exploitation is a surface phenomenon, however deep its explanation goes.[17] Moreover, though exploitation is arguably a form of distributive injustice, there may be more to distributive justice than the absence of exploitation. This and related issues come up again in the last section of this chapter.

Consider now the question of the criteria for fair exchanges. Since fair exchanges are those that take place in competitively efficient markets or on the leading edge of markets in transition, the question resolves itself into determining the criteria by which these markets can be identified. To begin with competitively efficient markets, recall that the price at which a good exchanges in a competitively efficient market approximates the price that would be found in an ideal market for that good. Ideal markets are defined in terms of some very strong structural assumptions (many firms, homogeneous product, perfect information, etc.). Though no real-world market may fit all of these defining features, some are reasonably close approximations to the ideal. Approximations to the defining features of an ideal market, then, are marks or criteria by which a competitively efficient market can be identified. One can identify such markets by looking for most of the following: many competitors, knowledgeable customers, low transactions costs, easy entry, cheap information about price and quality, and few or no externalities.

The basic idea is that if a market has many or most of the real-world analogs of the defining features of an ideal market, that is a good indication that this market is competitively efficient and that exchanges in it are fair. Consider, for example, the market in wholesale produce in most major cities. There are many suppliers and purchasers, price and quality information is easily available to both buyers and sellers (nearly all of whom are quite knowledgeable), barriers to entry are relatively low, the volume of transactions is high, price changes primarily reflect changing supply or demand conditions, and externalities and transaction costs are negligible. These are competitively efficient markets. What entrepreneurial profits there are (both positive and negative) tend to be relatively small and to be canceled out over relatively short periods of time, so that the owner-operators in the wholesale produce market earn about the equivalent of a wage plus a normal return on their capital investment. Exchanges in these markets are fair exchanges.

Approximation to an ideal market is a good criterion for competitively efficient markets, but there are two problems in applying it. First, it is unclear how many attributes of an ideal market must be approximated for a real-world market to count as competitively efficient. Having all those features would be highly restrictive. On the other hand, approximating only one defining feature of an ideal market is surely insufficient for saying that the market is competitively efficient. Second, it is unclear how closely a feature of a real-world market must resemble the template of the model for the approximation to hold. In short, the truth conditions for these approximation claims are indeterminate along two dimensions. This does not mean that there are no clear cases of markets that closely approximate the model (wholesale produce markets in most major cities do), but it does mean there are cases where there may be no way to say whether the market approximates an ideal market.

In addition, as was noted, markets need bear no structural similarity to ideal markets in order to be competitively efficient. So approximation to an ideal market cannot be the sole criterion. What else could serve? What all competitively efficient markets (including those that approximate ideal markets) have in common is that they are effectively invulnerable to successful entrepreneurship. No individual or firm is in a position to profit by reaping economies of scale; discovering a new, lower cost source of supply of inputs; instituting technological innovations that reduce production costs; making organizational changes that reduce transaction costs; expanding the market without incurring losses; appreciably increasing market share; repositioning their products in the market; or the like. These are the kind of things successful entrepreneurs do, but none of them can be done in a competitively efficient market.

There are other, less obvious ways in which a market may be invulnera ble to successful entrepreneurship. The next chapter will explain how some exchanges are supported by highly specific assets, that is, assets that are costly to redeploy once they have been committed. For example, a supplier might purchase a specialized piece of equipment to manufacture a product for another firm. This piece of equipment might be so specialized that it can be used for no other purpose than making that product. Furthermore, that product might itself be so specialized that the only firm that has any use for it is the firm that buys it. Initially, there might be a number of potential partners available for each side of this exchange relation. However, once the relationship between these two firms is engaged and begins to develop, the purchaser effectively has no other source of supply and the supplier effectively has nowhere else to sell his product. The situation is one of bilateral monopoly.

The "micro market" in which this exchange takes place may still be competitively efficient, however. Suppose that the original terms of the contract (i.e., the exchange) were crafted in such a way that neither side could have got a better deal from some third party over the life of the contract. For example, suppose that each side builds an expensive specialized piece of equipment that can only be used in conjunction with this contract. Following Williamson, this can be called an "exchange of hostages" (1985, 190–95). As a result, successive adaptations of the terms of the contract (which can be thought of as a sequence of exchanges) result in what one would have expected if there were many other sellers and buyers around whenever the contract was renewed. Under a contract like this, it could said that both parties are operating *as if* they were in an environment that approximates an ideal market. If that is what happens, then this "micro market" is effectively invulnerable to successful entrepreneurship and thus can be pronounced competitively efficient. (Exchanges supported by highly specific assets are quite common and will be discussed in detail in the next chapter.)

A clearer idea about what invulnerability to successful entrepreneurship involves can be got from considering how what were called stagnant markets are vulnerable to successful entrepreneurship. One kind of vulnerability is more hypothetical than real. The American sugar market is, in one sense, highly vulnerable to successful entrepreneurship. American sugar producers could be wiped out very easily by traders buying on the world market at the world market price and selling in the American market. However, tariffs and quotas make this illegal, thereby protecting domestic sugar producers from the rigors of the market. Producers of substitutes are also protected. For example, the Archer Daniels Midland Corporation is a powerful supporter of the domestic sugar industry because it can profitably sell a substitute for sugar (corn syrup) to soft drink companies, but only if the price of sugar is maintained at artificially high levels. Because of their political connections, these markets are, in one important sense, relatively invulnerable to successful entrepreneurship, but by ordinary economic criteria they are highly vulnerable.

On the other hand, some stagnant markets consist of firms or individuals who really could be undercut by more efficient competitors. These markets, however, can only be reliably identified in hindsight. American steel, clothing, and automobile manufacturers over the past twenty years have proved vulnerable in this sense. However, segments of these markets have become competitively efficient over the past ten years or so as some of these firms have shaped up, and others have gone out of business.

In the case where there are legal prohibitions or restriction on competition, the relevant markets are almost always hypothetically vulnerable to successful entrepreneurship. In the other type of case, it is harder to determine, at least ex ante. The reason for this is the simple fact that identifying this sort of vulnerability is what successful entrepreneurs do. Judgments that a market is vulnerable to successful entrepreneurship can be decisively confirmed only after the fact, that is, when that market has been successfully invaded, and entrepreneurs have initiated what Schumpeter calls their waves of "creative destruction" (1942, 81–86; 1961, chaps. 2, 4). If economists could readily identify these markets beforehand, they would not be hostage to the traditional American slogan, "If you're so smart, how come you're not rich?"

What follows from these observations is that invulnerability to successful entrepreneurship, which is the mark of competitively efficient markets, is difficult to identify. Structural similarity to an ideal market is not a necessary condition for competitive efficiency; it is simply a good indicator that the market is competitively efficient. There is, however, one additional uncertain indicator that should be mentioned: rates of return to equity owners. If government securities are conceived of as essentially riskless investments, then the rate on these securities is the social discount rate (the pure time preference rate). If all the equity owners of firms that compete in a given market are getting about this rate of return on their investment, then there is some reason to believe that there are no pure profits to be made. However, the failure to receive pure profits may also indicate that the managements of all these firms have simply not done a good job in acting on opportunities that are "there" for anyone in the industry to see. Also, most firms sell a mix of products (or, at least, they segment markets in different ways), so the fact that some equity owners receive only the social discount rate of return on their investment may represent offsetting positive and negative pure profits in different markets.

Unlike competitively efficient markets, markets in transition are easier to identify. If there is a more than one price for a product and if prices are trending in a certain direction, that indicates that the market in question is in transition to a new competitive equilibrium. It is not a guarantee, however, since the entrepreneurs initiating this change may be acting on mistaken beliefs about underlying conditions, and the market may end up heading in the other direction or returning to the old equilibrium. Finally, in chaotic markets, entrepreneurs' guesses are not reflective of the underlying economic realities; any pure profits that they make do not signal real changes in the economy: they are purely speculative in the pejorative sense of the term. But when transactions take place on the leading edge of a market that is in transition to a new equilibrium, the exchanges are fair and both parties are getting the value of their contributions.

Recall that the point of identifying competitively efficient markets and markets in transition was to determine in which markets buyers and sellers are getting the value of their respective contributions. Both sides are getting the value of what they are giving up when an exchange takes place in a competitively efficient market or on the leading edge of a market in transition. By implication, in these markets, reciprocity holds, and neither party is exploiting the other party. By contrast, in exchanges that are not fair—those in stagnant markets or those not on the leading edge of markets in transition—someone is getting more or less than the value of his or her contribution; in either case, reciprocity fails. Such exchanges may or may not be exploitative, depending on whether or not other conditions for exploitation hold.

It is worth pointing out that a fair exchange in the product markets does not presuppose fair exchanges in the factor markets and vice versa. Suppose that a given product market is competitively efficient, so that exchanges in this market are fair. Those who provide factors of production to participants in this market may or may not be getting the value of what they contribute. That would depend on whether or not the exchanges in these factor markets are themselves fair. For example, they may be colluding in charging their customers a higher price. The converse is also true. Fair exchanges in the factor markets may or may not be accompanied by fair exchanges in the product markets. For example, the U.S. government has imposed a system of tobacco allotments which restricts production of salable tobacco to specified lots. This allows farmers to charge more than a competitive rate, and yet their supply markets (for, e.g., farm equipment) may be fiercely competitive. However politically invulnerable they are, from an economic point of view, they are highly vulnerable to successful entrepreneurship.

Exchanges in stagnant markets, as well as those not on the leading edge of markets in transition, are not fair exchanges. Since the lack of fairness is a necessary (though not sufficient) condition for economic exploitation, the extent of economic exploitation in any market economy will be, in part, determined by the extent to which the product and factor markets are vulnerable to successful entrepreneurship. On a purely intuitive level, this seems perfectly reasonable.

Another implication of this account is that where and whether fair exchanges take place is a question that can only be settled by empirical investigation into how markets actually function, which means that the existence and extent of economic exploitation in market economies must be settled in the same way. This stands in sharp contrast to nearly all contemporary theories of exploitation in capitalist (free enterprise) economic systems, which require no real empirical investigation into how markets actually function. Instead, all one has to know is the basic relations of production (capitalists own the means of production and the workers have to sell their labor) to pronounce the system exploitative. That way of discovering the existence and extent of exploitation should have seemed too easy, too good to be true; but for those antipathetic to capitalism, the temptation to buy into that kind of analysis has probably been irresistible.

The Question of Alternatives

The theory of economic exploitation as it has been developed in this chapter up to this point is significantly incomplete. The discussion has proceeded on the presumption (indirectly supported by a variety of considerations) that a failure of reciprocity is a necessary condition for exploitation; the challenge has been to explain where and how reciprocity can fail in market exchanges. However, thus far, no other condition(s) have been identified that, together with the failure of reciprocity, would be sufficient for economic exploitation. There is one such condition. To identify it, let us return once again to the Marxist account of the capitalist's exploitation of the worker.

The standard Marxist account has it that the workers are forced to participate in the lopsided transaction that results in their contributing more value than they receive. The apparent problem with this claim is that on the face of it, it just does not seem to be true. The relation between the worker and the capitalist is not coercive. Indeed, Marxists would be unable to distinguish capitalist relations of production from those of slave societies unless they could distinguish the tie that binds the worker to the capitalist from the tie that binds the slave to his master.

There have been a number of responses to this problem from the Marxist community. G. A. Cohen (1983) has argued that while individual proletarians are free to leave the ranks of the exploited, the proletariat as a class is not. This means that the proletariat as a class is forced to participate in the system (and presumably that they are exploited in virtue of this fact). George Brenkert (1985) has called attention to a richer conception of freedom that is implicit in Marx's writings and that proletarians lack. On this view, positive freedom is not an absence of coercion; thus, the workers can be unfree (forced) even though they are not coerced. This lack of freedom is the real problem with exploitation; the maldistribution of income is a distinctly secondary issue on this account. But perhaps the most common view is that individual workers really are forced to work for the capitalists. However, this forcing consists not in coercion but in the basic or fundamental fact that individual workers really have no feasible alternative except to work for the capitalists (i.e., to work for some capitalist or other). This view is clearly expressed in the following passage from Jeffrey Reiman:

> Since workers in capitalism do not own means of production, they can be forced in a different way. Because access to means of production is access to the means of producing a living at all, those who own means of production have enormous leverage over those who do not. . . . The very structure

of property ownership itself provides the force by putting the worker in a position in which he has no real choice but to sell himself of his own free will. (1989, 309)

My purpose is not to resolve this dispute within the Marxist community about how to understand the claim that the worker is forced to work for the capitalist; nor is it even to address the question of whether or not the workers really are forced to work for the capitalists. (These two questions are repeatedly conflated in the secondary literature on Marx.) Rather, this dispute can serve as a heuristic device to gain some insight into the concept of exploitation.

To that end, suppose that there is a systematic failure of reciprocity between the capitalist and the worker in the sense that the capitalist is getting—and the worker is not getting—some of the value of the worker's contribution. Notice that what all of the aforementioned accounts of forcing (or some analog of forcing) have in common is that if they were true, they would *explain why* the workers would accept this lopsided arrangement; that is, they explain why the workers would accept exchanges that systematically fail to be reciprocal. Barring special explanation, no rational person who usually acts in his own self-interest would agree to participate in a system in which he regularly gives up more than he gets.

This provides some insight into what the other necessary condition for economic exploitation must look like: it must explain why someone who is both rational and usually acts in his own self-interest would accept less than the value of what he gives up. In short, one necessary condition for economic exploitation must explain why the other necessary condition holds, when it does hold. The assumption of rationality on the part of the exploited person directs one's attention to the alternative course or courses of action that are open to her to pursue. For a person to put up with a chronic failure of reciprocity, it must be that she does not have a significantly better alternative open to her; otherwise, she would not agree to this lopsided arrangement.[18] This means that the alternatives open to her are either significantly worse than, or about the same as, the one she chooses. As it is sometimes said, she had no real alternative to the option that she chose. This is encapsulated in the following schema, which shall be called the no real-alternatives-condition (for the record, the other condition can be called the failure-of-reciprocity condition):

DEFINITION. *X* economically exploits *Y* in exchange e only if (1) given *Y*'s end in view, the next best alternative available to *Y* is significantly worse than e or (2) given *Y*'s end in view, the alternatives to e available to *Y* (e.g., the deals that *X*'s competitors are offering) are about the same as e.

Both conditions 1 and 2 require some elucidation. The idea behind (1) is this: in entering into any exchange, a person has some goal or purpose in mind beyond that exchange. Following John Dewey, this can be called an *end in view* to distinguish it from the larger or more remote plans and purposes that an action may serve. In entering into an exchange, what *Y* would receive in the exchange is a means to that end in view. When condition (1) holds, *Y*'s next best alternative course of action is significantly inferior as a means of achieving that end in view. For example, suppose Smith's end in view is to support her family; she works in a company town and has few resources to engage in a search for other employment. Her next best alternative way to support her family is to beg on the street. Suppose that is significantly worse than continuing to work for the company.[19] In one sense, then, she has no real alternative but to work for the company.

Notice that if she has the resources to cover the costs of searching for a better alternative and if there really is a better alternative out there that she would find, then neither of the two disjuncts is satisfied (i.e., her next best alternative is not significantly worse and it not about the same as the exchange she accepts), and therefore she is not exploited by the company. Moreover, notice also that if she is getting the value of her contribution (i.e., her labor), then it also follows that she is not being exploited. This is so even if her next best alternative is significantly worse than working for the company. She might be getting the value of her contribution because other employees at the company are more mobile, and the company has to pay a wage to everyone that reflects what is required to retain these more mobile workers.

Disjunct (2) is intended to take care of exploitation that takes place when someone is not getting the value of what he is giving up, and the reason is traceable to one of two general causes: (1) artificial restrictions on alternatives, such as monopoly or state-imposed price controls, and (2) improperly functioning markets due to collusion, laziness, stupidity, and the like among potential competitors. As an illustration of cause (1), suppose that the state requires all farmers to sell their export crops to a state-owned marketing board at a fixed price that is less than the commodities are worth (i.e., what they would fetch in the world market, assuming the world market is competitively efficient). Suppose, further, that the next best alternative is to engage in subsistence farming, which gives him and his family about the same standard of living. (He may continue to grow the cash crop because of the costs of making the transition.) In this case, the farmers are exploited by the state.

As an illustration of cause (2), suppose that there are only two firms in a market—say, two airlines in the Bozeman, Montana to Fargo, North Dakota market—and they are charging people more than the value of the service. This might be because they collude or because they have simultaneously and independently settled into uncompetitive routines. (Suppose that the people in charge are former Civil Aeronautics Board bureaucrats.) The reason why passengers are regularly paying more than the value of the service is because the only two firms serving that market are offering about the same deal. Whichever of the two exchanges is chosen, the alternative would have been about the same. If all of this is true, it follows that the passengers are exploited by whatever airline they fly. The market is not competitively efficient; although there is an opportunity for successful entrepreneurship in this market, no one has seized it, and there is no guarantee that anyone will. Those in a position to do something about it may have other things to do with their resources, and those who want to do something about it may not have access to the resources needed to compete in that market. Some defenders of the free enterprise system make the unwarranted assumption that if a profit opportunity exists, it will always be seized—if not tomorrow, then at least by next month. But of course, it may not, and people will get exploited as a result.

On the other hand, note that except for cases like these and cases where there are state-enforced terms of exchange, if disjunct (2) holds, then the failure-of-reciprocity condition for exploitation is probably *not* met. In other words, if all competitors are offering about the same exchange rate, then barring the sort of explanations just adverted to, the market is competitively efficient, and people are receiving the value of their respective contributions; that is, reciprocity holds, and they are not being exploited.

The failure-of-reciprocity condition and the no-real-alternatives condition together are singly necessary and jointly sufficient conditions for economic exploitation. This definition and the supporting discussion constitute the theory of economic exploitation to be used in the rest of this book. It is time to consider some objections. One objection that comes readily to mind is that it seems that an unfair exchange (in the sense of 'unfair' employed here) must be exploitative. In other words, it seems that the failure-of-reciprocity condition is not just a necessary condition for economic exploitation but a sufficient condition as well. For example, suppose that Sally sells a family heirloom for much less than its true value—perhaps out of ignorance—to an antique dealer who knows about how much it will fetch at the next antique auction. By that fact alone, has the antique dealer not exploited her?

Not necessarily. To see why, it is necessary to fill out the story in a such a way that the no-real-alternatives condition is *not* met (i.e., she does have a real alternative). Suppose that this is not one of the usual sob stories philosophers like to tell. In other words, she is not selling this heirloom because she desperately needs some drug for her child with cancer or because she is starving, and no one else is willing to buy it. Sally just does not care enough about her family for this item to have much sentimental value, and she would like to have the extra money. Further suppose that some of the dealer's competitors would be willing to pay significantly more for the item.

The question is whether Sally is being exploited by the antique dealer. The answer is no. Although there is a definite sense in which she is getting less than the item is "really worth," she is nevertheless not being exploited. After all, she could look around a little more, go to some antique shows and flea markets—in short, pay some of the search costs to find out the market value of this item. She took a chance that this dealer would pay about what the item is worth and lost. This is not exploitation; this is just not being smart. However unfair the exchange is, it is not exploitative.

This example and the one about the woman working in the company town illustrate something about what is required for someone to have a "real alternative" to an exchange, that is, an alternative that defeats a charge of exploitation. Both examples suggest that for there to be such an alternative, not only must there be an alternative course of action that is both a satisfactory means to the particular end in view and "out there" to be found, but also, it must make sense for the person to pay the costs—in this case the search costs—associated with that course of action. If those costs, together with what it costs to purchase the item, significantly exceed the cost of the alternative chosen, then the person really had "no real alternative" to the exchange she made.

For example, if someone is working for next to nothing in Central America and could make considerably more as an illegal migrant laborer in the United States, that alternative may or may not be a real one, depending on the search costs involved in finding work in the United States. For many of these individuals, the search costs (pecuniary and nonpecuniary) involved in finding anything noticeably better than their current lot are so high that they have no real alternative to their existing situation. Such people may or may not be exploited, however, depending on whether or not they are getting the value of their contribution in their current situation.

A second objection begins with the observation—explicitly recognized earlier—that a fair exchange in the product markets is compatible with unfair exchanges in the factor markets. Suppose that José, a migrant farm worker who picks lettuce, is getting less than the value of his contribution and has no real alternative but to work for a particular grower. (Competing growers are colluding in offering about the same deal, and there are no other jobs around.) Accordingly, he is exploited. Suppose, further, that the farmer who hires him sells his lettuce for $6 a box in the wholesale produce market, instead of the $8 a box it would cost if he were paying José and the other workers what their labor was really worth, that is, what it would fetch in a competitively efficient market. The wholesale produce market is competitively efficient, so this latter transaction is fair and thus nonexploitative. But—so the objection runs—this is the problem. There is a temptation to say that the farmer is not the only one who is exploiting José. The wholesaler, the retailer, and the consumer are also exploiting him; it is just that some are more directly involved than others. Certainly, this is what the United Farm Workers Union wants people to believe. But is this really so?

In part, this possibility is ruled out by the way exploitation has been conceived in this discussion. Exploitation has been understood in terms of exploitative *exchange*, which means that an exploiter must be a party to the exchange with the exploited. Of course, this does not count as a reason for rejecting the objection, except insofar as the account provided here has other advantages over alternative accounts.[20] Nevertheless, there is an independent reason to reject the suggestion that José is exploited by those who are downstream in the production-distribution-consumption chain. It is quite possible to distinguish between being a beneficiary of exploitation and being an exploiter. For example, as part of some attempts to justify affirmative action, it has been claimed that existing white males have all benefited indirectly from slavery. Assuming that is true, it would be nonetheless quite odd to say of them that they are exploiting long-dead slaves, assuming that the latter were exploited. While benefiting from a situation may well be a necessary condition for exploitation, it is certainly not sufficient.

To return to the example of José, it is useful to distinguish the *truth conditions* for exploitation from the *explanation for* exploitation. It may be that there is something about a free enterprise system (e.g., private ownership of the means of production) that encourages the exploitation of José; but if that is so, the relevant facts *explain why* José is exploited by the farmer or even why exploitative exchanges are widespread or common in such a system, but they do not *constitute* the exploitation. By hypothesis, José is exploited by the farmer who hires him, but those further down the production-distribution chain are not the exploiters; they are simply the beneficiaries of the farmer's exploitation of José.

In the interest of conceptual clarity, it is important not to expand the boundaries of the concept of exploitation to encompass all or most of the ills one wants to attribute to a society. This applies even to the issue of distributive justice and injustice. Even if exploitation is a form of distributive injustice, it does not follow that all forms of distributive injustice are instances of the exploitation. Someone might want to argue, for example, that distributive justice requires that each person's basic needs be met; if those needs are not met, someone would thereby have a legitimate complaint of distributive injustice against society. But that complaint is not one of exploitation. Though it is plausible to conceive of exploitation as a form of distributive injustice, this book offers no general theory of distributive (in)justice. That must be left for another time.

The theory of economic exploitation developed in this chapter suggests (though it does not logically imply) that any market economy is going to play host to at least some economically exploitative exchanges. Though it is logically possible for there to be a market economy in which there are no economically exploitative exchanges, a little reflection on what that would require makes it evident that this is highly unlikely. Each and every transaction in such a system would meet one or the other of the following two conditions: (1) it would be in a competitively efficient market or on the leading edge of a market in transition, or (2) there would be a noticeably better alternative available to any person who fails to get the value of what she has to offer.

That seems unlikely. What is more likely is that in any market economy, some markets will be neither competitively efficient nor in transition and will, in fact, be stagnant. This entails that there will be some unfair transactions, that is, transactions in which people are not getting the value of their contributions. And in some of those markets, one of the parties to the exchange will have no real alternative but to accept the terms that person or organization does accept. The same will be true of some parties who make exchanges not on the leading edge of markets in transition. In short, it is likely that there will be exploitative exchanges in any market economy.

This means that it is likely that there will be some exploitative exchanges in any market socialist economic system. If this is so and if there is no viable socialist alternative to market socialism, then the socialist dream of a society without economic exploitation is a purely utopian fantasy. This does not mean that one must give up on market socialism, however. It just means that the dream, that is, the socialist vision of the good society, must be revised. The most obvious revision, in light of this discussion of exploitation, would be to maintain that the favored type of market socialist economic system would minimize exploitation, or at the very least, do better than a free enterprise system on this score. Indeed, it would be difficult to find a socialist who would deny this or even express any skepticism about it.

The main purpose of chapters 5–7 will be to show that this is not the case. Specifically, I shall argue that in point of fact, it is a free enterprise system that tends to minimize the incidence of economic exploitation, whereas the type of market socialist system identified in chapter 2 both permits and encourages forms of exploitative exchange that a free enterprise system precludes or minimizes. This argument depends crucially on some recent developments in economics. Over the past twenty years or so, the new economics of contracts and organizations, or *transactions cost analysis* (as it is sometimes called), has endeavored to explain some distinctive efficiencies of the various types of economic organizations found in a free enterprise system. Given the conceptual connection between inefficiency and exploitation established in this chapter, this has obvious relevance for the question of exploitation in market economies. The next chapter will provide an overview of these developments and indicates their relevance for the general thesis of chapters 5–7. Chapter 5 will explain the distinctive efficiencies of the characteristic organizational forms found in a free enterprise system and will indicate how these organizational forms preclude or tend to minimize the incidence of exploitative exchange. Chapters 6 and 7 will apply the principles of the new economics of organizations to the organizations of market socialism, notably, the self-managed cooperative and the associated state organizations that control new investment. The discussion in chapters 6 and 7 will be more explicitly comparative. The main argument of these two chapters seeks to establish that the characteristic organizations of a market socialist system permit—and indeed encourage—a range of exploitative exchanges that are prevented, precluded, or minimized by the characteristic organizations found in a free enterprise system. In short, market socialism is more exploitative than capitalism. Chapter 8 will consider some alternatives types of economic systems that look attractive from a socialist perspective. It argues that these alternatives are also inferior to a free enterprise system on the issue of exploitation or are not really forms of socialism, or both.

A traditional question of comparative economic systems, namely, the relative efficiency of socialist economic systems in comparison to free enterprise systems, has long been a matter of contention between the opposing sides in the capitalism/socialism dispute. One of the main points of this chapter has been to argue that there is an important conceptual link between inefficiencies (understood in terms of vulnerability to successful entrepreneurship) and exploitation. If an economic system suffers this sort of inefficiency and if it systematically prevents people from taking steps to remedy it, that system can be termed exploitative. This means that the debate about the relative efficiency of different types of economic systems takes on a new significance. The issue is no longer merely one of who can best deliver the goods; it is now connected with the question of exploitation—and ultimately the question of distributive justice—in economic systems.

4

Exploitation and
the Economics of Organizations

Comparing Types of Economic Systems

As was just indicated, the main argument of chapters 6 and 7 will seek to establish that the type of market socialist system described in chapter 2 permits and encourages a range of exploitative exchanges that are prevented or discouraged in a free enterprise system. The main purpose of this chapter and the next is to lay the groundwork for that argument. As a first step, some analytical questions need to be addressed. In particular, the objects of discussion need to be more clearly identified, and the exact nature of the claim being advanced needs to be made clearer. The purpose of this section is to discharge these two analytical tasks and to indicate a little more clearly how the case against market socialism in chapters 6 and 7 will be made.

Recall from chapter 1 that the objects of discussion are not particular economic systems, economic systems as they exist "on the ground." Instead, the objects of discussion are abstract objects—specifically, types of economic systems, which are distinguished by their type-defining features. Let us begin by reviewing the relevant type-defining features of the two types of economic systems that are to be compared. Here will be found what distinguishes the type of market socialist economic system described in chapter 2 from a free enterprise system.[1] It will be demonstrated that it is these differences that are responsible for the difference in the incidence of exploitative exchange in the two types of systems.

It might be thought that the key difference is that a free enterprise system permits and exhibits a variety of organizational forms, whereas in a market socialist system, there are only self-managed worker cooperatives. This is partly accurate but not entirely so. In chapters 1 and 2, it was pointed out that a market socialist system can permit organizational forms other than the self-managed worker cooperative. Firms that are wholly owned by the state and even some privately owned enterprises can exist in such a system.

The reason for this is that there may be special reasons why state or private ownership of some firms—or even entire industries—is desirable in a market socialist system. For example, economies of scale might make local telephone service a natural monopoly, and it might be best for natural monopolies to be wholly state-owned. In addition, state control of new investment requires, at some level, political organizations whose members are elected or appointed to register and implement decisions about the rate and direction of economic growth. On the other side of the coin, there may be compelling historical reasons for some segments of the economy to be entirely private. For example, historically well-founded distrust and hostility toward the state on the part of the peasantry may make it advisable for at least small-scale agriculture to be a wholly private sector operation in many countries. Market socialists need not—and should not—dogmatically insist that the worker cooperative be the only form of economic organization to be found in society.

However, both individually and collectively, wholly state-owned firms and private enterprises must be the exception and not the rule if the system is to realize the socialist conception of the good society sketched in chapter 2. The self-managed worker cooperative is the predominant organizational form in this type of market socialist system. This organizational form and the associated scheme of state control of new investment and intervention in the economy together are the chief instrumentalities by which various socialist goals (elements of the socialist conception of the good society) are to be realized. That is the motivation for this type of system, and these instrumentalities cannot be cast aside by permitting widespread private or state ownership of the means of production.

These observations suggest two important differences between a market socialist system and a free enterprise system. First, under a market socialist system, the self-managed worker cooperative will be far and away the most common form of economic organization, though not the only one. By contrast, if existing free enterprise systems are at all representative, the open corporation and the classical capitalist firm are the predominant organizational forms found in this type of system. A word needs to be said about these two kinds of organizations.

The classical capitalist firm is wholly owned and managed by one and the same individual. He hires and directs the firm's employees, decides what to produce and how much to charge for the product, and he negotiates all contracts with suppliers of inputs. He also provides most, if not all, of the firm's capital and gets the residuals, that is, what is left over after all input providers are paid. Finally, he can alienate any and all of these rights. In short, all the incidents of ownership that go to constitute full, liberal ownership of the firm are concentrated in this individual. On the other hand, the open corporation involves the partial separation of ownership and management of the firm. The open corporation controls large amounts of capital, too large for any one individual to supply; ownership of the corporation is dispersed among many shareholders. Most of these shareholders are not managers of the firm's assets, however. Managers (who often have some equity stake in the firm) are hired, usually by a board of directors, who in turn are answerable to the shareholders.[2] Ownership of shares in the corporation is ownership of the corporation's assets. This entitles shareholders to a proportional residual claim on the income stream generated by the firm and to some sort of ultimate decision-making authority over the firm's assets (e.g., a proportional vote on who serves on the board of directors). Ownership shares are freely alienable on a stock market, and shareholders' liability is limited to the extent of their investment.

The classical capitalist firm and the open corporation are the most common and important forms of economic organization in existing free enterprise systems, though they are not the only ones. There are closely held corporations, or "closed corporations" (Fama and Jensen 1983b), in which a few individuals own most of the stock and one of them is the manager. There are also partnerships, in which some but not all of those who work for the firm have a role in managing it and are its residual claimants. These other forms of organization, while not predominant, are at least common in existing free enterprise systems. By contrast, they would be quite uncommon under market socialism, as would the classical capitalist firm and the open corporation, all for the reasons indicated.

The discussion thus far has omitted one important type, or family of types, of economic organizations found in existing free enterprise systems— organizations that are owned and operated by the state. A significant percentage of people in existing societies with free enterprise systems are employed by the state in one capacity or another. These organizations have been deliberately omitted for a very simple reason: those who favor a free enterprise system are not in the least interested in defending state ownership or state control of the means of production subject to a few well-defined exceptions. They regard state ownership as an abomination, which, in their vision of the good society, would be eliminated or minimized by privatizing most existing government-owned enterprises.[3] What they are defending in this debate is private enterprise, private ownership of the means of production; in the private sector nearly all organizations are open or closed corporations, partnerships, or classical capitalist firms, with the first and fourth types predominating.

Are all free enterprise systems dominated by the classical capitalist firm and the open corporation? The answer in part depends on how one individuates economic systems. Historically, free enterprise systems have existed in which the open corporation was not a major factor. For example, early capitalism was dominated by classical capitalist firms and partnerships. However, in all existing mature free enterprise systems, these two types of organizations predominate. This could be a matter of historical accident, but there may be a deeper explanation for this fact. For reasons that will emerge later in this chapter and the next, it will be useful to proceed on the supposition that all free enterprise systems from now into the indefinite future will in fact be dominated by these two types of organizations. Alternatively, one side of the comparative discussion of market socialism and free enterprise systems could be restricted to free enterprise systems in which the classical capitalist firm and the open corporation predominate. Whatever option is adopted, the advantage of restricting the discussion to free enterprise systems dominated by these two types of organizations is that it allows a clear and sharp contrast to be drawn, based on the organizational forms that predominate in the two types of economic systems that are the subject of this discussion.

A second and related difference between a market socialist system and a free enterprise system is that a market socialist system must have and enforce laws prohibiting the emergence of these other forms of economic organization, subject to a few well-defined exceptions. By contrast, in a free enterprise system, people are free to organize production in any way they choose, subject to the standard prohibitions against slavery, serfdom, and so on. Why must a market socialist society prohibit alternative institutional forms? Recall that socialist critics of the free enterprise system trace the social vices of this type of system to concentration of the incidents of ownership (especially the management rights and income rights) in private hands. This, of course, is exactly what happens in the classical capitalist firm, the closely held corporation, and partnerships. And though management and income rights are separated in the open corporation, neither is widely dispersed among the population as a whole. So, from a socialist point of view, there are good reasons for a general prohibition on all these other organizational forms, allowing only a few exceptions.

It might be objected that there is no reason to suppose that such a legal prohibition would be necessary in a market socialist system. It might be said that the benefits of the worker cooperative will be so significant and self-evident that a legal prohibition on these alternative organizational forms would be wholly nugatory. It would be like outlawing slavery in modern America. There are two problems with this. First, absent a legal prohibition, the dispute between those who favor a market socialist system and those who favor a free enterprise system tends to dissolve. Those who favor the latter do not in principle have any special animus against worker cooperatives; they simply do not believe that the state should forbid alternative organizational forms. If people chose voluntarily to organize nearly all production through the cooperative form, those who favor a free enterprise system could hardly object (though of course they may believe this is unlikely to happen). Second, there are various incentives for individual firms to take on some of the characteristics of one or more of the above types of organizations.[4] For example, firms facing cyclical demand for their products or services (e.g., firms in the tourist industry) would be tempted to hire nonvoting wage laborers in the busy season and let them go in the off-season. Even if there is a general consensus that society is better off if the self-managed cooperative is the predominant organizational form, individual firms may find it in their own interests to be an exception to this general rule. To overcome the public goods nature of this problem, rational individuals facing this situation would seek a legal prohibition on alternative types of economic organizations.[5]

In general, socialists have not hesitated to call for a ban on what Robert Nozick has called "capitalist acts between consenting adults." The point of these observations is that a legal prohibition on these other organizational forms is well motivated from a socialist perspective. It prohibits the emergence of organizational forms that, while not the root of all evil, do account for many undesirable features of societies with free enterprise systems, at least according to socialist thought.

The other major difference between a free enterprise system and a market socialist system concerns the role of the state in directing the economy. In free enterprise systems, most new investment is financed by one or more of the following methods: (1) individuals' starting or expanding their own businesses through savings, (2) firms issuing debt, and (3) individuals or firms raising equity capital on the capital markets. By contrast, most new investment in a market socialist system is controlled by the state. This presupposes a set of political institutions responsible for setting the capital usage fee and disbursing investment funds. The details of these institutions were left indeterminate in chapter 2, which means that they could be filled out in a variety of ways consistent with the other type-defining features of this type of market socialist system. Finally, the state in a market socialist system is also more activist is preventing or correcting for the social irrationalities that would emerge or do emerge from the operation of the market, though this function has also been left institutionally indeterminate.

The discussion thus far makes it clear that the objects of discussion are two types of economic systems and that the crucial differences between them are organizational. But what exactly is to be proved about these types of systems? To say that a market socialist system permits and encourages a range of exploitative exchanges that are prevented or discouraged in a free enterprise system is less than completely clear.

To clarify what this means, some of the main points of later sections of this chapter need to be foreshadowed. The last two sections of this chapter will argue that in any market system, there are some very general and ineliminable features of the economic environment that create the potential for, or make possible, exploitative exchange. It is further argued that individuals, acting either for themselves or on behalf of their firms, have some predisposition to seize opportunities to exploit others if and when such opportunities present themselves.[6] Types of economic systems deal with this potential for exploitative exchange more or less well. What chapters 5–7 seek to establish is that a free enterprise system does a better job at this than does a market socialist system.

But what does 'better' mean in this context? Because the objects of discussion are abstract types of systems, it makes no sense to interpret this claim as a comparative quantitative judgment about the number of exploitative exchanges that take place "in" each of the two types of systems; that would have no meaning at this level of abstraction. What is needed is some natural way of classifying or categorizing exchanges that can be used to distinguish and compare the two types of systems.

The basis for such a typology is to be found in the fact that the kinds of organizations found in free enterprise and market socialist systems (and indeed in any market economy) can be defined in terms of a network of contracts (i.e., exchanges) among occupiers of a relatively small number of functionally defined economic roles. Each organizational type has a distinctive pattern of interrelations between and among the following roles:

1. laborers
2. capital providers, that is, those who furnish the capital the firm employs
3. other input suppliers, such as suppliers of raw materials, semifinished products, and specialty goods and services needed for production
4. monitors, that is, those who decide on the deployment of inputs in the productive process and evaluate the performance of laborers and other input providers
5. central contracting agents, that is, those in charge of negotiating contracts with all input suppliers
6. directors of the firm's output, that is, those in charge of determining the product that the firm produces, its characteristics, and its price,
7. ultimate decision makers, that is, those with final decision-making authority about the deployment of the firm's assets
8. residual claimants, that is, those with a claim on the residual income stream of the firm, which can be defined as what is left over after all other claims against the firm have been satisfied.

A terminological point: in ordinary parlance and among most economists, the term 'entrepreneur' is used to refer to someone who occupies roles 5 and 6, that is, someone who is in charge of the interface, on both the input and output sides, between the firm and the market.

Organizational forms (and, by implication, the two types of systems) can be defined and individuated by how these roles are interrelated. Consider the classical capitalist firm, the open corporation, and the market socialist worker cooperative in this light.

The classical capitalist firm. In the classical capitalist firm, one and the same individual occupies roles 2 and 4–8. Call this individual the boss. The boss also has the right to sell any or all of the rights implicit in these other roles, although for reasons detailed later in this chapter, they will normally be sold as a package. There are two variants on the classical capitalist firm: (1) firms that have small and short hierarchies of monitors, central contracting agents, and/or directors of the firm's output, with one and the same individual at the top of all these hierarchies; and (2) firms that borrow some of their capital (especially start-up capital) from outside sources; typically, however, the boss contributes a nontrivial proportion of the capital employed by the firm.

The open corporation. A distinctive feature of the open corporation is the separation of management from ownership. In terms of the eight roles, this means that monitoring and other management functions (viz., central contracting and directing the firm's product) are not carried out by those who are simultaneously the ultimate decision makers, suppliers of capital, and residual claimants. Those who simultaneously occupy these three roles, the *equity owners*, employ management, typically by choosing a board of directors which, in turn, hires and supervises the chief executive officer and/or the management team. Although ultimate decision-making authority and residual claimancy are linked to capital provision, sometimes others supply a substantial proportion of the firm's capital, either in the form of particular capital goods or more often in the form of loans or the purchase of other debt instruments. These capital providers are entitled to a contractually guaranteed rate of return on their investment, but they have no ultimate decision-making authority and receive none of the residuals. Their claims do, however, have legal priority over the equity owners in that they get paid off first in the event of bankruptcy. Another distinctive feature of the open corporation is that ownership shares are freely alienable on a securities market. Finally, the liability of the equity owners for execution of corporate debt is limited to the amount of their capital investment.

The worker cooperative. There are worker cooperatives in free enterprise systems and elsewhere. The concern of this book, however, is with the cooperative as it would exist in the type of market socialist system described and motivated in chapter 2.[7] In that type of system, the cooperative can be defined as follows: all and only the workers are ultimate decision-making authorities. Typically, this decision-making authority will be exercised in accordance with the one person–one vote rule. In that capacity, the workers either elect management (i.e., monitors, central contracting agents, and directors of the firm's product) directly or elect those who choose the managers. Workers and managers are all residual claimants, though there is no requirement that they all have the same income. Although the workers have physical possession of, and management rights over, the capital the firm uses, the state effectively owns all the firm's capital. State ownership of capital is manifested in the following four facts: (1) firms must pay the state a capital usage fee on a regular basis, comparable to an interest premium corporations pay to bondholders and other lenders of capital; (2) firms are required to maintain the value of their capital by following proper maintenance procedures and by paying into a capital reserve fund from which monies are withdrawn to replace capital goods whose useful life has expired; (3) firms may not sell off the capital they control; and (4) the state reassigns the firm's capital if and when the firm is dissolved. For these reasons, the state can be considered the provider of capital in a market socialist system.

In a free enterprise or market socialist market economy, exchanges among people occur in virtue of their occupation of one or more of the roles given in the list of eight, plus one role not mentioned in that list, namely, the role of customer. In both types of systems, customers include not only consumers but also other firms. A comparative analysis of a free enterprise system and a market socialist system can proceed by examining the types of exchanges that people make in virtue of the roles they occupy (i.e., where they stand) in the respective systems. But how is this comparison to be carried out for the purposes of arriving at some overall assessment of exploitation in these two types of systems?

Suppose, as was suggested, that in general, people have some propensity to seize opportunities for exploitation if and when those opportunities present themselves. Suppose, further, that there are background conditions in any market system that create the potential for exploitative exchange. Finally, suppose that the structure of roles in one type of organization precludes an opportunity for exploitation that another type of organization does not preclude and, furthermore, that a plausible story can be told about how people would seize this opportunity in the latter type of organization. For example, in the classical capitalist firm, the ultimate decision maker cannot exploit the provider of capital for the simple reason that the ultimate decision maker *is* the provider of capital. In this respect, the classical capitalist firm forecloses an opportunity for exploitation that might otherwise exist. By contrast, as chapter 6 will argue, the ultimate decision makers in the worker cooperative would have the opportunity to exploit the providers of capital, and some plausible stories can be told about how that opportunity could be seized. If this is right, the argument establishes motive, opportunity, and method for exploitation in a market socialist system. By contrast, in a free enterprise system, the motive is there, but the opportunity and a method are not. In the law, at least, that is good enough for convicting one defendant and freeing another. In this way, it will be argued that a market socialist system permits and encourages a range of exploitative exchanges that are precluded or minimized in a free enterprise system.

Before getting to these arguments, however, a considerable amount of preliminary work needs to be done. The next section will consist of an exposition of some of the seminal developments in economics (specifically, transactions cost analysis) in the 1930s and 1950s that underlie the discussion of chapters 5–7. The third section is an extended illustration of these developments; it will explain the distinctive organizational efficiencies of the classical capitalist firm. Implicit in this discussion are indications of how this type of organization prevents or minimizes a range of opportunities for exploitation that would otherwise exist. The fourth and fifth sections explain why that is a good thing, by identifying the general conditions that make exploitative exchange possible in any market economy. In other words, it establishes that there is the potential for exploitation in any market economy—a potential that is dealt with in one way or another (and more or less adequately) by the system's organizational forms. Chapters 5–7 explain in detail and compare how a free enterprise system and a market socialist system deal with that potential.

The Foundations of the Economics of Organizations

Why do existing free enterprise systems have the forms of organization that they do? One of the most interesting developments in economics over the past few decades is the articulation of a research program that attempts to answer this and related questions. Sometimes called the new institutional economics or the economics of organizations, this program seeks to explain why certain organizational forms, policies, and procedures predominate in a free enterprise system. Though some of the most important developments have taken place in recent years (notably, the publication in 1985 of Oliver Williamson's *The Economic Institutions of Capitalism*), the roots of this program are to be found in the 1930s and 1950s. This section begins with a discussion of two of the most important early contributions to this program: Ronald Coase's (1937) seminal contribution to transactions cost analysis and Armen Alchian's (1950) evolutionary theory of economic organizations. Perhaps more than any others, these two theorists laid the foundations for this research program by asking the right questions and indicating the general form the answers should take.

Traditional neoclassical economic theory treats the firm as a production function that transforms inputs into outputs. As such, the firm remains a kind of black box whose internal workings are ignored by the economic theorist. In a famous article, "The Nature of the Firm," Coase (1937) challenged this view. Coase maintained that one could not adequately understand a market economy without understanding the internal structure—the institutional structure—of the firm. The central question of Coase's article has an almost philosophical ring to it: Why are there any firms at all? There is a contrast implicit in this question, a contrast between the firm and the market as alternative ways of coordinating economic activity. Coase is asking why some economic activity is organized within firms as opposed to across markets.

The significance of this question can be appreciated by recalling the discussion in chapter 2 of the inefficiencies of central planning as compared to the market. In that discussion, the flexibility and responsiveness of the market was contrasted with the informational and incentive problems facing the hierarchies of a centrally planned economy. In light of that contrast, one might wonder, "If markets are so great, why aren't all economic relations market relations?" In other words, why do people come together in economic organizations (i.e., firms) instead of being independent contractors who buy inputs and sell outputs on the open market? The obvious answer—that modern production requires large manufacturing and distribution facilities—is inadequate, since the physical requirements of production do not uniquely determine how productive resources are owned. After all, each machine used in a production process could be owned by individuals, as indeed was the case in the putting-out system used in the early part of the Industrial Revolution (Landes 1966, 12).

Coase's answer to the general question of why there are firms is not particularly surprising. As is often the case, what is most important are the questions, not the answers. The hierarchical relation characteristic of the firm is sometimes more efficient than the market as a way of coordinating productive activity. Instead of having to find, negotiate, and reach agreement with various owners of factors of production at each and every stage of the production process and to do so repeatedly over time, an owner of some factor of production simply hires other factors of production, which are then subject to his direction. This line of thinking leads naturally to the opposite question, Why are there any markets? If it is less costly to bring transactions within the firm (i.e., under one ownership umbrella) why does this not result in an expansion of the scope of the firm to the point of extinguishing the market?

What Coase's article did was raise the question of the nature and determinants of the *transaction costs* of firms versus markets. In other words, Coase posed the question of the relative efficiencies and inefficiencies of coordinating productive activity within the firm or across markets. Prior to Coase, to the extent to which the matter had been given any thought, it had been believed that technology determined the firm-market boundary, that is, the extent to which the stages of production and distribution are integrated within a firm. Coase's argument, on the other hand, implied that transaction costs play an important, if not decisive, role in determining this boundary. An important task for economics became to explain the nature and determinants of this firm-market boundary by appeal to the relative transaction costs of each way of organizing economic activity.

This covers such issues as the kinds of contractual arrangements that govern relations between firms and their customers and suppliers, the make-or-buy decision, and the determinants of vertical and horizontal integration. Another area of research suggested by this article, which is most directly relevant to the purposes of this book, had to do with the structure of firms themselves. If the firm is conceived of as a nexus of contracts among its members, transactions cost considerations should be able to explain why firms are organized the way they are. In particular, there might well be transactions cost efficiencies in the classical capitalist firm and the open corporation.

These questions did not receive the immediate attention they warranted. The continued development of neoclassical economics, which treats the firm as a production function, served to divert attention and talent away from the research agenda suggested by Coase's article. It is only in the past couple of decades, as the neoclassical paradigm has come under increasingly heavy attack, that there has been renewed interest in the institutional perspective implicit in Coase's outlook.

The second seminal article for the new economics of organizations was Armen Alchian's (1950) "Uncertainty, Evolution, and Economic Theory." Alchian's article was responsible for two important contributions. First, he called into question the assumption, standard in neoclassical theory, that firms and individuals are maximizers. He argued that human action takes place in an environment of uncertainty and that in such an environment, there is no well-defined notion of an optimum. Furthermore, even if there is an optimum, it may be inaccessible to human actors. He says, "Uncertainty arises from two sources: imperfect foresight and human inability to solve complex problems containing a host of variables even when an optimum is definable" (p. 212). These observations called into question the applicability of standard neoclassical analysis to the real world, because it assumes that economic actors always maximize. He also suggested that any adequate analysis of economic activity had to find a place for this fundamental cognitive deficiency of human actors—a deficiency, it is worth noting, that cannot be modeled by assuming that economic actors know all the relevant probabilities.

The second contribution of Alchian's article is its adumbration of an evolutionary theory of economic organization. This theory starts from the observation that there is a competitive struggle for survival among firms. There are differences among firms in their internal organization, policies, procedures, and so on. Some of these differences are conducive to the firm's survival, and some are not. Those with the more efficient organizational forms, policies, and procedures will make positive profits (the criterion for success) and survive, while those with maladaptive features will not. The selection process is weak selection, not strong selection; that is, firms do not have to optimize to succeed or survive. Indeed, they need not be very efficient at all in any absolute sense. Consistent with making positive profits, they need only approximate the efficiency of their most efficient rivals.

The parallels with Darwinian evolution are striking. Firms evolve over time to become better adapted to their economic environment. But what corresponds in this system to heredity and mutation? Alchian's answer: imitation and innovation. Successful firms keep doing what they have been doing (they "imitate" themselves), and other firms adapt by imitating their more successful rivals. He says, "What would otherwise appear to be merely customary 'orthodox,' non-rational rules of behavior turns out to be codified imitations of observed success, e.g., 'conventional' markup, price 'followship,' 'orthodox' accounting and operating ratios, 'proper' advertising policy, etc." (1950, 218). In other words, various features of economic organizations (policies, procedures, and even organizational forms themselves) can be explained by an evolutionary process in which the more efficient features persist and the less efficient are weeded out. Those who adopt conventional markup policies in retail pricing of women's clothing, for example, may do so not from some complicated price projection models but just because that is the way it is done in the business. This policy has persisted because of its survival value, whether those who use it recognize that fact or not.

Innovation may be the result of a conscious search strategy for new and better ways of doing things, but it need not be. Innovation can come from imperfect imitation, trial and error, and even sheer chance. If an innovation is conducive to survival, it will tend to persist and become widespread. If not, it will die out.

As this example illustrates, one implication of Alchian's evolutionary model is that economic actors do not have to understand the efficiency advantages of the organizational forms, policies, and procedures in which they participate. How individual participants view their situation and react to it is immaterial from an evolutionary point of view. They may or may not believe that what they are doing is conducive to the survival of the firm. Indeed, they may have no opinion on the matter; they may have some other end in view.

For example, an executive may follow some standard procedure simply because he is too timid to try anything else. Or he may innovate by misinterpreting what his by-the-book superiors have told him to do or by miscopying a rival who is about to self-destruct. And on some occasions, executives actually reason their way to a better way of doing business. The theory does not require that individuals know the efficiency advantages of what they are doing. All that matters is that those advantages exist; competition does the rest.

For the economic theorist, an important attraction of Alchian's evolutionary approach is that the story of how a type of organization, policy, or procedure came into existence is irrelevant to explaining why it persists. The environment simply selects out those organizational forms, policies, and procedures that produce positive profits; those that do not are extinguished. Absent significant change in the external environment, this results in a measure of uniformity over time, as competitors who adapt by imitating successful rivals survive and competitors who do not go under.[8] The job of the theorist is to discover and elucidate the efficiency advantages of the object of study.

An example illustrates. Gilson and Mnookin (1988) argue that the up-or-out system for associates in law firms, which is similar to tenure in universities, has efficiency advantages over alternative employment practices. The policy says that after a probationary period, the firm must promote an associate attorney to partner or fire her. If the probationary period were of indeterminate length, firms would be strongly tempted, regardless of what they might have informally promised, to keep a good attorney on at the associate level indefinitely. The reason for this is that after five or six years, a good associate has built up a great deal of firm-specific knowledge (of operating procedures, of clients, etc.) and thereby has greatly increased her productivity; yet she is costing the firm relatively little. Because much of her value to the firm is due to this firm-specific knowledge, she is not in a good position to move on to another job at her current salary, which is nevertheless significantly less than the value of her contribution. This is why it is in the firm's interest to keep her on at the associate level indefinitely. However, by publicly committing itself to the up-or-out system, the firm is effectively precommitting itself to making the partnership judgment strictly on the merits of the case. The efficiency advantage of this arrangement is that in the absence of such a system, it would have to pay all associates a premium in compensation for the risk of being strung along. (And, because this example is about lawyers, the premium would undoubtedly have to be substantial.) Other, more costly alternatives might have been tried in the past, but if so, none has survived. All major firms now use the up-or-out system.

Within the evolutionary framework provided by Alchian, identifying or explaining these advantages would count as an explanation for why most firms use this employment practice. However, this does not mean that individual firms have instituted this policy because they saw that this was the most efficient way to do it; they might have simply been imitating more prestigious firms. Interviewers for the law firm tell prospective associates, "Just like at Cravath and Swain, we here at Dewey, Cheatham, and Howe use the up-or-out system for associates." Partners and associates need not be aware of these efficiency advantages. From their point of view, this is simply the way it has always been done. Moreover, Alchian would say that this system might have come into being for any number of reasons, including sheer chance. However, it survives and persists because of its superior efficiency properties.

Perhaps the most important implication of Alchian's evolutionary perspective is that there is a (rebuttable) presumption of efficiency in the common or widespread organizational forms, policies and procedures found in existing free enterprise systems. In other words, if an organizational form, policy, or procedure is common and has persisted for some extended period of time in a free enterprise system, then there is probably some efficiency advantage to it. This invites the researcher to discover and elucidate that efficiency. However, it is vital that this rebuttable presumption of efficiency not turn into the false Panglossian assumption that if something exists, then it must be efficient. There are a number of reasons why the Panglossian assumption is false. One is that economic systems do not exist in a vacuum. Other social institutions, such as the political system and the family, have pervasive and systematic effects on economic life; there is no guarantee, (despite Gary Becker and others) that economic principles can explain these other institutions and their effects on the economic system. In addition, noninstitutional cultural forces may have a profound influence on the economic environment in ways that the science of economics cannot fathom. Finally, some habitats in the economic environment may be so volatile and unstable that the forces of natural selection are unable to perform their winnowing function. So there is no guarantee that if something exists, it is efficient.

However—and on the other hand—these confounding influences are less likely to be a factor when the phenomenon to be explained is widespread and pervasive. For example, if the classical capitalist firm is an enduring fixture of free enterprise systems across a broad historical and geographical sweep, it is likely that it has substantial efficiency advantages over alternative organizational forms. Transactions cost analysis ought to be able to explain that by appeal to the efficiencies of that organizational form; as the next section shows, it can. However, since it is not the only type of economic organization, the transactions cost analyst has to identify the circumstances and conditions under which this organizational form will thrive and explain why alternative forms cannot prosper under those conditions.

Although for both Coase and Alchian, efficiency considerations are crucial to their explanations for a wide range of phenomena, those considerations enter into their explanations in fundamentally different ways. For Coase, there is the presumption that individuals are acting on the belief that the firm (or the hierarchical relations that characterize it) is more efficient than the market (or vice versa) as a way to handle some type or range of transactions and that this is why this way of organizing transactions is used.

By contrast, for Alchian, efficiency considerations functionally explain, via a natural selection argument, why organizations have the attributes they do, whether participants are acting on a recognition of those efficiency advantages or not. The environment has simply selected out those features which are conducive to survival. Such explanations are not genetic (i.e., they do not explain how that type of phenomenon came into existence in the first place), but they do explain why, once on the scene, that type of phenomenon persists. The next section provides just such an explanation of the classical capitalist firm.

An Illustration: The Classical Capitalist Firm

In an important article, Alchian and Harold Demsetz (1972) offered this sort of explanation for most of the distinctive features of the classical capitalist firm. This section will elucidate this explanation and supplement it with Yoram Barzel's (1987) account of the other defining features of this type of firm. What emerges in the end is an explanation of the concentration of roles 2 and 4 through 8 (see p. 98) in one individual, the boss.

According to Alchian and Demsetz, what is distinctive about the classical capitalist firm is that it is team production with a centralized contracting agent who is the residual claimant.[9] What explains this structure? Their explanation starts from the observation that "the economic organization through which input owners cooperate will make better use of their comparative advantages to the extent that it facilitates the payment of rewards in accord with productivity" (1972, 778). The idea is that if rewards were negatively correlated with productive contribution or if there were no correlation between reward and productive contribution, the organization would not survive in competition with others that positively correlated reward to productivity. So whatever organization exists, it must achieve a positive correlation between reward and productive contribution.

However, achieving this correlation is often no easy matter, especially in the case of team production where individual output is hard (i.e., costly) to meter. Team production involves several types of inputs whose product is not the sum of separable outputs of each cooperating resource (1972, 779). This mode of production can greatly increase total productivity, but at the cost of making individual contribution hard to ascertain. The reason that this is a problem—a cost—is that it creates an incentive for individual team members to shirk, that is, to reduce their input.

This can be modeled as a prisoner's dilemma or public goods problem. Each individual might prefer that no one shirks but because shirking is hard to detect, anyone who shirks gets all of the benefits but suffers only a fraction of the costs in the form of reduced output. Everyone reasons like this, and as a result, everyone chooses to shirk. Output falls and all are worse off, even according to their own schedule of preferences for income and leisure—that is, each member of the team would prefer less shirking and more output—and hence more income—than they actually end up with.

Before investigating how this problem is solved, it is worth pointing out that 'shirking,' the term Alchian and Demsetz use, has misleading connotations. It suggests that the input in question is limited to labor contribution and that shirking consists in avoiding labor by putting forth less than average—or less than expected—physical or mental effort. Both connotations are too narrow, however. A broader term is needed to encompass the range of behaviors that Alchian and Demsetz have in mind. Following Oliver Williamson the term 'opportunism' can be used to designate the broader range of behaviors of which shirking is a special case (1985, chaps. 1, 2). The inputs that can be reduced by opportunism are not limited to labor. Regular suppliers of any input may act opportunistically.[10] Providers of raw materials and semifinished products may shortweight deliveries, provide goods of substandard quality, or adopt policies that encourage or permit these things to happen. Even as it applies to laborers, the connotations of the term 'shirking' are too narrow. Workers may act opportunistically not only by hiding out in the restroom and taking longer breaks but also by such things as beating up on equipment to make the job go easier, working carelessly, pursuing office politics instead of doing the job, and in general, engaging in activities unrelated or only marginally related to the task at hand. Typically, opportunistic workers are not those who have nothing better to do with their time than to loaf on the job. Instead, they are those who have other plans, projects, or interests that they want to pursue—and they want to pursue them on company time. As a general proposition, the incentive to act opportunistically in the provision of labor services comes from the fact that in most jobs, when a decision has to be made, people can usually think of something better to do with their time—from the point of view of their own values and interests—than what they are being paid to do. This is true even if from a larger perspective, they prefer being gainfully employed to being unemployed.

The obvious solution to the general problem of opportunism among input providers is for one of the team members to specialize as a monitor of other input providers. What is monitoring? Perhaps what comes most readily to mind is metering outputs and administering discipline. Once again, however, there is much more to monitoring than the term might suggest. Alchian and Demsetz say, "We use the term 'monitor' to connote several activities in addition to its disciplinary connotation. It connotes measuring output performance, apportioning rewards, observing the input behavior of inputs as means of detecting or estimating their marginal productivity and giving assignments or instructions in what to do and how to do it" (1972, 782).

By hypothesis, metering (i.e., measuring) individual output is difficult in team production—though if one person specializes in monitoring, it should be somewhat easier than if each team member tries to meter the output of all the others. However, since metering individual output is difficult, what often happens is that the monitor makes his estimates based on some more easily observable substitute—usually his own or someone else's direct observation of individual input. For example, the monitor might make unannounced inspection trips to the work station or solicit the opinion of other team members who work in the immediate area as a way of evaluating the input of any given worker. These proxies will almost always be imperfect measures of productive contribution, but they will be superior to the feasible alternatives.

The obvious question this story invites is Juvenal's '*Quis custodiet ipsos custodes?*'—or, Who monitors the monitor? Monitoring is itself difficult to monitor, so does the problem not recur at the next level? Alchian and Demsetz maintain that this problem can be solved most efficiently by making the monitor the residual claimant; he gets what is left over after all other input owners have been paid. By closing the gap between principal and agent, this system gives the monitor a strong incentive to pay other inputs as close to their marginal value as possible. If he pays them less than their marginal value, other monitors will have an incentive to hire these input owners away for more than he is paying them. If he pays them more than their marginal value, then he ends up with less for himself. (It is not hard to guess which side is the "caution side" on which monitors seek to err.)

Observing and metering inputs is not the only way for the monitor to prevent shirking and other forms of opportunism. The quotation from Alchian and Demsetz suggests that the monitor might also redesign the production process (which presupposes that he has the power to do so) to make individual contributions more easily metered or else less in need of metering because they are more intrinsically interesting. And he must have the power to discipline input providers, including the power to terminate the contracts of those who cannot resist the temptation to act opportunistically or who cannot perform at a market-determined level of proficiency. This means that the monitor must be the central contracting agent with all the other input providers. Finally, so that the monitor pays due regard to the medium- and long-term wealth consequences of his monitoring (and other) actions, he has to be able to sell his monitoring rights and his rights of residual claimancy.

It is in the interests of all team members that this arrangement exist. In the absence of a monitor, the incentive to act opportunistically will be significant. The reason for this is that the extent of a person's opportunism is generally not widely known among all other input providers.[11] Because of this fact, in the absence of a monitor, it is not possible to reach agreement on an acceptable level of opportunism. It is easy to understand how a self-reinforcing process of increased opportunism could get underway, resulting in the dissipation of the benefits of team production. All team members will be worse off as a result—worse off than they would have been if they had been on a team whose members feel the occasional lash of the monitor.

This story is intended to explain a number of features of the classical capitalist firm:

1. why there is a single monitor
2. why that monitor has residual claimant status

3. why the monitor can determine (within a broad "zone of acceptance") how inputs are to be used or combined[12]
4. why the monitor is the central contracting agent (and ultimate decision-making authority) with all the other input providers, which entails that he can renegotiate the terms of the contract with each team member, up to and including firing any team member.[13]

There are two other defining features of the classical capitalist firm that this story does not explain: (1) why the monitor-residual claimant is the firm's entrepreneur and (2) why he is also the primary provider of capital.

Yoram Barzel (1987) has endeavored to explain both of these features of the classical capitalist firm. The basic explanation is the same as that advanced by Alchian and Demsetz: high monitoring costs make it most efficient for the residual claimant to be the entrepreneur and the primary provider of capital goods. What the entrepreneur does is set the terms and conditions for the interactions between the firm and the market. On the demand-side interface between the firm and the market, he decides what is to be produced and in what quantity and at what price the product is to be sold. On the supply-side interface, the entrepreneur in his role as central contracting agent makes deals with laborers, suppliers of raw materials and semifinished products, providers of credit, and so forth. In all of these activities, performance is very difficult to monitor. Part of the problem is that success in any of these endeavors can be profoundly influenced by luck, and it is very difficult to separate out what is due to luck and what is due to skillful productive effort. By assigning the entrepreneur's tasks to the residual claimant, the entrepreneur must bear the total wealth consequences of his decisions. This gives him an incentive to exercise good judgment—an incentive that would be weaker if he lacked residual claimant status and his compensation depended on the judgment of a monitor.

Barzel offers a similar explanation for why the entrepreneur-residual claimant is also the primary provider of capital. The explanation focuses on entrepreneurial decisions about which venture(s) to pursue. It is very difficult to monitor the investigation and assessment of possible ventures. This means that the risks of any venture are not independent of the entrepreneur's actions. If he is diligent in investigating and assessing opportunities for the firm, the risks go down; if he is not, they go up.

If the entrepreneur is operating entirely with the capital of others, then he has an incentive to pursue much higher-risk, higher-payoff ventures than he otherwise would. These risks are further enhanced if he is the sole residual claimant and the other providers of capital have the status of bondholders. In contrast, by putting up a substantial portion of the capital himself, he is, in effect, providing a bond that he will act diligently in investigating and assessing possible ventures, as well as in his monitoring tasks and in his other dealings across the firm-market interface. This bonding arrangement has the same consequences as good monitoring (Barzel 1987, 112–13).

This concludes a series of hypothetical rational choice explanations for the salient features of the classical capitalist firm. Seven comments on this series, in no particular order, are warranted:

• There are differences among classical capitalist firms; the series only explains what they have in common. In particular, it explains why all of the functionally defined economic roles except those of (labor and nonlabor) input providers are concentrated in one individual.

• These explanations are not genetic explanations; that is, they are not explanations of how the classical capitalist firm came into being. It is not necessary to suppose that someone or some group reasoned all of this out in the misty predawn of capitalism and decided to set up firms in this way. The true story of the genesis of this type of organization is undoubtedly messier and unpleasant in a number of respects. Nevertheless, how the classical capitalist firm came into being is simply not addressed in this account.

• These explanations are evolutionary in the sense that they explain why organizations that have this form would survive in competition with alternatives that lack this form in one or more respects. For example, suppose there is an environment in which there are two types of firms: those for which the entrepreneur-residual claimant does not provide most of the capital and those for which he does. The account explains why the latter type would tend to survive and prosper and the former would not. The actual competition may well not have been piecemeal in this way, however. Moreover, Alchian and Demsetz make no effort to document an historical struggle for survival among different organizational forms with the classical capitalist firm coming out on top, although, in point of fact, some sort of struggle must have taken place, since the classical capitalist firm has not been around from the beginning of civilization. Nevertheless, they have made no effort to dig up the organizational equivalent of the skeletons of the short-necked giraffes who did not thrive or prosper. Of course, the historical record does tell us something about how production was organized in the precapitalist era, but the Alchian–Demsetz–Barzel account does not rule out a role for extraeconomic (e.g., political) factors in the explanation of the rise of the classical capitalist firm. Indeed this account does not rule out a role for extraeconomic factors in explaining the persistence of the classical capitalist firm if the phenomenon is overdetermined. In other words, the efficiency considerations identified by Alchian, Demsetz, and Barzel may be sufficient to explain the persistence of the classical capitalist firm, but extraeconomic factors may enhance its stability.

• As the previous example suggests, these explanations are explicitly or implicitly comparative in that they suggest that alternative modes of organization (in this case, alternative ways of dealing with shirking and other forms of opportunism) are inferior from the standpoint of transactions cost efficiencies. For them to be fully convincing, the alternatives would have to be more explicitly and systematically articulated and compared.[14]

• All of these explanations contain implicit ceteris paribus clauses. And often, all else is not equal. Perhaps most important is the fact that capital requirements are sometimes too high for one individual to supply most of the firm's capital. In other words, the transaction costs of coordinating some activities across markets are sufficiently high to make it more efficient to bring under one roof more capital than any one person can supply. As will be explained in the third section of chapter 5, under such circumstances, it is more efficient to effect a partial separation of the roles of monitor, entrepreneur, provider of capital, and residual claimant—a separation of the sort that one finds in the open corporation. There are also special circumstances under which closed corporations, partnerships, and cooperatives minimize transaction costs and so are superior, from the standpoint of transactions cost efficiencies, to the classical capitalist firm. All of these exceptions and complications are covered by ceteris paribus clauses implicit in these explanations. These clauses will be systematically uncovered in the next chapter.

• Implicit in the various explanations of how opportunism is minimized in the classical capitalist firm are hints about how such a firm prevents or minimizes exploitative exchange. For example, since the entrepreneur provides most of the capital himself, he cannot exploit the primary providers of capital by pursuing an unconscionably high risk venture that will make him big profits if it succeeds and dissipate someone else's capital if it fails. To take another example, by reducing shirking, the monitor keeps the owner of the firm (viz., himself) from being exploited by lazy workers.

• Implicit in these explanations are the general features of the economic environment that create the potential for exploitative exchange. Specifically, the gains from team production, the penchant most people have for opportunistic behavior, and the informational asymmetries that allow people to practice the opportunistic arts are general phenomena that are ubiquitous in a modern market economy. The next two sections will systematically identify and discuss these general phenomena or background conditions that make exploitation possible in any market economy, and indeed perhaps in any economic system whatsoever.

The Empirical Preconditions for Exploitation

In his treatise on the current state of the new economics of organizations, or transactions cost analysis, Oliver Williamson identifies two behavioral assumptions on which this research program rests and three dimensions along which transactions can vary: the two behavioral assumptions are bounded rationality and opportunism; the three dimensions are uncertainty, frequency, and asset specificity. Transactions cost analysis seeks to explain the properties of transactions by appeal to these *features of transactions* and the *associated behavioral assumptions* which, not coincidentally, constitute the subjective and objective basis, respectively, for the possibility of, or opportunity for, exploitative exchange. Specifically, *bounded rationality* and *opportunism* explain why people are at risk for being on the short end and the long end of the stick, respectively, in an exploitative exchange. And given those behavioral postulates, transactions are more or less likely to be exploitative, depending on where they are located along the three dimensions of uncertainty, frequency, and asset specificity. The purpose of this section is to explicate each of these five factors and then to explain more explicitly how they create the potential for exploitative exchange—a potential that any market system must deal with in some way or other.

Bounded rationality. Standard neoclassical economics maintains that economic actors always maximize. This facilitates a formal treatment of a wide range of phenomena, but it is unrealistic as a description of existing human beings. (Whether or not that is a problem for neoclassical analysis is a controversial issue that will not be taken up here.) By contrast, Herbert Simon's notion of bounded rationality comes closer to a description of what human beings are really like: it assumes that human beings are "*intendedly* rational but only *limitedly* so" (1961, xxiv). In other words, it assumes that people intend to act in their own best interests but that they do not always do so because of a number of human limitations. These limitations include limited computational ability and a variety of defects in judgment and reasoning.[15] These limitations also make it reasonable to treat the human mind as a scarce resource. As Williamson says, "If the mind is a scarce resource, then economizing on claims against it is plainly warranted. Respect for limited rationality elicits deeper study of both market and non-market organization" (Williamson 1985, 46; cf. Simon 1978, 12).

What makes the assumption of bounded rationality (as well as the assumption of opportunism to be discussed shortly) so attractive is not simply its greater realism. It also suggests that human organizations and the rules or contracts by which they are defined can be understood as instrumentalities that are more or less useful for coping with these limitations of the human condition. This perspective on organizations is fundamental to transactions cost analysis and constitutes one of its great strengths. It invites the analyst to ask evaluative questions of a comparative nature, that is, how one type of organization compares to another as an instrumentality for dealing with a range of problems that would not exist but for various human limitations. This contrasts with the approach suggested by neoclassical economics, which holds up unrealizable ideals against which reality is to be measured.[16]

Opportunism. The other behavioral postulate of transactions cost analysis is opportunism. Specifically, the assumption is that most people are sometimes given to opportunistic behavior. What is opportunistic behavior? Williamson's definition—self-interest seeking with guile (1985, 47)—is suggestive but not very clear. To get a more helpful definition, consider the range of phenomena to which this term refers. Opportunism does not merely—or even primarily—consist in, lying, stealing, cheating, and bribing (though those are instances of the phenomenon par excellence). Opportunism also includes cutting corners, shading effort and quality, giving oneself the benefit of the doubt, creating a doubt where none existed and then giving oneself the benefit of it, shirking in all its manifestations, colluding in the shirking of friends and coworkers, hijacking an organization (i.e., redirecting it to serve one's private goals), expending organizational resources for the purposes of hijacking it,[17] pirating (i.e., exacting private benefits in exchange for facilitating, or even not interfering in, internal and external transactions involving the organization), and taking home office supplies.

As the term suggests, opportunism consists in the seizing of an opportunity. Specifically, it consists in seizing an opportunity for advancement (primarily for oneself but sometimes for others on whose behalf one acts as agent) at the expense of others not provided for in some contractual relation. This is what all of the listed behaviors have in common. Contracts (exchanges) are made against a background of legitimate expectations about how people will behave. The legitimacy of these expectations is partly normative and partly descriptive. In other words, the expectations derive, in part, from widely shared beliefs about how people ought to behave and in part from beliefs about how people do, in fact, behave. Consequently, opportunistic behavior includes not only violations of implicit and explicit provisions of the contract but also the violation of any legitimate expectation surrounding the transaction.

Two factors that complicate the problem of dealing with opportunistic behavior are that the penchant for it varies from one person to another and that it is not "stamped on their foreheads"; that is, not only do people differ in their penchant for opportunism, but those differences are, for the most part, not public information. This is why the threat of shirking—or opportunistic behavior generally—cannot be handled by a simple adjustment in the terms of the contract. In other words, a boss cannot say to a worker, "Your job is worth $x an hour but since I know you will shirk a certain amount, I will only pay you $x - n an hour." If people knew how much others would shirk, the problem of dealing with it would be easier.

As indicated, the assumption that drives transactions cost analysis is that most people are sometimes given to opportunistic behavior. It would be implausible to assume that everyone is always on the lookout for a chance to act opportunistically, nor will everyone push to extract the maximum benefit from whatever chances are presented. This suggests that opportunistic behavior can vary along two dimensions: frequency and utilization. Clearly, some people are more inclined to seize opportunities than are others. And, people differ in the extent to which they will utilize, or take advantage of, the opportunities with which they are presented. Though perhaps most people will take small advantage of a large opportunity (the temptation being so great), some people will take maximum advantage of every opportunity, even the smallest. These are the quintessential parasites of human society.

There is, of course, a general moral prohibition against opportunistic behavior. How frequently people act opportunistically is a function of (1) their penchant for opportunism, (2) the power that moral prohibition has over them, (3) their capacity for clear-headed thinking about what they are doing, and (4) the opportunities to violate this prohibition that transactions present. The first two of these factors are self-evident, but the latter two require comment.

Presented with a chance to act opportunistically, people often interpret the situation so that it does not appear that way. This is illustrated in a common saying among the workers in what used to be Yugoslavia, "They pretend to pay us, so we pretend to work." In this way, people can rationalize opportunistic behavior as nonopportunistic. The more given someone is to such rationalizations, the more she will act opportunistically. Of course, sometimes shirking is not opportunistic. It is often the only way workers have to prevent bosses from acting opportunistically toward them. This might be one of those rare cases in which two wrongs do make a right.

On the other point, transactions can be more or less vulnerable to opportunistic behavior. The employment contracts and associated governance structures characteristic of universities and government bureaucracies generally do a very poor job of monitoring workers. Part of the problem is that individual contributions (output) are inherently difficult to identify, but the problem is often compounded by institutional failure even to monitor inputs (e.g., professors "working at home"). These organizations are, therefore, highly vulnerable to various forms of worker opportunism (and would probably be wiped out in a competitive struggle for survival if efficiency were the criterion for survival). The more vulnerable an organization is to this behavior, the more it will occur, all else equal.

This is not a simple consequence of people's general penchant for opportunism. For one thing, organizations known to be vulnerable to some form of opportunism tend to attract the type of people who are given to that form of opportunism. (This phenomenon is called *adverse selection* and will be discussed in more detail shortly.) Second, there is something insidious about opportunistic behavior in that those who engage in it tend to prosper at the expense, in some way or other, of those who do not. When some form of opportunistic behavior reaches a certain threshold level, those who abstain begin to feel like "chumps" for their abstention. As a result, they begin to act opportunistically or to do so more frequently than before; in short, their penchant for opportunism changes. In this way, a self-reinforcing process gets under way that either destroys the organization or reaches a new equilibrium level—that is, a new low—of shirking and pay. For these two reasons, social organizations can be said to encourage opportunism to the extent that they do not embody structures and procedures to preclude or minimize it.

For example, the centrally planned economies of the former Soviet Union and communist China are so profoundly inefficient that it is extremely difficult to survive by living according to the rules. Not coincidentally, most people do not; over the years, the distribution system in particular has become hopelessly corrupted. It has reached the point where it is only by participating in the corruption that someone can move beyond bare survival. For this reason, these economic systems can be said to encourage corruption. It is in this way that opportunism is transformed from a human problem into a social problem.

People's propensity for opportunistic behavior would be less of a problem if all contracts were unambiguous, completely determinate, and costlessly enforceable. Not only does none of these conditions hold, but each varies considerably from transaction to transaction. Much of transactions cost analysis consists of understanding how parties to various types of transactions deal with these sources of friction and the associated potential for exploitation. For example, since legal enforcement of contract provisions is often very costly, a contract might contain a clause mandating binding arbitration by a specified arbiter for some range of disputes. Or one party might require some sort of bonding arrangement from the other party to ensure compliance with contract provisions.

What makes opportunistic behavior possible is almost always some informational asymmetry between contracting parties—an asymmetry that one party deliberately creates or at least maintains. As Williamson says, "Opportunism refers to the incomplete or distorted disclosure of information, especially to calculated efforts to mislead, distort, disguise, obfuscate or otherwise confuse. It is responsible for real or contrived conditions of information asymmetry, which vastly complicate problems of economic organization" (1985, 47–48). Although Williamson maintains that the informational asymmetry is a form of opportunism, it is also very often a necessary condition for other forms of opportunistic behavior. In other words, the creation or maintenance of informational asymmetries makes opportunistic behavior possible. For example, the fact that one worker has a fairly good idea of what he is contributing to team production and others do not makes it possible for him to shirk. Here opportunism takes the form of shirking.

Two forms of informational asymmetries in particular have been systematically investigated in transactions cost analysis: adverse selection and moral hazard. These concepts originally come from the insurance industry, but they have since been found to have much broader application. Adverse selection occurs when selection procedures systematically encourage people with undesirable characteristics to participate in a certain type of exchange without revealing that they have those undesirable characteristics. For example, suppose a retail firm hires security personnel based solely on an interview in which they are asked how they would deter and detect shoplifting. This firm might well fall victim to adverse selection because those who do best at this interview would probably include a disproportionate number of shoplifters. The general problem is that there are ex ante informational asymmetries that one party does nothing to dispel and that also work against the interests of the other party. Sometimes these problems can only be eliminated by procedures that are too costly to implement, but often they can be economically ameliorated. Efficient transactions are crafted to achieve just this result.

While adverse selection is an ex ante phenomenon, moral hazard is ex post. After a contract has been made, certain of its features can encourage— or not sufficiently discourage—violations of some of the terms of the contract or, at least, violations of legitimate expectations induced by the contract. This is a morally hazardous situation. In the insurance industry, for example, this problem arises when deductibles are too low or nonexistent so that the insured person is not sufficiently encouraged to exercise due care and caution. In the employment situation, the classic moral hazard problem is the incentive to shirk in unmonitored or loosely monitored team production. This, too, is a result of informational asymmetries. Other members of the team do not know what the shirker's output is, allowing the latter to take advantage of that fact and thereby violate legitimate expectations about performance. Perfect monitoring is usually impossible, so the only recourse is to find economical means to discourage the shirking. This, of course, is a large part of the rationale for the classical capitalist firm (more on this in chapter 5).

Inevitable informational asymmetries are responsible for the conditions of adverse selection and moral hazard. These problems are particularly important in principal-agent relationships, such as employer-employee, stockholder-manager, collective-individual worker. Much of transactions cost analysis seeks to understand how organizations and individuals craft transactions (e.g., the employment contract and even the job description) so as to avoid or mitigate these problems. We shall return to these issues later. Consider now the three key dimensions along which transactions vary.

Asset specificities. One of the most important features of transactions that transactions cost analysis considers is the specificity of the assets that support transactions. Physical and human assets have, or come to have, valuable but highly specific characteristics—characteristics that are most useful only in the context of a given contractual arrangement. Such assets are not easily redeployed once they have been committed.

There are three main types of asset specificities: (1) site specificities, (2) physical asset specificities, and (3) human asset specificities (Williamson 1985, 55). Site specificities would be illustrated by the example of an electric generating plant built at the mouth of an already existing coal mine so as to reduce transportation costs for coal (Joskow and Schmalensee 1983). The assets represented by this plant have the value they do only because of their proximity to the coal mine. If coal had to be brought in by rail from another source, the value of the plant would fall accordingly. Physical asset specificity would be illustrated by the fact that the chemical composition of bauxite varies from one source to another and that idiosyncratic technologies are required for chemical processing, materials handling, and waste disposal in connection with aluminum smelting (Stuckey 1983). Wholly dedicated assets represent the most extreme form of physical asset specificity. A supplier fabricates a specialized piece of equipment to manufacture a product that only one customer can use. This piece of equipment has the highest possible degree of physical asset specificity. Human asset specificity means that employees build up firm-specific knowledge and skills that have little value elsewhere. For example, the parts manager in an auto dealership knows where every part in the warehouse is. That knowledge is extremely valuable but only in that particular dealership.

Uncertainty. 'Uncertainty' in this context refers to the fact that many of the contingencies that arise in the course of a transaction or contractual relation (especially a long-term one) cannot be foreseen and negotiated beforehand;

often, even their probabilities cannot be known. For this reason and because of the inherent indeterminacy and ambiguity of language, complete contracts cannot be written to govern every contingency. Unanticipated disruptions in supply, transport, and so on can profoundly and adversely affect one of the parties to the exchange. Uncertainty is a serious problem in conjunction with asset specificities, bounded rationality, and opportunism. When highly specific assets have been committed and the other party to an exchange is given to opportunism, what are claimed to be disruptions beyond that party's control can, in fact, be disruptions induced by opportunism or strategic behavior. Because of informational asymmetries, there is often no cost-effective way to know whether this is the problem or whether the problem is due to some genuinely exogenous disturbance. Transactions have to be crafted so as to minimize these problems; otherwise mutually beneficial exchanges will be forgone or a premium will have to be paid to the party at risk.

Frequency. The frequency with which transactions take place is an important variable in determining the nature of the transaction, especially in conjunction with asset specificities. Frequent transactions involving nonspecific assets need only simple governance structures. For example, frequent purchases of wheat on the grain market require only ordinary contracts enforceable under contract law. On the other hand, infrequent transactions involving highly specialized assets require more complex governance structures. For example, the human capital that university professors bring to their jobs is highly specialized, and the market in this form of capital is fairly thin. At most universities, the terms and conditions of hiring and retention are governed by an expensive structure of formidable complexity. Generally speaking, frequent transactions serve as an effective counterweight to bounded rationality and opportunism. One's cognitive limitations and the potential rapacity of one's green grocer are not serious handicaps to transactions in retail produce. Both are much more serious problems and require correspondingly complex governance structures when the transaction is the purchase of a mainframe computer or the labor of a university professor.

Opportunism, Appropriable Quasi-Rents, and Exploitative Exchange

The next task is to consider how these attributes of transactions, together with the conditions of bounded rationality and opportunism, create the conditions for exploitative exchange. To begin, note that transactors tend to develop long-term relationships with each other. It is not only the firm's employees who get involved in long-term economic relationships with firms; firms develop comparable relations with each other. Long-term contracts are signed, short-term contracts are repeatedly renewed, and orders for goods and services become standing orders. What starts out as a large-numbers bidding situation is very often effectively transformed into something approaching a bilateral monopoly. This is what Williamson calls the fundamental transformation (1985, 61–62).

The fundamental transformation is a ubiquitous phenomenon; the main reason it occurs is that it permits transactions cost economies. One of the most important of these involves the development of valuable but relatively transaction-specific assets (both physical and human) that accompany a long-term commercial relationship. A supplier becomes intimately familiar with the needs of his customer. The supplier builds equipment or facilities to service a particular customer, and these investments cannot be easily redeployed. The purchaser finds he cannot easily purchase a particular input, tailored to his specifications, from another source of supply. Search costs would be quite high, alternative sources of supply would have to be developed from scratch, and production and sales would be disrupted. As contracts are periodically renewed, learning-by-doing economies are realized, and personal relationships among both principals and subordinates develop. These personal relations permit effective communication and foster trust. Once this fundamental transformation is under way, other bidders are effectively shut out. For these very good reasons, each side prefers to deal with its longstanding trading partner rather than go out into the marketplace.

When assets are nonspecific and transactions are frequent, the fundamental transformation does not occur, even if the parties repeatedly deal with one another. Wheat is a relatively nonspecific commodity (both physically and locationally) and is frequently purchased by its customers. If a particular grain supplier sells frequently to a particular miller, it is because each party effectively competes on a regular basis with alternative purchasers and suppliers. However, most transactions are not like these wheat transactions. Most are supported in some way by relatively specific assets. Some of the value of these specific assets constitutes what have come to be called *quasi-rents*. In an important article on vertical integration written in the late 1970s, Klein, Crawford, and Alchian explain this concept and the related concept of appropriable quasi-rents as follows: "Assume an asset is owned by one individual and rented to another individual. The quasi-rent value of the asset is the excess of its value over its salvage value, that is, its value in its next best *use* to another renter. The potentially appropriable specialized portion of the quasi-rent is that portion, if any, in excess of its value to the second highest-valuing *user*" (1978, 298).

To illustrate, suppose that the amortized fixed cost of a roller-skating rink is $500 a day and that a particular rink operator is willing to pay that much to lease it from its owner. Suppose, further, that the next most valuable use for this building is as a warehouse and that there are a number of warehouse operators would pay $100 a day (but no more) for it. This represents the salvage value of the asset. The difference between the revenue that the asset actually generates and the asset's salvage value is the quasi-rent (in this case, $400).

If this rink operator is the only rink operator in town, the entire quasi-rent is vulnerable to appropriation by the leaseholder. To see how, suppose that the rink was built by the owner with the intention of leasing it to this particular rink operator. The latter signs a three-year lease and agrees to renew it on those terms as long as the business is profitable. Renewal time comes along, and the operator reports that business is not good. Costs are much higher than expected, so he can only keep the business going if the rent is reduced to $120 a day. There are no other rink operators interested in leasing the facility. The building owner has no real alternative but to agree. Virtually the entire quasi-rent has now been appropriated.

It might be thought that value of the asset has been reduced (and along with it, the quasi-rent) because conditions in the roller-skating industry have changed for the worse and that therefore there has not been a massive appropriation of a quasi-rent. But the reader, like the owner of the building, does not know all of the details. The rink operator has recently fired his entire workforce and hired his family to replace them. He hired his wife as the bookkeeper for an annual salary of $38,700, although the going rate for bookkeepers is about $20,000. He has hired his five children to work in the concession stand, skate rental shop, and so on for $30,000 each per year, although the going rate for that labor is about half that. He hired his mother to play the organ for $75,000 a year; organists, suppose, make about $45,000. All this information is private and/or too costly for the owner of the building to obtain. All he sees is an audited financial statement, which supports the operator's claims. This asset (the building) still has quasi-rents associated with it; they have simply been appropriated by the operator's family—or the operator himself, to the extent that he gets kickbacks from his family members.

This opportunistic appropriation of quasi-rents is a instance of economic exploitation. To see why, recall that an exploitative exchange is one in which a person does not get the value of what he gives up in an exchange and is in a position in which he has no real alternative but to make that exchange. The exchange on terms of $120 a day meets both of these conditions par excellence. By hypothesis, the value of the asset is $500, of which the owner gets only $120. So he is getting significantly less than the value of what he is selling (namely, rink services for a day). Furthermore, he has no real alternative but to accept the exchange the operator offers. The actual alternatives are either to let the building stand unoccupied or to rent it as a warehouse. The former is significantly worse than renting it to the operator on the terms he offers, and the latter earns about the same return as he would get from renting it to the operator. Therefore, the owner has been exploited by the operator.

Suppose now that the story is changed a little. Assume that there is another rink operator in town who would be willing to pay $300 a day to rent the building. The quasi-rent remains at $400 a day, since the value in the next best use (which is still as a warehouse) remains at $100 a day. However, now only $200 of that quasi-rent is appropriable; if the renewal offer fell below $300 a day, the owner of the building would simply rent it to the other operator. The rest of the quasi-rent is effectively protected by the existence of the potential competitor.

It might be thought that in either case, no owner would be so stupid as to make such a deal initially. Because of the specialized value of the asset, he would insist on a much longer lease, or else he would require a penalty for nonrenewal before a certain time or the like. Suppose, then, that he has a thirty-year lease with the original operator. He could still have his quasi-rents appropriated by the lessee. The operator could simply state that the contract must be renegotiated because business has fallen off; unless the terms are altered, he will be forced out of business and thereby default on the lease.[18]

In principle, there are many possible solutions to the moral hazard problem that this case poses. The operator might be required to pay for the features of the structure that make it suitable for a roller-skating rink (but then the quasi-rents associated with this investment may be subject to appropriation by the owner of the building). Or the operator might be required to post a bond that could be used to hire more auditors and consultants to keep tabs on the operation—though that would probably be prohibitively expensive in an operation of this size. Another possibility is that the building owner might choose to operate the rink himself, or the rink operator might choose to own the building; this is the vertical integration solution.

Let us return for a moment to the original story. Suppose the building owner has his quasi-rents appropriated. He gets out of the business (too many sharks in the roller-skating industry for him), and the bank is left with the property. They then sell it—to the operator! At this particular roller-skating rink, then, there has been vertical integration. Imagine now that there are many different types of relationships between rink operators and building owners across the land. Suppose, however, that all relationships other than vertical integration are subject to such serious moral hazards that only the vertically integrated operations thrive. As time goes on, there are fewer and fewer of any other type of operation. People who are interested in getting into the business do some research and find that operators who own their own buildings tend to do much better than those who do not, so they figure that must be the best way to do it. They need not understand why that is so, but they imitate successful operations by owning the building themselves. In a few years or a few decades, all rinks are operator-owned.

This story has all the elements of a free enterprise thriller: appropriable quasi-rents, opportunism, exploitation, the extinction of a pattern of asset ownership, and the ascendancy of a better adapted pattern. With the passage of time, the quasi-rents of the relevant assets are protected and thus no longer appropriable, and justice reigns.

It is now possible to give a general statement of what makes exploitative exchanges possible in any market economy. Essentially, it is the following four facts:

1. The assets that support many exchanges are relatively specialized and thus have quasi-rents associated with them.
2. These assets get locked into a specific transaction or series of transac-

tions in the sense that they are costly to redeploy once they are committed. (This is the fundamental transformation.)

3. Owners of specialized assets suffer from bounded rationality, and they make transactions in an environment in which not all future contingencies can be foreseen.

4. Trading partners are sometimes given to opportunism—specifically the appropriation of quasi-rents, if and when quasi-rents are appropriable. The extent to which people are given to opportunism varies from person to person and is generally not knowable beforehand.

If any of these conditions (quasi-rents from relatively specific assets, the fundamental transformation, bounded rationality and uncertainty, and opportunism) were absent, it is unlikely that exploitation would occur. Consider each in that light, in reverse order.

First, if people had no penchant for opportunism, a "general clause" contract would suffice to prevent exploitation. This is a contract containing a clause to the effect that all parties will disclose all materially relevant information and act in a cooperative manner (Williamson 1985, 66). These clauses mean little in a world where people are given to opportunism and the extent to which they are so given is unknown—in other words, a world in which there are both lawyers and the need for lawyers.

Second, if rationality were unlimited and all future contingencies and their probabilities were foreseeable, all bridges could be crossed in advance in the contract. In other words, the contract would detail every contingency and specify how each party is to act in the face of that contingency. The terms of the exchange would reflect knowledge of the probabilities that these contingencies would eventuate.

Third, if transactions supported by relatively specific assets were frequently entered into with a variety of different parties, there would be "real alternatives" for the owners of these assets in the event that trading partners tried to appropriate their quasi-rents. In other words, if the assets were specialized but there were a number of other potential users to whom it was just as valuable, the quasi-rents would not be appropriable.

Finally, if the assets involved were so nonspecific that they had another use that was just as valuable as their customary use, there would be no quasi-rents to appropriate. On either of the latter two scenarios, the assets are easily redeployable, either to other uses or other users; they are what Williamson calls "assets on wheels," and their owners cannot be exploited.

These four facts make exploitative exchange possible in any market economy. One dimension along which types of market economies vary is how well their characteristic organizational forms deal with this potential for exploitation. The purpose of the next three chapters is to compare a free enterprise and market socialist system on precisely this point.

5

Transactions Cost Efficiencies
of Capitalist Organizations

Some Methodological Considerations

Transactions cost analysis attempts to account for or explain a wide variety of phenomena found in contemporary free enterprise systems by understanding these phenomena as efficient responses to the objective and subjective conditions for exploitation identified in the last chapter. Theorists proceed on the supposition—informed by Alchian's general evolutionary hypothesis—that the common or widespread organizational forms, policies, and procedures found in free enterprise systems are efficient responses to asset specificities, informational asymmetries, and opportunism found in the economic environment. Their task is to identify or elucidate these efficiencies. The presumption of efficiency functions much like the presumption of simplicity and order that guided planetary astronomy in the era of Kepler and Galileo. The theorist proceeds on the supposition that it is there to be discovered. However, as indicated in chapter 4, this is a presumption only, which means that it might be false in any particular case. For example, a commonly observed feature of all existing free enterprise systems might be explainable by some element of the tax codes that is common to all of the associated political systems. In general, there are a host of other potential confounding factors that might explain various features of existing economic systems. The proposition "If it exists, it must be efficient" is a Panglossian assumption that cannot be sustained when the object of discussion is the real world and not some economist's model.

How can the danger this assumption represents be guarded against? One way is for the theorist to elucidate the transactions cost efficiency in such a way that it supports the corresponding counterfactual conditional about what would happen if some other organizational form, policy, or procedure were to coexist. For example, Alchian and Demsetz's account of the superior monitoring properties of the classical capitalist firm makes an implicit comparative claim to the effect that if organizations with other monitoring arrangements existed and were in competition with classical capitalist firms, they would not survive.[1] The reason that this counterfactual supports the explanatory claim has to do with the nature of the fact to be explained. What is to be explained in these explanations—the explanandum—is the *persistence* of some phenomenon. In this instance, it is the persistence of a certain form of monitoring in a competitive environment in which people are free to experiment with alternative organizational forms. If a case can be made that alternative monitoring arrangements would be at a competitive disadvantage, that provides some reason to believe that existing monitoring arrangements persist because of their efficiency advantages. Relatedly, one can construe the explanatory claim as involving an appeal to some law that covers the phenomenon; one of things that distinguishes genuine laws from mere accidental generalizations is that the former—but not the latter—support counterfactual conditionals (Goodman 1965, chap. 1).

Plausible stories involving counterfactuals do not suffice to prove that a transactions cost explanation is correct, however. The reason is that while a transactions cost efficiency might be one factor in explaining some phenomenon, it may not be the only one. The phenomenon may be overdetermined, in which case there are a number of factors sufficient to produce the phenomenon, only one of which is the efficiency of the arrangement. For example, one factor responsible for the concentration of economic roles (monitor, entrepreneur, primary provider of capital, residual claimant) in the classical capitalist firm might be the transactions cost efficiencies of that concentration. But in America, the culture of rugged individualism might also be a factor in explaining the persistence of this organizational form. If this is true, the phenomenon would be overdetermined.

Yet another possibility (probably more common) is that there are a number of contributing factors that are singly insufficient, but together sufficient, to explain the phenomenon. In this sort of case, transactions cost advantages may be only one factor in accounting for the facts to be explained and possibly not a very important one. For example, the reputedly low incidence of shirking among Japanese workers may be partially explained by the superior monitoring arrangements of the predominant organizational forms in the Japanese economy. However, broader cultural forces may be at work; indeed, these forces may be more important than the monitoring properties of the organizations in explaining the work habits of the Japanese. Both of these examples cite noneconomic factors in explaining the facts to be explained; indeed, sociologists have criticized transactions cost analysis for ignoring noneconomic factors in its explanations of various features of organizations.[2]

These ways in which a transactions cost explanation could go wrong can never be ruled out once and for all. This is a simple consequence of the underdetermination of theory by the data. However, there are ways in which those who offer transactions cost explanations can reduce the likelihood that other factors are, in fact, significant in the true explanation of some phenomenon. Telling comparative stories about the inefficiencies of alternatives is one—though not the only—way to do this. Unfortunately, other ways require transactions cost analysts to do they have not yet done enough of—detailed empirical work. Key concepts need to be operationalized, testable hypotheses must be formulated, and real empirical data that would differentially support their hypotheses need to be gathered. This sort of work is not easy. Testing hypotheses about shirking in the workplace, for example, would be challenging and possibly dangerous. To date, transactions cost analysis has largely been an armchair enterprise of identifying the asset specificities, informational asymmetries, and so on and explaining how the policy or procedure in question is an efficient response to the situation so described. A related deficiency of this research program is that alternative hypotheses are often not explicitly considered and rejected. Some of the requisite critical work has been done (e.g., Williamson 1985, chap. 9), but more systematic comparative analyses and evaluations are needed.

On the other hand, the main strength of transactions cost analysis is that it offers a systematic and unified explanation for a wide range of phenomena that heretofore have either been ignored by economists or have not been adequately explained by other, more traditional approaches. In addition, the stories it tells usually have great intuitive appeal because they explain the phenomenon in question as a rational and efficient response to the expropriation hazards that asset owners face in various kinds of contractual relations—the kind of response one would expect to persist in a competitive environment in which transactors can experiment with different types of contractual relations. The explanation of the up-or-out system for associates in law firms discussed in chapter 4 is a good illustration of this point, as is the Alchian–Demsetz–Barzel explanation of the distinctive features of the classical capitalist firm.[3]

Fortunately, the aforementioned potential problems and deficiencies of this research program have a minimal impact on the discussion that follows, mainly because this chapter is only concerned with the predominant organizational forms to be found in a free enterprise system. As such, it is pitched at a very high level of abstraction, focusing only on the distinctive pattern of exchanges that define these widespread or common organizational forms. In other words, the explanandum is not some idiosyncratic fact about the shoe industry in recent years or even some distinctive feature of the American version of the free enterprise system. Instead, what is to be explained are phenomena that are common to all free enterprise systems. This reduces the likelihood that other, extraneous factors are wholly or even largely responsible for the phenomenon in question. This likelihood is further reduced to the extent that plausible stories can be told in support of the relevant counterfactual conditionals. Of course, this does not rule out the possibility that other factors are partly responsible for these organizational forms. In addition, there is no assurance that existing organizational forms are optimal. One reason for this is that though each of the distinctive features of these organizational forms may be more efficient than alternative ways of doing things, these individually efficient features may interact in such a way that the organizational form itself is less than optimal. This means that there might be other, superior organizational forms that would win out in a competitive struggle for survival. It is just that they have not been invented yet; or, perhaps they have been invented, but there is something preventing them from taking root and spreading in existing free enterprise systems. However, for the purposes of this study, the common organizational forms found in a free enterprise system need not be optimal; they need only do better in their transactions cost attributes than the organizational forms that would be found in a market socialist system. Proving this is the burden of chapters 6 and 7.

The plan for this chapter is as follows: The next section discusses more systematically and in more detail the transactions cost efficiencies of the classical capitalist firm. It explains how and why the structure of this type of organization economizes on transactions costs. Contained in this exposition (as well as in the discussions in subsequent sections) are indications of how the classical capitalist firm precludes opportunities for exploitation or makes it difficult for persons to take advantage of whatever opportunities for exploitation do exist.

The third section of this chapter discusses the transactions cost efficiencies of the open corporation. Recall from the first section of the previous chapter the distinctive features of this type of organization: Capital requirements are substantial, much larger than can be met by one individual. Those who provide most of the firm's capital are the ultimate decision makers and have the status of residual claimants.[4] These individuals are called stockholders or equity owners. Managers (i.e., those who exercise monitoring and entrepreneurial functions) are hired by a board of directors who are in turn answerable to the stockholders. Though managers may own stock, they are not substantial equity owners. Finally, the liability of the stockholders is limited to their original investment, and ownership shares are freely alienable on securities markets. There are transactions cost efficiencies associated with all of these features of the open corporation. The main purpose of this section is to explain these efficiencies and to indicate how they preclude or limit opportunities for exploitative exchange between and among occupiers of the various economic roles that were identified in the first section of chapter 4.

This section also contains a brief discussion of the transactions cost efficiencies of three other types of organizations found in a free enterprise system: the multidivisional corporation, the closed corporation, and the partnership. The multidivisional corporation is an important variant on the open corporation. It consists of semiautonomous profit centers in which operational control is delegated to division heads and top management exercises only high-level monitoring and broad strategic (i.e., entrepreneurial) functions. In the closed corporation, nearly all the stock is held by a small group of individuals (usually family members), and the firm is managed by one of those stockholders. The closed corporation is a kind of hybrid of the classical capitalist firm and the open corporation. Partnerships are characterized by profit sharing and collective management by the partners. If there is a managing partner, he or she is elected by the other partners and answerable to them. A partnership is not a cooperative because not all workers are partners. This third section ends with a brief discussion of the transactions cost efficiencies of these organizational forms.

These four types of firms do not exhaust all the organizational possibilities of a free enterprise system. For instance, there are mutual associations, such as savings and loans; nonprofit institutions, such as hospitals, universities, and charities; and, of course, there are state-owned enterprises. However, what distinguishes a free enterprise system from a market socialist system is that free enterprise systems have the four basic types of organizational forms (and one variant) just identified, two of which predominate. By contrast, in a market socialist system, the worker cooperative predominates, and the other types of organizations discussed in this chapter would be both uncommon and generally prohibited by law. For these reasons, only these four organizational forms will be discussed.

The fourth and final section of this chapter discusses the employment of labor in free enterprise systems. This topic warrants separate treatment because of the systematic differences between the types of contracts or exchanges between firms and workers in free enterprise systems and market socialist systems. This section investigates some of the transactions cost efficiencies of labor contracts as they have evolved in free enterprise systems. It also investigates the question whether or not workers in a free enterprise system are systematically exploited by the firms that hire them. The second section of chapter 6 contains a corresponding discussion of the possibility of the exploitation of labor in the market socialist cooperative.

The Classical Capitalist Firm Revisited

Recall from chapter 4 that the classical capitalist firm is owned by one individual.[5] The presumption is that the amount of capital involved is not so large that most of it must be raised in the capital markets. These firms can and do raise funds by borrowing—usually from friends or relatives—and some of the latter may have a minority equity interest in the firm, but the amount of outside debt and equity financing is not proportionately large in the classical capitalist firm. The firms that fall under this heading range from restaurants, repair shops, and other proprietorships, up to small to medium-sized corporations that are effectively owned and controlled by one individual.

The classical capitalist firm can be distinguished from other types of organizations by a distinctive pattern of interrelations among the set of functionally defined economic roles identified in the first section of chapter

4. Specifically, there is a single monitor (or a small and short hierarchy of monitors) who is the central contracting agent with laborers and all the other input providers (e.g., suppliers of raw materials and semifinished products). This presupposes that this monitor has the authority to negotiate the terms of these contracts, including the authority to terminate contractual relations between the firm and all input providers, including laborers. It also means that the monitor can determine, within a more or less broad zone of acceptance, how all inputs are to be used or combined in the production process.

In the classical capitalist firm, this monitor is also the sole residual claimant on the firm's income stream and is responsible for determining the product to be produced, its characteristics, and the price at which it will be offered for sale. Because of his control over the output side, as well as the input side, of the firm-market interface, this monitor-residual claimant is the firm's entrepreneur. In addition, this monitor-residual claimant-entrepreneur is the primary provider of capital for the firm and has ultimate decision-making authority about the firm's assets. Finally, this individual has the right to sell the firm, which is equivalent to selling any and all of the rights associated with the listed roles. What follows in this section is a series of explanations of the transactions cost efficiencies of these distinctive features of the classical capitalist firm; implicit in them are indications of how this type of firm prevents or limits opportunities for exploitative exchange that transactors would otherwise be subject to.

The Single Monitor

Recall that a monitor is needed when team production takes place. This is production in which several cooperating factors are used to produce a product that is not the sum of separable outputs of each factor (Alchian and Demsetz 1972, 778). As a result, the contribution of individual factors is difficult to ascertain. This measurement problem make it possible for a factor provider who shirks or otherwise opportunistically reduces output to get more than the value of what he contributes.

To see why, suppose that there is no monitor and the provider of factor F_1 opportunistically reduces her contribution (input) and thus negatively affects the team's output, whereas the providers of the other factors of production, $F_2 \ldots F_n$ do not. For example, F_1 might be labor and its provider might be a shirker. Supposing that team output is priced at the approximate marginal cost of production, it follows that the providers of these other factors are having some of the value of their assets appropriated by the shirking provider of F_1. Because the value of these other assets in non-team production is much less, they are specialized assets; thus, some of their value constitutes quasi-rents. Under these circumstances, the provider of F_1 can be said to be opportunistically appropriating some of the quasi-rents of other factors of production.[6] Why would these other input providers put up with this arrangement? Presumably, they would not, if they had somewhere else to go. But they would not have anywhere else to go if the same problem has arisen in other teams. (Suppose there is a law forbidding monitoring.) In the absence of a monitor, and of the opportunity to join other teams that do have a monitors, one factor owner (the provider of F_1) can exploit other factor owners.

Notice that the problem is stated in a completely general form so that it applies to all factor providers and not just to those who provide labor services. If those who provide capital or raw materials did so in exchange for a share of the output, they would also be subject to an expropriation hazard. And, depending on the nature of their contributions, they might also be in a position to reduce output by acting opportunistically (e.g., by short-weighting deliveries). One solution to the problem (perhaps the most obvious one) is for one individual to take on the role of monitor of team production. The monitor checks up on each member's provision of inputs to detect and deter shirking and other forms of opportunism. But it is, in fact, not so obvious that one individual should take on this role. Though some monitoring might be needed, it is not directly evident that one person should do it. There are other possibilities to be considered.

Clearly, it would be inefficient for everyone to monitor everyone else, since that would involve an enormous duplication of effort. But this is not the only way to involve everyone in monitoring. Each individual could devote part of his or her workday (or workweek) to monitoring the team. Or, team members could rotate in and out of the monitor's job, so that everyone gets an opportunity to crack the monitor's whip, so to speak. The first alternative is generally inefficient, because the activities involved in monitoring are, in general, more difficult to monitor than the other activities involved in team production. If an agent's job consists of two tasks, one of which is easier to monitor than the other, then, all else equal, she will devote more effort to the task that is easier to monitor (Holmstrom and Milgrom 1990). For example, when teachers are given incentive pay based on the test scores of their students, they will "teach to the tests" and neglect the teaching of higher-level cognitive skills—a type of teaching that is more difficult to monitor. Given that monitoring is, in general, more difficult to monitor than other facets of team production, one can anticipate that workers in this arrangement would direct their efforts away from monitoring and toward team production, which would make for inferior monitoring of this team.

The other way of involving everyone in monitoring would be to have one person to act as monitor in a full-time capacity but to rotate each member of the team in and out of this role on a regular basis. Generally speaking, however, this would be inferior to having only one person—or a small and short hierarchy of persons—specialize in the task of monitoring. To see why this is so, recall what the monitor does. According to Alchian and Demsetz, monitoring consists in "measuring output performance, apportioning rewards, observing the input behavior of inputs as means of detecting or estimating their marginal productivity and giving assignments or instructions in what to do and how to do it" (1972, 782). Doing well at these tasks is a matter of talent, tastes, and training; not everyone is equal in the first two and not everyone is equally disposed to undergo and profit from the third.

What the monitor does is prevent or minimize shirking and other forms of opportunism by other input providers. One way to do this in the case of labor services is to redesign the task (or even the product itself) to make the work more intrinsically rewarding, thereby making other forms of monitoring less necessary. There are, however, limits to what can be done to prevent shirking and other forms of opportunism in this way. Often, sterner measures are called for—in particular, the other elements of monitoring mentioned by Alchian and Demsetz: directly measuring output to the extent possible, metering inputs, and apportioning rewards and penalties as a result of other forms of monitoring.

These activities generally require those who do it to look upon others as potential shirkers and opportunists who have to be kept in line for their own good and the good of the team. Not surprisingly, there is a kind of adverse selection problem associated with this in that those who excel at these forms of monitoring often have other disagreeable characteristics. At the minimum, they tend to regard others as more given to shirking and opportunism than they really are. By contrast, kindly souls who are predisposed to think well of their fellows tend not to do as well at metering inputs, apportioning rewards and penalties, and the like. They systematically underestimate people's penchant for opportunism, and are reluctant to impose serious penalties on those who act opportunistically. However, successful monitoring tends to result in people's getting paid approximately the value of what they contribute. For this reason, good monitoring is essential to prevent the exploitation of some input providers by others. If everyone gets the opportunity to serve as monitor, the opportunists in the team will periodically get their golden opportunity to siphon off some of the value of other team members' contributions.

For all these reasons, the most efficient arrangement is to have one individual specialize as monitor of team production.[7] This arrangement is not limited to the classical capitalist firm. As Putterman says, "In the most egalitarian of producer cooperatives, the *kibbutz*, each work branch has its head, who supervises and tries to assure the effective work performance of its members. A relatively conventional supervisory structure marks many collective enterprises, such as those of the Mondragon network of cooperatives in Northeastern Spain" (1984, 173). Within the broad parameters suggested by Alchian and Demsetz's definition of monitoring, the rights and privileges associated with the monitor's role may vary from one type of firm to another. However, all classical capitalist firms have a single, full-time monitor or, at least, a small and short hierarchy of monitors.

The Monitor as Central Contracting Agent

The central contracting agent is the person in the firm who enters into contracts with suppliers of inputs (laborers, suppliers of raw materials and semifinished products, etc.) on behalf of the ultimate decision maker. Why would the monitor occupy this position of central contracting agent? Notice that the various tasks the monitor must perform presuppose that he has the authority to decide how inputs are to be used or combined, at least within a broad zone of acceptance. In other words, though there may be side constraints on what he may do with the assets to be used in production (labor, leased capital goods, and other inputs), the monitor has the authority to determine how inputs shall be used. The monitor cannot assign or design tasks, meter inputs, and so on without having that authority. The need for this basically open-ended authority comes from the fact that contracts with input providers governing every contingency cannot be written, and the costs of continually renegotiating contracts in response to unforeseen contingencies is prohibitive. This is perhaps the primary efficiency advantage of hierarchy, an advantage first noticed by Coase (1937). Grossman and Hart call this authority "residual rights of control" (1986, 717).[8] Because of the monitor's role in directing and regulating the flow of inputs, the contract between the input provider and the firm is effectively or essentially between the former and the monitor. Having these residual rights of control is even more essential if (as shall be argued shortly) the monitor also decides on the product to be produced and its characteristics. The general point is that the role of monitor effectively presupposes that the monitor is also the central contracting agent with all the other input providers.

Must the monitor have the authority to fire input—providers, in particular, the workers? It would seem so, if she is to exercise real authority in carrying out her tasks. This claim, as well as the monitor's authority, is subject to an important qualification, however. The zone of acceptance within which the monitor has the authority to fire input providers may be more or less narrowly defined. The state and collective bargaining agreements have narrowed that zone considerably over the past century. This erodes but does not usurp the monitor's authority to fire. This can best be appreciated by contrast with the situation in earlier times. In the good old days of capitalism—indeed, up until a couple of decades ago—the boss could fire workers for the most trivial and insubstantial reasons. Now many workers have protections so elaborate and extensive that they appear weak and tenuous only to civil service bureaucrats and tenured professors. Nevertheless, these protections have the form of side constraints in that they detail what a person cannot be fired for. They do not reassign what might be called "the residual right to fire." That right remains with the monitor, as it always has. The transfer of that right to the workers (as a collective) or to the state would be an important step toward socialism, which is why this measure is generally favored by socialists and opposed by defenders of a free enterprise system.

The monitor-central contracting agent's residual rights of control over inputs (whether labor or nonlabor) is what prevents input providers from forcing a renegotiation of their contracts when unforeseen contingencies arise. In other words, this authority relationship between the monitor-central contracting agent and the input providers prevents the latter from "holding up" the firm and/or its members by reopening negotiations in response to contingencies not explicitly covered in the contract (e.g., assigning one employee to do another's job when the latter is sick).[9]

Transactions cost analysis uses an iterated version of this explanation to explain decision-making hierarchies within firms generally (and not just the classical capitalist firms). Hierarchies economize on decision-making costs, if only because the agreements required by more consensual arrangements take time and other resources to achieve. This is not to deny that there may be offsetting efficiencies to more consensual arrangements; in a free enterprise system one would expect to see—and one does, in fact, see—more democratic methods of decision making in some circumstances and over some range of decisions. The militarylike hierarchies of nineteenth-century industrial capitalism have not disappeared entirely, but this is certainly not the norm in the late twentieth century, which has witnessed a proliferation of experimentation with alternative decision-making processes and structures.

Do transactions cost efficiencies wholly explain why hierarchies exist? Perhaps not. An alternative explanation, much favored by radical political economists, is that hierarchy serves the interests of power and that is why hierarchy in its many forms persists.[10] This explanation is often inferred from the fact that there are no production cost (i.e., technological) efficiencies to hierarchy (Marglin 1974, 46). This inference overlooks the possibility that there might be transactions cost efficiencies that attend hierarchy. Moreover, power has also proved to be a difficult concept to define and operationalize. Those problems to one side, however, the main difficulty with citing power as the sole or predominant reason why hierarchies exist is that there is no evidence to suggest that less efficient modes of organization that concentrate power win out—or would win out—over more efficient modes that disperse power more evenly (Williamson 1985, 231 and chap. 10). That is exactly the sort of evidence that would be needed to discredit transactions cost efficiency explanations at the expense of power explanations.

Power might be part of the explanation for the origins or genesis of the classical capitalist firm. Given the concentration of roles in one individual, that has a certain measure of prima facie plausibility. However, absent the kind of evidence just alluded to, there is no good reason to believe that hierarchies exist in the classical capitalist firm primarily because they concentrate power in the hands of some individuals (viz., classical capitalists) at the expense of others.

The Monitor-Central Contracting Agent as Residual Claimant

The discussion in the first subsection explained the need for a monitor to prevent the exploitation of input providers by other input providers and the advantages of having just one monitor (or a small and short hierarchy of monitors), and the preceding subsection explained the efficiency advantages of the monitor's being the central contracting agent with other input suppliers. But what are the efficiency advantages of this individual's being the residual claimant? As was pointed out in chapter 4, the explanation for this starts from the fact that monitoring is itself difficult to monitor. Task (re)design requires specialized knowledge of the production process and creativity; the deployment of both is hard to assess from the outside. The same is true of the design and implementation of more old-fashioned metering strategies. Not only are the inputs to the various monitoring modalities difficult for outsiders to judge, but so are the outputs. What does a well-monitored team look like? If the monitor lacks residual claimancy status, then she herself has an opportunity to shirk in the provision of monitoring services, which, all else equal, will lead to greater shirking and other forms of opportunism among all other input providers. In short, there will be a failure of leadership.

Another advantage to making the monitor-central contracting agent the residual claimant is that it gives her a better incentive not to expend too many resources on monitoring or on inputs generally. It is obvious that a central contracting agent will economize on production costs if she has residual claimant status. The same holds true of monitoring costs. Some forms of opportunism are simply not cost-effective to prevent. If the monitor-central contracting agent has residual claimancy status, she has to consider the costs of monitoring more carefully than she otherwise would. On the other hand, if this individual were to lack residual claimancy status, then she would have an incentive to expend more resources on monitoring activities (including task redesign) than is warranted, especially if those expenditures can be buried in such a way that whoever employs her has trouble identifying them.

By way of contrast, if monitoring were constituted by only intrinsically desirable tasks and consumed few resources, it would be unnecessary to make the monitor-central contracting agent the residual claimant. Though some elements of monitoring, (e.g., task design or redesign) might be inherently interesting, other aspects of monitoring (e.g., metering inputs and outputs, apportioning rewards) are not. The intrinsically interesting tasks could be farmed out to whoever is otherwise best suited to perform them. Indeed, this is done in many firms in advanced contemporary free enterprise systems (e.g., in Japan, the United States, and parts of Europe) where workers' input is sought in the redesign of their tasks.

But the other tasks that the monitor performs are often positively unpleasant for most people, and carrying them out makes the monitor an unpopular figure. These are generally not farmed out in private firms in existing free enterprise systems—perhaps because the temptation to shirk in this role would be overwhelming for most people.[11] (By contrast, casual observation suggests that shirking in the provision of monitoring services is pandemic in public enterprises.) In addition, those who delight in these forms of monitoring are inclined to do too much of it, which is counterproductive. Unlike most other tasks, one does not want the monitor to be someone who really enjoys her work. The best monitors are those who see much of what they do as necessary but disagreeable. Making the monitor a residual claimant eliminates the need for monitoring the monitor without at the same time creating an adverse selection problem that would attend hiring those who relish the opportunity to crack the whip.

The same sort of considerations explain why the central contracting agent should be the residual claimant. The central contracting agent exercises significant entrepreneurship in searching out the best and least costly input suppliers, considering alternative methods of organizing production, and so on. These activities, like the other forms of entrepreneurship to be discussed shortly, are difficult to monitor and are, for that reason, best handled by someone with residual claimant status.

A heretofore unnoticed consequence of making the monitor-central contracting agent the sole or primary residual claimant is that it facilitates the development of regular markets in other inputs. If every factor provider involved in team production were a residual claimant, the returns to a given factor of production would vary considerably across firms. Not only does this subject especially risk-averse input providers to risks that they would be willing to trade for a more definite income, but it also impedes the functioning of the market as a provider of information about the value of inputs. Returns to a factor owner would reflect not only the scarcity value of his factor of production but would also include an element traceable to his entrepreneurship, such as it is, as well as a purely stochastic element. This impedes the development of relatively stable prices in the factor markets, which, in turn, makes the payoffs of different production decisions even more uncertain than they would otherwise be.

The Monitor-Central Contracting Agent-Residual Claimant as Director of the Firm's Product

The high cost of monitoring is also a reason why it more efficient for the individual who is the monitor, central contracting agent, and residual claimant to exercise the crucial entrepreneurial functions of choosing a product and its characteristics and making the strategic decisions on marketing and pricing. Once again, specialized and costly knowledge is required to evaluate the quality and amount of effort put forth. In addition, as Barzel points out, luck has an imponderable influence on entrepreneurial success, which further aggravates the difficulty of monitoring entrepreneurial activity (1987, 104). A salaried director of the firm's product would have an opportunity to exploit her employer by shirking or by engaging in other forms of opportunism (e.g., entrepreneurship "on the side"). This opportunity can best be foreclosed by making her the residual claimant.

Finally, this arrangement allows for better coordination between the input and output firm-market interfaces. The central contracting agent is responsible for the input interface between the firm and the market; her task is easier to discharge if she is responsible for—or is directly in charge of whoever is responsible for—the output interface. The latter includes decisions on product, pricing, and marketing. In this way, the major entrepreneurial tasks are concentrated in one person.

The Monitor-Central Contracting Agent-Residual Claimant-Product Director as the Primary Provider of Capital

In chapter 4, it was noted that this arrangement, in contrast to an arrangement in which all capital is borrowed, serves the same function as good monitoring. Since the entrepreneur risks her own capital, she will pursue projects that maximize expected yield instead of excessively high-risk, high-yield ventures that she would be inclined to pursue if it were only other people's capital at stake.

But how does this preclude exploitation? If the venture succeeds, outside providers of capital would get the return on their investment that they were promised, and the entrepreneur would get the residuals. Supposing that they were promised the going rate for competitively efficient projects, they would be getting the value of what they contribute. No exploitation there: the problem comes if and when the venture fails. Not only can a salaried manager exploit her employer by doing less than she represents herself as doing in the provision of entrepreneurial services, but she is usually in a position to appropriate more than just the quasi-rents of the assets if a project is failing. In the real world, by the time sheriffs with padlocks show up, often everything not bolted down has somehow disappeared. This is a natural consequence of the physical control of the firm's assets exercised by the firm's head, coupled with a penchant for opportunism on the part of the latter. On the other hand, if this individual provides most of the capital herself, this potential moral hazard is averted.

There may be other transactions cost efficiencies to the practice of this individual's providing most or all of the capital. Barzel points out that this practice gives assurance to other factor providers that when business conditions appear to take a turn for the worse (whether or not they really have), the entrepreneur will not immediately terminate their contracts and hire or rehire factors at a lower rate on the spot market (another version of the holdup problem): "Employed factors will feel more secure if their contracts are structured so that an employer who fails to pay for the use of other assets stands to lose, which will happen . . . if a commensurate amount of the employer's own capital is idled when he lays off other factors" (1987, 114). By pledging to idle substantial resources of his own, the firm's owner assures these other factor providers that they will not be exploited in this way. Relatedly, if the central contracting agent has his own assets tied up in the project, it is much easier to get redress through the courts. An entrepreneur with no assets of his own at stake is what lawyers call "judgment-proof." Of course, this arrangement does not preclude bluffing or simply stonewalling, which, if successful, would permit the entrepreneur to appropriate some of the quasi-rents of others (i.e., to exploit them). Bluffing is not a stable strategy over the long haul, however, and reputation effects would likely mitigate this species of exploitation over time.

The Monitor-Central Contracting Agent-Residual Claimant-Product Director-Primary Provider of Capital as Ultimate Decision-making Authority

There is one final role to take account of—ultimate decision maker. The person who fulfills the role of ultimate decision maker has final say over the disposition of the firm's assets. It is this individual in whose interests the firm is operated. There are clear advantages to concentrating all of the hard-to-monitor roles (i.e., monitor, central contracting agent, product director) in this individual. Complete, costlessly enforceable contracts cannot be written, which means that separating any of these roles from ultimate decision-making authority makes it possible for those who occupy these roles to get paid more or less than the true value of their services and, when the one party has nowhere else to go, to exploit or be exploited. Making the ultimate decision maker the primary supplier of capital gives him something to lose if he exercises his authority poorly, and making him residual claimant gives him something to gain if he exercises his authority wisely.

The Right of Alienability and Liability to Execution of Debt

The final distinctive feature of the classical capitalist firm is that this individual who occupies all of these other roles can alienate any and all of the rights associated with these roles by selling them (usually as a package, for the reasons indicated in the preceding subsections). In addition, as owner of the firm, that individual is fully liable for execution of the firm's debts. The most important implication of this multiple-role occupier's also being able to alienate (i.e., sell) these roles and being liable for the firm's debts is that—externalities to one side—the economic consequences of all the decisions made in these roles accrue to, or are capitalized into, the value of the firm and thus fall squarely on the shoulders of the individual who makes them. If some or all of these rights are inalienable and held only temporarily, then the decision maker does not have to take account of the consequences that his decision will have on the long-term value of the rights in question. Suppose, for example, that the boss could not sell his right of residual claimancy but would, instead, have to give it up without compensation when he leaves the firm. Under these circumstances, he could enter into a venture that would generate short-term gains but net losses over the long term—losses that could be incurred after he leaves the firm and which would be borne by the owners of specialized assets (including labor) that are locked into the firm for the long term. The right of alienability and the liability to execution of debt together encourage responsible use of assets by the boss, since this right and the corresponding liability result in his bearing the full economic consequences of his actions.

The Open Corporation

The compact economic structure of the classical capitalist firm is responsible for significant transactions cost efficiencies. This naturally raises the question of how or why any other organizational form could survive in a competition with this organizational form. The following subsection will provide an answer. The general purpose of the present section is to discuss the other organizational forms to be found in the free enterprise system that would be effectively banned in a market socialist system, primarily the open corporation. It also includes a brief discussion of the multidivisional corporation (a variant on the open corporation), the closed corporation, and the partnership. Specifically, this section seeks to identify the transactions cost efficiencies of the distinctive features of these types of organizations and to indicate how they preclude or limit opportunities for exploitation that would exist if these organizations were structured differently.

The open corporation is characterized by the following five distinctive features:

1. The amount of capital it controls is generally too large for one individual to supply.
2. The primary suppliers of capital are the residual claimants and have ultimate decision-making authority with regard to the assets that the firm controls. Let us say that anyone who simultaneously occupies all three of these roles (primary supplier of capital, residual claimant, and ultimate decision making authority) is an equity owner of, or has an equity ownership stake in, the firm.[12] Typically, this amounts to proportional ownership of the firm's assets, a proportional claim on the firm's residuals, and a proportional vote on who serves on the board of directors, which, in turn, hires management. Individuals with all these rights are called stockholders.
3. The managers are neither the primary providers of capital nor the primary residual claimants, though they may have some equity stake in

the firm. They are hired by a board of directors, which is ultimately answerable to the stockholders.

4. Shares of equity ownership are freely alienable on a securities market.
5. Equity owners' liability for the obligations of the firm is limited to the amount of capital invested.

There are transactions cost advantages to all of these features, advantages that preclude opportunities for exploitative exchange that would otherwise exist. Let us begin with the first of these, large capital requirements.

Large Capital Requirements

It is widely believed that technology and/or mass markets dictate the need for large corporations in advanced industrial societies. This, however, confuses the physical requirements of production with ownership requirements. Modern mass production does indeed require large, expensive production facilities, but technology does not dictate that the facilities should all be owned by one firm. As was pointed out in chapter 4, the capital goods required for mass production could be separately owned by individuals and/or small groups, instead of a single firm. Why, in general, doesn't this happen? Why isn't every technologically separable stage of production separately owned? Indeed, why isn't every piece of equipment—or even every pipe and valve in a factory—owned by a separate individual or group? What is the principle of gravitation that explains the ownership of capital in a free enterprise system? Transactions cost analysis attempts to explain this phenomenon by arguing that the costs of organizing transactions involving large production facilities across markets exceed the costs of bringing those transactions within the firm. What are the costs of markets?

In his seminal article "The Nature of the Firm," Coase mentions the costs of gathering information about prices and negotiating contracts with the owners of cooperating factors of production as the main costs of using the market to organize transactions (1937, 336–37). Though this is part of the answer, it is not the whole story. Recent work in transactions cost analysis emphasizes the expropriation hazards (i.e., opportunities for exploitation) posed by asset specificities and opportunism as costs that can be avoided by removing transactions from the market. These hazards—or potential hazards—abound. Because long-term contracts governing every contingency cannot be written and because much of the value of many assets is so specific to a particular arrangement, expropriation hazards would be pandemic in a world of independent input providers or even of small to medium-sized companies. These hazards will not persist in a world in which large quantities of capital are brought together under the umbrella of very large firms.

This point bears further elaboration. Transactions cost analysis has been preoccupied with explaining the determinants of vertical integration, both backward into the supply stage and forward into subsequent stages of production or distribution (e.g., Klein, Crawford, and Alchian 1978; Williamson 1985, chaps. 4–7). Part of the reason for this is that this aspect of transactions cost analysis has important and immediate implications for antitrust policy.[13] But it also explains why large firms exist at all. To see why, notice that firms that control a number of stages of production (and the associated capital) have a number of transactions cost efficiencies in comparison to a sequence of firms and/or independent contractors in the production-distribution chain. The most important of these is that when unforeseen contingencies arise, contracts do not have to be renegotiated in a climate in which one party is highly vulnerable to exploitation by the other. Instead, those in charge can simply make whatever adjustments are required.

Suppose that firm S (the supplier firm) has a long-term contract to supply firm P (the purchasing firm) with an input that P cannot easily get elsewhere. After some time has gone by, the demand for P's product falls off precipitously, unexpectedly, and permanently. This means that P's product, as well as the specialized input supplied by S, is worth less than it used to be. P, unfortunately, is still obligated to purchase the input from S at the same price. Or perhaps the contract allows for some downward adjustment, but it is not enough (suppose the price is tied to an economic index that turns out not to reflect accurately the situation that P faces). If P owned S as a subsidiary, management could simply order a cutback in the production of S's product, thereby releasing factors of production for more highly valued uses elsewhere. Adjustments like this are absolutely essential if the market is to perform its signaling function properly. However, if P does not own S, P must keep taking delivery of the input and paying S more than the input is really worth. Unless P was getting a price discount initially to compensate for the risks inherent in this arrangement, P gets—or more exactly, P's equity owners get—exploited. They are paying more for the input than it is really worth, and they are doing so because the terms of the contract give them no real alternative. The potential expropriation hazards presented by long-term contracts may be mitigated in a variety of ways (including the two firms purchasing significant shares of stock in one another), but sometimes the best, simplest, and most efficient way will simply be to integrate vertically: S or P buys out the other firm. This is what happened when General Motors purchased the Fisher Body company, which had been an independent firm (Klein 1991).

The transactions cost efficiencies involved when large amounts of capital are owned by one firm (the open corporation) preclude or obviate opportunities for exploitative exchange that would otherwise exist. Intuitively, the idea is that under vertical integration, there are fewer firm-market borders that must be protected against potentially opportunistic input providers and customers. For this reason, fewer resources have to be expended to protect the quasi-rents of specialized assets when those assets are brought into the firm than would have to be expended if those assets directly supported market exchanges.

This point can be appreciated by imagining the passage of a law prohibiting firms from controlling more capital than any one individual or family could supply. What would happen as a result of the passage of this law (aside from a rash of adoptions of the owners of some firms by the aged parents of the owners of other firms)? The most important result would be that owners of specialized capital goods or ensembles of specialized capital goods (i.e., owners of these smaller firms) would face a risk of having their quasi-rents appropriated by their customers or input suppliers, or both. Some of these risks would eventuate, resulting in the exploitation of these owners. For the rest, costly safeguards of some sort would have to be developed (e.g., arbitration procedures to deal with unforeseen contingencies or even the renewal of long-term contracts). If such safeguards could not be developed, the only other alternative would be for those facing these expropriation hazards to charge a premium in the form of higher prices for their products to compensate for the risk of exploitation they face. Regardless of whether the safeguards were developed or the compensating premium was paid, the products these firms produce would be more costly than the cheapest alternative, namely, vertical integration, which has now been prohibited by law. Products would sell for more than their competitively efficient market price, and since other firms would face similar restrictions, buyers would effectively have nowhere else to go. In short, these exchanges would be exploitative. Either in this way or by way of the straight appropriation of the quasi-rents of the equity owners, exploitative exchanges would take place in this system that would have been precluded if the law had permitted firms to control large quantities of capital.

As with other transactions cost efficiencies, there is no need to suppose that those who invented the large corporation were responding to a recognition of the transactions cost efficiencies of vertical integration (notably, the avoidance of expropriation hazards). Indeed, a cursory examination of the historical record suggests that these individuals sometimes acquired much of their capital by engaging in just this form of exploitation! But by doing this, they created organizations so large that no one individual could effectively control them and so large that competitors had to raise capital from many different sources in order to compete. In any such market, once competing organizations raise the capital and are on the scene, they impose discipline on that market and prevent the original firm from continuing to exploit its customers. A good illustration of some of these points is to be found in the market in long-distance telephone service in the United States. AT&T enjoyed a legal monopoly on long-distance service for many years. Many people suspected, quite rightly, that AT&T was charging more for their service than it was "really worth." When the monopoly privilege was withdrawn, entrepreneurs amassed huge amounts of capital to form competitors such as MCI and U.S. Sprint. Prices fell, and AT&T cut out the fat in their operations and stopped exploiting their customers.[14]

The large corporation, far from being the main source of exploitation in the modern world (as the opponents of a free enterprise system would have it), is, in point of fact, a bulwark against exploitative exchanges that would take place in a world comprised exclusively of smaller organizations and independent suppliers and contractors.

These observations about the transactions cost efficiencies of bringing large amounts of capital under one decision-making roof lead to the question, Why aren't all economic organizations large corporations? In particular, why do classical capitalist firms (not to mention other types of organizations) survive—and indeed thrive—in a free enterprise system? A full answer to this question would go further into the details of transactions cost analysis than is necessary for the purposes of this chapter, but an outline of an answer can be sketched. Both environmental and organizational factors have a role to play in explaining the survival of the classical capitalist firm. When asset specificities are low or quasi-rents are well protected by competition and when there are no economies of scale to be realized, there are no transactions cost advantages to dissolving the firm-market boundary by amassing large quantities of capital within one firm.[15] Moreover (as will be explained later in this section), there are inefficiencies that attend the separation of management from equity ownership, and there are inevitable inefficiencies—bureaucratic inefficiencies—that go with large size in any organization. These include credit stealing, blame shifting, and in general, misrepresenting the nature or value of one's own contribution or the contributions of others.[16] The superior incentive alignments of the classical capitalist firm and its relatively nonbureaucratic nature give it efficiency advantages over its larger rivals that are decisive in some ecological niches.

There is no guarantee that the size of firms in a given industry is optimal. To put it another way, there is no guarantee that the boundary between the firm and the market is always—or even ever—drawn optimally. Nor is there any guarantee that the division of labor between different types of organizations is optimal in a free enterprise system. All that can be said is that there are competitive forces at work and that there is a tendency for those forces to select out the more efficient organizational modalities among existing competitors in a given economic environment.

The main purpose of this subsection has been to identify the transactions cost efficiencies of bringing together large amounts of capital under one decision-making roof. To summarize, the primary advantages are two. First, it allows capital to be deployed with a minimum of discussion, consultation, and negotiation; however many equity owners there are, there is an essential identity of interests among the owners of these large amounts of capital, an identity of interests that does not hold when transactions take place across markets. Second and relatedly, this capital structure eliminates the expropriation hazards (opportunities for exploitation) that would have to be faced if firms and individuals with highly specific assets—and potentially exposed quasi-rents—had to deal with each other in the marketplace.

Equity Ownership

A distinctive feature of the open corporation is that the primary suppliers of capital are also the residual claimants with ultimate decision-making authority over the assets of the firm. In practical terms, ultimate decision-making authority in the open corporation amounts to no more than a proportional vote on who shall serve on the board of directors. Despite the fact that this vote is rarely exercised in anger (so to speak), it is nonetheless an important right because, principal-agent problems to one side, it is the ultimate decision maker's interests that shape and constrain the firm's activities. What needs to be explained in this subsection are the transactions cost efficiencies of joining this ultimate decision-making authority to two other key roles in the open corporation: the role of residual claimant and the role of provider of most of the firm's capital. Consider first residual claimancy. On the face of it there is an obvious efficiency advantage to joining residual claimancy to ultimate decision-making authority: If the ultimate decision maker is the residual claimant, he has—or those who act in his interests have—an incentive to economize on all costs of production. In a competitive environment, this tends to result in factor providers' getting the value of what they contribute, which, in turn, minimizes exploitation.

The efficiency advantages of this arrangement can be further appreciated by supposing these two roles to be separate. What would this situation look like? The residual claimant is the ultimate risk-bearer in the firm. She gets the positive profits due to good fortune and/or successful entrepreneurship, and she suffers the losses due to bad luck and/or unsuccessful entrepreneurship. In order to suffer the losses, however, the residual claimant must pledge some assets that may be lost if a venture fails. Since it is difficult to pledge one's labor as security, the most plausible scenario is for the residual claimant to provide capital. Suppose now that this residual claimant-capital provider did not have ultimate decision-making authority in the firm. This scenario creates an obvious opportunity for the exploitation of the residual claimant-capital provider by the ultimate decision maker. After all, the latter controls the firm's assets (its capital), and the firm is managed in his interests, but by supposition, he gets none of the residuals and none of the returns to capital. However, because he is the ultimate decision-making authority, he would be in a position to siphon pure profits from the residual claimant and quasi-rents from the capital provided by the hapless capital provider into his own pocket (perhaps in the form of inflated payments for decision-making services). A real-world example of this might be American nonprofit hospitals. Whatever their legal status, they often make enormous profits, which are funneled into the pockets of the top echelon of decision makers in the form of inflated salaries, perks, and other forms of on-the-job consumption.[17]

An example of a profit-making organization in which rights to the residuals are held by people without any decision-making authority is the limited partnership. In this organizational form, the limited partner puts up an equity stake in exchange for a claim on the residuals but has no decision-making authority. What protects her assets, however, is that the person with decision-making authority, the general partner, is also a residual claimant, so that in theory at least, a harmony of interests is achieved.[18] One final example, this one hypothetical: imagine an economic system in which the state provides all the capital and is the residual claimant for certain firms and yet top management, answerable to no one, has ultimate decision-making authority in each of these firms. No one that this author is aware of has ever proposed such a system—and with good reason. This type of system would encourage widespread exploitation of capital providers by top management and would be an economic disaster.

These are the efficiency advantages—and the implications for exploitation—of joining ultimate decision-making authority to residual claimancy in the open corporation. What needs to be explained next are the transactions cost efficiencies of making those who jointly occupy these roles the primary suppliers of capital. In addition, something also needs to be said about why and under what circumstances corporations would raise substantial amounts of capital through the issuance of debt.

Making the residual claimant-ultimate decision maker the primary supplier of capital serves the same functions that it does in the classical capitalist firm. One of these is that it serves as a bond to other input providers in that if the ultimate decision makers are also the primary providers of capital, then, by pledging to idle some of their own resources in the event that they lay off workers or otherwise cancel contracts, they are giving some assurance to other input providers that this will happen only under seriously adverse economic conditions; it will not be part of a "holdup attempt" in which they try to appropriate some of the quasi-rents of other input providers by forcing the renegotiation of contracts once the latter are locked into the situation. In this way, the asset specificities committed to the firm by these other input providers are protected from exploitation by the residual claimants (Barzel 1987, 114).

There are other transactions cost efficiencies to be found in the residual claimants–ultimate decision makers' also being the primary providers of capital. To understand what they are, suppose once again that the former are not the primary providers of capital. Consider the extreme case in which the residual claimants with ultimate decision-making authority supply none of the capital that the firm uses. (Later, this assumption will be relaxed.) Under these circumstances, the firm is effectively leasing all of its capital. Whether the capital providers supply concrete capital goods or finance capital, these lessors are like bondholders in that they are promised a fixed rate of return in exchange for allowing their capital to be used. The capital providers in this scenario would be contractually on a par with other input providers, such as suppliers of raw materials and semifinished products. Call this a *pure rental firm*.[19]

Unlike firms that own their capital, the pure rental firm would be unable to pledge its capital to bond short-term obligations, such as those commonly incurred with suppliers and banks. Instead, it would have to pay a premium in its dealings with suppliers, banks, and possibly even workers—a premium that firms that owned their own capital could avoid. By contrast, when the ultimate decision makers are putting their own capital on the line, they are able to avoid this premium. To understand the true significance of this problem, it is necessary to identify who is de facto liable for the corporation's obligations in the pure rental firm, that is, who gets stuck if the firm does not show a profit. Suppose sales slow down and inventory piles up. What happens? After any undistributed residuals are used up, what do the residual claimants-ultimate decision makers do? Since they control management, they will order managers to look for ways to cut costs and raise revenues. One obvious way to cut costs is to cut back on scheduled maintenance of facilities and equipment. This way of meeting short-term obligations results in lowering the value of the capital goods that they control. On the revenue side, revenues could be raised by shifting working capital into high-risk, short-term ventures.

Suppose these measures fail. The residual claimants-ultimate decision makers are told by those to whom they owe money or have other obligations that since these decision makers have ultimate authority in the firm, the assets they have contributed are liable to execution for all outstanding debts. This is fine with the decision makers because, by hypothesis, they have contributed no assets at all to the pure rental firm. They are simply residual claimants with ultimate decision-making authority. And because this is a limited liability firm, their personal assets have not been pledged. Indeed, no one's personal assets have been pledged; the pure rental firm owns virtually no assets at all! The assets they employ are owned by someone else—capital providers, laborers, and other input suppliers. Some of the value of these assets (primarily the capital) will have been siphoned off, to the extent that it is possible, in hopes of keeping the firm going. And, of course, part of what is required to keep the firm going is to pay the ultimate decision makers and to make periodic payments to the residual claimants. One may suppose that those in charge will conform to Trotsky's dictum, "Those who have something to distribute seldom forget themselves."

The possibility of making these payouts is a consequence of the fact that firms must be able to make payments to residual claimants before all debt, long-term and short-term, has been discharged (Manning 1977, 9–10). This is especially true of the pure rental firm, which never really discharges its long-term debt. As Manning has pointed out, the only thing the firm can distribute to residual claimants are assets that it controls. As long as there is continuing debt, equity owners will receive payments before all debt is discharged. Indeed, the notion of a residual is something of an accounting fiction (1977, 33). It is not something that is automatically extruded by the firm at regular intervals but instead represents a decision made by management to turn over some of the firm's assets to a certain class of people, namely, the residual claimants. Even when the firm is in trouble, the ultimate decision makers in the pure rental firm can make payments to the residual claimants (i.e., to themselves), and they can get the money by siphoning value from the capital that the firm controls. If they are not imaginative enough to think of ways to do this, firms and individuals would undoubtedly set up shop to explain to them how they can get access to the value of the capital they effectively control. Clearly, in an ownership arrangement like this, the residual claimants-ultimate decision makers can exploit the capital providers.

Obviously, the capital providers can and will take steps, in the form of monitoring, to prevent or limit these opportunities for exploitation. The most obvious step would be to insist on a say in major corporate decisions, but that violates the supposition that outside capital providers are not the ultimate decision makers. Besides, even if they have a say on some delineated category of decisions, residual rights of control (as they were called earlier) remain with those who are the ultimate decision-making authorities, who are also the residual claimants. Finally, monitoring has costs associated with it, and there may be forms of exploitation of capital owners that are not cost-effective to prevent. Once again, one comes up against the fact that complete, unambiguous, and costlessly enforceable contracts cannot be written. These forms of exploitation are precluded if the role of capital provider is joined to the other two roles.

This discussion illustrates a peculiarity in the structure of the pure rental firm that merits some additional attention. It seems natural to define the residual claimant as the one who gets what is left over after all input providers have been paid, whether those residuals are positive or negative. The problems inherent in letting those with no assets at stake determine what is "left over" are apparent. There is, however, a more fundamental problem with this conception of residual claimancy. To say that a person gets the negative residuals is to say that that person is liable to execution of debt. However, that liability cannot be personal liability, since that is inconsistent with the status of corporations as limited liability organizations. If these individuals put up no capital at all, their role as negative residual claimants is—quite limited. In actual fact, as the discussion indicates, the capital providers (and to a lesser extent, other input providers) would be de facto liable for any obligations the firm incurs, which is another way of saying that the assets they have lent the firm are unsecured. If these lenders also lack decision-making authority, one has a situation in which there is a group of people with ultimate decision-making authority who will receive all of the positive profits—and suffer none of the losses—associated with the business. It is completely obvious that this situation creates significant opportunities for exploitation.[20] These opportunities are foreclosed if the exchange between the capital providers and the residual claimants is eliminated by combining these roles. If the residual claimants-ultimate decision makers are the primary supplier of capital, then they have accumulated wealth to lose if they act unwisely. For all of these reasons, there are significant transactions cost efficiencies to equity ownership, that is, to uniting the roles of ultimate decision maker, residual claimant, and capital provider.

An objection that might be raised to this account is that it does not explain the existence of substantial debt financing by corporations, such as leveraged buyouts. Indeed, it is unclear why there is any debt financing at all. Consider the latter question first. When the ratio of debt to equity is relatively low, it is not difficult to see the attractions of debt financing, as compared to equity financing, from both borrower's and lender's perspective. The borrowing firm gains leverage to pursue profit opportunities that would otherwise be beyond its reach. If those opportunities are ephemeral or if the firm is reluctant to share its prospective good fortune by taking on additional equity owners, it is in its interests to finance new or expanded ventures by issuing debt instruments that pay a fixed rate of return to the debt holder.[21] The lenders, if the firm has a relatively thick equity cushion, have some protection against loss, since in bankruptcy proceedings, debt holders are paid off before equity owners. Unlike the pure rental firm, a well-capitalized firm has substantial assets to secure the debt instruments that it issues.

Corporations that are highly leveraged are another matter.[22] Suppose a manager of a division of a large corporation seeks debt financing to take his division private through a leveraged buyout. The incentive for the manager to take on all this debt is that he believes there are significant profit opportunities that he can seize if he is out on his own. For example, he may believe that there are (transactions cost) inefficiencies in the bureaucratic structure of the parent company that would be avoided if the division were a freestanding entity. But doesn't this arrangement pose significant risks for the lender—risks of having the value of his assets dissipated in an unsuccessful venture or even appropriated by the manager-entrepreneur(s) who have only a small equity stake? Indeed it does, and to cope with these risks, the lender will insist on some ultimate decision-making authority (e.g., veto power on major decisions) and will incur a variety of other monitoring costs to protect his investment (Jensen and Meckling 1976, 337–42). Moreover, in return for all these risks, the lender will demand and receive a risk premium. This is what "junk bonds" are all about. This sort of arrangement makes sense, however, only when both sides are convinced that there are large entrepreneurial profits to be made and that they can only be made by a particular manager or management team. Otherwise, safer investments are indicated, either in the form of debt or equity.

The general point is that there are advantages and disadvantages to debt versus equity financing; in a free enterprise system, there will be a tendency for the transactions costs associated with each to be minimized. However, there is no guarantee that in the real world, the debt-equity structure of an industry or in any particular firm will be optimal. Indeed, it often will not be, given the bounded rationality and other imperfections of the human beings who make the relevant decisions.

The main purpose of this subsection has been to explain how and why there are significant transactions cost efficiencies to equity ownership, that is, to tying together ultimate decision-making authority, residual claimancy, and the provision of capital. Though it is sometimes advantageous to have some capital provided by outsiders through debt financing, it is rarely efficient for all or nearly all capital to be borrowed. Equity ownership is a way of reflecting the consequences of the actions of ultimate decision makers back onto themselves in a way that cannot be accomplished if residual claimancy is radically separated from the provision of capital. However, there is an apparent problem with this arrangement in the open corporation in that the equity owners do not exercise strategic or operational control of the firm's assets. Prima facie, this seems to create opportunities for exploitation in the open corporation. Let us turn, then, to the third distinctive feature of the open corporation—the separation of ownership and control—to see whether or not these opportunities do exist and if so, how they are dealt with.

The Separation of Equity Ownership and Managerial Control

One of the most important distinctive features of the classical capitalist firm is its concentration of management functions (monitoring and entrepreneurship) in the hands of the individual who is the primary residual claimant, the ultimate decision-making authority, and the provider of capital (i.e., the equity owner). This eliminates the need to monitor these hard to monitor functions. These transactions cost efficiencies of the classical capitalist firm preclude exploitative exchange between the managers and the capitalist-residual claimant of the firm by precluding the exchange itself. By contrast, the open corporation reintroduces the exchange relation—and thus, at least, the potential for exploitative exchange—between management and the equity owners. What, then, is the advantage in this separation of management and equity ownership?

Part of the answer is implicit in the large capital requirements of the modern open corporation. Those requirements are so substantial that many equity owners have to be involved; obviously, not all of them can be managers. For reasons discussed previously (see pp.137–42), bringing large amounts of capital under one decision-making roof has significant transactions cost efficiencies and, by implication, precludes a significant range of opportunities for exploitative exchange that would otherwise exist. The separation of equity ownership and management and what that entails is simply the price that must be paid for these efficiencies.

These considerations are suggestive as far as they go, but they say nothing about whether or how exploitative exchange takes place between equity owners and managers as the result of the separation of these two roles and how it might be prevented. In particular, something has to be said about how management is monitored in the open corporation. This is especially pressing in light of the fact that management consists of essentially two tasks that are very difficult to monitor: (1) the monitoring of other input providers and (2) entrepreneurship on the input and output interfaces between the firm and the market. This would seem to open the door for management to exploit the equity owners, a door that the classical capitalist firm closes by joining these tasks to equity ownership.

A further difficulty with the open corporation is that equity owners, who have the right to hire the managers, seem to be in a poor and weak position to judge the value of the managerial services they are purchasing. How, then, can equity owners monitor management and prevent the latter from appropriating some of the value of the firm or its assets (i.e., some of its quasi-rents)? If they cannot and if all firms of comparable size have the same basic structure, these equity owners effectively have nowhere else to go. Under these circumstances, if management appropriates some of the quasi-rents of the firm, that appropriation would meet both of the conditions for exploitative exchange. This is a stylized picture of what many critics of the free enterprise system believe, in fact, happens.[23] A defense of the free enterprise system on this point requires an explanation of how management can be effectively monitored in the large corporation to minimize the proportion of the firm's quasi-rents that go into managers' pockets.

It might seem that the obvious solution to this problem is to make the managers stockholders; indeed, that is usually done, up to a point, by making stock or stock options part of the pay package. This would make pay reflective of entrepreneurial contribution and would provide an excellent incentive for management not to shirk. But it is not the entire solution for two reasons.

First, the basic problem of shirking (or more generally, opportunism) in an environment of team production still exists, only now the team has been enlarged to include the monitor. As before, the opportunist gets all of the benefits but suffers only a fraction of the costs. In a very large corporation, that fraction of the costs that residual claimants-managers must pay for their opportunism might be vanishingly small, especially in comparison to the benefits. Opportunism is not limited to shirking in the provision of an input: it can take the form of on-the-job consumption (lavish offices and various other perks), buying inputs from friends who may not be the best suppliers, hiring one's friends and relatives, and so on. The costs that these activities impose on a corporate executive in his role as stockholder of a large company are likely to be vanishingly small in comparison to the benefits he receives from these forms of opportunism.

Second, there is the problem of risk diversification. The performance of a firm is not entirely determined by the actions of its top management, and the idea that the latter completely controls what goes on in the firm is as much a myth as the idea that the top management in any large organization (e.g., a large government agency, the military) exercises complete control. If top management's pay were strictly determined by the firm's profits, they would be unable to diversify the risks they face. As Fama and Jensen point out, "Risk aversion tends to cause them to charge more for any risk they bear than security holders who can diversify risk across many organizations" (1983a, 330). As Arrow (1964) has shown, one of the advantages of the open corporation is that it allows for the diversification of risk by equity holders. So, if managers' entire pay were determined by their status as residual claimants, risk would be inefficiently distributed, and managers would have to receive extra compensation for bearing the full risk consequences (though obviously not the full wealth consequences) of their entrepreneurial decisions. In consequence, they would likely shirk in the provision of entrepreneurial services by acting much more cautiously than conditions warrant. This problem is addressed by paying managers a basic salary and giving them bonuses in the form of stock and stock options on top of that salary. Tying management's pay to firm performance is one way of mitigating the moral hazard (and thus the potential for exploitation) inherent in the separation of equity ownership and managerial control in the open corporation, but it does not eliminate the problem. Moreover, it not appropriate or efficient as an exclusive instrument to deal with the opportunity for exploitation presented by this separation of ownership and control.

Fortunately, there are other factors that play a role in mitigating this moral hazard. Perhaps the most important of these is the board of directors. Elected by the stockholders, the board of directors hires, fires, and sets the pay of management. Because members of the board are much more knowledgeable than ordinary stockholders about the market for managerial services, they are better positioned to set management's pay at about the market-determined rate. The board also plays an important role in monitoring management's performance. One way this is accomplished is through the audit committee of the board. The internal audit department reports directly to the audit committee, not to management. In addition, the audit committee also hires a public accounting firm to audit the firm's financial statement. The primary concern of the public accounting firm is to certify that the financial statement management prepares gives an accurate picture of the firm's financial condition to the board, the stockholders, and other interested parties (e.g., securities analysts and government agencies such as the Securities and Exchange Commission). Though auditors will detect large-scale misuse of funds, they will not detect fraud below a certain level of materiality or significance, nor is that the purpose of the audit. When audit differences are posted by the public accounting firm, they are saying to these audiences that management is trying to make the firm's financial condition look better than it really is. Misrepresentations of this sort at the margins are much more common than outright fraud. Finally, the public accounting firm also makes recommendations to the board and to management about ways to improve internal controls (i.e., monitoring).[24]

Another way that the board monitors management's performance is through what Fama and Jensen call *decision control*. They identify four steps in the decision-making process:

1. *initiation*—generation of proposals for resource utilization and structuring of contracts
2. *ratification*—choice of the decision initiatives to be implemented
3. *implementation*—execution of ratified decisions
4. *monitoring*—measurement of the performance of decision agents and implementation of rewards. (1983b, 303)

They call steps 1 and 3 *decision management* and steps 2 and 4 *decision control*. Decision management roughly corresponds to entrepreneurship and is exercised by the firm's managers. The board of directors, however, monitors the major entrepreneurial moves that management makes by exercising the decision control functions of ratification and monitoring.[25]

The exercise of decision control functions does not require that management be excluded from the board. In his discussion of corporate governance, Williamson identifies three benefits to management membership on the board of directors: (1) the board has access to the decision-making process as well as the results; (2) management's participation on the board can give the board access to more and better information than would be forthcoming in a more arm's-length relationship; (3) management participation on the board can serve to protect the otherwise-difficult-to-protect employment relation between the firm and management—for example, top managers usually have no formal grievance procedures if the board disciplines or dismisses them (1985, 317).

Participation by management on the board of directors is sometimes accompanied by the participation of other board members in the management of the firm; this allows the firm to draw on the expertise and connections of well-placed outsiders. However, the dangers of both management participation on the board and board participation in management is that the monitoring function of the board will be compromised and management or the board (or both) will engage in self-dealing or otherwise exploit the stockholders.

Indeed, though the board has superior information and expertise to monitor management, Juvenal's question once again obtrudes: '*Quis custodiet ipsos custodes?*' The principal-agent relationship between the board and the equity owners is itself in need of monitoring. How can this can be accomplished? Harold Demsetz has suggested that this may be the role of the large shareholder, that is, the individual—or even an organization, such as a pension fund—that has a substantial proportion of its own wealth tied up in a particular firm. Demsetz says, "No owner of a trivial fraction of equity has enough interest or power to take the problem of control [i.e., monitoring] seriously; leaving this task to someone else makes more sense. However, this someone, if he or she is to exist, must own a large personal stake in the firm. An undivided large equity stake requires considerable personal wealth when the efficient size of the firm is large" (1988a, 231).[26] Often, of course, this individual is on the board of directors. And whether he or she is on the board or not, that individual has substantial power and a strong incentive to oust poor managers and/or colluding directors. In this manner, the monitoring problem is addressed—if not completely solved—in the same general way it is solved, for the classical capitalist firm, namely, by making the monitor a residual claimant.

Another part of the solution to the monitoring problem is to be found in the market for corporate control (Manne 1965). If the management of one firm (or a wealthy individual) believes that the management of another firm is not making good use of its assets, they have the incentive to buy up enough shares of the firm to take control and oust ineffective management and/or board members.[27]

An insufficiently appreciated player in this game, who provides valuable information for the equity owners, is the securities analyst. Securities analysts for brokerage firms make it their business to know what managers are doing (or, at least, what they have done in the recent past) with the corporate assets that they control. Because of their connections to players in the securities markets, analysts' judgments of corporate decision making are reflected in the price of stock in the corporation. Corporate managers have been known to make moves (e.g., layoffs, restructuring) to "satisfy the analysts." If a firm's management makes a series of poor decisions, it is usually reflected in the price of the firm's stock on the securities exchanges in short order. Capital markets are like other markets in their knowledge-transmitting properties. A fall in share prices sends a message to all of those who want and need to know—in particular, to equity holders, who are having the value of their assets dissipated. This provides a signal for them to bail out or to get more involved in monitoring than they otherwise might. This service is provided by the securities markets at a nominal cost.

None of this operates perfectly and without opportunistic behavior on the part of all concerned. Indeed, in recent years it seems that many managers of large American corporations have been exploiting stockholders by getting paid—paying themselves—much more than they are worth (though there is some dispute about this). Small investors can get out before they have had too much of the quasi-rent value of their contributions (i.e., equity) leached out by opportunistic corporate executives, but large pension funds and other institutional investors may effectively have nowhere else to go. So the exploitation can continue until and unless the law or the evolution of the open corporation puts a halt to it. On the other hand, this problem does not seem to be endemic to free enterprise systems, since Japanese and German firms do not make the kind of inflated payments to management that their American counterparts do. This suggests that there is something peculiar to the American system that permits this problem to fester. In general, much of what goes under the heading of monitoring management has the form of damage limitation, which is what one would expect in a world of asset specificities, informational asymmetries, and opportunistic players. However, this discussion has identified the means by which the management of large corporations can be monitored in the most effective way possible—by tying the monitoring function to equity ownership.

Free Alienability and Limited Liability of Equity Ownership

All these processes presuppose an effectively functioning securities market in which equity shares are easily tradable. Unlike partnerships, where other equity owners must approve the sale of ownership shares, shares in an open corporation may be freely bought and sold. The buying and selling of shares in the securities market helps to create an informed (though temporary) consensus as to how well a company (i.e., its management) is doing in managing its assets. The securities market also plays a crucial role in the institutional mechanism by which someone or some group can pull the plug on bad management. The lure of entrepreneurial profits that goes with residual claimancy provides the incentive for players with proven ability (viz., those who have won big profits in the past or who have risen to positions of power and authority in other corporations) to act expeditiously to rid the firm of bad management and begin to realize the full potential of the firm's assets.

The limited liability of equity holders consists in the fact that their liability to execution of corporate debt and other obligations is limited to the amount of their investment. By contrast, partners in a partnership are fully liable for all the debts incurred by the partnership. It would not be sensible for individuals with a normal degree of risk aversion to entrust their entire wealth to hired managers without engaging in very extensive monitoring—monitoring that would have to be duplicated by other investors. Moreover, investors would have to investigate how deep their coinvestors' pockets were in order to assess the extent of their potential liability and thus the risk that they face as investors. Limited liability solves both of these problems in a single stroke (Jensen and Meckling 1976, 331; Demsetz 1988b, 114). It also significantly reduces the litigation costs of bankruptcy that would have to be borne by someone if each investor's liability were unlimited. The problems that limited liability creates (primarily, the threat of opportunism from management) are dealt with in the ways already outlined.

This completes the discussion of the transactions cost efficiencies of the open corporation. The cumulative account of these transactions cost efficiencies explains how various role occupiers (capital providers, monitors, etc.) eliminate or limit their exposure to exploitation by others when capital requirements are too large to be met by one individual. What remains to be done is to consider the three additional organizational forms mentioned at the outset of this section: the multidivisional corporation, the closely held or closed corporation, and the partnership. The rationale for discussing these types of organizations is that each would be effectively banned in a market socialist system.

The multidivisional corporation is an open corporation composed of semiautonomous profit centers. A central office monitors the management of the divisions, allocates cash flows among them, and engages in strategic planning.[28] Top management is freed from operational responsibilities and can concentrate on major entrepreneurial and personnel decisions. The divisions themselves are responsible for implementing major decisions, and monitoring of the divisions is largely carried out by a general staff (Williamson 1985, 278–90). This type of corporation represents a kind of scaled-up version of the open corporation. Top management plays a role analogous to a board of directors, though it may take a more active role in what Fama and Jensen call the initiation and ratification steps in the decision-making process (1983b, 303–11). It is a way of bringing still larger amounts of capital under a more spacious decision-making roof while keeping the divisions and divisional managers directly accountable to the market.

To close this section, it would be appropriate to take a brief look at the transactions cost efficiencies of two other types of organizations commonly found in a free enterprise system: the closed corporation and the partnership. The closed corporation is one in which residual claims are restricted to a few individuals who have some special relationship with the main decision agents (e.g., blood or family relations). These relationships either permit better monitoring or lessen the need for monitoring—though when business conditions deteriorate, these very relationships often exacerbate monitoring problems, for familiar reasons.

Because the main decision agents are substantial residual claimants yet do not supply all of the capital, the closed corporation has many of the advantages of both the classical capitalist firm and the open corporation. For example, as in the classical capitalist firm, the chief executive officer bears a considerable proportion of the wealth consequences of his decisions. On the other hand, the closed corporation allows access to larger amounts of capital than the chief executive officer can provide. This permits the firm to realize the transactions cost efficiencies that can attend bringing together large amounts of capital under unitary management. However, as Fama and Jensen point out, the closed corporation also suffers the disadvantages of both these organizational forms (1983b, 306). Restricting residual claims to a small number of individuals forgoes some of the benefits of risk diversification. In addition, restricting decision making to those with wealth who are willing to bear risks limits the pool of decision makers. Finally, minority stockholders, like stockholders in larger corporations, are subject to the usual expropriation hazards (e.g., on-the-job consumption by managers) that go with attenuating the connection between monitoring and residual claimancy.

Partnerships involve consensual decision making by a number of coequal decision agents who share in the residuals. Partnerships have efficiency advantages over alternative organizational forms when most of the firm's capital is human capital embodied in the partners themselves, the deployment of which is difficult to monitor. This organizational form is most common among professionals in fields such as consulting, law, medicine, engineering, and accounting, although medicine may be headed toward the open corporation form as treatments become more standardized and the physical capital requirements associated with advanced medical technology grow increasingly large.

A common feature of partnerships is that there are significant complementarities that each partner brings to the partnership. In these situations, the quasi-rents of the human assets that partners bring to the firm are substantial; without partnership status, those quasi-rents would be highly vulnerable to appropriation. For these reasons, management and residual claimancy are limited to and spread among the partners. It is not completely clear why liability is unlimited in the partnership. Perhaps what is going on here is that the partners are effectively pledging the value of their human capital (which constitutes most of the firm's assets) as a bonding device, that is, as a way of assuring clients and input suppliers (e.g., professional staff who are not partners) that they will fulfill their contractual obligations. In this respect, it plays the same role as nonhuman capital does in a more traditional firm.

The classical capitalist firm, the open corporation, the closed corporation, and the partnership are not the only organizational forms to be found in free enterprise systems. However, existing free enterprise systems are dominated by the first two, and there are numerous instances of the other two types. All four would be essentially prohibited in a market socialist system. From an organizational standpoint, this is the crucial difference between a free enterprise system and a market socialist system. The purpose of this and the preceding section has been to explain the transactions cost efficiencies of these organizational forms as a way of explaining how they preclude or limit opportunities for exploitative exchange. The points of contrast with the worker cooperative are implicit in this discussion; they will be made fully explicit in the next two chapters.

The Employment Relation in a Free Enterprise System

The discussion of the central contracting agent in the classical capitalist firm explains how the authority relation can prevent input providers from exploiting the firm by forcing contract renegotiations when unforeseen contingencies arise, but it does not explain what prevents the firm from exploiting input providers. This raises a prior—and, from a socialist point of view, a more important—question: Are workers in a free enterprise system systematically exploited by the firms that hire them? The "systematically" qualifier is important, since the discussion is about free enterprise systems in the abstract not particular free enterprise systems as they exist "on the ground." Historical accident and a host of nonsystemic contingencies can be responsible for any number of exploitative exchanges in any particular free enterprise system or, indeed, in any other economic system. The question at issue in this and all other discussions like it is whether or not there is something about the system itself that is responsible for all, or nearly all, workers' being exploited in a free enterprise system.

Another reason for addressing this question at the systemic level is that the employment relation in a free enterprise system is fundamentally different from that relation in a market socialist system because of differences in the structures of the predominant organizational forms. For these reasons, a comparative evaluation of the two types of systems on the question of exploitation requires an examination of this relation in both types of systems. This section discusses the question of whether or not firms in a free enterprise system systematically exploit labor; the second section of chapter 6 will discuss the same question in reference to a market socialist system.

It has been a staple of socialist and leftist thought for the past century and a half that the workers are systematically exploited in a free enterprise system. Chapter 3 critically discussed in a cursory way, some of the standard Marxist and socialist arguments for this.[29] All of these arguments have been found wanting. The main problem is that the alleged exploiter, the capitalist, is making a contribution as a provider of capital, and so the requisite failure of reciprocity has not been established. Even if all these arguments fail, however, that does not prove that the workers are not systematically exploited in a free enterprise system. It just means that these particular arguments do not show it. Some other argument might establish this conclusion. How then to proceed?

The framework for discussing exploitation provided in the last chapter will prove useful in this regard. Let us begin by identifying the general conditions that would have to be met for a worker to be exploited by a firm in a market economy generally. It will then be possible to address the question of whether or not these conditions are standardly met in the employment relation in a free enterprise system.

A worker's asset is his or her capacity to labor. Either that asset has appropriable quasi-rents attached to it or it does not. Suppose it does not. This implies one of two things: either his assets have no quasi-rents at all or the quasi-rents are not appropriable. If the former is the case, the worker would earn about the same wage he would get if that asset were deployed in its next best use; this would be the case with unskilled labor in a tight labor market. If there are quasi-rents associated with his labor assets but they are not appropriable, that means that there are competitors willing to offer the worker about the value of what he is selling. For example, doctors have highly specialized skills, and the next best use for their capacity to labor is generally not nearly as attractive; nevertheless, the quasi-rent value of their assets is well protected because demand for their services as doctors is high, and alternative employers are relatively easy to find.

Notice that given the way the concepts 'quasi-rent' and 'appropriable quasi-rent' are defined (Klein, Crawford, and Alchian 1978, 298), there is no implication that the asset owner in question knows about the other potential purchaser(s) of what he is selling. All that matters is that there are other potential purchasers out there, so to speak. There does seem to be a tacit supposition to the effect that if an asset owner's quasi-rents are nonappropriable, then both the asset owner and the purchaser of the asset's services know this and act accordingly. If this were the case, then if the worker's assets have no appropriable quasi-rents, then ipso facto he gets the full value of his assets. However, suppose that the quasi-rents meet the definition of nonappropriability in the sense that there are other purchasers out there willing to pay the full value of the asset, but the asset owner does not know about these other purchasers out there waiting to be found at a reasonable search (and asset redeployment) cost. Such an asset owner has simply failed to search out these other purchasers. This means that while the quasi-rent value of his asset may not be appropriable according to the definition, some of that asset's value may get appropriated anyway, since the asset owner did not avail himself of his next best opportunity.

In the case of a worker, this means that a worker may fail to get the full value of his services because he does not know about, or has not sought out, better alternative employment opportunities. As in the case described in chapter 3 of the woman who sold the heirloom, this worker does not get a "fair" price for what he is selling, since part of the value of his labor has been appropriated by the purchaser. However, even though he is not getting the value of his contribution, he is not being exploited in this situation because there are available alternatives that he has simply failed to investigate or discover. Recall that there are two necessary conditions for exploitation: the person is not getting the value of what he contributes, and he effectively has nowhere else to go. In this situation, though he is not getting the full value of his contribution, he does have somewhere else to go, namely, to another purchaser of his services who is willing to pay him the full value of his services.

The upshot of all this is that if the workers are systematically exploited in the employment relation, part of the value of their labor assets must be appropriable quasi-rents. If the quasi-rents of their assets are nonexistent, then they are getting the full value of their contribution. On the other hand, if their assets have associated quasi-rents but they are not appropriable in the sense implied by the definition, then whether or not they are paid the full value of their respective contributions, the workers are not being exploited. Conversely, if a worker's assets have quasi-rents and they are appropriable, then some of the value of those assets can be appropriated without his being in a position to do anything about it; that is, he is in a position to be exploited.

The question now becomes, Does this happen on a regular basis and for systematic reasons in a free enterprise system? What is needed to sustain a positive answer to this question is some structural feature of free enterprise systems that leaves all or nearly all workers' quasi-rents permanently exposed. One apparently promising candidate for that feature is the alleged fact that firms exercise disproportionate bargaining power in contract negotiations with prospective workers. The way this is usually explained is that it is easier for employers to find workers to accept a low wage (i.e., one that is less than the value of the worker's labor) than it is for a worker to turn that offer down. Unlike the firm, the worker has nowhere else to go. This is why workers are in general exploited by the firms that hire them. The problem with this is that as an explanation, it is a non-starter: it simply restates the allegation to be proved. The reason is that to say that an employer actually exercises (and not merely has) disproportionate bargaining power in contract negotiations with worker X is to say three things: (1) the employer's offer is less than the value of worker X's labor, (2) the employer's next best alternative to hiring worker X at the offered rate is as good or better than hiring worker X (suppose it is to hire a comparable worker at the same wage); and (3) worker X's next best alternative is about the same or significantly worse than accepting that offer. In this way, X would be in a position to have the quasi-rent value of his assets appropriated. But the problem is to explain how or why this comes to pass and what sustains this phenomenon once it does happen. It is of no explanatory help to assert that it does. In other words, the claim that the worker is systematically exploited by his or her employer cannot be justified by the proposition that employers exercise disproportionate bargaining power in their contract negotiations with employees. The latter proposition simply restates the former.

One phenomenon that might do some explanatory work in this context (and thus serve to justify the claim about exploitation) is that free enterprise systems produce downturns in the business cycle that bottom out in recession or depression. It might be argued that when macroeconomic conditions take a turn for the worse, workers are not in a position to flee if and when firms make a grab for their quasi-rents, which they could do by, for example, asking for give-backs or by not giving raises to match the rate of inflation. It might be further argued that continued erratic economic performance, including high rates of unemployment, makes it possible for firms to persist in offering workers less than the value of their contributions.

There are two problems with this line of argument. One is that it assumes that free enterprise systems are inherently unstable at the macro level. Among economists who favor the free enterprise system, there is a long tradition of disputing this. They have argued that depressions and recessions in existing societies with free enterprise systems are state-induced destabilizations brought on by the latter's inflation or deflation of the money supply.[30] If their analysis is correct, free enterprise systems are not inherently unstable at the macro level, so that even if the workers are exploited in the way suggested, it is not the free enterprise system that is responsible. It is instead the state or the political system that is to blame.

But even if that is not true and a free enterprise system (i.e., any free enterprise system) is inherently unstable at the macro level, the conditions that accompany depressions and recessions do not allow the workers to be exploited by the firms that hire them. Vulnerable though they may be, the workers' problem under these circumstances is not exploitation. To see why, recall from chapter 3 that the value of an asset is determined by what it would fetch in a competitively efficient market or on the leading edge of a market in transition, where a competitively efficient market is defined in terms of a local equilibrium in the determinants of the scarcity value (e.g., natural resources, labor skills, technology, distribution of wealth and income) of the asset in question.[31] In times of changing economic conditions, the value of assets, including labor assets, is changing; in a depression or recession, that change is usually in the direction of a decline.

This means that if an asset earns a lower return than it used to, it does not follow that its owner is having some of its value appropriated by the purchaser of that asset or the asset's service. The terms of the exchange may be on the leading edge of a market in transition. For example, if aggregate demand has fallen precipitously in a depression, workers may find they have no choice but to take a cut in wages. Since the underlying value of their assets has declined, however, this cut reflects a revaluation of their assets and not the appropriation of quasi-rents by their employer. Indeed, if their wages are contractually guaranteed for a period that extends into the new macroeconomic environment, they are in a position to exploit their employers; they would be getting more than the value of what they are contributing, and their employer would have nowhere else to go. To take another example, population growth or immigration may make the workforce grow faster than new workers can be absorbed by the economy; once again, workers may find that they have no choice but to take a cut in wages. Although the workers are suffering a decline in wages, they are nonetheless getting the full value, including the quasi-rent value, of their assets. It may be unfortunate—indeed, it may even be unjust according to some conceptions of justice—that workers undergo the accompanying hardships while (one may suppose) their bosses or the firm's owners do not. But the former are not being exploited by the latter. The firm's owners or managers are simply bringing the workers the bad news about the declining value of what the workers are selling, namely, their labor. Employers get this bad news when they sell the firm's products in the market; they then pass the news on to workers as quickly as possible. As has been repeatedly urged in this book, markets serve an important information-transmitting function in a world of changing economic conditions.

The general point here has other applications. Suppose that the market for teachers in a free enterprise system is competitively efficient, as that notion was defined in chapter 3. Someone might nevertheless believe that teachers are exploited because their pay is so low relative to jobs that are, or seem to be, much less socially valuable. According to this socialist, this is a classic example of a "social irrationality" thrown up by the operation of the market. However, whether or not it is a social irrationality, it is not an instance of exploitation. Why not? It may be true that if the distribution of wealth and income were different, teachers would make much more—and others with jobs judged less important, much less—than under the existing system. It may even be that at some level, justice requires a different distribution of wealth and income. However, neither proposition changes the fact that the teachers are getting the value of their contributions and thus are not exploited.

Indeed, the complaint against this society can be usefully rephrased as a complaint against its values, as those values have emerged in and through the market. The free enterprise system is the messenger which brings the news about the value of people's contributions. Sometimes the news is not good. A paradoxical way of making this point is to say that what is wrong with this society, according to our hypothetical socialist teacher, is that its values are so twisted that teachers can make paltry salaries and yet not be exploited![32] This is true even if a free enterprise system is responsible for creating those values, which (supposing all of this to be true) constitutes yet further grounds for criticism of this type of system. A general lesson here, as in chapter 3, is that it is important that the charge of exploitation not be conflated with other charges a social critic might want to make against a free enterprise system.

Is there any other way that workers might have their quasi-rents systematically appropriated? Perhaps the most promising place to look is cases in which employees make relatively specific investments in developing their skills or knowledge; then, once the fundamental transformation has taken place and they have entered into a long-term employment relation, they may have no comparable alternative employment opportunities. Under these circumstances, their quasi-rents would be vulnerable to appropriation by opportunistic employers.

However, a number of policies or procedures have evolved in existing free enterprise systems to protect workers' quasi-rents under these circumstances. One form of protection is the collective bargaining agreement. Some features of collective bargaining serve to limit the exposure of the quasi-rents of employees' relatively specific assets, whether they are intended to have this effect or not. Union contracts typically require that the company observe due process before firing workers. This serves not only to protect workers who have built up firm-specific assets but also as a counterweight to the fact that dismissal imposes disproportionate costs on workers (of whatever skill level) because of its disruptive effects on family and social life. Unions also negotiate other personnel practices and evaluate wage and benefit offers (Reid and Faith 1980; Freeman and Medoff 1979). In this way, knowledgeable negotiators can help to ensure that workers are receiving the approximate value of their labor assets; if they are getting that value, then despite the fundamental transformation that locks them into that employment relation, they are not being exploited.

Indeed, it is possible to give a transactions cost explanation for the existence (or persistence) of unions.[33] What unions do is bring large amounts of human capital under one decision-making roof. When workers are unionized, firms bargain not with individual workers but with the larger collective entity that represents them. Unions effect a kind of horizontal integration of human capital. This can serve to protect the quasi-rent values of their members' assets in a manner that parallels the protection provided by vertical integration of the quasi-rent values of nonhuman assets. Of course, unions own neither their members nor their members' human capital, so they are not the asset owners but their agents. This raises the possibility of principal-agent problems, problems that have been serious in cases where the union leadership has used the assets at its disposal to further a personal or political agenda not endorsed by the membership. In some cases, their only real monitor has been the Mafia (an organization known for its effectiveness in monitoring).

These problems to one side, the efficiency functions that unions serve are, of course, not their only functions; they also serve a monopoly function and a more political, "voice" function (Hirschman 1970)—which leads, among other things, to reduced income inequality among workers (Freeman and Medoff 1979). Arguably, both functions are, at bottom, exploitative. The coercive and quasi-coercive power that unions wield effectively closes off alternatives for employers and prospective nonunion employees, and it allows unions and their members to appropriate the quasi-rents of the firm's equity owners.[34] If unions or their members are exploiters, however, it would not be the first time that an organization that serves to mitigate some social vice in one respect aggravates that very problem in some other respect.

Absent unions, what institutional structures are available to employees to protect the value of the relatively specific assets they bring to the job? As a way of enticing prospective employees, employers will often voluntarily adopt personnel policies and procedures (such as due process rights) to ensure that workers will not be fired or have their pay cut unless it is warranted by changes in economic conditions and thus in the value of their services. Another way that firms can bond their promises not to act opportunistically toward employees is to pay substantial severance pay to those whom it lets go. This serves the double function of providing the dismissed employee with a cushion against the blow of temporary unemployment and of binding the employer to a policy of laying off employees only if business conditions require it. These and other "up-front" policies are usually more effective than a firm's general reputation, which may be distorted or not widely known among prospective employees. Reputation effects do, however, have their role to play in purely local markets.

Sometimes the ways in which employees' transaction-specific assets are protected are not directly evident; the up-or-out system in corporate law firms (also common in other professions), which was discussed in the last chapter, is a case in point. To put this in terms of the protection of quasi-rents, recall that associate attorneys develop substantial firm-specific assets during the probationary period leading up to the partnership decision. Toward the end of that probationary period, the associate is being billed out at a relatively high rate and yet is not making anything close to what she is earning for the firm (even taking into account overhead, etc.). Because some of her assets are so firm-specific, her next best alternative employment opportunity might be significantly worse than staying on as an associate at that particular firm. Clearly, no one would want to leave her quasi-rents exposed for too long, especially to lawyers. Commitment to the up-or-out policy prevents this from happening. By publicly adopting this policy, the firm effectively commits itself to making the partnership decision on the merits of the case, since it cannot opportunistically deny the associate promotion and then turn around and offer to keep her on indefinitely at her current rank and pay, thereby appropriating the considerable quasi-rents that she has built up over the years.

Notice that just as employees are potentially vulnerable to opportunism by firms, so, too, are firms potentially vulnerable to having the quasi-rents of their assets opportunistically appropriated by employees. The firm may make a capital investment in equipment especially designed for a particular employee, or, more commonly, it may spend resources to train an employee for his or her job. This training, which the employee gets to keep, as it were, may consist wholly or in part of knowledge and skills that can be redeployed elsewhere. It is as if the firm gives the employee a tool that it cannot take back when the employee leaves the firm. How do firms protect investments like this from being opportunistically appropriated by their employees?

One way is by not vesting workers in a pension until they have accumulated many years on the job (Mortenson 1978; Becker 1962). This gives workers a strong incentive not to quit before retirement. Other ways include tying pay to positions, instead of to individuals, and promoting from within on the basis of merit (Putterman 1984, 176). This encourages individuals to stay with the firm and use the skills they have acquired to benefit the firm. Finally, a firm may involve the employee in a process of social conditioning so that he or she identifies with the firm and its goals. This is especially important in team production, which requires a high degree of cooperation among its members. Foulkes contends that the fiercely egalitarian treatment of managers and workers in many Japanese firms and some American firms is an instance of this type of conditioning and serves to protect the firm's investments in human capital and the value of other specialized assets employed by the team (Foulkes 1981).

Alternatively, when these values or investments cannot be protected, the firm simply pays the employee less than the value of her services for as long as it can as a way of recouping its investment in the employee that will be lost when the employee quits. For example, the career path in major public accounting firms provides opportunities for staff accountants to acquire extremely valuable knowledge of the workings of various industries (financial institutions, real estate, manufacturing, health care, insurance, etc.), as well as knowledge of how particular client firms operate. This involves not just learning by doing but also specialized and costly training sessions paid for by the firm.

These accountants are very often hired away in two or three years by the very firms and industries they have audited. Accounting firms compensate themselves for this lost investment in their employees by underpaying and overworking everyone on the professional staff below the rank of partner. They also benefit by having former staff accountants in client firms because their former employees can shape the client firm's accounting policies and procedures to facilitate the yearly audit, thereby making it possible for the accounting firm to underbid its rivals. Staff accountants who stay on to become partners in the public accounting firm recoup this underpayment, as do those who leave the firm in a few years with their newly acquired human capital for more lucrative opportunities outside of public accounting. Very few stay on the career path in public accountancy for more than few years but less than what it takes to be nominated for partner. Though these employees are not being paid the value of their services, they are not, in general, being exploited because they have alternative employment opportunities. Up to a point, the longer they stay on, the better those alternatives get. This way of dealing with the problem of unsecured human capital must be carefully handled, however, if the firm is not to create a bad reputation and, as a result, suffer an adverse selection problem when they go to recruit new staff accountants.[35]

Policies and procedures such as those just described protect the quasi-rent values that both firms and workers bring to the exchange that constitutes the employment relation. The real question now becomes: Are policies and procedures of this sort the exception or the rule? In other words, are the quasi-rents of firms and their employees in general protected from each other in free enterprise systems? The answer in large measure depends on whether or not the evolutionary hypothesis that underlies transactions cost analysis is true, at least as it applies to the employment relation. This hypothesis starts with the observation that in a free enterprise system, people are free to craft whatever contractual arrangements they find mutually beneficial. Competitive pressures in such a system will tend to select out those policies and procedures that minimize transactions costs. One the main types of transactions costs to be minimized are the potential expropriation hazards that each side faces from the other side. If employment policies and procedures evolve that minimize these costs, then workers (and the firms that hire them) will tend to get the value of what they bring to the employment transaction. In such circumstances, the quasi-rent values of workers' specialized assets will tend to be protected, as will the quasi-rent values of the assets that support the wage offers that employers make.

While it is likely that there is a tendency for this sort of thing to happen, it is not obvious how strong it is or whether there are any countertendencies or other factors at work in the other direction. In other words, while there may be a tendency for workers to get the value of their labor contribution and thus not be exploited, no evidence has been offered that this tendency always or usually works itself out rather than being held up or counteracted by some countertendency or some other endogenous factor operative in any free enterprise system. It is at least possible that this happens and that those affected have nowhere else to go. In short, it still seems at least possible that most or nearly all workers are systematically exploited in a free enterprise system.

Though this remains a possibility, it can be argued that it is nevertheless quite unlikely. The argument proceeds by reductio ad absurdum. Suppose that most or nearly all workers (the "most or nearly all" qualifier will henceforth be suppressed) are exploited by their employers. According to the definition of exploitation developed in chapter 3, this means that they are not getting the value of their contributions and have no real alternative but to accept the wage they have been offered. If they are not getting the value of their respective contributions, it is either because they are in a stagnant market (i.e., a market that is neither competitively efficient, nor in the process of becoming competitively efficient, nor highly volatile) or because they are in a market in transition but the exchange they are making is not on the leading edge of that market. Suppose the latter. Given that the market is in transition, it is on the way to becoming competitively efficient. Therefore the workers will be getting the value of their contributions and thus will not be exploited. Moreover, if they are not on the leading edge of a market in transition, an exchange on the leading edge will often be available or accessible at a reasonable search and redeployment cost, in which case they do have a real alternative to their current situation and thus are not being exploited.

Realistically, the only way that the workers could be systematically exploited is if labor markets are and always have been stagnant, that is, neither competitively efficient nor in transition to becoming competitively efficient.[36] Suppose, then, that this is the case. Further suppose that the workers have no real alternative but to accept the terms they do accept. This means that all of the alternatives are about the same or much worse. Suppose, first, that they are about the same. This means that, in general, workers are getting less than the value of their contributions and that everywhere they turn, the prospects are about the same. How could this happen? One way is through collusion among employers.[37] They could have all got together and agreed to hold down wages. The problem with that scenario, aside from the lack of any empirical evidence to support it, is that it ignores the fact that a cartel-like arrangement of this sort creates obvious incentives to violate it. An entrepreneur who offered workers slightly higher wages and charged slightly lower prices could increase sales, market share, and net profits. A self-reinforcing process would get underway, which means that the market would be in transition and on its way to ensuring that workers got the full value of their contributions. This is not to say that collusion never happens, but it is unreasonable to posit it as a permanent and universal feature of free enterprise systems. What makes it unreasonable is the internal dynamics of the quest for entrepreneurial profit in this type of system. Admittedly, collusion is not the only possibility. Nevertheless, whatever explanation might be offered, the fact remains that if labor markets are consistently stagnant, there are profit opportunities there to be seized— opportunities that entrepreneurs are consistently unwilling or unable to seize. On the face of it, this seems quite implausible.

Still operating under the supposition that labor markets are stagnant, consider now the possibility that the workers' alternatives to their present situation are much worse. Perhaps their only alternative is to accept public relief, which is much worse than continuing to work at their jobs for less than the value of their labor. But if this were true of most workers most of the time, one would observe very little labor mobility throughout the history of free enterprise systems. (Indeed, the same phenomenon would be observed if their alternatives were all about the same.) Having no real alternative but to accept the positions they are currently in, most workers would not change jobs, except insofar as such changes are occasioned by the gyrations of the business cycle. In point of fact, however, this has not been the case. Historically, free enterprise systems have been remarkably dynamic, especially when government involvement has been minimal. People change jobs often even when macroeconomic conditions are relatively stable, and such systems have set off some of the largest and most successful peaceful migrations in human history. Labor mobility is a fact of life for large segments of the population who do not have the security of tenure or the civil service.[38] The fact of labor mobility refutes the idea that all, or nearly all, workers in a free enterprise system are usually in a situation where all the alternatives are considerably worse than continuing to do what they have been doing.

Whatever the alternatives, the possibility that workers are consistently being paid less than the value of their labor presupposes that there are persistent profit opportunities that innovative entrepreneurs are unwilling or unable to seize. This sits uneasily with a widely shared belief, even among socialists, that a distinctive feature of free enterprise systems is a prodigious capacity for innovation on the part of entrepreneurs. It is hard to believe that at least some of the creative, clever, and highly self-interested people who control productive resources in these systems are not innovative enough to discover a way to exploit workers a little less than they are being exploited, thereby setting in motion a self-reinforcing process that ends up with workers getting about the value of their contributions. Socialists have yet to come up with a plausible explanation of what would repeatedly stop this process short of equilibrium.

If the picture of the employment relation sketched in this section is accurate, it does not follow that no worker is ever exploited. What is at issue is the claim that all or nearly all workers are consistently or persistently exploited in a free enterprise system. The denial of this claim is consistent with the proposition that some workers are sometimes exploited in such systems. Indeed, the latter would be difficult to deny. Exploitation of workers can and does take place. Labor markets are sometimes stagnant, which results in workers' not getting the value of their labor contribution and some of these workers effectively have nowhere else to go. In addition, exogenous changes, or shocks, can uncover previously protected quasi-rents, which employers are then in a position to appropriate. However, as employees in a firm, industry, or region have their quasi-rents appropriated by their employers, they and others eventually "wise up" and develop their talents and abilities in other directions or else migrate, as the case may be. If a clever entrepreneur can develop a governance structure to protect these quasi-rents, that firm will be able to prosper at the expense of its "greedier" rivals who cannot resist grabbing for their workers' quasi-rents. Workers will develop specialized talents and abilities and mutually beneficial exchanges will go through that otherwise would not, or else exchanges will take place at a lower rate than they would if they had to include a premium to compensate workers for placing firm-specific assets at risk. Though exploitation will take place in any free enterprise system and, indeed, in any market economy, it will not be a pervasive and systemic phenomenon afflicting most workers for most of their working lives, as socialist critics of the free enterprise have maintained down through the years.

6

Exploitation in a
Market Socialist Economy I

More Methodological Considerations

Worker cooperatives can be found throughout the world and are not a new phenomenon. Two that are most prominently mentioned in the socialist literature are the self-managed firms in what used to be Yugoslavia and the collection of cooperatives near the town of Mondragon in the Basque region of Spain. There are significant differences between the two types of cooperatives, as well as differences in the larger economic environment in which these organizations are found. More important for the purposes of this book, there are also significant differences between them and the organizations that would exist in the type of market socialist system outlined in chapter 2. After all—and in contrast to free enterprise systems—this type of system has never existed before. It is worth spending some time explaining these differences and exploring the significance of the fact that the type of socialist system under discussion has never existed anywhere in the world before.

In the years since World War II and prior to the country's dissolution in the 1990s, the Yugoslav economic system underwent a number of profound and dramatic changes.[1] Indeed, the constitution changed so often that the suggestion has been made that it should have been kept, along with the French constitution, in the periodicals section of libraries. In its least Stalinist incarnation, most of the firms in the Yugoslav economy were (and at this writing, still are) self-managed cooperatives. The workers do not have unrestricted rights of self-management: not only are they required to maintain the value of their capital, but they have also had to share ultimate decision-making authority with political officials. Local government officials (and especially the Communist party) have had significant influence in choosing the managers. However, through their workers' councils, workers have also had a say about who the managers are and about other matters (e.g., work rules) that directly affect them.

In the Yugoslav cooperative, the workers have been the residual claimants—after a fashion and subject to various restrictions (Sirc 1979,

18–19, 45). The economy is a market economy, which means that firms are free to set prices at whatever the traffic would bear, subject to state veto and other forms of state interference. In point of fact, the state has often intervened and set prices that reflected various other economic and, indeed, political concerns (Estrin and Bartlett 1982, 88–89). So although it has been officially a free market economy as far as prices are concerned, in point of fact, it has been a regulated market with many prices set outside of the market process. New investment has been funded by the cooperatives and the state in varying proportions over the years, with some funds generated by a tax on the cooperatives' capital assets. This tax is analogous to the capital usage fee of market socialism. When these funds are disbursed by political organizations, both market and nonmarket decision-making criteria have been used.

Despite some similarities, there are four substantial differences between this system and the type of market socialist system described in chapter 2. First, unlike the Yugoslav system, in a market socialist system only those who work in the firm have ultimate decision-making authority. This means that the enterprises cannot be state-controlled. Second, the price system is supposed to work relatively unhampered—about as unhampered as it does in existing free enterprise systems. Proponents of market socialism implicitly recognize that the market has important information-transmitting capabilities that are seriously impeded by various forms of administered prices, so widespread interference with the pricing mechanism is not supposed to happen in a market socialist system, as it did in Yugoslavia. Third, the extent of state control of new investment has varied considerably over the years in Yugoslavia, whereas under market socialism, the state is supposed to control most new investment. Also, the mechanism of control has been left unspecified for market socialism, which makes the relevance of the Yugoslav experience less clear in this respect. Finally, perhaps the most profound difference between a market socialist economic system and the Yugoslav economic system is that the former is assumed to exist within a democratic political framework. By contrast, the latter existed in a nondemocratic political framework dominated by the Communist party, which, in its various national manifestations, has been arguably the preeminent economic wrecking crew in all of human history.

The fact of communist political control of the economy (not to mention the smoldering ethnic hostilities) obviously had something to do with the various economic disasters that befell Yugoslavia before its dissolution. Perhaps one of the most harmful aspects of communist rule was their unwillingness and inability to stabilize property rights. This manifested itself in two ways: (1) the basic constitution, which specified how property rights in the means of production were to be specified and distributed, was frequently revised; and (2) residual rights of control in the firm (as well as rights to the firm's residual income) have never been clearly defined. The party always reserved the right to intervene in the affairs of firms and entire industries in arbitrary and unpredictable ways. Even a cursory study of the Yugoslav economy makes it evident that considerable time and effort were devoted to trying to anticipate, encourage, and/or thwart various forms and manifestations of state intervention. This resulted in a situation in which the question, Who is really in charge of the means of production? had no answer. At least in theory, these problems are not supposed to afflict a market socialist system. Property rights are assumed to be stable and the role of the state is assumed to be relatively clearly defined, that is, about as clearly defined as the state's role in existing free enterprise systems. In light of these considerations and because of the other, more purely organizational, differences between the Yugoslav economic system and a market socialist system, the evidence from what used to be Yugoslavia will be of limited usefulness in what it can tell us about exploitation in a market socialist system of the sort described in chapter 2.

The evidence from Mondragon is also likely to be of limited usefulness but for rather different reasons.[2] The Mondragon experiment is a collection of interrelated cooperatives, including an investment bank, in the Basque region of Spain. These cooperatives have enjoyed some measure of success over the years and are often pointed to as real-world exemplars of socialist ideals. There are some important similarities and differences between them and the Yugoslav cooperatives. As in the case of the latter, the workers in Mondragon have decision-making authority in the cooperatives, which means that they elect a supervisory board, which appoints management. However, unlike the situation in the former Yugoslavia, only the workers have ultimate decision-making authority. This means that political authorities have no representation on the supervisory board. Another difference is that the workers of Mondragon have an equity stake in the firm. They are required to pay an entry fee roughly equivalent to one year's pay when they join a cooperative in the system. Some of this goes into a collective equity account for the cooperative, and some goes into their own individual equity accounts. Each year, individual equity accounts are credited with 6 percent interest. This represents a "normal" rate of return on capital and is a way of taking account of the scarcity value of capital. The firm pays out these accumulated individual equity accounts when the worker leaves the firm or retires. Equity accounts cannot be sold to outsiders or to other workers. Each year, some funds, including part of any entry fees collected in that year, go into a collective equity account, which is never paid out. Residuals over and above these capital usage payments are distributed to the workers according to various formulae. Outside debt financing comes from a cooperative investment bank, the Caja Laboral Popular, which is part of the larger Mondragon system.

One obvious and important difference between Mondragon and market socialism concerns the ownership of capital. In the Mondragon cooperatives, the ultimate decision-making authorities (the workers) are the owners of the firm's capital (subject to certain limitations and restrictions). Although the workers are also the ultimate decision-making authorities in a market socialist system, they do not own the capital their firms employ; the state does. This means that in such a system it is at least possible for those who control the means of production to exploit the capital providers. This possibility is foreclosed in Mondragon by the fact that the workers *are* the capital providers. A second important difference between market socialism and Mondragon is that the external economic environment for Mondragon consists of conventional firms (open corporations, classical capitalist firms, etc.). If the cooperatives do not perform well, either for their clients or for their workers, they will lose business and workers to these more traditional organizations. The latter provide an actual or potential disciplinary force of alternative organizational forms for the Mondragon cooperatives that would be absent in the one-organization environment of market socialism. This is especially important for assessing the potential for exploitation in the system because if someone has real alternatives to his situation, then he is not being exploited, even if he is receiving less than the monetary value of his contribution (something to which he might acquiesce because of other, nonmonetary benefits that attend membership in the cooperative).

These points touch on an issue that goes beyond the scope of this book but have a bearing on the broader question of the material relevance of Mondragon for modern industrial economies. The broader question, which has been systematically investigated by Bradley and Gelb (1982), is whether or not the Mondragon experiment could be replicated and sustained on a much larger scale. Their conclusions can only be described as pessimistic:

> Basque ethnicity per se does not appear to be so major a factor as to prevent the replication of Mondragon. More problematical are linkages with local communities and limited labor mobility: first, these two factors appear to contribute to the maintenance of consensus; second, they partially insulate the cooperatives from competitive pressures from the external labor market, permitting a more compressed payments scale; third, limitation of the cooperateur horizons helps to retain capital by reducing the desire to remit savings to distant areas while working. Fourth, low labor turnover is vital for the maintenance of cooperative equity capital. Cooperative survival may not be easy in a fluid labor market with general labor mobility and technology changes. (1982, 168)

The authors also point out that various screening procedures adopted by the cooperatives, including a substantial entry fee, produce an unrepresentative sample of workers, even when contrasted to a control group of Basques in the Mondragon region (1982, 163–67). This type of cooperative might be hard pressed if it had to take on the highly heterogeneous and mobile labor force (not to mention some of the charmers from capitalism's underclass) that exists in the rest of the world. These three factors—different organizational structure, a different external economic environment, and a selection bias that shapes the membership of the Mondragon cooperatives—should serve as a warning about making inferences from what has happened in the Mondragon experiment to what would happen in a market socialist system. And, as noted, similar considerations apply in the case of the Yugoslav experience. In contrast to free enterprise systems, which exist in many versions around the world, market socialism is a fundamentally different type of economic system that has never existed anywhere in the world before. Of course, this does not mean that the empirical records of Yugoslavia and Mondragon are irrelevant, but those records do not tell us as much as one might initially suppose.

How, then, shall we proceed in the absence of significant empirical evidence that has a direct bearing on what would happen in a market socialist system? Fortunately, the theoretical apparatus developed in chapter 4 and deployed in chapter 5 is well suited to providing a basis for reasonable and informed speculation, at least about the incidence of exploitation in a market socialist system (the main concern of chapters 6–8). Recall from the end of chapter 4 that there are four general features of any market economy that make exploitative exchange possible: (1) assets that support many exchanges are specialized and thus have quasi-rents associated with them, (2) these assets get locked into transactions in the sense that they are costly to redeploy once they are committed, (3) the owners of these assets suffer from bounded rationality and make agreements in an environment in which not all future contingencies can be foreseen, and (4) transactors are sometimes given to opportunism on behalf of themselves or on behalf of others (e.g., the firms they represent). This penchant for opportunism is variable across individuals and is not easily knowable. Chapter 5 makes it clear that organizational forms, by virtue of their transactions cost attributes, deal with this potential for exploitation more or less satisfactorily.

This provides the basis for an evaluation of a market socialist system on the question of exploitation because the predominant organizational form—the worker cooperative—has been specified in enough detail in chapter 2 to permit an identification and discussion of its transactions cost attributes and thus its potential for exploitation. This is the topic of chapters 6 and 7. Specifically, it will be argued that the organizational structure of a market socialist economy would permit and encourage forms of exploitation that a free enterprise system precludes or minimizes. Before developing that argument, some objections to the approach being taken here need to be ventilated and discussed. This will simultaneously address some legitimate concerns about the essentially theoretical approach to these questions advocated here and permit a better appreciation of the argument that is to come.

The four background conditions identified, which make exploitative exchange possible, are assumed to hold for any market economy. But suppose this is not true. Then it would not matter whether the organizational structure of a market socialist system is vulnerable to exploitation, since it would be vulnerable to a problem that would not arise. This means that it is important to verify that these conditions would, in fact, hold. The first and second—that many assets are fairly specific and costly to redeploy—

are noncontroversial. Any economic system will face that fact. The third assumption—that people suffer from bounded rationality and limited foresight—is also fairly obvious. Trotsky once said that the *average* new communist human being would be capable of the intellectual achievements of Aristotle and Marx and that new peaks would rise above these heights. But even if that were true of market socialist men and women, it would not be of much help in, say, negotiating the merger of two firms. Not only would each side have their Marxes and Aristotles, but some third party might have a razor-sharp mergers-and-acquisitions lawyer who would take both sides to the cleaners. This brings us to the only controversial assumption— the assumption about opportunism. Is it plausible to assume that the people in a market socialist economy would be about as opportunistic as people in free enterprise systems? This, I suspect, is an assumption most proponents of market socialism would be reluctant to grant. And unless it is granted, the problem of the potential for exploitation in a market socialist system simply goes away.

To evaluate this concern, it is important to be clear about exactly what is being assumed. First, the assumption is not that people would be about as opportunistic in a market socialist system as they are in any existing free enterprise system. There are a number of reasons for this. One is that the incidence of opportunistic behavior (including exploitation) in any actually existing economic system, whatever its type or subtype, is likely to be a function of a number of factors, some of which have little or nothing to do with the economic system. For example, popular wisdom has it that Japanese workers are much less given to shirking than their American counterparts. In addition, executive pay scales in Japan seem to indicate that corporate managers are less opportunistic in their dealings with shareholders than are many American executives whose pay seems to bear little relation to their contributions. If these two observations are correct, then the incidence of exploitation differs in these two actually existing free enterprise systems. However, it is likely that historical and cultural factors explain much of these differences in the incidence of exploitation. The basic point underlying this illustration is important for understanding the nature of the main argument of chapters 6 and 7 and so warrants further elaboration.

The discussion that follows does not predict how much exploitation (or, more generally, opportunistic behavior) would take place in a *society* with a market socialist economic system. The reason for this is that a society with this type of economic system, like any other society, would have other social institutions in addition to its economic system. Moreover, other noninstitutional social forces would also be at work in such a society. These other institutions and forces interact with the economic system in unimaginably complex ways. The actual incidence of exploitation in any society will be a function of many factors, some of them extraeconomic. What chapters 6 and 7 focus on are opportunities for and methods of exploitation in a market socialist economic system, considered in abstraction from these other factors or disturbing influences. Proponents of market socialism might want to argue that other institutions (notably, the political system) or other forces in a socialist society would preempt the exploitation that would otherwise take place because of the nature of the economic system. However, this is not an argument that market socialists, qua socialists, are in a good position to make. As chapter 2 indicates, most of the motivation for a market socialist economic system is to be found in a widely shared diagnosis of the ills of capitalist society. What makes them ills of *capitalist* society is that the economic system is to blame for these problems. The promise of market socialism is that the favored type of economic system would preclude, extinguish, or significantly reduce these social ills. The problems are alleged to be in the economic system, and that is where the solution is supposed to be found as well. After all, this is why radical change in the economic system is being advocated. Independent of these ad hominem considerations, it would be implausible to maintain that the actual incidence of economic exploitation would not be significantly determined by factors intrinsic to the economic system, even though it is difficult to say exactly how important other factors might be in fostering or inhibiting exploitation.

Returning to the assumption of opportunism, what is being assumed, from chapter 4 on, is that people are given to opportunism and that the extent to which they are so given is both variable across individuals and not easily known. Nothing else is assumed about this tendency to act opportunistically, except that it is nontrivial. To achieve a better understanding of this assumption, it would be useful to consider the various ways in which it could be false. One way it could be false is that everyone's penchant for opportunism, whatever its strength, could be easily discovered. It is hard to imagine how that could be the case, since behavioral dispositions are unobservable, and the behaviors in question necessarily involve deception and/or failure to disclose relevant information; also, reputation effects are not perfect (i.e., sometimes people get away with it). Besides, even if the strength of people's propensities were well known, organizations would still have to deal with those propensities. It is just that the problems occasioned by the penchant for opportunism would be more tractable.

Another part of the assumption is that people's propensity to act opportunistically is variable across individuals. This means two things: some individuals are more inclined than others to seize a chance to act opportunistically if and when such a chance presents itself, and some are more inclined than others to take maximum advantage of whatever chances do present themselves. It is difficult to imagine that people would all be about the same along either or both of these dimensions, since all manner of contingencies would have an influence on where people ended up along these dimensions (e.g., the propensities of one's parents). Even if people were about equal along either or both of these dimensions, however, this, too, would only mitigate the problem of opportunism that institutions would have to cope with, because, once again, the behaviors are necessarily unanticipated and masked by a cloak of ignorance. Even at a pickpocket's convention, it is necessary to take steps to protect one's wallet.

The one part of the assumption whose falsity would make the problem of opportunism (and thus the potential for exploitation) go away is the assumption that most people do have at least some disposition to act opportunistically. Actually, a slightly weaker—and equally vague—assumption will do, namely, that at least a substantial minority of people have this disposition. Suppose this were false. This would mean that at most a small minority would be given to opportunism and a substantial majority (i.e., most people) would not. In short, suppose that most people simply have no propensity to act opportunistically. To understand how implausible this proposition is, recall from chapter 4 the range of behaviors that fall under the heading of opportunism: in the provision of labor services, opportunism includes not only loafing on the job (except to the extent that it is expected) but also pursuing any other interests or activities on company time that are not explicitly or implicitly permitted by the formal or informal rules of the firm. This includes (1) redirecting the organization to serve private interests (hijacking), (2) exacting private benefits in exchange for doing one's job or not interfering with others doing their jobs ("pirating" or "tax collecting"), (3) engaging in any other activity that misrepresents the nature or value of one's contribution (i.e., credit stealing, blame shifting) and (4) colluding in any form of opportunism practiced by friends and coworkers. To assume that most people in a market socialist system have no *propensity* to do any of these things is to assume that these behaviors would almost never occur, *no matter what the monitoring arrangements*. In other words, the following counterfactual conditional would have to be true: "If the cooperative engaged in no monitoring at all (including so-called horizontal monitoring by coworkers), then opportunistic behavior on the part of the workers would be negligible." This is an implication of the disappearance of the *propensity* to act opportunistically, which is not to be confused with the disappearance of the behavior; the behavior might disappear because of effective monitoring even if the propensity remains. Of course, defenders of market socialism may well want to claim that monitoring arrangements within the cooperative would be likely to make this happen or at least that those arrangements would be superior to monitoring arrangements in capitalist firms, but to make that claim is to presuppose that there is some penchant for opportunism on the part of the workers that monitoring arrangements would check. To take this approach is to concede that the problem of the potential for exploitation cannot be avoided and indeed must be engaged as it has been framed in chapters 4–6.

The assumption that most people in a market socialist system have no penchant for opportunism is more implausible still when one considers how individuals in this system will act as agents for their cooperatives in dealing with organizations and individuals across the boundaries between the firm and the market and between the firm and the state. Someone is going to have to be the central contracting agent with input suppliers, someone is going to have to be in charge of the firm's product (including advertising!), and someone is going to have to deal with the state on the issues surrounding the maintenance of capital goods and the payment of the capital usage fee. To assume—or even to entertain seriously—the possibility that most of these individuals, acting in their capacity as agents for their cooperatives, would refrain from acting opportunistically if and when opportunities present themselves is truly heroic. Once again, if the propensity does not exist, the corresponding counterfactual conditional would have to be true, namely, that if no steps were taken to prevent opportunistic behaviors on the part of these agents (e.g., the appropriation of a supplier's quasi-rents), those behaviors still would not occur.

Finally, as pointed out in chapter 4, the extent of people's opportunism is in part a function of how they view the situation in which they find themselves. If a worker believes she is not getting paid the full value of her contribution and has nowhere else to go, then shirking would seem to be both a rational and moral response to the situation. If a purchasing agent believes she is overpaying for some input and has no real alternative, then she would surely take advantage of her supplier if the opportunity presented itself. Since people are notorious for being biased in judging in their own cases, to take seriously the possibility that the penchant for opportunism will disappear is to assume that biases that are responsible for mistaken beliefs such as these will also disappear. This is simply not credible.

But (a socialist might respond) might not a market socialist economic system foster trust and solidarity among all the workers in such a way that the penchant for opportunism would be extinguished? This is certainly a possibility and will be investigated in due course. However, while the system is removing this stain from the human soul (so to speak), its institutions—and, in particular, its organizations—need to do a good job at preventing, precluding, or minimizing opportunities for people to act opportunistically. The reason for this has to do with the dynamics of adverse selection and moral hazard.

To understand these dynamics, consider the following hypothetical example. Suppose a law is passed prohibiting a certain form of monitoring of employees in a certain type of business—say, surveillance cameras in retail clothing stores. Suppose this seriously impedes employers' ability to detect employee theft of merchandise. Employees in these stores who are antecedently given to stealing from their employers would reap a bonanza in the form of stolen clothes. This is the moral hazard problem. As losses mount, employers would try to cut costs, and at some point (probably very early on), they would cut all workers' wages or perhaps not increase them at the rate of inflation. This does not restore the status quo ante, however, because not all employees are stealing the same amount, and some are not stealing at all. The latter begin to feel taken advantage of, as indeed they are. Their wages have been cut to compensate for the theft engaged in by their fellow employees. Some would begin to steal to offset their lower wages, and others would leave the retail clothing business for other jobs.

Who would be hired to replace them? The answer is obvious—clothes-horses with weak consciences. These are the people who most want the job and would be willing to work for the lower wages, which, of course, they will supplement. This is the adverse selection problem, and it is especially difficult in this case because one's love of clothes (and, indeed, the size of one's wardrobe), are private information, as is the strength of one's conscience. Let us suppose, then, that there is no cost-effective way to screen these people out. After a time, all retail clothing stores will be staffed by people who either were antecedently, or had become, clotheshorses with weak consciences.

This example shows how the dynamics of adverse selection and moral hazard systematically alters people's behavior and behavioral dispositions. The same considerations apply if the object of discussion is organizational form. If a type of organization is vulnerable to opportunistic behavior, it will attract those whose penchant for opportunism is greatest. Because of its vulnerability, it will not effectively punish the opportunistic behavior, which puts the nonopportunists at a distinct and noticeable (to them) disadvantage. As time goes on, they begin to feel like "chumps" for passing up—or taking less than full advantage of—the opportunities with which they are presented. As a result, if they do not leave, their resistance to acting opportunistically wears down, which means that their penchant for opportunism increases. Differences among individuals in their dispositions to act opportunistically may still exist, but those differences are not as significant because the institutional environment has systematically promoted opportunism at the expense of more honorable behavior. In this way, the incidence of opportunistic behavior tends to be set by the limits imposed by the institutional environment.

In response to these observations, it might be pointed out that although the unjust have always prospered at the expense of the just, the latter have not disappeared. This is true, and it is true because of the differential action of other institutions and noninstitutional forces. For example, if some people really do believe that opportunists will go to hell when they die, that is likely to have a significant effect on their penchant for opportunism.[3] The force of this objection is to raise once again the question of the ultimate significance of economic factors as determinants of social life. As was suggested, while no precise and general answer to that question may be forthcoming, few doubt that economic forces are very important, both now and as far into the future as it makes sense to look. This means that people's penchant for opportunism in the economic realm is significantly shaped by the vulnerability to opportunistic behavior of the economic system (specifically, the economic organizations) in which they find themselves.

These considerations indicate that it is necessary to take seriously the potential problem that the penchant for opportunism and the other three background conditions pose for a market socialist economic system. It is appropriate to investigate the relevant organizations and the way they structure exchanges, including the transaction costs of these exchanges. It follows that there is no way to preempt an investigation into how well the organizations of a market socialist system handle the potential for exploitation that faces market economies generally.

The same point can be approached from a slightly different angle. According to the terms of the debate defined in chapter 1, market socialism is supposed to be the successor to existing free enterprise systems, and it is supposed to be inaugurated within the next few generations. This means that individuals who inhabit this system will be close lineal descendants of existing individuals, with all the psychological continuities that entails. These continuities do not rule out significant changes in consciousness as a market socialist system takes hold. However, proponents of market socialism seek (or at least should seek) to eschew the utopianism of nineteenth- and early twentieth-century socialist thought and practice—a utopianism that has led to serious credibility problems for socialism in the late twentieth century. Thus, they must not assume that the people who inhabit this type of system are at the outset radically different from existing individuals, especially in their propensity to act opportunistically or, more generally, in their self-interestedness. Indeed, some of the appeal of market socialism trades on motivational continuities between the current system and market socialism. If one assumes that at least at the outset, people in a market socialist system have a nontrivial penchant for opportunism, then the potential for exploitation would be found in the hearts of the inhabitants of this type of systems; accordingly, it would be apposite to investigate how the organizational forms of a market socialist economy handle that potential. It is to this task that we now turn.

Exploitation among and by the Residual Claimants in the Cooperative

Recall from chapter 4 the organizational structure of the worker cooperative in a market socialist system. All and only the workers are residual claimants and ultimate decision-making authorities. Typically, that decision-making authority is exercised according to a "one person–one vote" rule. In this capacity, the workers elect management (i.e., monitors, central contracting agents, and directors of the firm's product) directly, or else they elect a workers' council, which chooses the managers. Although workers and/or their managers have physical control over the firm's assets, there are four important respects in which they do not own those assets and the state does, namely, (1) the workers must pay a capital usage fee to the state; (2) they must maintain the value of the assets they control by following proper maintenance procedures and by paying into a capital reserve fund from which monies are disbursed to replace capital goods as they are used up; (3) they may not sell off the capital that the firm controls and pocket the proceeds; and (4) the firm's assets revert to the state if the firm goes out of business. Finally, though firms may undertake new investment from retained earnings, most new investment would be under the control of the state.[4]

This organizational structure creates numerous opportunities for exploitation. Moreover, plausible stories can be told about how those opportunities could be seized. By contrast, either these opportunities do not exist in the classical capitalist firm and the open corporation, or else there are superior damage-control mechanisms in place that limit the extent to which these opportunities can be seized. So it will be argued in the remaining sections of chapter 6 and in chapter 7. The purpose of this section is to argue that some workers, in their capacity as ultimate decision makers and residual claimants, would exploit other workers within the cooperative, whether the cooperative is small or large. It also argues that the cooperatives (or the workers in their capacity as the ultimate decision-making authorities and residual claimants of the cooperative) would be able to exploit their customers in ways that the classical capitalist firm and the open corporation could not. The next section will consider the opportunities and methods by which workers can exploit managers and vice versa and how both can exploit the providers of capital. The focus in the next section will be on the small-to-medium-sized cooperative—a type of organization comparable in size to the classical capitalist firm. Chapter 7 will consider distinctive modes of exploitation in the large cooperative, which is comparable in size to the open corporation. It will also discuss how exploitation could occur through the state organizations that are charged with determining the capital usage fee that each firm must pay and those that are responsible for controlling new investment. The discussion throughout will be explicitly comparative, with the other term of the comparison being the parallel organization and/or procedures found in free enterprise systems. Without further ado, let us turn to a consideration of the workers in the cooperative in their dual role as ultimate decision makers and residual claimants.

The workers' status as ultimate decision-makers and residual claimants means that they get to decide how to divide up the revenues of the firm net of nonlabor expenses. How will they do it? Let us suppose, just for the sake of discussion, that they decide to divide it up equally. Under these circumstances, each worker in the firm is getting the same income, yet the value of each worker's contribution is obviously not the same. In the diamond-cutting cooperative, for example, those who sweep the floors make a much less valuable contribution than those who make the cuts. (How diamonds are cut makes an enormous difference to their value.) In a purely egalitarian distribution, the ratio of income to the value of workers' respective contributions would vary considerably from worker to worker within the firm. Some workers, namely those with more valuable talents and abilities, would be getting far less than the value of their contribution as compared to those who lack valuable talents and abilities. To be sure, the latter contribute, but they are paid all out of proportion to the value of that contribution. This constitutes a clear failure of reciprocity.

Let us further suppose that all the workers' cooperatives are like this. By hypothesis, the private (i.e., capitalist) sector and the state sector are insignificant in a market socialist system, so the workers with talent and ability really have no feasible alternative but to be members of cooperatives. So they (or at least most of them) effectively have nowhere else to go. It follows that in a society composed of radically egalitarian worker cooperatives, workers with talent and ability would be exploited by those with neither.

But why suppose that a market socialist society would consist of purely egalitarian firms? Indeed, it seems that the workers would have one compelling reason *not* to vote for equal distribution of income, namely, that those workers with especially valuable talents and abilities would go elsewhere. Without key personnel, the firm could not survive. This is what lies behind Saul Estrin's speculations quoted in the final subsection of chapter 2 about the market position of those with special skills. On his view, income differences within firms would not disappear; those differences, especially as they pertain to managers, would simply be reduced relative to what one finds in capitalist societies. If the workers collectively chose an unequal distribution that roughly matches income to the value of workers' respective contributions, the skilled workers would be getting the value of their contributions and so would not be exploited.

It is probably correct to say that an equal distribution of income would not characterize most cooperatives, but this just refocuses our speculations: would the income distribution that emerges from the discussions and bargaining among the workers approximate equality closely enough that some of the workers would not be getting the value of their respective contributions? Or would the workers be paid approximately in accordance with the value of their contributions, thereby precluding this form of exploitation?

The short answer to these questions is that it is difficult to know with certainty what would happen. But this does not mean that all answers are equally likely. There are three pieces of empirical evidence that indirectly support the more egalitarian scenario. In addition, there are some more prosaic, commonsense considerations that also favor that scenario. Together, they make it reasonable to believe that the distribution of income within the cooperative would fail to reflect the value of workers' contributions and thus that reciprocity among the workers would fail.

To begin with the empirical evidence, some studies of existing cooperatives suggest that income differentials are noticeably smaller than they are in more hierarchical organizations.[5] Second, an exhaustive study of wage differentials in academic departments in colleges and universities found that departments that are similar in organizational structure to cooperatives have more egalitarian wage structures than hierarchically organized departments (Pfeffer and Langton 1988, 592–94). Finally, there is significant wage compression in the Mondragon firms (Thomas 1982, 136).[6] All of this evidence is, of course, not conclusive for the question at issue, since existing cooperatives and the more egalitarian academic departments may not tell us what the distribution of income would be like in a market socialist system because the latter is so profoundly different from any existing system. This evidence is, nevertheless, suggestive.

Common sense and casual empiricism lend additional support to the judgment that income distribution within the market socialist cooperative would probably be relatively egalitarian. There is a well-known tendency for human beings to be biased when judging in their own cases. In a market socialist cooperative, this means that workers without relatively scarce and valuable skills (who will be in the majority) would tend to overestimate the value of their own contributions.[7] Because the workers are collectively the ultimate decision makers, these misjudgments would be reflected in the criteria that determine the distribution of the firm's net income. In addition, because workers are collectively the residual claimants, these relatively unskilled workers are in a zero-sum game with the skilled workers. (This fact of a zero-sum game would also do little to enhance solidarity and fraternal feelings among the workers.) This means that the overestimation of the value of their own contributions entails the underestimation of the value of the contribution of the skilled workers. For this not to happen, the majority is going to have to be unbiased enough to appreciate and recognize the nature and value of the contributions of those who have more to offer the firm than they themselves do. (Of course, the skilled workers are also likely to have an inflated opinion of the value of their contributions, perhaps even more so than the unskilled, but they are in the minority.) In deciding on pay scales or the criteria that determine pay scales, each worker is going to have to ask herself, How much am I worth to this firm? or How much are those who do the same sort of job as I do worth to this firm? Faced with this question, who among us believes that we would not overestimate the value of our own contribution?

Another factor that would conspire to lead unskilled workers to overestimate the value of their own contributions is that in a market economy, self-esteem is often tied to relative incomes.[8] To put this point more starkly and less charitably, in a commercial society, which market socialism surely is, people tend to confuse economic worth with personal worth or worth as a human being. Economic success or failure is conflated with success or failure as a person. A relatively egalitarian income distribution within the firm would be less injurious to the self-esteem of the unskilled workers.

Finally, and in a related vein, most people are not very adept at—and, indeed, are often plainly incapable of—marginalist thinking about economic value.[9] For example, farmers in search of subsidies admonish us to imagine what the country would be like without farmers, when the real question is what the country would be like if the current number of farmers was reduced by a few, including, quite possibly, the ones who are asking for subsidies. Teachers' unions defiantly ask us to consider just how important teaching our children is—to which the appropriate response is that it is very important but also something relatively many people are capable of doing satisfactorily. It is not unreasonable to expect that unskilled workers in the cooperatives would be similarly given to nonmarginalist thinking about the value of their labor services.

None of this predicts the degree of equality that would result from the vote within the firm. The discussions and bargaining might be extremely complicated, and there is no way to predict the exact outcome. However, this discussion has pointed to some likely factors that would influence how the unskilled workers, who are in the majority, would perceive the situation. Although it is not possible to predict the precise distribution of income that would emerge over time, it is likely that the disproportionalities between income and value of contribution would be nontrivial if only because the biases responsible for them are nontrivial.[10] If this is true, then the failure of reciprocity requisite for exploitation would exist.

In fact, the most likely scenario is that if market socialism were inaugurated, the relative incomes of skilled and unskilled workers within the firm would not change very much. (By contrast, management's income might well tumble significantly.) However, as the workers or their representatives on the workers' council repeatedly voted on income or the criteria by which income is determined, the systematic bias just mentioned would emerge, thereby resulting in a decline in the relative income of skilled workers. Though strict equality would probably not be the end result, at some point, the disproportionality between the value of their respective contributions and their respective incomes would entail a failure of reciprocity. If this happened in all or nearly all the firms, the skilled workers would effectively have nowhere else to go. According to the account of exploitation developed in chapter 3, they would be exploited by their less skilled coworkers.

How might the defender of market socialism respond? At least two responses come to mind. One would be to concede the point about the relative flattening of incomes but go on to argue that the discussion assumes an excessively narrow, economic conception of the benefits of working in a cooperative. It might be pointed out that what the worker receives from working in the cooperative is not merely income. There are other, nonpecuniary benefits that must be taken into account; when these other benefits are considered, there is no overall failure of reciprocity. The other response would be to deny that this egalitarian tendency would, in fact, work itself out. It might be argued that markets in skilled labor could and would operate to check this tendency toward equality in the distribution of net income. In other words, it could be admitted that an excessively egalitarian distribution of income *would* emerge if nothing else interfered, but that in point of fact, market forces would do just that. The services of skilled workers would be bid up to the point where they would be remunerated approximately according to the value of their contributions. At the very least, there would be no systematic difference between free enterprise systems and market socialist systems on this score. Let us consider each of these objections in turn.

The first calls attention to the nonpecuniary benefits of working in a cooperative. Such benefits may well exist and may be substantial. To ignore them would be like complaining about the high cost of living in the San Francisco Bay area without mentioning the substantial benefits that attend living in that pleasant environment. For evidence about the cooperatives, one only need to turn to Mondragon, where there is significant wage compression, yet the labor force is relatively stable (Thomas 1982, 136). Since the workers have alternatives in the noncooperative sector, there must be nonwage benefits that make it worth their while to stay in the cooperatives.

There are three problems with this response, however. First, the evidence from Mondragon may not provide much evidence about how most skilled workers would view their situation in a market socialist system. There is the selection bias mentioned in the last section. Because of this, the skilled workers in Mondragon might be the type who find the benefits of working in a cooperative adequate compensation for the effects of wage compression. It may be that most skilled workers in a market socialist system would not find the attractions of cooperatives adequate compensation for the diminished income they are forced to accept, just as not everyone finds the considerable attractions of the San Francisco Bay area sufficient compensation for the exorbitant cost of living there.

Second, the wage compression in a market socialist system might be significantly greater than what is found in the Mondragon cooperatives because in a market socialist system, there would be very few alternative employment opportunities in the non-cooperative sector. Freed from the discipline imposed by alternative organizational forms, a highly egalitarian wage structure might evolve. Independent of all these considerations, however, there is one problem that cannot be avoided. Presumably, the benefits that attend membership in a cooperative are available to all workers, skilled and unskilled alike. Assuming these benefits are equally (or at least randomly) distributed, the disproportionality between the value of the skilled worker's contribution and what he receives would still exist.

Finally, the concern of this book is with economic exploitation, not exploitation in some broader, more generic sense. Economic exploitation (and, for that matter, distributive justice) is concerned with the distribution of economic wealth and income—exchangeable goods and services and the claims thereto. There is a utopian tradition in socialist thought, exemplified by Marx's occasional musings about life in communist society, in which the economic sphere is downgraded in importance or significance. In communist society, everyone's needs are met, and the economic system has done its job by noon, or even by ten o'clock in the morning. I have argued in detail elsewhere that this scenario could not exist for as far into the future of the human race as it makes sense to look (Arnold 1990, 167–81, chap. 8). One of the attractions of market socialism is that it constitutes a decisive break with that utopian strain in the socialist tradition. By exhibiting a willingness to talk seriously about how to manage scarcity, market socialism takes economics—and the material wealth economic systems distribute—seriously.

Though the noneconomic benefits of a market socialist system might be substantial and, indeed, constitute an important reason to prefer it to a free enterprise system, economic benefits, construed broadly to include the reduction or minimization of economic exploitation, are part of the market socialist conception of the good society. So it was argued in chapter 2; this topic will be taken up again in the final section of chapter 8.

Consider now the second objection. It might be argued that markets in various kinds of skilled labor would prevent the development of an exploitative income structure within the firm. If skilled workers are being underpaid relative to the value of their respective contributions at a given firm, other firms would have an incentive to bid up the price of their services, probably by offering them bonuses to switch. The compensation committees within these cooperatives would simply have to tell the rank-and-file that the firm must make adequate counteroffers to retain these workers. Incomes of skilled workers would thereby come to reflect more accurately the value of their contributions. A perfect match between income and the value of their contributions would probably not be achieved, but it would at least be approximated to the point where reciprocity would be established and exploitation thus eliminated or prevented.

What makes this response especially attractive is that it parallels exactly the kind of argument that a defender of the free enterprise system would give in response to the charge that workers are exploited in that type of system. After all, the boss in the classical capitalist firm is the ultimate decision maker and sole residual claimant, and managers in the open corporation who make wage offers are often substantial residual claimants—so there is the same conflict of interest between workers and those who decide on their pay. If these type of organizations pay their skilled workers about the value of their contributions, it must be because market forces prevent them from paying much less. The same thing would happen in a market socialist system.

The problem with this response is that it ignores four factors that would prevent the robust operation of labor markets in a market socialist economy—factors that do not impinge on a free enterprise system. Because labor markets would not operate as well in a market socialist system, the egalitarian tendency described would have some room to work itself out.

The first factor is rooted in the fact that the workers are collectively both the ultimate decision-making authorities and the residual claimants. A cooperative is unlikely to delegate to its management decision-making authority when it comes to adding workers, because the addition of new workers can significantly affect their own income, since all workers are residual claimants. Assuming that decision making is democratic, this means that a consensus must be reached among a relatively large group that it is in the firm's best interests to bring new members on board before expansion will take place. By contrast, in capitalist firms it is unnecessary to achieve wide consensus on the need to expand: only one person or a small group of people needs to be convinced that it is a good idea. This suggests that cooperatives in a market socialist system would be slower to expand than their free enterprise counterparts.

Second, market socialist firms would be slower to let workers go when the market called for it. If the cooperative structure reduces alienation as advertised, it will do so, at least in part, by providing greater job security for its members. It is also likely that workers would be able to insist on more elaborate due process safeguards than are found in capitalist organizations to prevent firings motivated by office or shop floor politics. For these reasons, in a market socialist system it is likely that there would be fewer layoffs than one would find in a free enterprise system.

These two factors mean that cooperatives in a market socialist system would not be as responsive to changing conditions as capitalist firms in a free enterprise system are. One consequence of this is that labor markets would be much thinner or less robust. Firms are simply not hiring and laying off as much as they would be in a free enterprise system.

The third factor is that it will be harder to start new firms than in free enterprise systems because entrepreneurs who believe they see a profit opportunity will have to share any profits they make with all the other workers in the firm. If it is more difficult to start new firms, then, all else equal, there will be fewer opportunities for workers to leave their present place of employment.

The final factor that would reduce labor mobility in comparison to free enterprise systems is the absolute uncertainty that all workers face about their annual income. Workers' income does not come solely from their labor. As residual claimants, they are entitled to a share of the firm's total income net of nonlabor expenses. This means that a skilled worker in a marginal firm may make less than an unskilled worker in a more prosperous firm. Because of the inherent uncertainties of a market economy, the net income of all firms will vary from year to year. This means that all workers' income will fluctuate, though the firms may adopt some internal distributional measures to moderate the swings from one year to the next. For example, they might set wage rates for job categories and then pay out residuals every quarter like the quarterly dividends that corporations pay to stockholders. Whatever the particulars, however, there is no getting around the fact that the remuneration a worker receives will vary more than the remuneration of his counterpart in a free enterprise system.

This feature of a market socialist system will make it more difficult for workers to evaluate offers from other firms. These offers would have to be couched in terms of bonuses or perhaps shares of income rights in the firm, but it will be unclear what these offers really mean in a dynamic market economy. This uncertainty is dramatically compounded by the lack of a stock market in a market socialist society. One function of a stock market is to offer a market-based assessment of a firm's profitability, especially estimates of future profitability. Since ownership shares in the cooperatives are not bought and sold, there is no market-based assessment of a firm's prospects. Though there may be financial reports about past performance, those reports offer a highly incomplete or misleading guide to the future; a prospective worker considering an offer of employment would be gullible indeed to rely too much on what the firm says about its own future prospects. The ignorance and uncertainty is asymmetrical, however, since most workers (especially the skilled ones) will know—or will think they know—the prospects of their own firm better than that of other firms they may be asked to join. This informational asymmetry will make workers more reluctant to change jobs.

Returning now to the situation of the skilled workers, at some point, of course, they would be willing to change jobs, and at some point, existing firms contemplating expansion would be willing to hire them. In addition, new firms will be started, even if less frequently than in free enterprise systems. So, it is not as if labor markets would not exist. This is why a purely egalitarian income distribution would probably not result or would be unstable if it did. Nevertheless, these labor markets would not be as robust or active as labor markets in a free enterprise system. The relevance of all this to exploitation is that firms that pay their skilled workers less than they are worth (for reasons indicated, this is likely to include most cooperatives) would be relatively insulated from the pressures of labor markets. In consequence, the tendency toward equality that operates within the firm would have some room to work itself out. This would insure a failure of reciprocity in the relationship between the skilled and the unskilled workers within the firm. Given that many of these skilled workers would have no feasible alternatives, it follows that they would be exploited.

By contrast, in a free enterprise system this systemic problem does not arise because the four factors are absent. Decisions to expand or contract the firm's workforce are made by one or a small number of people. Whether or not they tend to do a better job at this than cooperatives is irrelevant for present purposes. The crucial point is that labor markets are likely to be more active than in market socialist systems because of the decision-making mechanisms and the incentive structures in the respective systems. Because successful entrepreneurs can keep the pure profits that they earn, new firms will be started more easily than under market socialism. Finally, since workers have no nonwage income, they are better able to evaluate alternative pay offers. Of course, in a free enterprise system, labor markets, like other markets, are not always competitively efficient; some workers will be exploited in any free enterprise system. However, in a free enterprise system (without any qualifying predicates), unlike a market socialist system, there are no distinctive structural features that tend to push skilled workers' pay below what it would receive in a competitively efficient market.

To this comparative assessment it might be objected that according to the account of the market process given in chapter 3, stagnant markets are vulnerable to successful entrepreneurship, so that the market process ought to be able to rectify the situation. The problem is that vulnerability to successful entrepreneurship can be very hypothetical (i.e., difficult to "exploit") if structural impediments prevent entrepreneurs from seizing the profit opportunities that stagnant markets represent. State-enforced monopoly is one such impediment, and the preceding paragraphs have described others. It is not at all obvious how an entrepreneur could get labor markets to function better, given the kind of institutional restrictions a market socialist system would impose.

These considerations do raise other possibilities that merit some attention. Since market socialism is a competitive market economy, evolutionary pressures that tend to minimize transaction costs in a free enterprise system should also be at work in a market socialist system, at least so far as the general framework of market socialism permits. The last section of chapter 5 briefly discussed some of the methods that have evolved in free enterprise systems to protect workers' quasi-rents. Of these instrumentalities, perhaps the most important are unions. Might not unions develop among the skilled workers in a market socialist system to protect their quasi-rents? Upon reflection, there seems to be no reason, in principle, why they would not; if the preceding account about what might happen initially in a market socialist system is at all plausible, they probably would. However, this possibility raises some puzzles and complications. If some subgroup of the workers in a cooperative unionize and threaten to strike, whom are they threatening and what are they bargaining for? They are, after all, part of the larger group that has ultimate decision-making authority and residual claimant status. Presumably, they would want more income at the expense of the rest of that group. This could take the form of increased residual shares; but it could also take the form of a guaranteed wage in exchange for which they would give up, or allow to be attenuated, their status as residual claimants. Whatever form this took, their nonunionized fellow workers would surely begin to have some concerns about the vulnerability of their own quasi-rents. One can easily imagine them saying to each other, "Might not our unionized fellow workers overestimate the value of their contributions when formulating wage demands? Maybe we ought to form a union ourselves."

If this were to happen, complex bargaining would ensue, and while there is no way to predict the exact outcome, there is no reason to think that the outcome would match income to the value of contribution. Bargaining power, which would crucially depend on how exposed a group's quasi-rents are, would determine the outcome. Although all labor markets are relatively stagnant in a market socialist system for reasons indicated, some are more stagnant than others. It is a safe guess that generally speaking, those with more specialized talents and abilities would be more exposed than those with less specialized talents and abilities. In any case, the opportunities for all workers would tend to be fewer and more inaccessible than they would for workers in a free enterprise system because the latter does not have the structural barriers to well-functioning labor markets found in a market socialist system.

The adversarial climate that would be found in the unionized cooperative would also bode ill for reducing alienation and encouraging attitudes of trust and solidarity necessary for dampening the penchant for opportunism. This climate is traceable to the fact that the workers are collectively the residual claimants and ultimate decision makers, which in a cooperative means that all the income of the firm, net of nonlabor expenses, is up for grabs. Depending on whether they think of themselves primarily as individuals or as members of a subgroup, they are in a zero-sum game with other individuals or other subgroups over this revenue. Obviously, this problem does not afflict the classical capitalist firm, since only one person is the residual claimant and the wage fund is more completely determined by market forces.

Similar forces confront the open corporation, which also allow it to avoid or minimize this problem with its workers. The open corporation avoids a parallel problem among equity owners because of proportional sharing rules among shareholders. As Jensen and Meckling say of the open corporation: "It severely restricts the opportunities for any individual shareholder or group of shareholders to reallocate wealth away from other shareholders to themselves. The proportional sharing rules which govern distributions [of residuals] . . . make it difficult to benefit some shareholders at the expense of others" (1979, 494).

Theoretically, the cooperative could precommit to a distribution rule that would reflect shadow market prices for labor services, but in practice, this could not happen because in the absence of reasonably well-functioning labor markets, there is no way to know what those prices should be. The operation of reasonably well-functioning markets is a discovery process that gropes toward revealing what the market clearing price really is. Absent such markets in human labor, it is highly unlikely that firms could (1) know what those prices would or should be or (2) make the necessary adjustments required by the frequent changes in the underlying determinants of scarcity value. To sum up, the fact that the workers are collectively the residual claimants and get to decide how to divide up the net income of the firm (i.e., the income of the firm net of nonlabor expenses) creates opportunities for workers to appropriate the quasi-rents of their fellow workers who have nowhere else to go. In short, it creates opportunities for exploitation—opportunities that tend to be foreclosed or minimized in a free enterprise system by the more robust operation of labor markets.

The fact just noted that firms in a market socialist system would not be as sensitive to changes in market conditions means that all product markets in a market socialist system would tend to be less responsive to changing conditions that their free enterprise counterparts.[11] This fact of shared residual claimancy creates opportunities for exploitation in a market socialist system that either do not exist or would be minimized in a free enterprise system. The reasoning can be explained as follows. Suppose that demand for a cooperative's product increases and as a result of some combination of the four factors the cooperative decides not to add additional workers.

They might, for example, try to increase production by substituting capital for labor, but this will not always be profitable, and there will usually be time lags until new capital investments come on stream. If all firms in this market reach the same decision, the rational thing for each firm to do would be to raise its price in response to this increase in demand. By contrast, firms in free enterprise systems would be more likely to hire additional workers, and increase production but not increase price, since these retarding factors are not operating in this type of system.

With regard to the market socialist system, in subsequent exchanges in this market, cooperatives would be exploiting their customers, because the price is not competitively efficient, and their customers have nowhere else to go. The price is not competitively efficient because this market is vulnerable—albeit hypothetically—to successful entrepreneurship. Its vulnerability consists in the fact that instead of raising prices, some firms could—and presumably would—hire nonvoting wage laborers to meet the increased demand (assuming there are people willing to be "wage slaves") if they were legally permitted to do so (which they would not be). The legal prohibition on wage labor acts like a state-imposed prohibition on competition with a monopolist. However, instead of ruling out all competition, it simply rules out competition from organizations that do not have the prescribed form. As in the case of the monopolist, the customer has nowhere else to go and is exploited when she pays the higher price.

The defender of market socialism has a response to this, which Saul Estrin explains as follows: "If existing cooperatives do not react adequately to changes in consumer demand, the resulting misallocations can be tackled by brand new cooperatives. And the system provides economic incentives, in the form of higher incomes, to entrants attracted to meet shortages" (1989, 176–77). Entrepreneurship is exercised, then, by the formation of new cooperatives. The problem with this response is that it assumes that new cooperatives can be formed relatively easily, when, in point of fact, this is not the case. There are two reasons for this, one of which has already been discussed.

First, as has been pointed out, someone has to exercise the requisite entrepreneurship in spotting and acting on these profit opportunities. Because of the structure of the cooperative, however, successful entrepreneurs in a market socialist system must share with their fellow workers any pure profits they capture; the incentive to try to take advantage of perceived profit opportunities would be correspondingly diminished. Clearly, a market socialist system will be less responsive to these profit opportunities than its free enterprise counterparts would be.

Second, one of the reasons why firms exist at all is that they permit the development of complementarities among the assets the firm employs—complementarities that do not exist when a new firm is formed. By the time these complementarities have developed, (i.e., by the time the new firm is up to speed), it may be too late. In 1940, the French military, ensconced in defending the Maginot Line, faced increased demand for the service they provided to the French nation (namely, national defense). At that time, there were adequate resources in America to meet this increased demand, but it did no good—at least until 1944.[12]

If cooperatives in a market socialist system would be less responsive to changing conditions, this means that product markets would be stagnant (i.e., neither competitively efficient nor in transition) more often than in free enterprise systems, leaving customers with nowhere else to go. Since these inefficiencies are induced by the fact that the ownership structure of the cooperative requires that all and only the workers share ultimate decision-making authority and residual claimancy, it can be said that a market socialist system would permit or encourage a form of exploitation that tends to be minimized in a free enterprise system.

Other Forms of Exploitation in the Small-to-Medium-sized Cooperative

The purpose of this section is to consider other distinctive opportunities for and methods of exploitation that would be found in small-to-medium-sized market socialist cooperatives. These organizations are about the size of classical capitalist firms in existing free enterprise systems. The first section of the next chapter considers the case of larger cooperatives, which are comparable in size to open corporations. The reason for making this distinction here and not in the last section is that a difference in the size of firms made no difference to the argument in the preceding section, whereas it will make a difference henceforth.

With regard to these smaller firms, the first subsection will concern exploitation of nonopportunistic workers by opportunistic workers and monitors; the second is about exploitation of and by central contracting agents and directors of the firm's product; and the third and final subsection considers how the cooperative might collectively exploit the capital providers, that is, the state and ultimately the taxpayers.

Exploitation by Opportunistic Workers and Monitors

It might seem that the cooperative would not face the problem of workers shirking or engaging in other forms of opportunism because, unlike the situation in capitalist organizations, workers are the residual claimants. But that inference is unsound. Production is still team production, which means that individual contribution (and thus its value) is hard to ascertain. This means that the opportunistic worker gets all of the benefits but suffers only a fraction of the costs of his foul deeds. In very small organizations (those with under a dozen, or perhaps twenty, members), this may not matter very much. The income and wealth consequences of shirking and other forms of opportunism by even one member may be so significant for every other member of the cooperative that everyone has a strong incentive to do whatever monitoring is necessary to reduce it to an absolute minimum. Under these circumstances, exploitation by opportunistic workers would be correspondingly insignificant. Notice that in very small classical capitalist firms the boss is also a worker and does the monitoring in conjunction with his other work, which suggests that monitoring is usually not too serious a problem in very small classical capitalist firms either. On the other hand, because workers in these organizations are not residual claimants and thus have less incentive to monitor fellow workers, some opportunistic behavior may occur (e.g., stealing supplies) in very small classical capitalist firms that would be detected or deterred in the very small cooperative (though it is hard to say how much). In this respect, then, there may be less exploitation in a market socialist system than in a free enterprise system.[13]

It might be thought that cooperatives would require less monitoring than their capitalist counterparts because the cooperative form of organization would have a legitimacy in workers' eyes that their capitalist counterparts lack in a capitalist system. The problem with this hypothesis, however, is that it overlooks the fact that economic systems (and thus types of organizational forms found in them) that persist tend to be in harmony with widely shared views about what kinds of economic relations are legitimate. This is an implication of Marx's insight that a society's base (economic structure) determines its superstructure (ideology).[14] Indeed, one of the striking failures of the socialist movement in the past century and a half has been its inability over a protracted period of time to persuade large numbers of people of the illegitimacy of the capitalist system and its organizational forms. The fact is that most workers in existing free enterprise systems do not regard the economic system under which they live as fundamentally illegitimate, despite the herculean efforts of its ideological opponents.

These observations notwithstanding, it is likely that the very small cooperative will be somewhat better monitored than the very small classical capitalist firm because all the workers have the status of residual claimants. Superior monitoring is not the only benefit in respect to exploitation that attends small size. It is also quite possible that relations of trust and solidarity would also be easier to foster in relatively small organizations. Might this not be a reason for the state in a market socialist economy to restrict cooperatives to a very small size, especially since (as shall be demonstrated shortly) there are significant opportunities for shirking and other forms of opportunism once cooperatives get beyond the mom-and-pop (or brother-and-sister) stage?

The short answer to that question is no, and the reasons are to be found in the transactions cost efficiencies of bringing large amounts of capital under one decision-making roof discussed in the last chapter. The main advantage of expanding the boundary of the firm at the expense of the market is that it yokes together the interests of the ultimate decision-making authorities who control complementary assets. When these assets are not brought together within the firm, they are controlled by groups or individuals with disparate interests, and contracts have to be negotiated across the market. For reasons discussed on a number of occasions in this book, expropriation hazards (i.e., opportunities for exploitation) can exist in this environment that would otherwise not exist if the firm-market boundary were dissolved at that point. So there would be significant avoidable risks of exploitation if firms were restricted to an artificially small size. To put this in more concrete terms, consider what would happen if a large manufacturing facility were broken up into numerous very small cooperatives. If the boys in the paint booth had to negotiate a contract to supply the ladies down in final assembly, somebody's highly specialized assets would be seriously at risk. At the very least, extremely complex contracts would have to be negotiated and written. Inevitably, such a society would end up saying to its lawyers what American society has said to its doctors: "Here is the wealth of the nation: take what you think is fair."

In light of these observations, it is possible to assume for the sake of discussion that there would be no artificial barriers to firm size in a market socialist system and that transactions cost efficiencies would play about the same role in a market socialist system as they play in a free enterprise system in determining where the firm-market boundary would be drawn.[15] Because of the conceptual connection between transactions cost inefficiencies and opportunities for exploitation established in chapters 3 and 4, this assumption implies that the opportunities for exploitation that arise or exist because of where the firm-market boundary is located would be about the same in both types of systems. This proposition, in turn, implies that at least as far as this discussion of exploitation is concerned, it can be assumed that a market socialist system would have about the same mix of very small, small-to-medium-sized, and large firms as would be found in a free enterprise system. This assumption has an important methodological implication for this section and the first section of chapter 7: in the comparative assessment of the potential for exploitation in and through small-to-medium-sized cooperatives, the comparable free enterprise organization is the classical capitalist firm; similarly, the comparable free enterprise organization for the large cooperative is the open corporation.[16]

One final methodological assumption: in what follows, no distinction will be made between very small firms and small-to-medium-sized firms unless there is some reason to believe that there would be systematic differences between them as it pertains to exploitation. (The issue at hand— monitoring—is a case in point.)

Returning to the problem of monitoring in the small-to-medium-sized cooperative, when firms are employing, say, twenty-five or more workers, it will make sense to have a full-time monitor. Unfortunately, monitoring is likely to be significantly less effective in small-to-medium-sized cooperatives than in comparable classical capitalist firms. To see why, notice that there are two important differences between these two types of organizations. One is that in the cooperative, the workers are the ultimate decision-making authorities. This means that the monitor is either directly elected by the workers or is chosen by a workers' council elected from their ranks. By contrast, in the classical capitalist firm, the monitor is not responsible to the workers. A second difference is that in the cooperative, unlike in the classical capitalist firm, each of the workers is a fractional residual claimant. Given some plausible assumptions about human behavior, these two facts are responsible for three weaknesses in the cooperative's monitoring arrangements—weaknesses that do not afflict the classical capitalist firm.

First, unlike the classical capitalist firm, cooperatives face a problem of adverse selection in choosing a monitor. The monitoring job will disproportionately attract those with the essentially political skills required to get elected to the job of monitor. Obviously, these skills need not be positively correlated with the ability to succeed at the often disagreeable tasks that a good monitor must do. In point of fact, these political skills might well be negatively correlated with what is required to be a good monitor. Workers would be inclined to vote for those who appear to promise to go easy on them individually (or on their subgroup) and to go hard on everyone else. Convincing people of this sort of thing is the consummate political accomplishment of successful politicians in a democracy. This is an adverse selection problem because the system encourages people like this (i.e., undesirable types) to come forward to seek the job of monitor.

Second, a distinctive moral hazard problem is associated with monitoring the cooperative. To the extent that opportunism cannot be prevented by redesigning tasks to make them more agreeable, a successful monitor must create a climate in which opportunism is not tolerated. It is hard to see how this could be done without creating a relationship between the monitor and the workers that would be to some extent adversarial. Such a relationship would be difficult to sustain in a context in which the monitor is elected by the workers. In short, it will be difficult for the monitor to put the fear of God in the workers if the workers get to elect God.

Third, monitoring is itself difficult to monitor; the cooperative's monitor has only fractional residual claimant status. This is significant in light of the fact that for most people the monitor's tasks of metering inputs, apportioning rewards, and administering discipline are often intrinsically disagreeable—especially for the cooperatives' monitors, who have the requisite political skills to get elected to the job. Given these facts, fractional residual claimant status in a cooperative of, say, twenty-five to a hundred workers would provide a much weaker incentive for the monitor to avoid shirking in the provision of monitoring services than his classical capitalist counterpart. The costs of his shirking (and other forms of opportunism) are spread widely among many residual claimants. The main cost associated with shirking by the monitor is the shirking and other forms of opportunism that are encouraged in the ranks.

By contrast, the classical capitalist firm faces none of these problems. Getting and keeping the job of monitor does not depend on the good will of those who are being monitored. The job tends to attract and reward those who are best at running companies, a crucial facet of which is monitoring team production. Popularity with the workers is neither necessary nor sufficient for getting and keeping the job. In addition, since the monitor is the full residual claimant, he bears the full income and wealth consequences of his shirking, including the consequences of the shirking and other forms of opportunism of his employees. In the classical capitalist firm, every dollar that the shirking worker filches is filched from the boss. For all these reasons, monitors in the classical capitalist firm would generally be more effective at ferreting out and getting rid of parasitic, opportunistic workers (i.e., the exploiters) than their counterparts in the worker cooperative.

How might the defender of market socialism respond to these observations? In the first place, it might be objected that the empirical evidence does not support these theoretical speculations. Bradley and Gelb have found that in the cooperatives of Mondragon (where managers are elected by the workers), monitoring by management is, in point of fact, quite effective; there is even some horizontal monitoring by fellow workers (1981, 211). This evidence is ambiguous, however. The basic problem, which was noted in the general discussion of Mondragon in the first section of this chapter, is that three other factors may be responsible for the low incidence of shirking in Mondragon: (1) these firms compete with capitalist organizations and so must be effectively monitored or in need of little monitoring if they are to survive; (2) there may be selection biases that draw relatively nonopportunistic managers and workers to the Mondragon cooperatives and repel more opportunistic prospective workers and managers; (3) the fact that the Mondragon workers have something approaching equity ownership in their cooperatives may be an important factor in accounting for effective monitoring. None of these factors would operate in a market socialist system.

Another objection would be to call attention to the fact that market socialism is a competitive economy, which means that firms with serious internal weaknesses would not survive in competition with firms that have avoided these weaknesses. Cooperatives that are taken in by opportunistic monitors would tend not to survive, whereas those that chose more hard-nosed monitors would survive and prosper. Though this is possible, there is little assurance that it will happen, since the undesirable behaviors are largely unobserved and the character traits that are responsible for those behaviors are unobservable. In addition, because one basic type of organizational form is mandated, there is much less room for experimentation in organizational structure than in a free enterprise system. In other words, since cooperatives in a market socialist system have to compete only with firms that face similar potential problems, there is no assurance that these problems would be solved by market forces. (On this point, consider public bureaucracies which have no competition from alternative organizational forms.)

Finally, this response overlooks the fact that what is at issue is a comparative assessment of the classical capitalist firm and the small-to-medium-sized cooperative. Even if market forces provided some check on the factors that lead to weak monitoring in cooperatives, those factors will still exist and would still have some effect. Monitoring may not be a disaster in the small-to-medium-sized cooperative, but what is at issue is whether or not it would be generally less effective than in comparable classical capitalist firms where the monitor is the full residual claimant (and thus requires no monitoring herself). In this connection, notice that the entrepreneurial gains that can be realized by reducing shirking and other forms of opportunism cannot be fully captured by the person who provides these superior monitoring services in the cooperative. Instead, she must share those gains with all who work in the cooperative. This weakens her incentive to come on board and put up with the inevitable unpleasantness that would attend turning a firm around.[17]

Another objection might be that the observation presupposes the absence of trust and solidarity among workers in the cooperatives. The presence of those sentiments would lessen the need for monitoring by making the workers less disposed to shirk. This means that the internal weaknesses of the cooperative's monitoring arrangements are less of a concern. While this possibility cannot be ruled out, there some reason to be skeptical of it. It is not at all clear what it is about the cooperative that would ground this increased trust and solidarity. It might be thought that the basis for this would be the fact that the firm belongs to them; it is *theirs*. But there is an important sense in which the firm does not belong to them: they don't own it! More exactly, all of the firm's nonhuman assets belong to society at large and are entrusted to the workers only for as long as they happen to be using those assets. Though they exercise operational control over those assets, at the deepest level, this control is conditional. Indeed this conditionality of control is, in some sense, the essence of social ownership.

Two other reasons to be skeptical of the potential for solidarity within the cooperative are related to the workers' status as residual claimants and ultimate decision makers. As was argued in the last section, a source of friction in the cooperative is the fact that the workers collectively get to decide how the net income of the firm will be divided up (or the criteria that determine how the firm's income will be divided). Disagreement about this matter is very likely. More generally, as ultimate decision makers, some workers will undoubtedly disagree with the direction the company is taking, who the managers should be, and so on. Indeed, a whole range of issues and decisions are up for discussion and a vote in the cooperative that are up for neither in the classical capitalist firm. It would be unduly optimistic to suppose that there would be no *sore losers* in these disputes. Sore losers in this context are workers who shirk or otherwise act opportunistically in response to being on the losing side of these contentious issues that the workers must address as a collectivity.

Indeed historically, solidarity has been best and most impressive when a group is confronted by a clear and direct threats to individual and group interests. Such threats produce cognitive agreement and a harmony—or even an identity—of interests. Such agreement and harmony would not exist when workers were debating among themselves (being possibly at each other's throats) about what policies and procedures a firm should adopt and how income should be divided up. The existence of competitor firms may suppress these problems up to a point, but as long as a firm's back is not to the wall, or as long as its competitors are facing the same problem, it is likely that this basis for solidarity would not exist. These considerations suggest that whatever the forces at work on the monitor, the monitor's task of preventing shirking and other forms of opportunism may be more difficult, not less difficult, than that of her capitalist counterpart.

Let us suppose, however, that the fact that the workers are collectively the ultimate decision makers and residual claimants would not weaken solidarity within the cooperative. Suppose further that the problem of shirking among the workers was small and insignificant. Even if things started out that way in market socialist economy, it would become a genuine problem because of the systematic weaknesses in the cooperative's monitoring arrangements. As explained in the first section of this chapter, the dynamics of adverse selection and moral hazard systematically shape behavior to conform to the constraints imposed by the institution. In other words, as long as *some* penchant for opportunism remains in the hearts of the workers, the human material in the cooperative will be placed between the anvil of adverse selection and the hammer of moral hazard, resulting in a rise in opportunistic behavior and a strengthening of the penchant for it. It is in this way that shirking—and the exploitation it represents—is transformed from a human problem into a social problem.

Exploitation of and by the Firm's Managers

Management consists of monitoring, acting as central contracting agent, and being the director of the firm's product. Monitoring has already been discussed; this subsection considers the other two management functions. The central contracting agent represents the ultimate decision makers in dealing with suppliers of inputs. However, when it comes to labor inputs, it seems reasonable to suppose that in the small-to-medium-sized cooperative, the hiring of new workers would be done by a committee of the whole or a large and representative subcommittee. The decision to hire a new worker is the decision to cut each worker's share of the firm's income, so it would undoubtedly be taken with care and only after thorough discussion. Contracts for other inputs, however, would be handled by a central contracting agent. The director of the firm's product manages the output side of the firm-market interface. This includes making decisions about what product(s) to produce, what quality characteristics it shall have, and how it shall be marketed and priced.

It is hard to know how all of the tasks associated with these two roles would be divided up in the small cooperative, though if the classical capitalist firm is any guide, it is likely that they would be assigned to one person—in fact, to the same person who is the monitor.[18] There are obvious efficiency advantages to having one person in charge of both the input and output interface between the firm and the market and to be in charge of the deployment of factors of production within the firm. (The latter is part of the monitor's job.) This observation is subject to two important qualifications. One is that when the firm reaches a certain size (the medium-sized cooperative), one person will not be able to execute all of these tasks; as in the comparably sized classical capitalist firm, a small and short hierarchy (democratically selected, no doubt) will be needed. The second qualification is that the cooperative would probably involve the workers in more of the decision making, since this is supposed to be one of the principal virtues of the cooperative in comparison to capitalist firms. However, since complete contracts governing every contingency cannot be written, it is likely that the way this would work is that the membership would have to be consulted on a specified range of decisions (e.g., the introduction of new products), while managers would be granted residual rights of control, that is, all management rights not otherwise assigned to the workers. They would have these residual rights for as long as they occupy the manager's position.

Though this looks to be a cozy arrangement in which no one could get exploited, in point of fact that is not the case. The numerous opportunities for exploitation implicit in this arrangement are traceable to the nature of the manager's tasks, coupled with his status as fractional residual claimant. To understand these opportunities, it is necessary to get clearer about what the cooperative's residuals represent. These residuals are the income of the firm net of nonlabor expenses. For analytical purposes, this income can be conceived of as consisting of two parts: (1) the returns to ordinary labor (this can be thought of as a wage fund) and (2) the returns to entrepreneurship, which are zero when the market for the firm's inputs and outputs are competitively efficient. The firm's manager, in each of her three roles (monitor, central contracting agent, and director of the firm's product), can be conceived of as providing the firm with labor in the form of (1) routine decision-making services and (2) extraordinary decision-making services (entrepreneurship) in which pure profits for the firm, either positive or negative, hang in the balance. Pure profits in this scenario can be thought of as the returns that the firm gets over or under the going rate of return on its labor assets, just as pure profits in a capitalist firm are the returns that the equity owners get over or under the going rate of return to capital.

The firm's manager, in her role as central contracting agent and monitor, can exercise significant entrepreneurship in searching out the best and least costly input suppliers, in considering and implementing alternative methods of producing the product (including different methods of organizing production), and so on. In her role as director of the firm's product, she can exercise entrepreneurship by developing new channels of distribution for the firm's product, restructuring pricing policy, changing the attributes of the product to position it differently in the market, and making any number of changes in the selling effort, such as putting salespersons on commission or taking them off commission. Entrepreneurial activity on both sides of the firm-market interface is extraordinarily important for the success of the firm. If a manager seizes the right opportunities, the marginal difference can be enormous. On the other hand, if she does a poor job, either by making changes that do not work out or by failing to make changes to keep up with the competition (the equivalent of shirking), negative profits and even ruin can result.

It is now possible to see the significance of the manager's status as fractional residual claimant. If the firm does well as a result of entrepreneurial actions on the part of its manager, the manager gets only a fraction of the value of her contribution. On the other hand, if her entrepreneurial actions (or inactions) fail, the manager pays only a fraction of the costs. These facts create opportunities for exploitation that do not exist in the classical capitalist firm where the manager is the full residual claimant.

Consider some of the ways in which the cooperative's manager(s) can exploit the rest of the firm. The central contracting agent can buy inputs from inferior cooperatives of which, for example, her friends or relatives are members and suffer only a fraction of the costs this imposes on the firm. She may fail to exercise due diligence in searching for the best combination of price, quality, and reliable supply of inputs. Similar problems can arise on the output interface. She may fail to seek out new markets for the firm's product, fail to keep up with innovations, not pay sufficient attention to changing demographics, and so on. In other words, on both fronts, managers may shirk in the provision of routine decision-making services, which can result in real losses for the firm in a changing environment— losses that are spread among all the firm's members.

In its effects on the firm, this shirking is equivalent to, but conceptually distinct from, poor entrepreneurial judgment on nonroutine questions. Managers may not shirk but can still do a poor job at either or both interfaces between the firm and the market. Factors that are crucial to a decision may be overlooked or not given appropriate weight. Obvious solutions to new and pressing problems may not be seen, and the cooperative suffers losses as a result. Whether the decisions are routine or not, since managers cannot sell their claims on the residuals, they do not bear the long-term consequences of their decisions. If a cooperative's manager makes a disastrous decision that will cost the firm money for the next ten years and she will be leaving in five years (or sooner), then others (future residual claimants) must pay for her mistake.

Of course, cooperatives will make efforts to monitor managers and so prevent shirking and poor entrepreneurship. In addition, they themselves will be called in for advice and consent on major decisions. This would certainly mitigate these problems and it would mean that the membership bears some of the responsibility for whatever decisions are made.[19] But that is not in dispute. The crucial issue is a comparative one, and there can be no doubt that the classical capitalist firm is superior to the small-to-medium-sized cooperative on these points. The various forms of on-the-job consumption detailed earlier are all found in existing classical capitalist firms and indeed constitute a prime cause of business failure. However, since the manager is also the sole residual claimant, he cannot exploit others through his choice to consume on the job. He must bear the full wealth consequences of his decisions, not only in the present period but into the future as well. This is because, unlike the cooperative's manager, the classical capitalist can sell his claim on the future residuals of the firm, which means that the value of his decisions tends to be capitalized into the value of the firm.

In a related vein, it is worth pointing out that monitoring management is costly and imperfect. It is a mistake to think that the physical proximity of workers and management in the small cooperative would make monitoring either relatively easy or less necessary. To keep an eye on management requires something other than an unobstructed line of sight. A good evaluation of managerial decision making requires access to the information that the decision maker had, as well as knowledge of the costs of gathering more information. This is part of what makes it difficult and costly to monitor managerial decision making; another part of the problem is that luck can have an imponderable influence on the results of following through on any decision. All of this means that the monitoring activities by the membership of the small-to-medium-sized cooperative will be highly imperfect. This, in turn, implies that it will often be the case that these cooperatives will effectively have nowhere else to go when they suffer at the hands of bad management that misrepresents to the workers the value of their contribution; in other words, they do not know that they are having their pockets picked, because they have no cost-effective way to find out that their managers, rather than conditions beyond their managers' control, are responsible for the firm's misfortunes. All of this implies that the members of firms with poor managers are exploited by these managers.[20] It is worth reemphasizing that these problems simply do not come up in the classical capitalist firm because of the structure of roles of that organization. As full residual claimant (and primary provider of capital), the manager suffers the full income and wealth consequences of her decisions.

A defender of market socialism might point out that all of these problems are also faced by the large open corporation. And indeed that is true. A comparison between the small cooperative and the open corporation would prove less unfavorable to the small cooperative because of this. However, one of the assumptions of this discussion, which was ventilated at the beginning of this section, is that a market socialist system would have about the same mix of very small, small-to-medium-sized, and large firms as a free enterprise system. This means that the fact that the open corporation suffers some of the defects of the small cooperative is of no comfort to defenders of market socialism: what matters is that it has decisive advantages over its counterpart, the small-to-medium-sized cooperative.

Turning now to the case of managers who do an exceptionally good job, exploitation would take place in the other direction. Managers who turn routine decisions into nonroutine decisions by exercising initiative and managers who use nonroutine decisions to innovate can position the firm to capture pure profits in the factor markets or in the market for the firm's product. Moves of this sort are crucial to the operation of the competitive process. In the language of chapter 3, these actions turn stagnant markets into markets in transition. However, in a market socialist system, the successful entrepreneur must share whatever pure profits he earns with everyone else in the firm, since the members of the cooperative are the residual claimants. This is also true of those who conceive and develop entirely new products, services, and production processes. Clearly, under these circumstances the successful manager does not get the value of his contribution.[21] Nor does he really have anywhere else to turn. All cooperatives require those who exercise the crucial entrepreneurial functions to share the wealth they are responsible for with all other members of the firm. Since, by hypothesis, the private sector is insignificant in a market socialist economy, these managers have no real alternative but to work for a cooperative. In short, they are exploited. This exploitation is mitigated, however, to the extent that the members of the cooperative assist in or monitor decision making. But the workers cannot collectively make or monitor all decisions when the cooperative reaches a certain size (of, say, about two dozen workers).

It is a common observation made by friends of the free enterprise system that socialism is deficient in encouraging innovation and does not sufficiently discourage hidebound, timid (i.e., shirking) management. This is true, and the inefficiencies and wealth losses that this occasions are quite real, but the purpose of this discussion has been to tie these deficiencies to exploitation of and by management. It is not just that people do not have some new products they otherwise would have and that their standard of living is a little lower than it otherwise might be. Another consequence is that some people are getting exploited by others because of this defective economic structure.

By contrast, the manager in the classical capitalist firm experiences the full wealth consequences of his decisions. If he innovates or otherwise exercises successful entrepreneurship, he will be able to capture all of the gains of that innovation because he is the sole residual claimant. To these observations it might be responded that the structure of the classical capitalist firm rewards equally the wise and the lucky and punishes equally the foolish and unlucky. Indeed, that is true, and if as I have argued elsewhere (Arnold 1987c), people's deserts are determined by their contributions, then to the extent that the deserts of classical capitalists are attenuated by good or bad luck, these classical capitalists get more or less than they deserve.[22] But this has no consequences for exploitation. Lucky classical capitalists are not exploiting anyone, and the unlucky ones are not being exploited by anyone. The only failure of reciprocity is between them and the gods.

Exploitation of the Capital Providers

For reasons explained in the preceding subsections, the exploitation of some members of the cooperative by others is likely to be more serious or significant than comparable forms of exploitation in the classical capitalist firm. However, suppose this is not the case. Suppose that other factors, such as solidarity among the workers, would prevent these forms of exploitation. Workers would rarely think in terms of "I," "me," and "mine"; instead, they would think in terms of "we," "us," and "our." Under those circumstances, there could still be exploitation across the boundary between the firm and other organizations, including, notably, state organizations. Indeed, in a market socialist system, it is at the boundary between the firm and the state that those who would be opportunists in the service of their cooperatives would find the mother lode of quasi-rents to be appropriated. This is a consequence of the fact that unlike the classical capitalist firm, in which the residual claimant owns most of the capital that the firm employs, the state effectively owns all the capital that the market socialist cooperative uses.

To understand how exploitation takes place at this boundary, it is helpful to recall how ownership of the nonhuman productive assets of a society is conceived of in a market socialist system. It is also necessary to understand in more detail just what those assets are. In a society that has a market socialist economic system, the public is supposed to own these assets collectively. Since the state is democratically controlled, the state stands in for or represents (albeit imperfectly) the public on this matter. Members of cooperatives are temporarily entrusted with a portion of society's productive wealth to use for their own benefit and for the benefit of society, but these assets are really owned by society as a whole. That ownership is manifested in four distinctive features of a market socialist system noted at the beginning of the second section of this chapter: (1) the cooperative is required to maintain physical plant and equipment and must make payments into a capital reserve fund to replace these goods when their useful life has expired, the former being comparable to maintenance requirements imposed by lessors on rented equipment in a free enterprise system, the latter to principal on a loan or the replacement cost of a rented capital good; (2) the cooperative must pay a capital usage fee to the state, which is like interest on a loan or a premium paid on a leased capital good over and above the replacement cost; (3) just as a firm cannot sell a leased piece of equipment to someone else or to some other firm and pocket the proceeds, so too a cooperative cannot sell off the assets it uses; and (4) control of the firm's assets reverts to the state if the firm goes out of business, just as control of a rented piece of equipment would revert to the lessor in the event that the lessee went out of business.

Feature 1 raises a point about accounting that warrants some clarification.[23] Accountants would prefer the term, 'capital reserve fund' to 'depreciation fund' to describe the fund the cooperative must set up and to which it must make periodic payments. Depreciation is a way of calculating the value of an asset at any particular point in its life. If a machine that costs $x has a useful life of ten years, its value after one year is $.9x. Depreciation schedules are used by accountants to determine the cost of producing a unit of the firm's product and, of course, these schedules have tax purposes. In the accounting sense, however, there can be no such thing as a depreciation *fund*, since depreciation is simply a way of calculating the value of assets at a given time. A capital reserve fund, on the other hand, is a fund set aside to replace capital goods as they are used up. The difference is important in the present context because the historical cost of an asset may not reflect accurately the current value of that asset. An obvious reason for this is that replacement costs may have changed, but there may be other reasons as well (more on this later). The general point is that if the assets of the firm are conceived of as a portion of society's wealth that the cooperative has the use of on a temporary basis, it is appropriate to demand of the cooperative that it maintain the value of that portion of society's wealth to which it has been entrusted. In other words, society is not providing the cooperative with chunks of metal and wire and the like, but instead with some social wealth. This means that firms do not necessarily discharge their obligations to society simply by paying a portion of the historical costs of an asset into a capital reserve fund.

This conception of social wealth and the cooperative's relationship to it has some additional implications for the purchase and sale of capital goods. When a firm wants to initiate a major expansion, it will presumably borrow money from the state (perhaps through state-controlled banks), with which it will purchase capital goods. The firm will then make capital usage payments on those assets. However, firms cannot be required to clear every purchase of equipment with the banks or with the state. If a firm outgrows its copier machine, it has to be able to sell it on the used copier market and use the proceeds and its reserves or its working capital to buy a larger one. The system could not function if purchases like this had to be cleared through the "owner" of the capital (i.e., the state). What the members of the cooperative cannot do, however, is to sell the copier and pocket the money. So although firms can sell capital goods they control, they cannot sell them off, that is, sell them and divert the proceeds to the residuals. What the state can require, then, is that they not reduce the value of the assets of the firm.

The social wealth controlled by the cooperative is not limited to a collection of specific capital goods (and the labor assets that work them). As Jensen and Meckling point out in their discussion of the pure rental firm, there are some assets that cannot be rented from others (1979, 481). These include product design and engineering, specialized training of the labor force, distribution systems, advertising, and the brand-name loyalty of customers. These assets are very hard to assign a value to, at least in ongoing operations, and markets in them are fairly thin, to say the least. This creates a valuation problem for the state. How much must the firm include in its capital usage payment to cover the value of, for example, the distribution system for its products? After all, it is in effect renting that distribution system from society, so some payment is due. However this problem is resolved, the state would undoubtedly mandate that these intangible assets be properly maintained. On the other hand, in most cases, no monies would have to be paid into a capital reserve fund for these intangibles because they have no finite life if they are properly maintained.

The sum of the salvage value of a firm's (nonhuman) assets, both tangible and intangible, is almost always much less than the value of the firm itself. The reason for this is that there are significant complementarities among these assets. Indeed, that is part of the explanation for why firms exist at all. This additional value can be imputed to the particular assets of the firm, in which case each of these assets has quasi-rents attached to them. Let us define the quasi-rent value of the firm as the sum of the quasi-rents of its assets, both tangible and intangible. The quasi-rent value of the firm reflects its location—its niche—in the larger economic system of which it is a part. Accountants call this "good will" (Kieso and Weygandt 1983, 572–74), but the term is misleading because the value it represents is something more than the value of intangibles such as customer loyalty. A firm that is making a profit is meeting a certain constellation of needs of its clients and is providing a source of revenue for its input suppliers. Persons and organizations on both the input and output sides of the firm-market boundary will have made at least some investments in their relationship with that particular firm, and the firm will have made corresponding investments in its relationship with them. These investments would be lost if the firm went out of business. When the market socialist state abolishes private ownership and turns firms over to the workers, organized as cooperatives, part of the social wealth with which the workers are entrusted is the value associated with the firm's position in the economy and thus the quasi-rent value of the firm. To maintain this value, the management of the cooperative must maintain the position of the firm (in the broadest sense of that term) in the economy.[24]

To summarize, there are three forms of social wealth owned by society at large (through its representative, the state) that are entrusted to the cooperative: physical assets (e.g., plant and equipment), intangible assets (e.g., product engineering and distribution systems), and the firm itself, whose value is more than the sum of the salvage value of its parts.

This structure of ownership rights to a firm's nonhuman assets is responsible for a number of opportunities for exploitation by and through the worker cooperative that do not exist in the classical capitalist firm.[25] They all stem from the fact that the workers have no equity stake in the firm and thus have a limited time horizon when it comes to the firm and its assets. Unlike the workers in Mondragon, whose members receive an equity pay-out when they quit or retire, when members of a market socialist coopera-tive leave the firm, they receive no payout, since they are not equity own-ers. This limited time horizon attenuates their interest in the firm (specifi-cally their interest in its financial well-being after they leave), at least in comparison to a classical capitalist, who can sell both the particular assets of the firm and his rights to the residuals (i.e., the future cash flows that the firm generates).

It would be implausible to maintain, as Jensen and Meckling (1979) sometimes seem to, that the workers in a cooperative would have no inter-est whatever in their firms after they leave. Ties based on fraternal feelings and solidarity may well serve as a basis for an interest in the well-being of the cooperative that extends beyond their own tenure. Indeed, that interest would very likely be more substantial than the interest of workers in a clas-sical capitalist firm, since the latter are neither its ultimate decision-making authorities nor its residual claimants.

On the other hand, the point of comparison is not between the two sets of workers, but between the workers in the cooperative and the classical capitalist. The latter's ties based on sentiment are often quite strong, more so if his offspring can inherit the firm—which brings us back to the finan-cial interests involved. As indicated, the financial interests of the workers in the cooperative are systematically different from the classical capitalists, because the former do not own the firm's assets and have a limited claim on the firm's residuals. This means that the current workers in a cooperative, who are both ultimate decision makers and residual claimants, have both opportunities and a motive for exploiting capital providers (the state) and possibly future residual claimants (future workers)—opportunities and motives that do not exist in the classical capitalist firm. These opportunities can be found in (1) the maintenance rules for capital goods, (2) the capital reserve requirements, (3) the rule requiring them to maintain intangible assets, and (4) the rule requiring them to maintain the quasi-rent value of the firm itself. Let us consider each of these in turn.

The first of these opportunities involves what Jensen and Meckling call the *agency costs* of the rental arrangement (1979, 480). To understand what these costs are, consider rental arrangements for capital goods in existing free enterprise systems. Long-term rentals that cover the entire useful life of a capital good are, in point of fact, quite rare; the asset is usually owned outright by the firm that uses it. There is a transactions cost explanation for this. It is difficult to write complete, easily enforced, long-term rental con-tracts governing every contingency for most capital goods. In a long-term contract, acceptable maintenance becomes harder to define, and the replacement cost of the asset becomes more speculative and problematic. For these reasons, it is usually more efficient for the firm to own capital goods outright.

Consider now the cooperative. As explained, it effectively leases all of its capital goods from the state. Although the state requires the cooperative to maintain its assets properly, as was just noted, what counts as proper maintenance becomes increasingly problematic over the length of the life of an asset. The state would have to set standards to try to ensure that capital goods are properly maintained. The interests of the cooperative's members lie elsewhere, however. Because their (financial) time horizon does not extend beyond their employment at the cooperative, it would sometimes be in the interests of the cooperative and its monitor—but not the classical capitalist firm and its owner-monitor—to defer or skimp on maintenance whenever doing so would increase net revenues (i.e., residuals) in the short term at the expense of net revenues beyond their time horizon. The state would undoubtedly incur monitoring costs to try to prevent this, but since monitoring is both imperfect and costly, there would be an opportunity for the residual claimants (members of the cooperative) to exploit the capital providers (the state) that would not exist in a classical capitalist firm where these two roles are joined.[26] There is no need to suppose that the ultimate decision makers in the cooperative (i.e., the workers) are bent on running the firm into the ground. The issue is never faced like that. Rather, there are many small decisions that have to be made about maintenance, and all that is being supposed here is that the workers would tend to favor decisions that benefit them at the expense of the state.

The obvious agency costs of the rental arrangement are those associated with the maintenance of capital goods; the unobvious ones are those associated with the capital reserve fund. One way of thinking about the rule requiring firms to pay an amount equal to replacement costs into a capital reserve fund is that it is a way of keeping the cooperative from consuming its capital by funneling wealth from the capital providers (i.e., the taxpayers) into its pocket. The problem with this rule is that it could be manipulated by the cooperative because of its highly indeterminate content. This indeterminacy stems from the fact that economic conditions are always in a state of flux, and firms must take this into account when they are planning to replace equipment and other capital goods at the end of their useful lives. What does it mean to set aside enough money to replace your cooperative's mainframe computer when computer technology is being continually revolutionized? Presumably, the firm is supposed to set aside enough funds to replace a capital good with something that is functionally equivalent, which means that the firm would have to exercise some judgment on this question.

Is the firm itself going to be the same size next year? Is the product mix going to remain unchanged? Has technology changed in ways that affect production facilities? These and countless other questions affect plans to replace—or not to replace—capital goods. Even the decision to continue to produce the same item in the changing world of a market economy is a speculative one, requiring judgment and business acumen. If, for example, a firm is producing home movie cameras at the dawn of the age of the camcorder, what should they be paying into their capital reserve fund, given that their product is about to become obsolete? And does it really make sense to incur substantial maintenance costs for specialized production equipment that will soon have to be scrapped?

In light of this, it would not be at all surprising if the firm systematically underestimated both maintenance costs and what needed to be paid into the capital reserve fund for those items whose useful life would expire beyond their time horizon. After all, if they underestimate those costs, the bottom line is correspondingly improved in the near term. (Independent of the implications for exploitation, the cumulative effect of this would be to shorten the useful life of all equipment, which would distort the capital structure of the economy even further.)

It is important to understand that the state cannot simply stamp its foot and tell the cooperatives not to "cheat." Not only are there significant informational asymmetries that cannot be overcome or can only be overcome with monitoring efforts that are not cost-effective, but (as the preceding discussion shows) the facts of the matter are themselves inherently contestable and highly speculative. In summary, then, the epistemological fog surrounding the replacement value of firm's assets creates opportunities for the cooperative's residual claimants to appropriate for themselves some of the value of those assets when those assets have to be replaced at a time that is beyond their time horizon. In other words, they can exploit the owners of the firm's capital—the state and through it, the taxpayers.

What about assets that do not have to be replaced—intangible capital such as a brand name, a distribution system, product design and engineering, and so on? Since some of the value of these assets would be realized in the future, that is, beyond the current workers' time horizon, they would have less incentive to protect the long-term value of these assets. Imagine a situation in which control of the firm is effectively in the hands of older workers (who are going to retire in, say, the next five years) in an alliance with those who are planning to move on to other firms in the near term. It would be in the interests of these older workers and the short-timers to sell off, for example, a distribution system to a rival and then lease it back for five years. Or they could sell another firm's products under their brand name as a way of selling their brand name or customer loyalty. Of course, they are not supposed to be able to sell off capital goods, but the distinction between selling off assets and simply making the adjustments necessary to maintain the position of the firm in the economy is a difficult one to draw. For firms unsure about where to draw the line, consulting firms would doubtless spring up to help them do it to the best of their advantage.

To this it might be objected that these older workers would not sell their younger counterparts down the river. But there is no need to assume an unusually strong penchant for opportunism on the part of the old-timers and the short-timers: transactions that have the effect of selling off intangibles could be folded into other transactions that arguably make good business sense. The systematic bias responsible for selling off intangibles may be a cognitive bias as much as a bias of the heart. In other words, the short-timers (whose ranks would swell as the firm headed toward bankruptcy) and the old-timers may genuinely believe that they are doing what is best for the firm when, in point of fact, what they are doing is best only for themselves. It would not be the first time that people's beliefs were profoundly shaped by their interests.

Finally, the quasi-rents of the firm itself constitutes a store of wealth that can find its way into the pockets of the firm's ultimate decision makers. How could this wealth be tapped? One way would be to borrow funds and use the proceeds to invest in projects that expand current cash flows at the expense of future cash flows where the loan is repaid in constant amounts over a period of time (Jensen and Meckling 1979, 496). This period of time could extend beyond the termination date of most workers—or of older workers who exercise disproportionate ultimate decision-making authority. In this way, income would be shifted from the future to the present and thus from younger workers—and even from future workers—to older workers.

A second way to tap this quasi-rent value would be to issue long-term bonds (or borrow money from the state designated as working capital) and use the proceeds to increase that year's payout or fringe benefits. Or workers could vote themselves large pension benefits with no funding provisions, just as politicians do in dealing with state employees (1979, 484).

Finally, current workers in the cooperative could get access to the quasi-rent value of the firm through the improper exercise of entrepreneurship. It was pointed out previously that the firm has a responsibility to maintain its position in the economy. Presumably, if it improves the firm's position, it would reap the benefits in the form of increased residuals. But what happens if it retreats from its position in the market? Who bears the losses? Presumably, the residual claimants. But suppose the latter can shift those losses—in effect, the costs of poor entrepreneurship—beyond their time horizon. They would certainly have some incentive to do this. One way that this could happen is that firms could take on excessively risky projects whose benefits accrue in the near term if all goes well and whose costs, if the venture fails, would be spread out over a time period that extends beyond their time horizon.

In these and other ways, present members of the cooperative could access the quasi-rent value of the firm and thereby exploit those to whom it belongs—society at large, or more exactly, the taxpayers. Other groups whose quasi-rents would be appropriable under some of these scenarios are younger workers and future workers in the cooperative because of their residual claimant status. These groups, as well as the taxpayers, are the ones that will have to foot the bill when payment comes due.[27]

There is some empirical evidence that has a bearing on these issues. Many of these problems have afflicted what used to be Yugoslavia, where the state and not the workers owned the capital of the firms. As Jan Vanek has said in his discussion of the worker cooperative in Yugoslavia,

The danger often referred to in the Yugoslav experience of the work col-
lectivities 'eating up their factories' can therefore be seen not merely in its
crude form of lack of maintenance and of replacement of physical assets,
excess distribution [of residuals] . . . but also in the more subtle form of
greater or lesser depreciation of all assets in real terms through improper
or inadequate operation of the enterprise. (1972, 220)

Obviously, in a market socialist system, various forms of monitoring
would be instituted to try to prevent these and similar predations. These
will be discussed in some detail in the second section of the next chapter.
Moreover, if real solidarity among the workers existed, it would likely
dampen the penchant for opportunism, though it is less plausible to suppose that this solidarity would extend easily or completely beyond the
boundary of the cooperative to the state bureaucracy charged with monitoring the firm's use of society's capital. After all, the natural human reaction to audits and auditors is on par with the natural human reaction to
root canal procedures and the endodontists who perform them.

However—and this brings us to the crucial point of this discussion—
none of this potential for exploitation exists in the comparable organization
in a free enterprise system, the classical capitalist firm. The manipulation of
maintenance and capital replacement does not create opportunities for
exploitation in the classical capitalist firm because the residual claimant also
provides the capital and can sell his interest in the firm at any time.
Because of that, he suffers the full wealth consequences of any decisions
about maintenance, capital replacement, and the sale of intangibles. This is
true even of the wealth consequences that are realized in the distant future
because those consequences are capitalized into the value of the firm.
Moreover, since he owns the firm, he owns its quasi-rent value, so he cannot
exploit someone by appropriating this wealth in his capacity as ultimate
decision maker. For all these reasons, there are opportunities and motivations for exploitation in a small-to-medium-sized cooperative that simply
do not exist in the classical capitalist firm.[28]

7

Exploitation in a
Market Socialist Economy II

Exploitation in and through the Large Cooperative

In the large cooperative, just as in the small cooperative, the workers are collectively the residual claimants and the ultimate decision makers. Although in theory they could elect managers directly, most discussions of market socialism envision a workers' council selecting a manager or management team. And indeed, that makes sense: monitoring management in the large cooperative (which is what the council does) is something that most workers are not in a good position to do, at least beyond the level of their immediate supervisors.[1] In general, the task of monitoring management is likely to be more difficult in a large cooperative than in a smaller cooperative if only because management's job is much more complex in a large organization. A smaller group, elected from the ranks of the workers, would be better positioned to monitor management, since they could develop the specialized knowledge and acquire the sheer experience required to do a good job in assessing how well management performs. Notice that the rationale for the existence of this intermediate body is the same as the rationale for having a monitor in the small cooperative instead of having everyone monitoring everyone else.

Capital provision in the large cooperative would be from the state, as in the smaller cooperatives. Other than sheer size, the differences between the large cooperatives and the smaller cooperatives do not appear to be that great. Indeed, in principle, smaller cooperatives could also have a workers' council, although that possible complication was ignored in the discussion in the last section of chapter 6. Though the two types of cooperatives are similar in many respects, the comparable capitalist organization, the open corporation, is dramatically different from its smaller cousin, the classical capitalist firm. And that difference makes a difference in the subject of this section—the comparative evaluation of the large cooperative and the open corporation on the topic of exploitation. Some of the weaknesses of the small cooperative are relative weaknesses only, that is, weaknesses relative to the classical capitalist firm. Those weaknesses do not exist when the terms of comparison are the two types of larger organizations. For example, the fact that the manager is a fractional residual claimant is a weakness of the small cooperative in comparison to the classical capitalist firm, but it is not a weakness of the large cooperative vis-à-vis the open corporation, since the manager of the large cooperative is also a fractional residual claimant.

Indeed, there are four important similarities between the governance structure of the large cooperative and that of the open corporation: (1) ultimate decision-making authority is joined to residual claimancy and both are spread widely among many different individuals; (2) there is a partial separation between these two roles on the one hand and managerial control on the other (i.e., in both types of organizations, management has only fractional residual claimant status and only fractional ultimate decision-making authority); (3) there is a mediating body between management and the ultimate decision-making authority—for the cooperative, the workers' council, and for the open corporation, the board of directors—whose main task is to monitor management; and (4) in neither case do the members of these intermediate bodies provide most of the firm's capital.

As notable as these similarities are, there are important differences as well. In the open corporation, unlike the cooperative, ultimate decision-making authority and residual claimancy are joined to the provision of capital. In other words, there are equity owners, and most of the firm's capital is provided by them. By contrast, in the large cooperative there are no equity owners; it effectively rents all of its capital from the state. This difference means that the governing boards represent the interests of very different ultimate decision makers. Specifically, the governing body of the corporation represents the interests of the capital providers; the governing body of the cooperative does not. Another difference between the two types of organizations is that in the open corporation, shares of equity ownership—and thus proportional claims on the firm's residuals—are freely alienable on a stock market. On the other hand, a worker's residual claims on the large cooperative's cash flows are inalienable and must be given up when workers leave the firm. These differences are significant; indeed, the governance structure of the large cooperative either creates opportunities for exploitation that do not exist in the open corporation or else has inferior damage control mechanisms to deal with forms of exploitation that are endemic to both types of organizations. Making the case for this is the main purpose of this section.

Fundamentally, the issue is about how to monitor management. How effectively could this be done in the large cooperative? In the last section, it was argued that monitoring arrangements in the small-to-medium-sized cooperative would be weakened by adverse selection and moral hazard problems. Politically astute but relatively ineffective managers would be chosen and would be compromised by their status as elected officials. Managers' status as fractional residual claimants would also affect their incentive to do a good job as manager, at least in comparison with the classical capitalist who gets to vacuum up every residual dollar.

However, it is not obvious that a large cooperative would be at a comparative disadvantage vis-à-vis the open corporation on these points. If the workers' council developed some expertise and experience at choosing and evaluating managers, they would be no less easily taken in by smooth-talking political types than the average board of directors is. Furthermore, if management is appointed by the workers' council, the former may not be compromised by the democratic structure of the firm in the way that the manager of the small cooperative would be. Finally, in both the open corporation and the large cooperative, managers are only fractional residual claimants, so any diminution of incentives that go with this status would afflict both types of organizations. (This is likely to have an impact on forms of opportunism such as unauthorized on-the-job consumption.)

Notice, however, that if the large cooperative is going to avoid the weaknesses of the small cooperative and do about as well as the open corporation in monitoring management, it will have to look more like a corporation and less like a cooperative in two respects. First, the workers' council will have to have people on it with the experience and specialized knowledge to assess managerial performance, since managerial tasks or functions are, in general, hard to monitor. (More on these functions shortly.) The need for people with experience and specialized knowledge can be appreciated by considering the problems that the council faces. Although shirking by management is a always a potential problem, perhaps a more important form of opportunism is managers' efforts to make it appear that they, the managers, are doing a better job than they really are. The inherent difficulties in monitoring the particular tasks of management are aggravated by the natural human desire to put the best face on a situation. In other words, managers (like other human beings) are prone to indulge in credit stealing and blame shifting. The monitoring problem is further compounded by the fact that much of the information needed to assess management's performance is developed and provided by the management itself. Insofar as it concerns financial information, this problem can be dealt with in the same way that corporations deal with it: the workers' council would hire an independent public accounting firm to audit the firm's financial statement that management prepares. Also, as in the corporation, the cooperative's internal auditors would report to the audit committee of the workers' council, instead of to the managers. Of course, the audit committee is going to have to have someone on it with expertise in accounting. The same considerations apply in assessing nonfinancial information submitted by management (e.g., plans for expansion, repositioning). Usually the best sources of the requisite knowledge and experience are people who themselves have had significant managerial experience, which is part of the reason why corporate boards are dominated by other executives.

These observations are obvious enough to anyone with a basic understanding of how large, profit-making organizations are run. Unfortunately, many socialists seem insensitive to these facts in their enthusiasm for democratic governance. It is certainly possible for workers to have ultimate decision-making authority without any special expertise. Stockholders in large corporations are a perfect example of this. But ultimate decision-making authority is different from actual governance, and the latter is what the workers' council has to do. The problem is that it is unclear where, within the firm, all of this specialized knowledge and experience is to be found. The obvious solution would be to employ outsiders (e.g., executives from other cooperatives) in an advisory capacity, though this means the reintroduction of wage labor, at least for these advisors. That problem to one side, the council must be careful to prevent its power and authority from being effectively ceded to these outsiders, who may have important informal ties with those being monitored. Though this need not lead to the reintroduction of power elites, there would be important structural continuities between governance in the large cooperative and governance in the open corporation.

The second respect in which the large cooperative would resemble the open corporation is that the workers' council would interpose itself between the workers and management. If the management team is to be effective in preventing shirking down through the ranks, it must be at least partially insulated by the council from the white heat of democracy. This, of course, creates the risk of management becoming unaccountable to the workers, though that risk may be manageable. In sum, the workers' council will have to walk a fine line if it is to be true to the ideals of the self-management and at the same time get good performance from its managerial team. In a competitive environment, firms that do a good job in monitoring management will tend to survive and prosper at the expense of rivals whose monitoring of management is less effective.

The large cooperative is, however, less likely to overpay its executives than its corporate counterpart. Boards of directors in free enterprise systems are dominated by executives who are themselves highly paid. Obviously, they have little interest in keeping down the average pay for executives. (Imagine what would happen if professors set the pay of their opposite numbers at other institutions.) If enough people with dirty fingernails sat on the compensation committee of the workers' council, it is doubtful whether top management would get the kind of compensation package that corporate officers sometimes get, at least in America in recent years. Conspicuous on-the-job consumption would also likely be diminished in a large cooperative. This is one case where physical proximity does make a difference in monitoring management.[2] On the other hand, it is not clear that executives of corporations in free enterprise systems are, in general, overpaid. Those who complain (rightly, in this author's view) about the fact that the compensation of some American executives has nothing to do with their performance often point to the more modest compensation packages received by Japanese and European executives. This suggests that the problem is an American problem, that is, a problem with the American version of the free enterprise system and not a defect of free enterprise systems in general.

Still, it may be true that the market for managers of large corporations are not competitively efficient. It is certainly "thinner," in the sense that there is not as much buying and selling going on as there is, for example, in wholesale produce markets. And the product is definitely harder to evaluate. These two facts together do not guarantee that markets in executive services are not competitively efficient and that managers are generally paid more than they are worth, but it could turn out that way. However, this problem of thin markets for managers (if it is a problem) would also face the large cooperatives. Indeed, it might be worse in them because of the structural impediments in all labor markets in a market socialist system, discussed previously. It is more likely, however, that managers would be underpaid for the reasons that were discussed in the first section of chapter 6. So it is not clear in the final analysis if the relationship between firms and their executives is inherently more exploitative in the open corporation than it would be in the market socialist worker cooperative.

Monitoring Management in the Large Cooperative

Let us turn now to the particular tasks that management is responsible for—monitoring, central contracting, and directing the firm's product—and see how they would be monitored in the large cooperative. Let us assume that top management in the large cooperative discharges its monitoring functions by instituting performance evaluation policies for other workers and by hiring and monitoring lower-echelon managers, all with the consultation and participation of the workers themselves. Whatever the benefits of widespread participation, the problem with it, from the council's perspective as monitor of top management, is that it entails a diffusion of responsibility for monitoring. (The same holds true for the other aspects of management to the extent that they are shared with the workers.) If monitoring is done poorly, blame is less easy to assign, and if it is done well, credit is more difficult to attribute. This provides some incentive for managers to shirk in the provision of monitoring services. More generally, this diffusion of responsibility smudges the record of managers' contribution, thereby making it more difficult to reward them according to their contributions. The open corporation solves this problem by permitting executives to employ whatever methods of monitoring they choose (from the whip to the solicitation of advice from those being monitored) and then holding them personally responsible for the results. Of course, it does not always work that way: many executives are master blame shifters and credit stealers in all of their tasks. As the firm lurches from one disaster to another, they are able to convince the board that those disasters are not their fault. Credit stealing is, if anything, even more prevalent. However, the same possibilities for opportunism would exist in a market socialist system. What is at issue here is the susceptibility of organizational structures to shirking and other forms of opportunism in the provision of monitoring services by top management and the relative ease with which management can be monitored. On this point, it seems that the less hierarchical, more consultative structure envisioned for the large cooperative is decidedly inferior to—and thus more vulnerable to exploitation than—the open corporation.

Although, in theory, the same problem arises when the council seeks to monitor management's work on the input and output interfaces between the firm and the market, in point of fact, this problem probably would not arise. There is some empirical evidence from what used to be Yugoslavia supporting the proposition that workers in large cooperatives in a market socialist system would be relatively uninterested in these matters, at least in comparison to matters such as income policies and work rules.[3] Indeed, that makes sense, since the issues that management must deal with on these fronts are more remote from the workers' knowledge and immediate interests and require experience and more specialized knowledge to deal with. Should the firm challenge the Wordperfect Corporation in the desktop publishing market? Should it sell semifinished products to competitors? Do changes in the regulatory environment necessitate the redesign of products or production processes? Do changes in the tax code require changes in maintenance procedures or investment strategies? It is facile to suppose that workers can easily acquire the requisite specialized knowledge and the sheer experience required to have meaningful input on issues and questions such as these.

How, then, would the workers' council monitor these aspects of management, since the council is composed of workers? As indicated before, they would likely hire other executives in an advisory capacity before ratifying major entrepreneurial decisions proposed by management. The question now becomes, Would the workers' council do about as well as (or better than) a corporation's board of directors in monitoring in management's entrepreneurial activities? Putting aside the principal-agent problems posed by the outside advisors, it seems that the council would have an incentive to monitor management as well as or better than corporate boards. After all, members of the workers' council are all much more substantial residual claimants —substantial in the sense that their own financial well-being is intimately connected with the fate of the cooperative—than the average board member in the open corporation. Though the incentive to monitor might be superior, the interests being protected are systematically different, and it is for this reason that there are distinctive opportunities for systematic exploitation in a market socialist system that are not found in a free enterprise system. These opportunities are traceable to the peculiar structure of ownership rights to the firm's capital and the nature of the workers' status as residual claimants.

As in the case of the small cooperative, three facts are of decisive importance in this connection: (1) neither members of the workers' council nor the workers themselves own any of the firm's capital; instead, the state effectively owns the cooperative's capital; (2) the workers' claim on the residuals is limited to their tenure at the firm; (3) the workers' claims on the residuals are inalienable—that is, their claim on the residuals cannot be sold to outsiders or indeed to anyone. What this means is that the workers' council, unlike the board of directors, represents only current residual claimants—not the capital providers and not the future residual claimants. There is no reason to suppose that the council will be any more solicitous of the interests of future residual claimants (i.e., future workers) and the capital providers (i.e., tax-payers) than the managers would be. Indeed, they could all conspire to exploit these voiceless citizens of market socialist society. Like the small-to-medium-sized cooperative, the large cooperative would be characterized by poor maintenance, dubious formulas for calculating replacement costs of capital, and income shifting from the more distant future to the present.

By contrast, the board of directors of the open corporation represents, albeit imperfectly, the interests of the equity owners (the shareholders). The latter not only own have a claim on the firm's residuals that extends indefinitely far into the future but can also sell their ownership shares at any time. Those shares represent a claim on all the assets that the firm owns (net of its debt obligations), as well as future residuals that these assets can be used to generate. Debt holders are protected because in the event of bankruptcy, they get paid off before the equity owners do, which means that the board cannot protect the initial investment of equity owners without also protecting the investment of those who hold corporate debt instruments. In the cooperative, there are no equity owners at all to protect the major debt holder—the state. The state has no equity owners to suffer the blows of financial misfortune. Moreover, to the extent that a corporation's board of directors represents the interests of the shareholders as opposed to those of (merely) current residual claimants, it is concerned with the long-term consequences of management's decisions for the equity value of the firm. In other words, it protects the interests of the capital providers and the future residual claimants.

This is not to say that the board always does its job. Sometimes incompetent management is protected, top managers effectively choose the board that oversees them, and various other forms of self-dealing take place. But putting principal-agent problems to one side for a moment, it is clear that the open corporation's board of directors protects the interests of future residual claimants and capital providers better than the group whose institutional function is to represent only the interests of the current residual claimants. Through their agents—management and the workers' council—the ultimate decision makers in the cooperative (i.e., the workers) can appropriate the quasi-rent value of the firm and, to a lesser extent, the quasi-rent value of the assets that future residual claimants might bring to the firm (i.e., the quasi-rent value of future worker's human capital). By contrast, the ultimate decision makers in the open corporation cannot exploit the capital providers because they *are* the capital providers. And they can sell their claims on the future residuals. As in the case of the classical capitalist firm, equity ownership closes down avenues of exploitation that are wide open in a market socialist system.

An obvious solution to the problem of the workers' limited stake in the firm is to include representatives of the capital providers on the workers' council. This proposal bears affinities to the codetermination movement, which seeks state-mandated representation of labor interests on corporate boards in free enterprise systems (Pejovich 1978). However, this body cannot properly be called a workers' council. One of the most important rights of workers, the right of self-management, has been attenuated. In other words, the workers no longer collectively have ultimate decision-making authority in the firm, since representatives of the provider of the firm's capital (i.e., state officials representing the public) now have a say in who the managers will be and how the firm will be run. But perhaps that is not such a bad thing. There appears to be a serious weakness in the structure of the market socialist system, and the most natural way to deal with it would be to put state officials on the council. Besides, there is no reason for socialists to recoil in horror from partial state control of the cooperatives. That is an anathema only to those on the Right.

Various forms of state ownership of the cooperatives will be discussed in chapter 8. For present purposes, it is sufficient to point out that the public officials who serve on such boards or those who appoint them may well have an even shorter time horizon than their counterparts in the cooperative, at least under the assumption that the political system is democratic. Since political actors can be turned out of office at the next election, their time horizons tend to be fairly limited. This does not mean that it never pays for political authorities to take the long view, but at least in recent decades, democratically elected politicians and those who answer to them have not been known for their patience and farsightedness on economic matters. In sum, it is far from clear that appointing political authorities to the governing council of the large cooperative would provide much protection for the interests of the capital providers, the taxpayers (not to mention the future residual claimants).[4]

Equally important, the systematic difference in interests between the residual claimants and the providers of capital would probably make this arrangement ultimately unstable. Representatives of one or the other group would likely achieve a position of dominance (perhaps by changing the laws that set the ground rules) from which it could serve its own interests at the expense of the losing group. If, for example, the workers' representatives maintained hegemony, the problem of the exploitation of taxpayers would remain. On the other hand, if the state achieved dominance, the system would be one of effective state ownership of most the means of production, which is incompatible with the type of market socialism under discussion.

Returning to the workers' council as it was originally described, it is not even clear that it offers current residual claimants (the workers) better protection against exploitation by bad management than a board of directors offers its equity owners against the same threat. The reason why has to do with the nature of the assets that the respective groups put at management's disposal. For the workers, it is their knowledge and skills, and for the equity owners, it is their capital. The quasi-rent value of the capital contributed by equity owners tends to be relatively less than the quasi-rent value of the workers' assets because it is easier for equity owners to withdraw from the firm by selling their equity shares on the stock market and redeploying those assets elsewhere.[5] Indeed, an important consequence of the creation of the modern corporation and the associated stock markets in which equity shares are freely traded is that the quasi-rent value of investors' capital is significantly reduced; this makes these investors less vulnerable to exploitation than they would be if their capital contribution were less fungible. By contrast, workers' assets (their respective capacities to labor and specialized skills) are, in general, more difficult to withdraw and reposition. If managers make some bad decisions to the point where a worker wants out, the latter cannot easily withdraw some or all of her labor assets from the firm the next day and park them somewhere else. She does, of course, have other avenues of redress in the large cooperative, but it is not obvious that they are more effective, from her point of view, than the investor's option of selling stock. Selling one's stock is a way of sending a message; if the message does not get through, the sender is at least no longer exposing her assets to dissipation by poor managers. It is the economic equivalent of voting with one's feet; while it carries costs with it, those costs are generally much less than the costs workers incur in changing jobs.

The stock market in a free enterprise system is an extremely sensitive—albeit imperfect—device whereby the value of a firm is constantly assessed and reassessed. It represents the collective judgment of an enormous number of people who have a vital personal interest in making a correct assessment of the equity value of large corporations. If poor managers start to dissipate that value, the market tends to register that fact and thereby invites equity owners to withdraw. This outside monitoring of management, assisted by securities analysts, cannot be provided in a market socialist system because there is no equity ownership, and for obvious reasons there could be no stock market in workers' labor assets.

A related liability of a market socialist system is a weak or nonexistent market for corporate control. For example, members of the Yezhov cooperative and their workers' council might not realize how poorly their management is doing relative to the firm's potential. Corporate raiders from the Beria cooperative cannot buy control of the Yezhov cooperative, oust the latter's ineffective management, and bring the Yezhov cooperative up to its full potential. The most they can do is offer to join the Yezhov cooperative and run for office, in exchange for which they would get an equal share of the residuals, if elected. The prohibition on a market for corporate control serves to insulate ineffective managers and their workers' councils from market-based accountability. This permits the exploitation of the other residual claimants (namely, the other workers), not to mention the capital providers.

It is tempting to think that the workers' council, because it is composed of workers, would serve faithfully the interests of the cooperative's members. While their hearts might be in the right place (the incentive alignments are, after all, quite good), there is no guarantee that they will do a good job at monitoring management. Monitoring very large profit-making organizations is difficult to do, and good intentions are not enough. Outside monitoring by people who specialize in that task and who stand to make a great deal of money if they discover that a firm is being poorly managed is a better damage-control mechanism than whatever internal recall mechanisms might be developed in a large cooperative to deal with poor management or poor oversight from the workers' council. One reason for this is that to the extent that hierarchy exists in the cooperative, disaffected workers would be at an obvious disadvantage in launching an effort to replace management or council members. (Imagine corporate raiders on Wall Street being employees of their takeover targets.) In addition, disaffected workers would also be easier to buy off than corporate raiders. Of course, hostile takeovers in the open corporation are often costly and not easy to execute. Proxy fights, whereby dissident shareholders try to oust incumbent management through votes of the equity owners, tend to be even less successful, though how much of this is an artifact of the legal system is unclear. Nevertheless (subject to a few exceptions), in neither case are dissidents going up against people who can take their jobs away from them. It is naive to suppose that managers of large cooperatives would not develop mechanisms to neutralize dissidents within the firm, whatever the cooperative's charter says.

Because it is difficult to monitor management of large, complex organizations, opportunistic managers can get away with much more exploitation than can workers down on the assembly line, where monitoring is easy and effective. This fact might explain some of the resentment that has been historically directed at those at the top in business organizations; it might also explain why many people find management jobs so attractive. Both large cooperatives and open corporations must face this fact, which is inherent in the institutional role. However, at least in the open corporation, though the ill-gotten gains to individuals may be substantial, the overall losses are probably not too serious. The reason is that if losses were significant, it is likely that the open corporation would have succumbed, like the dinosaurs, to its smaller, warm-blooded rival, the classical capitalist firm. Whether a similar fate would befall the larger cooperative at the hands of its smaller rival is less clear since both types of firms have the same organizational structure.

Exploitation along the Firm-Market Boundary

Before closing this section, it is worth discussing briefly some distinctive opportunities for exploitation that could occur along the firm-market boundary in a market socialist system. This requires a relaxation of some assumptions made in the last chapter, namely, that transactions cost efficiencies would play about the same role in drawing the boundary between the firm and the market in a market socialist system as in a free enterprise system and that both systems would have about the same mix of small, medium, and large firms. One reason the latter might be false is that there could be an ideological bias for smaller organizations in a socialist society. In addition, an endogenous (i.e., economic) reason is that in this type of system, it would be much more difficult to effect mergers and acquisitions than it is in a free enterprise system, which means that average firm size would likely be smaller. The reasons for this, and its implications for exploitation, warrant some elaboration.

Imagine the situation facing the management of two firms contemplating a merger or one firm contemplating an acquisition. Putting one of these together would be much more difficult and problematic in a market socialist system than it would be for an open corporation in a free enterprise systems. This is so for three reasons. First, in the case of an acquisition, the management of the acquiring company need only seek the approval of the board of directors and not the stockholders, whereas a majority of both cooperatives would presumably have to agree in a market socialist system. In an open corporation, the acquiring company simply acquires controlling shares of the stock. The situation is a little more complicated in a merger, but the merger of cooperatives would still require a broader consensus. Second (and perhaps more important), one common result of either type of change is that jobs are eliminated because of the attending efficiencies that the acquisition or merger realizes, and it is often unclear at the outset which jobs will go. Most—indeed nearly all—of the equity owners of the firms in a free enterprise system have no interest whatever in preventing a shrinkage of the workforce when a merger or acquisition goes through. By contrast, the ultimate decision makers of cooperatives would have every interest in world in preventing just that.[6] Finally, since the cooperative seeks to maximize net income per worker rather than net income, some mergers and acquisitions that would go through in a free enterprise system would be blocked in a market socialist system.

The fact that some mergers and acquisitions do not take place that from an economic point of view should take place has some important implications for exploitation in market socialist system. As pointed out in chapter 5, one of the principal costs of organizing transactions across markets rather than within firms is that transactors can have their quasi-rents exposed to their trading partners. If the size of firms in a market socialist economy were held down by ideological bias or by a bias traceable to the structure of cooperatives, expropriation hazards (i.e., opportunities for exploitation) induced by asset specificities would exist that otherwise would not.

The same considerations apply in the other direction. Sometimes organizations are too large. The major costs of the firm, as opposed to the market, are the costs associated with bureaucratic inefficiency that is endemic to hierarchy.[7] The manager of a division within a large multidivisional corporation or of a unit in a conglomerate may take his division or unit private through a leveraged buyout. This cuts out some of the cross-subsidization (and exploitation) that is inevitable in these large organizations; it also introduces the superior incentive alignments of the classical capitalist firm or, at least, shortens and narrows the bureaucratic hierarchy responsible for the original inefficiencies.

This would be a much more problematic undertaking in a large cooperative. Presumably, a unit could not secede without the concurrence of the larger cooperative of which it is a part; otherwise, some units would face serious expropriation hazards, in the form of threats to secede, from other units within the cooperative. Suppose that an unusually efficient unit believed that it was responsible for more "value added" than were other units. If that were true and widely known, workers in other units would be reluctant to let it go. In a market socialist system, large cooperatives might well be composed of factions held together by a strongman or by an uneasy truce—Titoism at the level of the firm.

These observations do not presuppose that free enterprise systems always draw the line between the firm and the market optimally. Rather, this type of system permits experimentation with organizational forms within very broad limits (e.g., no slavery); the competitive process tends to select the efficient experiments and reject the inefficient ones. This openness to experimentation in free enterprise systems, which would be curtailed in a market socialist system, also plays a role in the evolution of new and different contractual arrangements. In recent years, a hybrid of the classical capitalist firm and the open corporation has become an increasingly important organizational form in free enterprise systems: the franchise arrangement. Individuals enter into contractual agreements with large corporations (e.g., McDonald's) to market and sell the latter's products. The franchisee is the residual claimant on the franchise, but he is significantly constrained in how he operates his business by policies and procedures imposed by the franchiser. This type of business arrangement, which has never, to this author's knowledge, been investigated and evaluated by socialist theoreticians would create a real problem for a market socialist system. Must the franchisees be ultimate decision makers in the parent company, or would that role be limited to the members of the latter? And who, after all, is to count as member of the cooperative? Some of the most interesting recent work in transactions cost analysis explicitly recognizes that the boundary between the firm and the market is often blurred or arbitrary. The study of the economics of organizations is being transformed into the study of the economics of contracts. As they scrutinize novel and exotic contractual arrangements for conformity to the principles of market socialism, socialist theoreticians run the risk of looking like Islamic fundamentalists trying to devise a civil code for a modern state by applying the Koran.

To summarize, opportunities for exploitation will exist along the firm-market boundary in both free enterprise and market socialist economic systems. And free enterprise systems do not draw that boundary optimally so as to minimize, in any absolute sense, those opportunities. (For a better alternative, imagine an economic system in which God is in charge of determining the boundary between the firm and the market.) However, free enterprise systems encourage experimentation on where and how to draw the boundary, whereas market socialist systems prohibit or discourage experiments for structural, legal, and/or ideological reasons. Because of this, a free enterprise system tends to do better than a market socialist system in removing or minimizing opportunities for exploitation along the boundary between the firm and the market.

Exploitation through State Organizations

The state in a market socialist society would exercise some of the same economic functions that states in free enterprise systems exercise. For instance, it would provide for some goods and services such as defense and education through state-owned enterprises, and it would use fiscal and monetary policy as instruments to try to achieve macro level goals for the economy. But it would also do some things that the state in a free enterprise system does not do. It would serve as steward of all of society's capital, and it would control nearly all new investment. States in free enterprise systems take actions that affect society's capital structure but not in the comprehensive way envisioned for the market socialist state.

In a market socialist system, these two functions of the state are interrelated. It is because the state is the steward of society's capital that it receives the capital usage fees from the cooperatives; those funds represent the returns to capital, and it is with them that the state controls new investment. Recall from chapter 2 that the motivation for state control of new investment is twofold. First, it subjects the rate and direction of economic development to collective decision making. The priorities for new investment do not just emerge as the unintended consequences of disparate plans and interests of groups and individuals, as they do in free enterprise systems; instead, those priorities are consciously and collectively chosen through the political process. Second, state control of new investment prevents or corrects for various "social irrationalities" tossed up as unintended by-products of the operation of market forces. Perhaps the most important of these is unemployment, but this category also includes externalities such as pollution, and specific undesirable patterns of investment and/or consumption. For example, if a region has been especially hard hit by unemployment, investment funds can be targeted to that area. If a certain kind of pollution becomes an important problem, the state can spur innovation in pollution control by directing new investment to firms and industries that make pollution control devices. Finally, if a situation has developed in which a society, according to its own collective judgment, is producing too much of one type of thing (e.g., luxury goods) and not enough of another type of thing (e.g., health care), this collective preference can be incorporated into the plan for new investment.[8] The state in free enterprise systems tries to deal with some of these problems too, but it is not very effective. One of the reasons is that it simply does not have the resources at its disposal, at least in comparison to a market socialist state. All it has at its disposal are its regulatory and taxing authority, whereas a market socialist state has not only these instruments but also nearly all of that portion of society's wealth that is directed toward economic growth and development. There is, of course, the danger that the state will not represent the public interest; the primary way this danger is supposed to be dealt with is by ensuring widespread participation in the political process.

Despite the attractions from a socialist perspective of state stewardship of society's capital and state control of new investment, both of these features of a market socialist system create distinctive opportunities for exploitation. The purpose of this section is to investigate these opportunities. The discussion is focused narrowly on exploitation, omitting treatment of other problems, including some significant inefficiencies, occasioned by these features of a market socialist economic system. For example, unlike in a free enterprise system, where smaller firms are rarely audited, all smaller firms in a market socialist system would have to be audited. Compared to the free enterprise alternative, this is a significant inefficiency simply because of the substantial resources that would have to be committed to these audits on an ongoing basis. There are other problems with any form of noncomprehensive state planning of new investment that would need to be ventilated in a comprehensive discussion of market socialism.[9] Some of these problems will be alluded to in what follows, but a full discussion of them is beyond the scope of this section and, indeed, this book. The main concern of this book is the potential for exploitation in types of economic systems. This section is divided into two subsections. The first concerns opportunities for exploitation that arise in determining the value of the assets on which firms would pay the capital usage fee. The second subsection examines the distinctive opportunities for exploitation that arise as a result of state control of new investment.

Exploitation through the Valuation of Assets

The last subsection of chapter 6 discusses the ways in which cooperatives could exploit the providers of capital. This subsection discusses how exploitation might take place in the other direction. Because of the potential for exploitation by the cooperative, the state in its role as capital provider will have to audit the cooperatives on a regular basis. Many people think that the primary task of the auditor is to detect fraud and malfeasance on the part of corporate officers. But that is not the case. Perhaps the most important task the auditors must discharge in a market socialist system is to verify that the value of tangible and intangible assets has been properly maintained. And, of course, they must ascertain that the cooperative has maintained the quasi-rent value of the firm itself, the asset that accountants misleadingly call *good will*. All of this is important for the obvious reason that society wants to prevent the dissipation of the assets that it has entrusted to the workers in the cooperative. But it is also important because the total value of the firm is the figure on which the capital usage fee is calculated. The higher that figure is, the higher the capital usage fee will be. As noted earlier, it is difficult to ascertain the value of physical assets, and there are enormous problems in ascertaining the value of intangibles, such as product engineering and brand-name loyalty. Furthermore, the problem of determining the value of good will is theoretically insurmountable, since good will is the difference between the selling price of the firm and the salvage value of its assets—and firms are not bought and sold in a market socialist system. Western accounting firms facing comparable problems in trying to assess the value of firms in Eastern and Central Europe essentially threw up their hands. Though the problem may not be solvable in theory, it must be solved in practice because firms *do* have a quasi-rent value attached to them because of their "niche" in the economy, and (as indicated earlier) there are ways that firms can appropriate that value if the auditors do not do their job.

The epistemological indeterminacy of the value of all these assets creates a devil's playground in a market socialist system. Clearly, there is an inherent conflict of interest between the cooperatives and the state on this. For reasons discussed earlier, the cooperatives will tend to undervalue their assets. The auditors will have to act aggressively to protect the interests of society at large. How this would be played out is impossible to say without a more detailed specification of the relevant state institutions and their incentive structures. For example, if auditors were paid a commission on the value of the assets of the firms they audited, they would have a strong incentive to overvalue those assets. If they themselves were members of independent profit-making accounting cooperatives and were hired by the firms they audit, they would have an incentive to undervalue the assets.[10] Whatever the incentives, however, it is fair to say that it would be truly astonishing if the auditors came up with an accurate valuation of the firms. Independent of the incentives implicit in the structure of the organizations of which they are members, the multiple indeterminacies identified previously would make it much more likely that they would undervalue or overvalue the firms rather than assess them accurately.

This has important implications for exploitation: neither the state nor the cooperative has anywhere else to go if the other party is appropriating value from them. If the cooperative is siphoning value from the firm's assets into the residuals that the auditors do not catch, then obviously the state will not be able to do anything about it. Moreover, even if the state discovers it, there may not be much that it can do. Penalties might cause the firm to go under or cause the workers to abandon the firm and go elsewhere. Also, whatever its legal authority, the state cannot easily strip the workers of their firm and turn it over to a new group of workers. Similarly, if the state has unwittingly (or perhaps wittingly, depending on what motivates the auditors) overvalued the cooperative's assets and set the capital usage fee too high, the workers would likely have no real alternative but to turn over to the state what is, in effect, their residuals or the return on their labor. This is so for three reasons. First, getting a second opinion from another state auditing team would, in general, be too costly, and there are moral hazards in permitting firms to shop around for auditors. Second, it is likely that some of the quasi-rents associated with their labor really are appropriable because they will have developed some firm-specific assets (knowledge and skills) that would be lost if they left. And it would likely be difficult to redeploy those assets because of the sluggish labor markets that characterize market socialism. Finally, even if these workers could go somewhere else, it may not matter. Depending on the incentive structure under which the auditors are working, these workers might well be facing essentially the same situation at their new jobs. It follows from all this that if the cooperatives are not exploiting the state, the chances are very good that the state is exploiting the membership of the cooperatives.

These observations would not count as a serious objection against market socialism if the same problem afflicted capitalist organizations. However, the latter do not face this problem. The classical capitalist firm escapes it entirely because the classical capitalist supplies most of her own capital. The equity cushion is usually thick enough to secure short-term obligations and any money they borrow from friends and relatives. This is one reason why these firms are rarely audited. The open corporation on the other hand is audited, but it has an equity base to secure its creditors. By certifying that the financial statement is accurate (subject to the usual disclaimers), the auditors are assuring stockholders and debt holders that the equity base is intact. The exact value of corporate assets is less of a concern to debt holders (and not something the auditors try to ascertain), as long as the firm's equity cushion is thick enough to protect its debt. Only when a firm is highly leveraged is the debt holder at risk. This risk is handled by giving the debt holder veto power over major moves by the corporation and by attaching a risk premium to the interest the corporation must pay on its debt.

Exploitation through State Control of New Investment

In general, those who favor market socialism have provided little detail about the institutional structures by or through which state control of new investment would be exercised. The presumption that the state would be characterized by a high degree of participatory democracy tells us little about the details—or even the broad principles—of institutional design. Chapter 2 provides a rudimentary sketch of a way in which new investment might be controlled through the political process. It would be useful here to recall that sketch and augment it further. Suppose that the national legislature sets the capital usage fee, which determines the amount of funds that will be available for new investment. If, for example, it is set at 5 percent, then every firm must pay 5 percent of the value of the firm, as the latter has been determined by the auditors. The priorities for how these funds will be spent are also determined through the political process. At the national level, those priorities might be expressed in very broad terms (e.g., so much for the tourist industry, so much to develop new sources of energy). Political authorities might also designate funds to certain regions, for example, to those areas suffering from high unemployment.

However, because the political process at this level can only produce general guidelines, there must be various planning agencies to implement investment policy and priorities, presumably at different levels (e.g., national, regional, and local) of the society. These agencies receive their marching orders from the political process, but they themselves must determine the more specific guidelines to be followed in disbursing the funds. Lower-level planning authorities might make finer distinctions within the broad parameters set by the national legislature, and they might get input from lower levels of government. Actual funds could be disbursed through state-owned (national, regional, or local) banks, which would evaluate proposals from existing firms and from groups of workers who want to start up new firms. These proposals would be evaluated for their fit with the investment plan for the economy, their contribution to sovling regional or local problems (e.g., pollution) that did not receive priority at higher levels of government, and their financial soundness. By accepting these funds, cooperatives agree to pay the capital usage fee on the assets they purchase with them.

This method of determining new investment creates substantial opportunities for exploitation in a market socialist society that do not exist in a free enterprise system. To see what they are, notice that in a market socialist system, profitability is not the decisive or determinative criterion for new investment decisions that it is in a free enterprise system. At every level, governmental organizations charged with formulating and implementing policy use multiple decision criteria to determine where and how investment funds should be channeled. This use of multiple decision criteria creates a number of distinct moral hazard problems.

Suppose, as seems reasonable, that one of the most important goals of the investment policy formulated by the legislature is to reduce or prevent unemployment. This creates a moral hazard problem of colossal proportions. In the last subsection of chapter 6, it was pointed out that the ultimate decision makers in a cooperative have an incentive to shift costs into the future and shift income from the future to the present. One thing that might constrain these forms of exploitation is the concern that the cooperative, to which these decision makers have ties of fraternity and sentiment, might go out of business if they go too far. However, if they believe that state authorities in control of new investment would not let this happen, that constraint evaporates. This allows firms that have been poorly run to be bailed out at the expense of—and thus to exploit—society at large.

There is some empirical evidence that bears on this. In what used to be Yugoslavia, even when the state did not completely control new investment, it had some control of investment beyond what can be achieved by manipulating tax and fiscal policy. It also had responsibility for reducing unemployment. It is perhaps not a coincidence that the state was used to bail out failing firms. As Janos Kornai observes,

> state money is regularly used to rescue consistently loss-making firms [documented in an accompanying table]. . . . A high proportion of consistently loss-making firms are not merely kept alive with state subsidies or soft credits; their capacity is increased further. There is only a loose relation between the firm's past and future (expected) profitability and its investment, growth, and technical development. (1992, 490)

Kornai does not specifically address the question of whether there is a causal connection between the state's responsibility for dealing with unemployment and the bailouts, but the evidence he offers is very suggestive, to say the least. Moreover, as Kornai notes, the problem of bailouts is further aggravated by elements of socialist ideology such as solidarity with those who are in economic difficulty or about to lose their jobs (p. 493). It seems reasonable to suppose that any economic system in which state control of new investment is conceived of, at least in part, as an instrument to deal with unemployment will face a serious moral hazard problem in this respect. The problem could not be avoided by simply passing a law whereby badly managed firms would not be bailed out, since the distinction between a badly managed firm and one that is the victim of circumstances beyond its control is inherently contestable. In addition, as a practical matter, what counts as a badly managed firm and what counts as a bailout must be defined, and one could well imagine the lobbying effort that failing firms (as well as firms that might fail in the future) would mount when some subcommittee of the national legislature marked up that piece of legislation.

The problem just discussed is not limited to a system in which state control of new investment is an instrument to deal with unemployment. The problem arises as long as any criterion other than profitability is used to determine new investment. Any firm in financial difficulty and in a position to appeal to these other criteria will have an obvious incentive to propose new investment that would cover up their mistakes or make up for risks that turned out badly. In other words, firms that have not managed their assets wisely can exploit society at large by appeal to these other criteria to keep them in business. For example, a failing chemical company can argue that it is best positioned to deal with the toxic waste problem it has created but only if it is lent the money it needs to expand production of its best-selling pesticide or to gear up a promising research project to create and market products to deal with this problem. They might point out that if they do not get the money, they will be forced out of business, and the taxpayer will have to foot the bill anyway. By contrast, in a free enterprise system the state can go after the company's equity owners, and as liability lawyers can attest, there is money to be found there. Indeed, the lack of an equity base in market socialist cooperatives, coupled with free labor mobility, encourages firms to run risks they otherwise would not take. If and when those risks eventuate, the workers can move on; society as a whole loses the assets.

If the system were able to deal with the externalities and other "social irrationalities" in a satisfactory manner, socialists might regard the inevitable exploitation perpetrated by poorly run cooperatives as a reasonable price to pay. However, the morally hazardous aspect of the situation means that these problems are effectively encouraged by the system. The root of the problem is the fact of multiple decision criteria for new investment. If unemployment or pollution or any other social problem traceable to the operation of the market is supposed to be addressed through new investment controlled by the state, this creates incentives for people to do things that risk causing the very problems the system is supposed to address or prevent. In sum, the system is self-defeating, and it allows—and indeed encourages—firms that have run their operations badly to exploit society at large by getting bailed out by the infusion of new investment monies.

By contrast, in a free enterprise system, perceived profitability is the main determinant of new investment, and if a firm is failing, it is generally not able to force others to contribute capital to keep it in business. In the classical capitalist firm, new investment that might rescue a firm comes from the savings of the classical capitalist or perhaps from money lent by friends and relatives. If the firm subsequently goes under, the classical capitalist has not exploited herself. But what about friends and relatives? Might not they be exploited under these circumstances? Perhaps. But on the other hand, maybe people who make loans to friends or relatives whose businesses are in trouble deserve whatever happens to them.

The ultimate decision makers in the open corporation are also not in a position to exploit those who provide capital for new investment because, with the exception of debt holders, they *are* the capital providers. Debt holders are protected by the equity cushion of the firm, since in bankruptcy proceedings debt holders are paid off before equity owners. In both types of organizations, equity owners, who have ultimate decision-making authority, are legally last in line to get paid and thus first in line to suffer whatever losses they are responsible for. In general, for debt holders, whatever losses they suffer merely represent the downside of the risk premium they receive; assuming that they bought debt instruments with their eyes open, those losses can hardly be termed exploitative. But what about the state as a source of capital for firms that would otherwise fail?

It is true that in existing free enterprise systems, some firms have been judged "too big to fail" (e.g., the Chrysler Corporation a number of years ago), but this is "the exception that proves the rule" in two respects. First, these bailouts are not vices of the free enterprise system with no qualifying predicates. They are vices (or virtues, depending on one's perspective) traceable to the political system and are far from universal, especially by historical standards. Second, bailouts by the state that occur because of the fear of unemployment are rare enough to create no appreciable moral hazard in the system. Whatever else can be said about the unhealthy relationship between government and business in existing free enterprise systems, those in charge of large private corporations have little reason to believe that the government will bail them out by investing taxpayers' money in them if they do not manage the assets they control wisely. In societies with a free enterprise system, there is a gulf between the economic and political system that would not— and indeed could not—exist in a market socialist system. Whatever problems this gulf occasions, one salutary consequence is that generally speaking, firms that do not meet the test of the marketplace do not get to exploit society at large by forcing the latter to invest more in them when they are in trouble.[11] The same cannot be said of publicly owned organizations.

This explains some of the ways in which the ultimate decision makers in failing cooperatives can exploit the capital providers (i.e., society at large or the taxpayers) by manipulating the multiple decision criteria that are the inevitable accompaniment of planning. No special assumptions were made about the government agencies charged with implementing whatever plans were arrived at through the political process. One reason for that is that defenders of market socialism have not been very forthcoming about the nature or structure of the state organizations that they envision controlling new investment in a socialist economic system. Despite this paucity of detail, something can be said about the organizational structure of the public bureaucracies (namely, the planning agencies and banks) charged with implementing the will of the legislature about new investment.[12] This, in turn, permits an identification of some additional distinctive opportunities for exploitation in a market socialist system.

In a series of articles, Terry Moe, a political scientist, has called attention to some systematic differences between economic organizations and their political counterparts, public bureaucracies (Moe 1989, 1990a, 1990b). Transactions cost analysis proceeds on the assumption that the structure of economic organizations is largely determined by considerations of (transactions cost) efficiency. Economic actors often consciously seek to arrive at efficient, mutually advantageous arrangements when they create a business organization, and even if they do not, competitive pressures tend to weed out inefficient structures. However, no such presumption of efficiency applies in the case of public bureaucracies. In the political arena, other factors are determinative.

To see what they are, notice that one crucial difference between business organizations and public bureaucracies is that the creators of the former are the ultimate decision-making authorities for as long as they want to be and can sell their rights in the firm at any time. By contrast, in the case of public bureaucracies, the political lives of their creators—the politicians—are relatively short or at least of uncertain duration. The ultimate decision makers in business can undertake and execute (or have managers undertake and execute on their behalf) plans and projects without worrying that someone else (notably their opponents or rivals) will usurp them in a few years and do something entirely different with the firm. This is a luxury that political actors do not have.

In a democracy, when a decision is made to create a public bureaucracy, there are winners and losers among the political actors. The latter did not want the organization created at all, or they wanted it to have a very different mandate. Even if one assumes that the winners had to make no compromises with the losers to get the agency created, the former must deal with the fact that their hold on political power is uncertain; their rivals may come to power in the next election or the one after that. In addition, the winning political actors have a specific agenda they want to advance through the agency. That is why the agency is created in the first place. So they want to get their agenda enacted, but they may not be able to hold onto political power indefinitely. How will they design the agency to cope with the fact that their own political power may evaporate and reappear in the hands of their rivals?

Moe discusses a number of strategies they can and do use (Moe 1990b, 136–37). One that is especially important for present purposes is that in writing the agency's charter, they can put more emphasis on technical expertise and professionalism than is warranted. Professionals tend to be more resistant to political pressure, and they desire autonomy. Some autonomy is inevitable in any case, since political authorities can only give the agency general guidelines, which it must then interpret. However, not just any professionals will do. Political actors need to find high-level bureaucrats who will "do the right thing" once they are in the agency. Professionals know this, so they strive hard to create reputations that will make them natural choices to staff the upper levels of new bureaucracies. If the right people are chosen, the agency can run itself and fulfill the desired goals of the political actors who created it without extensive political oversight. Additional methods by which the independence of the agency can be ensured include circumscribing the authority of the political appointees who are sometimes nominally in charge of the agency, ensuring that agency decisions are immune from legislative veto, and preventing the agency from being subject to sunset provisions, which requires legislative reauthorization of the agency after a certain period of time.

Once the agency has been created, there is a new group of players on the scene, namely, the bureaucrats themselves. Whatever their ends or goals, the inherent uncertainty of the political environment creates problems for them, just as it does for the political actors who created the agency. The bureaucrats can deal with this problem in a number of different ways. One is to encourage mutually beneficial exchanges with political actors and their supporters who can help or harm them, including groups who were originally hostile to the agency (Moe 1990b, 144). This strategy can only go so far, however, since the agency's actions are bound to favor some interests at the expense of others; those who are harmed, or fear being harmed, have an interest in mobilizing political support to thwart or redirect the agency's (and thus the bureaucrats') agenda. So there is no way for the bureaucrats to eliminate the political uncertainty in their environment.

This motivates a second, complementary strategy—isolation. As Moe says:

> Bureaucrats . . . can promote further professionalization and more extensive reliance on civil service. They can formalize and judicialize their decision procedures. They can base their decisions on technical expertise, operational experience, and precedent, thus making it "objective" and agency-centered. They can try to monopolize the information necessary for effective political oversight. These insulating strategies are designed, moreover, not simply to shield the agency from its political environment but also to shield it from the very appointees who are formally its in-house leaders. (1990b, 144–45)

In addition, as time goes on, bureaucrats develop agency-specific knowledge and skills, which makes them increasingly difficult to replace, at least at the wholesale level. Political actors of whatever persuasion are increasingly forced to deal with them. Political actors, including the agency's creators, can foresee some of this (though one should be careful not attribute omniscience to them) and will take steps, both in the initial phase and subsequently, to prevent these agencies from running amok. But the potential for significant principal-agent problems remains because of the dynamics of the politics of bureaucratic structure.

Let us consider how all this applies in a market socialist system to that part of the state concerned with the control of nearly all new investment for the economy. Various planning agencies would be created in an environment characterized by opposition and political uncertainty. After all, this takes place in the aftermath of the transition from a free enterprise system to a market socialist system, and presumably there would be many people around who would have been recently pried loose from their equity ownership in capitalist firms. In the period of the transition, investment bankers, urban planners, and (above all) economists would be developing their expertise and reputations so that they will be in a good position to be selected to staff the various banks and planning agencies that would be created to implement investment policy. Political actors on the winning side—the socialists—would obviously have an agenda to pursue. However deep and sincere their commitment to the democratic process, it is virtually certain that those who fight the political battles necessary to achieve victory for socialism will believe that society's investment priorities under the old order were significantly out of line with what was and is in society's best interests. (Concerns about the environment, for example, might be a major source of that conviction.) In light of this, they will seek out experts who share their particular vision about the direction the economy should take, and they will create bureaucratic structures that insulate the relevant agencies from political meddling. As time goes on, the bureaucrats themselves become major players in the policy game and seek to protect and insulate their agencies from political interference in the manner indicated.

This insulation enhances the discretionary authority implicit in the mission of the agencies and their relationship to the political process. This latter point warrants some elaboration. Because of the sheer size and complexity of modern market economies, the political process, at whatever level, can only produce general guidelines for economic planning, perhaps coupled with a few specific directives. These guidelines will have to be interpreted and applied by the relevant agencies. For example, the national legislature may decide that the nation should use more renewable sources of energy, but they may not know what investment policy best meets that objective. How much should go into research and development of new technologies? How much should production of existing modalities be stimulated? How are decisions on these questions affected by tax policy? These and a host of related questions require highly specialized knowledge and expertise, and some of that knowledge and expertise is located in the planning bureaus. Another factor feeding into this discretionary authority for the agencies is that compromise in the political process is often best achieved through vague or ambiguous language. It will be up to the agency to give form and substance to that language.

For these reasons, some individuals in the planning agencies and the banks will have real discretionary authority to decide which investments—or which kinds of investments—best meet whatever guidelines emerge from the political process. So, if the national investment plan calls for $10 million of new investment in tourism in California, someone is going to have to decide what the boundaries of the tourist industry are, what the boundaries of California are (Does it include any firm whose headquarters are in California? How are headquarters to be defined? and so on).

What are the implications of all this for exploitation? To see what they are, notice that the considerable discretionary authority that the bureaucrats have, in conjunction with the politics of bureaucratic structure, together create truly significant and probably intractable monitoring problems for political authorities. After all, the nature of their tasks makes the bureaucrats difficult to monitor, the agencies themselves will have been deliberately designed to be difficult to monitor, and the bureaucrats have both the motive and methods to exacerbate the monitoring problem. A further potential problem concerns the monitoring of the monitors. It is likely that the political authorities responsible for monitoring the bureaucracies (e.g., members of the legislature) would themselves be difficult to monitor. Politicians are accountable to the voters (and taxpayers), but, as public choice theorists point out, it is often difficult and not cost-effective for citizens to monitor their elected officials, especially on the minutiae of legislative oversight of the bureaucracy.[13] People knowledgeable in the ways of government know all of this, at least after a fashion. This raises the adverse selection problem: What kind of person would volunteer for morally hazardous duty in the planning bureaucracy? What would be the likely result?

At the very least, the potential for corruption would appear to be significant. Socialists do not talk much about corruption in a socialist system, either because they believe it would not exist or because they believe it could not be worse than it is in a free enterprise system. The former is naive, and the latter ignores the fact that the vulnerability of institutions to corruption is an important determinant of the actual level of corruption in any society.

The issue of outright corruption aside, the likelihood is high that the public organizations responsible for new investment decisions would develop an unhealthy symbiotic relationship with the cooperatives affected by their decisions. Cooperatives would, of course, have a strong incentive to mount lobbying efforts at the agencies on behalf of their investment projects. A revolving door between the cooperatives and the agencies would begin to spin. In short, a whole range of evils of the modern welfare state would be replicated in this new branch of government. The stakes in all this are very high: around 2 to 10 percent of the entire wealth of the nation would be up for grabs each year.

The revolving door problem is both important and particularly intractable.

If the wall between the cooperative sector and the planning sector is so high that bureaucrats in the planning agencies are legally prohibited from selling their talents and abilities in the cooperative sector, the government risks an adverse selection problem: it will be able to attract only those who are not attractive to private industry (i.e., the cooperative sector). The alternative is to pay everyone in the planning bureaucracy a huge premium for working in the public sector, which would mean that the taxpayers would be forced to pay many of these bureaucrats far more than they are worth. In this way, the latter could exploit the taxpayers. On the other hand, if the wall between the two sectors is low (a more likely scenario), the bureaucrat's incentive is relatively strong to act opportunistically and serve the interests of potential employers in the private sector instead of the public interest.

Another incentive for those in the agency to act opportunistically involves what might be called the private agenda problem. Bureaucrats in the planning agencies, especially at the higher levels, are likely to have their own ideas about what the investment priorities should be for the economy as a whole or for their particular sector. Since they are poorly monitored, they will have the opportunity to steer a sector of the economy, more or less blatantly, in the direction they believe it should go. The revolving door and private agenda problems involve a misrepresentation of the inputs or outputs or both on the part of the bureaucrats in the agency, and so can be conceived of as forms of opportunism. In both these ways, bureaucrats can exploit the taxpayers who pay their salaries.

The harm done to the taxpayers in the form of exploitation by the bureaucrats would likely be relatively minor in comparison to the larger harms done to society as a result of these forms of opportunism. First, if the bureaucrats' favoritism toward certain firms or industries temporarily props up cooperatives that eventually fail or if it bails out cooperatives that would otherwise fail, then society has had some of its capital stock dissipated, even though, in this case, the main exploiters are the members or the management of the failing cooperative, rather than the bureaucrats (the latter being simply collaborators). Second, the bureaucrats' private agenda may not serve the public interest. (Indeed, the same thing might be true of the politicians' agenda.) This is not specifically a problem of exploitation, however, except to the extent that the outputs of bureaucrats are misrepresented. Finally (and again independent of the exploitation issue), it looks as if the idea of using political control of new investment as a way of giving expression to people's collective preferences (not to mention dealing with the social irrationalities of the market) is truly utopian. Even assuming that some version of the democratic process best discovers what those collective preferences are,[14] their implementation in a market socialist system requires the cooperation of people who have some (and perhaps a significant) penchant for opportunism and who work in very poorly monitored organizations.

To complete this discussion, it is necessary to examine briefly the extent to which analogous problems afflict capitalist organizations. One factor that complicates a comparative analysis on this point is that there is no organizational equivalent to the planning agencies in the free enterprise system. New investment decisions are made "in-house," although debt financing brings outsiders into the picture.[15] However, there is a genuine issue here: just as bureaucrats in the agencies can exploit the capital providers (society at large) in a market socialist system through their decisions on new investment, so, too, it would seem that the decision makers in the open corporation (though not in the classical capitalist firm) could exploit the capital providers in their decisions about new investment.

Indeed, it might be argued that in the open corporation, profitability is not always the sole criterion for investment decisions. Other factors, which can be grouped under the heading of bias or favoritism, can play a role in management's decisions about new investment. It certainly seems possible for equity owners to be exploited by managers insofar as these other factors are determinative of the investment decisions managers make. For example, if a firm launches an ambitious expansion program to satisfy the ego of its chief executive officer and not because of sound business reasons, the equity owners may have the quasi-rent value (or worse) of their assets dissipated. Business persons, just like bureaucrats, can have a private agenda and can use their power to their own strategic advantage.

This possibility for exploitation of the equity owners in the open corporation cannot be denied, but the real issue here is the quality of monitoring and the damage control mechanisms; on both counts, the structure of the open corporation is markedly superior to the corresponding structures in a market socialist system. Recall from chapter 5 that one of the functions of the board of directors is to ratify major investment decisions. Sometimes, board members have significant residual claimant status (Demsetz 1988a), which gives them a strong incentive to protect the interests of the equity owners. Other monitoring instrumentalities include the ability of equity owners to sell their shares on the stock market. Securities analysts also have an interest in monitoring new investment decisions. Finally, there is the market for corporate control. In all these cases, there are people with a significant personal financial interest in accurately assessing and monitoring managerial decisions.

On the other hand, this is not the case in the corresponding political institutions. Not only are the organizations inherently highly vulnerable to shirking and other forms of opportunism, but the only true residual claimant is the taxpayer, and the only residuals for which the taxpayer is eligible are the negative ones. If the bureaucracy squanders money, either on itself or through bad investments, the taxpayer must pay up. If an investment is hugely successful, however, the cooperative reaps the residual gains. How to monitor large government bureaucracies has always been problematic, and it may not be cost-effective for a citizen to do it. An assumption to the effect that there would be widespread participation in the political process produces the illusion that there is no monitoring problem because it presumes that decision makers are monitors and vice versa. But this ignores the complexities of modern life in which both decision making and monitoring require highly specialized knowledge and skills. Moreover, talk about participatory democracy obscures the question of institutional design.

The other major problem with state investment is the sheer size of the errors that can be made. Market socialist systems, unlike free enterprise systems, would have "energy czars" and the like, who could squander social wealth on a grand scale. Only central planners and invading armies can put more social wealth to the torch. When these czars lose their heads and make bad decisions, everyone pays. Taxpayers, unlike equity owners, have unlimited liability.

This completes the comparative evaluation of free enterprise systems and the type of market socialist system outlined in chapter 2 on the question of exploitation. This evaluation was done through a comparison of the characteristic organizational forms of the two types of systems, namely, the classical capitalist firm and the open corporation on the one hand and the worker cooperative (both small and large) and the associated state organizations on the other hand. The organizations of market socialism have proven to be consistently more vulnerable to exploitation than their free enterprise counterparts. Distinctive opportunities for exploitation were found in the structure of economic roles (residual claimant, ultimate decision-making authority, capital provider, entrepreneur, monitor, economic planner, politician) that define market socialist organizations. Before final judgment can be passed, one potential complication must be addressed. Might not some forms of exploitation cancel out other forms of exploitation? For example, managers can exploit and be exploited by their fellow residual claimants; cooperatives can exploit and be exploited by the state. If these forms of exploitation canceled each other out, the relative disadvantages of market socialism vis-à-vis a free enterprise system would disappear or at least diminish.

Though this possibility cannot be ruled out (and indeed would undoubtedly occur in particular cases in real-world economic systems), there is some reason to believe that this canceling-out effect would not be a systematic phenomenon. The reason for this is that successful opportunistic behavior (which is what exploitation is) is necessarily deceptive and not anticipated. Indeed, it need not even be easily discoverable after the fact.[16] This means that the distribution of income will tend to be skewed toward those who are more opportunistic and whose assets have well-protected or low quasi-rent values and away from those who are less opportunistic and whose assets have the highest quasi-rent values (e.g., workers with highly specialized skills and knowledge). There is no assurance the latter will be compensated in other ways. For example, workers with highly specialized knowledge and skills might be exploited by their unskilled coworkers; they may get some of the value of their contribution back if the firm's management is especially slick in its dealings with the state's auditors, though these managers are more likely to siphon their ill-gotten gains into their own pockets. (People who hire exceptionally vicious lawyers face a similar adverse selection problem.) On the other hand, if their management team is relatively nonopportunistic, then the skilled workers would lose out—not once but twice.

All that can be said at this level of abstraction has to do with the dynamics of adverse selection and moral hazard, since these systematically affect people's penchant for opportunism. Given the comparative weaknesses of organizations of market socialism, one could predict that if market socialism replaced capitalism in a given society, there would be a tendency for workers with more highly specialized human capital and workers who are not given to opportunism to emigrate from the society. In short, there would be a brain drain and virtue drain, and those who remained would become more cynical in response to the likely increase in exploitation throughout the economy—hardly an encouraging prospect from a socialist (or indeed any other) perspective.

Though the just always prosper at the expense of the unjust, the really important question is, How much? It seems that the answer will depend crucially, though not exclusively, on the vulnerability of economic organizations to exploitation. I have tried to explain the vulnerabilities of market socialist organizations in such a way as to make it evident that there is no way to prevent the various forms of exploitation that have been identified, at least within the framework for a market socialist economy as it has been specified in this book. This raises an obvious question: Why this system? Or, more exactly, why this particular configuration of market socialist property rights? The answer to this question is to be found in the third section of chapter 2, which motivates each element of the system of property rights that has been the subject of this chapter and chapter 6. These motivations are to be found in a socialist vision of the good society—a vision that ultimately derives from a widely shared socialist critique of capitalism—and are summarized in Figure 2.1.

At this point, it would be appropriate to locate the results of the discussion in chapters 5–7 in the framework of the larger capitalism/socialism dispute outlined in chapter 1. The primary aim of these chapters has been to give a limited criticism of a well-motivated type of socialism and a limited defense of a free enterprise system. Roughly, the argument has been that this type of market socialist economic system is more exploitative than free enterprise systems. This is a comparative judgment about types of economic systems pitched at a level of abstraction that transcends particular economic systems. This means that there is no way to say how serious the problem would be in any particular society that has this type of market socialist system, since the extent of exploitation in any actually existing society depends on a whole host of factors, only one of which is the system of property rights in the means of production. Nevertheless, there is a substantial literature on the economics of property rights which indicates that "property rights matter."[17] At the level of abstraction at which this discussion has been carried out, all that can be said with assurance is the legal prohibition on alternative organizational forms both permits and encourages forms of exploitative exchange that are precluded or minimized by the characteristic organizational forms found in free enterprise systems. Since the good society is defined in terms of what it is reasonable to hope for, and since it is reasonable to hope that a society would not permit persistent and avoidable exploitation (a form of injustice), it can be concluded that this type of market socialist system is not the economic system of the good society.

What remains to be determined is how much progress this conclusion represents in the capitalism/socialism dispute. The answer to this question depends on how well motivated this type of market socialist system is. This in turn depends in large measure on whether or not there are socialist alternatives to the form of market socialism that has been under the microscope in this book—alternatives that do not have the defects that afflict the latter.

Indeed, one might wonder why other configurations of socialist property rights have not been considered, especially if a change in the system could eliminate or minimize some form of exploitation. Part of the answer to this question is that when discussing alternatives to a free enterprise system, it is extremely important to have a clearly specified alternative on the table that can be subjected to a thorough evaluation. For too much of the past century and a half, socialism has been like a three-year-old at the dentist's office unwilling to sit still for a thorough examination. If different socialist alternatives are to be discussed, they need to be specified and evaluated seriatim.

Still, it is legitimate to ask whether any other version of market socialism might realize the socialist vision of the good society. The first two sections of chapter 8 will systematically address this question by considering plausible alternatives to the version of market socialism that has been the main topic of this book. These alternatives are intended to deal with the organizational weaknesses identified in this chapter and the preceding one that make this form of market socialism so vulnerable to exploitation. The argument will be that each of these alternatives is either (1) also inferior to a free enterprise system on the question of exploitation, (2) unable to realize other social virtues that are part of the minimal socialist vision of the good society, or (3) not really a form of socialism. Chapter 8 will also explore the larger significance of this conclusion by connecting the conception of exploitation employed in this book to concerns about distributive justice and by reconsidering the socialist vision of the good society.

8

Other Options for Market Socialism?

Equity Ownership and Market Socialism

The problems with exploitation identified in chapters 6 and 7 raise the question of whether there are forms of market socialism that would not face these difficulties. The purpose of this section and the next is to address this question in a systematic way. Perhaps the most natural way to proceed is to consider the comparative weaknesses and vulnerabilities in the version of market socialism that has been under discussion thus far.[1] The central question is whether these weaknesses can be addressed by organizational changes that are compatible with the system's remaining market socialist and that are consistent with the socialist conception of the good society identified in chapter 2.

One of the most serious weaknesses of the worker control–state ownership model is that the capital provider is not the ultimate decision-making authority and residual claimant. By contrast, one of the salient advantages of the characteristic organizations of a free enterprise system is that these three functions are all joined. In other words, the latter organizations, unlike the organizations in the worker control–state ownership model, have equity owners. Thus, in the classical capitalist firm and the open corporation, those who are ultimate decision makers and residual claimants cannot exploit the primary providers of capital because they *are* the primary providers of capital.[2] By contrast, in the cooperative, although the workers are both the ultimate decision-making authorities and the residual claimants, they are not the providers of capital. The state exercises that function or responsibility. Since this division of functions or responsibilities is a source of numerous opportunities for exploitation, a natural proposal would be to join these three roles in a market socialist system to create equity owners. In principle, this could be done in one of two ways: either the workers in the various cooperatives or the state could be the firm's equity owners. The purpose of this section is to investigate these and related possibilities.

If the workers own most of the firm's capital, they are unable to siphon wealth from the capital providers into their own pockets, since they are the capital providers. This proposal effectively solves the so-called horizon problem because the workers' equity ownership requires them to have a time horizon that is as long as the ultimate decision-making authorities in capitalist organizations. If capital equipment is not maintained properly, if adequate reserves are not set aside to replace used up or worn out capital goods, if intangible assets are sold off, or if the quasi-rent value of the firm itself is dissipated, then the workers in their capacity as the firm's equity owners suffer the full wealth consequences of their decisions on these matters. There would be no need for armies of auditors to fight pitched battles with cooperatives over the valuation of assets. Indeed, small firms would not have to be audited at all, and large firms would be audited to gather the same kind of information as auditors seek from corporations in a free enterprise system.

This model has another advantage over the worker control–state ownership model. Since the workers are the equity owners, they receive the returns to capital; assuming those returns are not taxed away, the cooperatives will have both the means and the incentive to finance most new investment. If this model puts control of new investment in the hands of the cooperatives, it closes down or minimizes the opportunities for exploitation that come from total state control of new investment. There would be no opportunistic bureaucrats in poorly monitored state organizations with control over vast portions of social wealth. Failing cooperatives would have no better chance of being bailed out by the state than do firms in a free enterprise system. Groups of workers would be putting their own wealth on the line in making investment decisions, which precludes the need for state monitoring of these decisions.

Despite the advantages of equity ownership by the workers in comparison to the worker control–state ownership model, the former remains inferior to a free enterprise system with respect to exploitation in at least three respects. First, there is still the opportunity for the unskilled (or some other majority of) workers to exploit the skilled (or some minority of) workers within the cooperative. Since the workers are the ultimate decision-making authorities, pay differentials would still reflect majority opinion (assuming a one person–one vote rule) about the value of different workers' contributions. For reasons explained in the second section of chapter 6, this means that it is likely that the value of some workers' contributions will be systematically underestimated relative to the value of the contributions of others. Labor markets would also be more sluggish for the same reasons they would be in the worker control–state ownership model: firms are reluctant to expand and contract their membership in response to changing economic conditions; it is harder to start new firms because entrepreneurial gains are widely distributed; and because of variations in a firm's income, it is difficult for prospective members to evaluate job offers from other firms. Because labor markets do not function as well as under free enterprise systems, workers who are not getting the value of their contributions would be less likely to have anywhere else to go and thus would be exploited.

Second, monitoring arrangements in small-to-medium-sized cooperatives would suffer the same systematic weaknesses of adverse selection and moral hazard those organizations suffer in the worker control–state ownership model, since, in both cases, the workers are the ultimate decision-making authorities. This means that nonshirking workers would be exploited by shirking workers and shirking monitors. These problems are less serious in the classical capitalist firm for reasons indicated in chapters 5 and 6. More generally, the diffusion of responsibility for monitoring, which is a necessary concomitant of self-management (whatever the size of the firm) makes it more difficult to assess the contributions of those appointed to the job of manager. This in turn permits and effectively encourages shirking among managers and, as a result, among workers as well. By contrast, in the classical capitalist firm and even in the open corporation, responsibility for monitoring is more perfectly concentrated in management's hands.

Finally, this system requires the equity owners of the smaller cooperatives to monitor the entrepreneurship of managers in the latter's roles of central contracting agents and directors of the firm's product. This is a problem because it is difficult for the membership of the cooperatives (or indeed for anyone) to evaluate the entrepreneurial contributions of managers in these two roles. Because of the (partial) separation of equity ownership from management in the smaller cooperative, there is a monitoring problem in the smaller cooperative that does not exist in the classical capitalist firm, since in the latter the equity owner is the entrepreneur. This can result in productive entrepreneurs being exploited by being forced to share the extra residuals they bring in; on the other hand, ineffective entrepreneurs can exploit their fellow workers in the cooperatives by forcing them to pay for their mistakes.

But what about larger cooperatives in which the workers are equity owners compared to the open corporation? Are they more vulnerable to exploitation than their corporate counterparts? To answer this question, it is necessary to investigate the monitoring arrangements of the large cooperative; this requires us to confront the issue of equity markets in this model of market socialism. A central question in this connection is whether or not ownership of equity shares is restricted to members of the cooperatives. If the sale of equity shares is not restricted, then outsiders could acquire ultimate decision-making authority in the cooperative. Indeed, this is likely to happen for two related reasons.

One is what has been called "the portfolio problem." It has been widely remarked that a system in which the workers have equity shares only in the firms of which they are members presents them with risks that could be avoided by portfolio diversification (e.g., Jensen and Meckling 1979, 485–88). To put the point informally, if workers have all of their nonlabor assets tied up in their own firm, they are taking risks that could be avoided by owning equity shares in a diverse portfolio of companies.[3] Since it would be rational for them to diversify their risks, it is reasonable to suppose that they would do just that. It is easy to see how a process of diversification could reproduce a free enterprise system over a relatively short period of time.

David Ellerman has called attention to another reason why these firms are likely to degenerate into open corporations (Ellerman 1984, 263). At some point, older workers (and perhaps managers) in successful firms would want to realize the capital gains on their equity accounts. Those accounts would have been built up to such an extent that new workers would not be able to purchase their shares; only outside investors, perhaps by pooling their resources, would be able to do that. As time goes on, these outsiders would acquire a controlling interest in the firm. Indeed, the more profitable and better managed the firm is, the more quickly this would happen. All of the workers, not just the older ones, would want to realize at least some of their capital gains before they retired or left the firm and thus would want to sell some of their shares. However, allowing outsiders to have voting rights, which is implied by equity ownership, is incompatible with worker self-management (Bonin and Putterman 1987, 61–62; Estrin 1989, 174). This means that unrestricted equity ownership could not be endorsed by any socialist for whom self-management in the workplace is instrumentally or logically related to the socialist vision of the good society.[4] But even those socialists for whom self-management is not central to their conception of a socialist system could not endorse this proposal, since this system would effectively permit widespread private ownership of the means of production, thereby violating a necessary condition for any economic system to be socialist.

Suppose, therefore, that only workers in a firm could buy equity shares. The market for equity shares, then, would be restricted to present workers and those who wished to join the firm. In effect, the latter would involve a market for memberships in the cooperative. As Putterman points out, these would be a fairly thin markets, that is, there would be very little trading going on (1988a, 258–59). The reason for this is that these markets would really be labor markets, and the latter are sluggish in this type of system for the same reasons they are in the worker control–state ownership model. While current members of the firm might buy and sell shares among themselves, those markets and the markets for memberships would certainly not be very brisk in comparison to equity markets in a free enterprise system. This suggests that the superior monitoring afforded by an active stock market in which equity shares are frequently traded would be lost. In addition, the system precludes a market for corporate control, which allows bad management to be ousted as the result of a hostile takeover. Internal rebellion would be the only option short of quitting for dissatisfied workers. As explained in chapter 7, this is less likely to be effective than hostile takeovers or proxy fights. All this suggests that the monitoring of management would be less effective in the large cooperative than in the large open corporation. Less effective monitoring creates opportunities for poor managers to exploit other workers in the large cooperative and for especially good managers to be exploited by other workers in cooperatives.

Perhaps a more serious difficulty with this form of market socialism is that it seems to be unstable. If a worker leaves the cooperative and a new member is not there to buy that equity stake in the firm, it is not clear what would happen. If the firm had to pay out the accrued equity value of workers who leave, it would create a serious strain on firms in which many workers are approaching retirement around the same time or in which there is high labor mobility (a fact that would not be lost on the more opportunistic workers who can credibly threaten to leave). There is also a problem if workers in especially profitable firms want to get access to some of the capital gains their firm has enjoyed before they quit or retire.

An interesting way of dealing with these difficulties has been suggested by David Ellerman (1984; 1986; 1990, 81ff). To understand Ellerman's suggestion, it is necessary to explain some of the rather novel details of his model. This model is especially interesting because it may be the most plausible way to combine self-management and equity ownership by the workers. In this model, members of the cooperative have individual equity accounts and the firm itself has a collective equity account.[5] Together, these accounts are credited on a quarterly or yearly basis with the returns to the firm's capital and any undistributed residuals. (Workers also receive a conventional wage.) Both types of equity accounts serve to secure the cooperative's debt obligations, both short and long term. New investment is financed internally from these accounts and from external debt; individual and collective equity accounts appreciate in value to reflect the firm's growth and other increases in the value of its assets.

Workers establish their individual equity accounts by paying an entry fee when they join the firm. These accounts are periodically "paid down" to the workers, though they are not fully paid out. For example, each year after an initial lag-time of say, five years, workers would receive the equivalent of their share of the returns to capital (and any other appreciation in the value of the firm's assets) for one year, less any amounts credited to the collective equity account. This "pay-down" prevents members from building up very large equity accounts that the firm might have trouble paying out when workers leave; it also equalizes the risks between older workers and younger workers who would otherwise have significantly different amounts of equity at risk in case the firm were unable to meet its debt obligations. When a worker left the firm or retired, the balance of his individual equity account would be paid out in the form of a perpetual debt instrument that would be fully marketable (Ellerman 1990, 82–85). Equity is converted to debt because debt holders have no control rights, and this system restricts control rights to the firm's current members (i.e., the equity owners). On the other hand, the collective equity account is never paid out. This means that some of the returns to capital are "lost" to workers as individuals. The collective equity account is quite important and must be maintained, however, since it serves as part of the security for the cooperative's external debt—short term, medium to long term, and perpetual.

The principal advantage of this structure of equity rights and this method of financing new investment is that it give the worker an essentially unlimited time horizon, since he must be concerned with capital gains or losses that he will suffer on retirement or when he leaves the firm (Ellerman 1986, 65–66). Any debt instruments that he receives will be fully marketable and thus will tend to reflect the value of the firm. Not coincidentally, this proposal bears a striking resemblance to arrangements in the Mondragon cooperatives.

Two questions can be asked of this system: (1) is it in fact stable? and (2) is this a solution to the more serious problems of exploitation that face versions of market socialism in which there are no equity owners? With regard to question 1, it may not be possible for the firm to keep a large enough equity cushion to meet the equity (i.e., internal) financing needs of the cooperative and to secure all of its debt, including the perpetual debt instruments issued to retiring workers. One reason for this might be relatively high turnover. Recall that the Mondragon cooperatives have very low turnover among their members, which gives their equity base a stability that could not exist in a more mobile society. Cooperatives in more mobile societies may become highly leveraged, especially if the collective equity account is allowed to dwindle or if it is not adequately built up. They might also become highly leveraged because of high capital-to-labor ratios and the passage of time. Consider, for example, how much perpetual debt might be outstanding for a large, capital-intensive firm, such as a mining company after forty or fifty years. Highly leveraged firms are very vulnerable in difficult economic times, since debt holders must be paid periodically no matter how slow business is. Thus, it is unclear whether an economic system composed primarily of these types of cooperatives would be able to survive the ups and downs that any firm in a market economy faces over the long term.

On the question of exploitation, the answer would seem to be mixed. Equity shares are not freely alienable, and (as noted) there is no market for corporate control. Some aspects of management (notably, entrepreneurship) would likely not be as well monitored as they are in the open corporation, since there are no outsiders who can make a great deal of money by buying and selling equity shares or by making takeover bids. This means that it would be easier for bad managers to exploit cooperatives, and good managers of cooperatives would be more easily exploited than their corporate counterparts. However, this problem might be mitigated to some extent by the market for corporate debt.

On the other hand, in theory at least, Ellerman's model avoids the moral hazards of substantial debt financing by cooperatives. Recall that these hazards involve opportunities for exploitation having to do with maintenance and replacement of capital goods in a system in which the ultimate decision makers have a limited time horizon. This model elegantly solves this horizon problem in a way that is compatible with the requirement that only present workers are ultimate decision-making authorities. If the opportunities for exploitation created by a combination of substantial debt financing and the workers' potentially limited horizon are the really serious defects of the worker control–state ownership model, then assuming that substantial debt financing can be avoided, the other forms of exploitation identified might look like a price worth paying for the benefits of self-management. The only problem is that this is a price that a socialist, qua socialist, cannot afford to pay. Fundamentally, there are two reasons for this. One is that it is arguable that this economic system is not really socialist. The other is that it cannot realize a number of important elements of the socialist vision of the good society. These are logically distinct issues.

The social character of this form of ownership might be called into question on the grounds that the disposition of the net social product (the returns to capital plus the residuals) is done to serve private interests, not the public interest. In other words, decisions about what to do with the firm's earnings, including, most notably, new investment decisions, still represent the interests of disparate groups, even though in this case, the groups are the respective memberships of the cooperatives. In this type of system there is no economic organization or family of economic organizations that is intended to represent the interests of society as a whole.[6] As Saul Estrin has said, "The concept of collective ownership must . . . preclude any direct ownership . . . by the workers of the machines upon which they work. Ownership of cooperatives in a market socialist economy must therefore be *social* in the sense defined earlier" (1989, 185). Social ownership is explained a few pages earlier by reference to the Yugoslav system, in which the state, as the representative of society as a whole, owns the cooperatives or at least their capital (p. 172). Similarly, in the worker control–state ownership model, the social character of ownership of the means of production is located in the fact that the state effectively owns the means of production because it receives and disburses the returns to capital, thereby controlling most new investment. Assuming a highly participatory democratic state, the latter is supposed to represent, albeit imperfectly, the interests of society as a whole.

Ellerman shows some sensitivity to this issue and argues for the social character of ownership in his model on the grounds that each worker has a voting right in the firm of which he is a member; because of this, the firm represents the interests of its members (1990, 51–58). He compares the cooperative to a government in this respect:

> Governments are "all-inclusive" in that they represent everyone who legally resides in a certain *geographical* area. . . . But the management of a democratic firm is *also* "all-inclusive" in that it represents everyone who works in the enterprise. . . . Why shouldn't a grouping of people together by common labor be just as "social" as the grouping of people together by a common area of residence? The genuinely "social" aspect of a democratically governed community is that the community itself is not a piece of property. (1990, 75)

This might establish the social character of the ownership of the cooperative's capital and even possibly the socialist character of the cooperative itself. However, it does not establish the socialist character of the larger economic system of which it is a part. To infer the latter on the basis of the former is to commit the fallacy of composition. The legitimacy of this worry about the socialist character of the entire system is strengthened by the important similarity that this model has with a free enterprise system: in its control of the social product, this system seems to be guided by a swarm of essentially private interests instead of a collective expression of the public interest that state control is supposed to represent.

Ellerman might have a response to this, however. In his discussion of the democratic principles that underlie his model, he advocates something he calls the *affected interests principle*, which states that "everyone whose rightful interests are affected by an organization's decisions should have a right of indirect control (e.g., a collective or perhaps individual veto) to constrain those decisions" (1990, 47). This is a principle that I suspect most contemporary socialists would assent to. If an economic system follows this principle, then the interests of others are taken into account in all decisions, including those concerned with control over the social product.

The problem—and it is an enormous one—is that Ellerman nowhere explains how this principle is to be implemented in a way that goes beyond respect for market relations. Indeed, he admits (with considerable understatement) that this principle would be difficult to implement (1990, 47). This principle is an end or a goal, not a means. Unfortunately, he provides no details about the organizations or institutional structures beyond the cooperative that would implement or realize this principle. Without some idea of how this principle is to be implemented (especially when its realization conflicts with the decisions of the cooperatives about, for example, pricing, investment, distribution of residuals), the whole system of property rights in the means of production must be judged radically underdetermined. In consequence, both the socialist character of this system and its feasibility remain in doubt.

But even if these doubts could be resolved, there is another family of reasons for calling into question the socialist character of this proposal. These reasons can be approached by considering why it even matters whether this is a socialist economic system. The answer argued for in chapters 1 and 2 is that socialists believe that a socialist economic system is responsible for realizing a vision or conception of the good society, a minimal version of which was identified in chapter 2. Unfortunately, the Ellerman model is unlikely to realize three crucial elements of this vision of the good society. Two of these elements or goals that a socialist economic system is supposed to achieve are (1) collective control of the rate and direction of economic growth and (2) the prevention or correction of the social irrationalities of the market (e.g., unemployment and pollution) in a way that is categorically more effective than what a state in a free enterprise system can do.

It might be argued that this is what the affected interests principle is supposed to do, but to reiterate, the principle is an end, not a means. Absent some account of the institutional means by which this principle is to be realized, there is no reason to believe that either of these elements of the socialist conception of the good society could be achieved in this type of system. After all, the rate and direction of economic growth cannot be the subject of collective choice because control of new investment is left to the individual cooperatives. It is also unclear how or why this type of system would be in a better position to deal with the social irrationalities of the market than is the state in a free enterprise system. This is not to deny that states in free enterprise systems can affect the rate and direction of economic growth by a combination of subsidies and discriminatory tax policies. Nor can it be denied that these and other instrumentalities could be used to treat various social irrationalities in a market socialist system. The problem is that there is no reason to believe that the state in such a system would be categorically more effective in these matters than it is in a free enterprise system. The promise of socialism is not one of modest improvement on one or more of these fronts; instead, it is the promise of truly radical beneficial change on all of these fronts. Nothing short of that would justify the enormous institutional changes that socialists advocate. How such changes could occur in a system in which control of new investment is highly decentralized is unclear, at best. Certainly the current state of the art in macroeconomic analysis and policy gives no cause for optimism.

Finally, perhaps the most serious problem of all from a socialist perspective is that it is very doubtful that this type of system would be able to realize the achievement of relative equality of material condition. The reasons for this can be explained as follows. As a technical matter, firms differ widely in their ratio of capital to labor. Oil refineries, for example, are very capital-intensive whereas truck farming is very labor-intensive. If workers received the returns to capital, as this proposal implies, workers in highly capital-intensive industries would be much wealthier than those in less capital-intensive industries. Thus, the refinery workers would be much wealthier than the vegetable growers, and both would be paupers in comparison to the members of some large financial cooperatives.

To this it might be responded that the state could adopt a progressive income tax to equalize incomes or at least to reduce inequality of incomes (though this would leave inequalities of control over productive resources relatively untouched). There are two problems with this. First, it is unlikely to succeed for roughly the same reason it has not succeeded in democratic societies with a free enterprise system: one of the things that people do when their wealth or income is threatened by the state is to invest resources in the political process to ensure that the state does not expropriate them. The oil refinery workers would undoubtedly form a political action committee or something similar to help elect people or parties who believe that workers are entitled to the returns to capital that they control. Instead of "All Power to the Workers' and Soldiers' Soviets," their slogan would be, "All Returns to Capital to the Workers' Cooperatives." Marx (not to mention Lenin) could hardly be pleased with these developments. Second, this policy would undercut the whole point of giving equity ownership to the workers, namely, to give them a financial stake in maintaining the value of the firm and in making wise investments for the future. One cannot maintain the form of equity ownership while eviscerating its reality by high capital gains and/or income taxes.

Whatever the virtues of the Ellerman model (and I think they are considerable) there is nothing in it to ensure relative equality of material condition, at least across firms. Indeed, for the reasons indicated, wide interfirm variations in income are quite likely. And, as noted, it is doubtful whether the rate and direction of economic growth could be a matter of collective choice in the society, given that individual cooperatives have the resources and incentives to finance internally new investment through retained earnings and to finance externally by borrowing. Finally, it is unclear how the social irrationalities of the market could be handled in a categorically more effective way. For all these reasons, even if this type of economic system is socialist, it is not capable of realizing the socialist vision of the good society.

In fairness to Ellerman, he does not make a sustained effort to establish his socialist credentials. Indeed, he suggests that his proposal is a "third way" between capitalism and socialism—though the form of socialism he has in mind is state socialism (1990, 206). One of the themes of this chapter is that models of economic systems that avoid the problems of the worker control–state ownership model are either nonsocialist or unable to realize the socialist conception of the good society, or both.

Another form of equity ownership for a market socialist system is full state ownership of the means of production. Making the state the ultimate decision-making authority, residual claimant, and provider of capital has some obvious advantages over the worker control–state ownership model in preventing exploitation. First, since workers are not ultimate decision-making authorities and residual claimants, the exploitation of skilled workers by unskilled workers would not take place. Workers are not voting on the criteria whereby pay is determined; instead, they are hired by state-appointed managers. Labor markets would be about as robust as they are in free enterprise systems, and the various protective devices (notably, unions) found in free enterprise systems could and presumably would persist in this type of market socialist system. Second, since the managers are not answerable to the workers, the adverse selection and moral hazard problems that plague management of the small-to-medium-sized cooperative would not arise in these state-owned firms. Finally, managers who are poor entrepreneurs could not exploit the workers, nor could the workers exploit managers who are good entrepreneurs.

However, full state ownership is both inferior to a free enterprise system on the issue of exploitation and problematical from the point of view of the socialist conception of the good society. The main vulnerability to exploitation arises in connection with the monitoring of management. It is an implication of full state ownership of the firms that managers are ultimately answerable to political authorities. The problems associated with monitoring by political authorities were outlined in the last section of chapter 7: multiple decision criteria and structural impediments to accurate monitoring (not to mention sheer political patronage) create numerous opportunities for exploitation by and through political organizations—opportunities that do not exist in the classical capitalist firm or that tend to be minimized by the superior monitoring mechanisms available to the owners of the modern open corporation in free enterprise systems.

Some of the more important avenues of exploitation in a state-owned market socialist firm are those relating to successful and unsuccessful entrepreneurship on the part of managers. Because the state is the residual claimant, if a firm's management (perhaps with the advice and active cooperation of its workforce) earns large entrepreneurial profits, those profits are shipped off to the state. Though the state might pay its managers performance bonuses, managers' pay cannot be largely determined by their entrepreneurial contributions, for then they would effectively be the residual claimants. Unlike their counterparts in free enterprise systems, who can start their own firms or take their respective divisions private through a leveraged buyout, successful managers of large, state-owned firms can only work for other state organizations, which are relatively poorly monitored and politicized; that is, they effectively have nowhere else to go. For these reasons, the managers of successful firms would be exploited by the state. If, however, the firm suffers losses and the state pumps more resources into it to keep it afloat, the taxpayers are exploited. By separating residual claimancy from operational control, the rewards and penalties that go with successful and unsuccessful entrepreneurship are systematically misallocated. Finally, it is hard to see what the incentive is for workers and managers to be good stewards of the portion of social wealth over which they have operational control (if not ownership). A version of the horizon problem would undoubtedly face this type of system.

Independent of these problems of exploitation, this form of state ownership is likely to be unable to realize other elements of the socialist vision of the good society. Recall from chapter 2 that one of the motivations for self-management is that it is supposed to ameliorate alienation. In a self-managed firm, the workers are not working for someone else since they appoint the managers, or at least the managers are ultimately answerable to them. Because of this, there is a fundamental sense in which their productive lives are unalienated. Self-management is supposed to reduce alienation in the workplace in more concrete terms as well: in self-managed firms workers decide on matters such as plant layout, work schedules, and even trade-offs between income and more intrinsically satisfying work. This control over their working lives is also supposed to have other good effects, including dampening the us-versus-them mentality between managers and workers. However, no matter how democratic the state is, when the latter has complete ownership of the means of production, these benefits are no longer assured. The reason for this is that whatever the institutional details, the locus of ultimate decision-making authority—and thus ultimate power—shifts out of the firm and into the political arena. Politicians are effectively the ultimate decision makers, and they are in turn answerable to a diverse electorate. The problems involved in monitoring politicians aside, it is clear that workers will not have as much of a say in the operation of their firms as they would in the worker control–state ownership model. Thus, there is no assurance that management will be as responsive to the potential causes of alienation as their counterparts in the worker control–state ownership model would be.

This observation touches a final difficulty with complete state ownership of most firms. In light of the experience of communist societies in the twentieth century, full state ownership of most of the means of production may no longer be a serious option in the capitalism/socialism dispute. It is true that some socialists see the failures of the communist world as failures of a certain type of state—a centralized, nondemocratic state that has been alienated from the rest of society. They believe that if only these states had been truly democratic—in the sense of widespread participation in the political process—the problems of communism would not have existed or, at least, would not have been nearly as severe as they were and are. But the fact is that most people do not seem to view it that way. There is the widespread perception that state ownership of the means of production has been a large part of the economic problem with former communist systems. Evidence for this comes from the fact that former communist countries are experimenting with various forms of nonstate ownership and not merely various forms of a market economy. In addition, throughout the developed world there seems to be little enthusiasm for state ownership. In general, complete state ownership of most of society's means of production just does not seem to be on the agenda anywhere in the world today.

Perhaps the most compelling reason to be deeply suspicious of complete state ownership of the means of production is that it unites in the state both political and economic power. It is plausible to maintain that one of the most important lessons of the twentieth century is that this arrangement is inherently totalitarian. Indeed, most socialists in the last third of the twentieth century have abandoned full state ownership in favor of some form of cooperatives. Experience with totalitarian state socialism is surely part of the reason—and a good reason—for that.

Given the serious deficiencies of these forms of equity ownership from a socialist perspective, there seems to be not even a prima facie case for combining them by putting representatives of the state on the board of directors of the cooperatives in the Ellerman model. On the other hand, a case might be made for putting state representatives on the board of the cooperatives in the worker control–state ownership model to provide better monitoring of the firm's use of society's capital. This in turn would attenuate the opportunities for exploitation that would otherwise face a system in which the ultimate decision-making authorities are not the primary capital providers.

The problem with this suggestion is that it assumes that a board of directors composed in this manner would represent a kind of blending of the various interests board members represent, whereas, in point of fact, it is likely that the board would represent the interests of the dominant group. This has sometimes been called the "law of one majority" (Ellerman 1990, 47). So if the workers are the predominant ultimate decision-making authorities (and it is hard to see how any other arrangement can ensure the benefits of self-management), their interests will decisively determine the policies and procedures of the firms. On the other hand, if state representatives are the ultimate decision-making authorities (and it is hard to see how any other arrangement could effectively deal with opportunities for exploitation), then their interests will be determinative.

To conclude, equity ownership has some undeniable advantages in precluding or minimizing forms of exploitation that would flourish in the worker control–state ownership model that has been the main focus of this book, but making the workers or the state the equity owners creates other serious difficulties from a socialist point of view. The alternatives are either unstable, not socialist, or incapable of realizing the socialist conception of the good society. The next section considers some other alternatives that do not involve joining the roles of capital provider, residual claimant, and ultimate decision-making authority, that is, some alternatives that do not involve equity ownership.

Other Forms of Ownership and Market Socialism

Self-managed cooperatives are virtually a sine qua non for late twentieth-century socialists. In recent years there have been at least two other proposals (aside from the worker control–state ownership model) for economic systems composed of self-managed cooperatives that warrant some discussion. Both of them try to take advantage of some desirable features of free enterprise systems without losing their socialist credentials. Peter Jay (1980) has proposed one of these systems. Some elements of this system have also been endorsed or discussed by others (e.g., McCain 1977; Bonin and Putterman 1987, 61–79; Putterman 1988a, 1988b). As in the other models, firms in Jay's model are self-managed cooperatives (1980, 9). Workers do not—or at least need not—provide most of the capital; yet the cooperative does not borrow it. How is this possible? This model countenances something like outside equity financing. Outside investors who supply this type of financing would be entitled to a claim on the firm's residuals, unlike the state in the worker control–state ownership model. However, just like the state in the latter model, they would have no rights of control; those rights are vested exclusively in the workers. In other words, in this system the workers are the ultimate decision-making authorities, yet outside investors are both the primary suppliers of capital and the primary residual claimants (p. 14).[7]

There are a number of motivations for this equitylike financing (or *quasi-equity ownership*). Jay cites some of the problems with worker provision of equity financing just discussed: the inability of individual workers to supply enough equity, the portfolio problem, and the problem of the compatibility of worker control and free alienability of equity shares (1980, 13). He also believes that traditional capital markets are the most efficient vehicle for bringing investors and entrepreneurs together. It is just that on this proposal, investors cannot be offered any rights of control in the firm. What they can be offered are the residuals. Jay says, " 'Equity-type' investors will be entitled to receive all of the 'profits' of the enterprise; and it may also prove desirable to assign them a mortgage on the relevant assets. The 'profits' will correspond to the distributed earnings of a limited liability company and will amount to whatever the board of directors, appointed by the employees, says they amount to" (1980, 14).

On the face of it, this arrangement would seem to pose a very serious expropriation hazard. Since the workers are the ultimate decision-making authorities, it seems that they would be in a position to appropriate the equity value of the firm by paying themselves inflated wages and skipping dividends. Jay maintains that this would not in fact happen because the firm has to raise capital on both the debt and quasi-equity markets to finance new investment. To do so at a reasonable cost, it must have a track record of paying dividends comparable to traditional corporations. The debt and quasi-equity markets, then, are supposed to provide the necessary discipline for the firm's management (p. 14).

This type of system has a number of advantages over the worker control–state ownership model. The most important is that capital provision is through the capital markets and not through the state. Quasi-equity ownership avoids the vulnerabilities to exploitation that go with state ownership of capital; it also appears to have the monitoring advantages of the capital markets in a free enterprise system. Shares could be traded just as freely as in free enterprise systems. In addition, even if the workers have to put up some of their own capital, their status as residual claimants would be relatively insignificant. This means that this model would avoid the fight over the firm's net income that would be found in the cooperative in the worker control–state ownership model. The workers are not dividing the total income of the firm, net of nonlabor expenses. Because of this, wages could and probably would be more nearly determined by labor markets, which makes it more likely that workers would get paid in accordance with their contributions, thereby curtailing intrafirm exploitation.

These advantages of the system notwithstanding, it remains relatively inferior to a free enterprise system on the question of exploitation. The reason is that despite Jay's assurances, the quasi-equity owners really are at risk of having some of the value of their assets appropriated. Managers could do this by skipping dividends, paying the workers inflated salaries, and encouraging various forms of on-the-job consumption (e.g., lavish company picnics and office parties). Jay maintains that the managers would not do this because if they did, it would be more difficult for them to raise money in the debt and quasi-equity markets to fund new investment. If they were not looking out for the interests of the quasi-equity owners, that would be reflected in the price they would have to pay for investment funds. Share prices, then, are supposed to serve the same signaling function in this system that they do in a free enterprise system. The problem is that it is not at all clear why funding new investment should be so important to the managers.

The ultimate decision makers are the workers, so they are the ones who elect the board of directors or hire the managers directly. While they may have some equity stake in the firm, their holdings would not be substantial for reasons already indicated. Thus, they would have less of an interest in long-term investments that would come to fruition after they leave the firm than do the quasi-equity owners. In short, because the workers' association with the firm is limited, this type of organization faces the horizon problem, though perhaps not in as serious a form as the cooperative in the worker con-trol–state ownership model.

Managers answer to the workers, not to the quasi-equity owners, so when the interests of the two conflict, it would not be surprising if managers acted in a way that systematically favored the former at the expense of the latter. This means that managers need not worry as much about low share prices on the quasi-equity markets as their counterparts in a free enterprise system, since they are not hired and fired by the shareholders, and they are in no danger of losing their jobs through a corporate takeover. If they inflated wages and permitted various forms of on-the-job consumption by the work-ers, they would only cement their position as head of the firm. Moreover, since all cooperatives have the same structure of ownership rights, all man-agers would face this incentive structure, so the quasi-equity owners would effectively have nowhere else to go. For these reasons, the quasi-equity own-ers could and would be exploited by the ultimate decision-making authori-ties (i.e., the workers) in the firm. This form of exploitation cannot take place in the comparable capitalist organization, the open corporation, because in the latter, the capital providers are the ultimate decision-making authorities.

The appropriation of the equity value of the firm would not go on indef-initely, however, because at some point it would negatively affect the ability of the firm to satisfy its needs for short-term and medium-term credit. Main-taining this form of creditworthiness would be extremely important from the workers' point of view, since this type of credit is essential for day-to-day and month-to-month operations. To do this, the firm needs an equity base to secure its loans. Fortunately, the quasi-equity owners provide an ideal reser-voir for this purpose, so long as the workers do not bleed them white. Thus, while the workers would have some incentive to exploit the quasi-equity own-ers, there are limits to what it would be in their interests to do. The upshot of all this is that although this form of capital provision is superior to what is found in the worker control-state ownership model so far as exploitation is concerned, it remains inferior to ordinary equity ownership, which joins ulti-mate decision-making authority to the provision of capital.

Jay might have a response to this but only at the price of calling into ques-tion the socialist credentials of his model. He suggests that "the existence of alternative investment outlets offering attractive returns abroad may be regarded as a necessary and proper protection of savers at home and as a desirable incentive to workers' cooperatives to make reasonable distributions" (1980, 15). Jay's proposal is intended for Great Britain, and what he is here advocating is an "open borders" policy for capital. This quotation and the surrounding discussion suggest that in response to the worry that investors will have nowhere else to go, Jay would say that quasi-equity owners should be permitted to sell their shares and invest in conventional open corporations overseas. In consequence, if managers in the cooperatives started to appro-priate some of the value of the quasi-equity owner's investment on behalf of the workers or on their own behalf, share prices would fall so quickly that firms' ability to secure short- and medium-term credit would be imperiled, which would threaten the ability of the cooperatives to survive. Foreign capital markets, then, provide the alternative needed to keep the cooperative's managers and their bosses (the workers) from exploiting the quasi-equity owners.

What all this means is that Jay envisions market socialist islands in a larger free enterprise sea that would constitute the world economy. The external environment, then, is similar to the external environment of Mondragon in this respect. Whether or not this could be called a socialist system depends on how economic systems are individuated, but it certainly seems odd to predicate a socialist economic system on the presumption that it is part of a larger system in which investors can have the full equity ownership found in the large open corporations of a free enterprise system. This gives new meaning to the phrase, "socialism in one country." It also means giving up the universalist pretensions that have historically been associated with socialism.

Further suspicions about the socialist credentials of Jay's model arise when one considers his views on smaller firms. The cooperative form is supposed to be mandated only for firms that have more than one hundred employees (1980, 9). Jay recognizes some of the efficiency advantages of the classical capitalist firm, in particular, its rewarding entrepreneurs according their contributions (1980, 26). This means that a large sector of the economy could be effectively private. Given this and given also that there are quasi-equity owners who need not be laborers, it is pertinent to ask whether this is a really a form of social ownership of most of the means of production, a necessary condition for a socialist economic system.

Even if it is a socialist system, however, it is highly questionable, on a number of distinct grounds, whether this type of system could realize the socialist vision of the good society.[8] Two related social virtues that a socialist economic system is supposed to realize are the collective control of the rate and direction of economic development and suppression or correction of the social irrationalities of the market. In this model, there seems to be no room for an economic organization to execute either of these tasks. New investment is thoroughly decentralized and controlled by the cooperatives in consultation with the quasi-equity markets and the market for debt instruments. As in a free enterprise system, the state would bear some of the responsibility for dealing with the irrationalities of the market, but there is nothing in this proposal to suggest that these problems could be dealt with in a way that is categorically superior to how they are handled by states in free enterprise systems.

Finally, one of the chief social virtues that a socialist economic system is supposed to realize is a significant reduction in inequality of material condition, at least in comparison to what one finds in a free enterprise system. There is nothing in Jay's model to ensure that inequality of material condition would be significantly reduced. Indeed, it is possible that the transition to his system would involve nothing more than notifying current equity owners of large corporations that they have now become quasi-equity owners of the new-style cooperatives and that the workers will henceforth appoint the boards of directors in these large firms. However, at one point, he does suggest that currency controls to prevent capital flight might be necessary for a brief period after the transition, at least until the people who have now become quasi-equity owners stop hyperventilating and adjust to their new status (1980, 15–16). Trading on the London Stock Exchange or on Wall Street could then resume.

The idea of outside equitylike financing is attractive for a number of reasons, not the least of which is that it stabilizes the cooperative and gives it an equity cushion to survive economic downturns and to secure short- and medium-term debt. However, if capital flight is prohibited, the workers, through their managers, could exploit the quasi-equity owners in a way that could not happen in an open corporation. On the other hand, if capital providers had real alternatives in the form of foreign investment opportunities or a smaller purely private sector at home, it is doubtful whether the system should be called "socialist." Finally, even if it should be called "socialist," it cannot ensure the realization of key elements of the socialist vision of the good society.

One of the problems with Jay's model from a socialist perspective is that it has too many people in it who look suspiciously like capitalists. Not only are there many classical capitalists, but the quasi-equity owners of large firms will function much like ordinary stockholders, except they do not get to vote on the membership of the board of directors. Saul Estrin (1989) believes that social ownership requires an economy more dominated by the cooperative form and one in which the individual private investor has a much diminished role. In addition, he has little faith in the state, either as a full owner of the means of production or as an owner in the truncated sense found in the worker control–state ownership model. But, as noted, he also believes that social ownership of the means of production precludes equity ownership by the workers. Who, then, should own the capital that the cooperatives employ? Estrin's answer is holding companies, created specifically for that purpose and for the purpose of creating new firms in response to perceived profit opportunities (pp. 186–88). The latter point warrants a brief digression.

Estrin is concerned about the responsiveness of cooperatives to changing economic conditions on account of their ownership structure—specifically, the workers' status as collective residual claimants. As was explained in the second section of chapter 6, cooperatives are less likely to expand production and hire new workers in response to increased demand. They need the spur of competition to "do the right thing." However, if all established firms face about the same conditions and cannot hire wage labor, they would all react by raising prices instead of increasing production. Under these circumstances, customers effectively have nowhere else to go and thus are exploited, unless other firms can enter the market and make it competitively efficient. According to Estrin's model, this is precisely the role that new firms are supposed to play; this is why it is important for there to be easy entry for new firms.

Assuming that individuals cannot start up new firms (classical capitalist firms being generally prohibited), there needs to be a type of organization whose mandate includes the creation of new enterprises to compete with established firms. Estrin proposes that the holding companies carry out this function. They are in the best position to do this because, as owners of society's capital, they receive the returns to capital from all other firms in the economy. Because of this, they have the resources to fund new entrants. Their general mandate can be thought of as the promotion of economic growth and development. They would launch these new firms, and they would also lend financial capital to existing enterprises to finance new investment. Although the new firms would start out as creatures of the holding companies, after a time they would become regular cooperatives.

Since the holding companies own the cooperatives' capital (both physical and financial), their other main function would be to collect interest on this capital (society's return on its investment, so to speak), which they will use to fund new investment. Estrin believes that there should be many such holding companies, who would compete among themselves to hold the mortgage notes (as it were) on the capital of the various cooperatives, as well as fund new investment proposed by existing firms, and create new enterprises. This raises the crucial question of the ownership of the holding companies. Estrin considers a number of alternatives, each of which he finds unsatisfactory for different reasons (1989, 190–91). Clearly, ordinary private ownership of the holding companies would be inappropriate; these holding companies would be open corporations, and all of society's capital would be privately owned! What about the state? Estrin wisely puts little faith in the state bureaucracy as an engine of entrepreneurship, and so he rejects state ownership of the holding companies. Nor would it be a good idea for the holding companies themselves to be cooperatives, since the whole point of assigning primary responsibility for starting up new firms to the holding companies is that the cooperatives, by their very nature, tend to be deficient in their responsiveness to changing market conditions; that is, if the holding companies were also self-managed cooperatives, it is likely that there would be some serious shirking going on down in the New Firms Department of each of these enterprises. Also, this does not settle the problem of ownership of the holding company itself.

In the end, what Estrin favors is ownership of the holding companies by the cooperatives themselves! He says, "It is instead feasible that self-managed firms might become shareholders in the holding companies, creating a circularity of ownership. . . . This would be the most attractive solution from my point of view" (1989, 190). He also believes that private individuals, workers, and the government could be shareholders in the holding companies, though presumably most shares would be held by the cooperatives. These shares would be publicly tradable on the stock market, and shareholders would have proportional voting rights in the holding companies, which means that they would be the ultimate decision-making authorities. In this way, the ownership of capital would be ultimately monitored by the same array of instrumentalities found in a free enterprise system.

One can ask the same questions of this model as of the others. Is it in fact a socialist system? Can it realize the socialist vision of the good society? The first question can be rhetorically rephrased as follows: Is it really a socialist system if the holding companies that own all of the society's capital are themselves privately owned? Estrin might respond by saying that the socialist character of the system is assured by a combination of the self-management structure of the non-financial enterprises and by a wide dispersion of ownership of the equity shares in the holding companies.[9] It is hard to know whether this response is adequate. As with the Ellerman model, it seems that social wealth is managed for the benefit of private interests, though the network of those interests would perhaps be broader and systematically different from what exists in a free enterprise system. It is possible that this system is socialist at the micro level but not socialist at the macro level.

Putting to one side the issue of the socialist character of this system, wide dispersion of ownership of the holding companies is also important for another reason. If cooperative C owned controlling shares in holding company H and if H held the note on C's capital, this would create a clear conflict of interest that could result, among other things, in the exploitation of minority stockholders in H. For example, H could be ordered to renegotiate C's debt or to fund projects that H's management thinks are unwise; or, perhaps most importantly, C could prevent or discourage H from funding firms that might be competitors to C. Each of these would involve forms of exploitation. Estrin would undoubtedly favor laws prohibiting this, but it is unclear whether these laws could prevent the inevitable logrolling and vote trading among the cooperatives that would emerge to achieve the same ends as would be achieved by direct control of the holding companies' boards of directors.

Supposing that this problem could be solved, there is a further difficulty with this model from a socialist perspective. Some of the cooperatives are going to do much better than others in the stock market (i.e., the market for standard equity shares in the holding companies). At some point, some of this wealth is going to go into private hands (viz., to members of cooperatives that have good portfolio managers). There is nothing in the system to ensure that significant inequalities of wealth and income would not emerge from trading in these markets. Once again, it will not do to propose that these gains be taxed away. Either the affected parties will act through the political process to prevent this from happening, or the stock market will wither because, in the end, there is little to be gained by buying and selling shares in the holding companies. When that happens, the superior monitoring afforded by the stock market will also be lost. One cannot get this monitoring without providing the opportunity for some people to become rich.

Notice that the cooperatives are highly leveraged, since all of their capital is in the form of debt, which is held by the holding companies. It seems likely that there would be opportunities for exploitation at this interface between the cooperatives and the holding companies—opportunities that do not exist in the classical capitalist firm and the open corporation, both of which have equity bases to secure their debt.[10] At this interface, perhaps the most important challenge for the holding companies is to ensure that the value of the physical capital and the quasi-rent value of the firm are properly maintained. Because the members of the cooperative have a limited time horizon, all of the opportunities for exploitation associated with state ownership of capital in the worker control-state ownership model would exist in this system. Because the holding companies are private firms whose shares are publicly tradable (and not public bureaucracies) these opportunities might be smaller and less easy to seize; however, there is no getting around the fact that there is a monitoring problem in this arrangement that does not afflict the classical capitalist firm and the open corporation.

Finally, it is questionable whether this system could really provide the requisite entrepreneurship to keep markets from stagnating (to use the language of chapter 3). Stagnant markets are, of course, the breeding grounds for exploitation, since one party to an exchange in a stagnant market is not getting the value of his or her contribution and often has nowhere else to go. Estrin recognizes the importance of entrepreneurship. However, his proposal to deal with the problem does not appear to be as good as what one would find in a free enterprise system. As explained in the first section of chapter 6, it is almost always more difficult to create a new firm to meet increased demand for a product than it is for existing firms to expand production by hiring on wage labor. This is true independent of the mechanisms by which new firms are created. A comparison of these mechanisms reveals a further disadvantage of the Estrin model in comparison to a free enterprise system. In a free enterprise system the primary mechanism by which new firms are created is by individuals' starting up classical capitalist firms. These individuals can capture the full value of their entrepreneurial insights, something that cannot be done in Estrin's model. The importance of these considerations is that if cooperatives are less sensitive to profit opportunities than their free enterprise counterparts, then the economic system that Estrin favors is likely to be more exploitative than a free enterprise system on this score.

To summarize, the basic ownership structure of Estrin's model separates ultimate decision-making authority and residual claimancy (both of which are vested in the workers) from capital provision. In this respect, it resembles the worker control–state ownership model. Despite the arguably superior monitoring afforded by profit-making holding companies, this system still creates distinctive opportunities for exploitation—opportunities that do not exist in classical capitalist firms and are minimized in open corporations in a free enterprise system. In addition, it is questionable whether this system could really reduce inequality of material condition, which is one of the elements of the socialist vision of the good society.

This concludes the discussion of alternatives to the worker control–state ownership model of market socialism. With the exception of the full state ownership model, all of the models or types of economic systems considered in these two sections are ones in which the self-managed worker cooperative is the predominant organizational form. In the last third of the twentieth century, the prominence in socialist thought of this organizational form in the context of a market economy is perhaps best understood as a natural outgrowth of the repudiation of central planning and its top-down organizations, together with the belief that the hierarchy found in capitalist firms is, in one way or another, responsible for many of the ills attributable to the capitalist economic system.

An important issue that this book has addressed concerns the ownership structure of the capital in these cooperatives. This discussion is not exhaustive and is not intended to be. For example, a system in which the state is the residual claimant and the workers are both capital providers and ultimate decision-making authorities has not been considered. Another possibility that has not been discussed is a variant on the Estrin model in which the holding companies are residual claimants as well as capital providers, but the workers are the ultimate decision-making authorities. An account of the relative deficiencies of these types of system can be left as an exercise for the reader. However, this chapter, together with chapters 6 and 7, tries to cover some of the major options that have been proposed or discussed in recent years and that have some obvious attractions from a socialist perspective. Other writers have discussed various desirable features that a socialist society ought to have, but relatively few have said anything about a set of property rights in the means of production other than that they favor self-management. Fewer still have discussed property rights in the firm and its capital in enough detail to make possible the kind of comparative institutional evaluation offered in chapters 6 and 7 and the first two sections of this chapter.

One of the most important lessons of the preceding two chapters and this section is that equity ownership precludes forms of exploitation that would otherwise exist. By joining the roles of ultimate decision-making authority, provider of capital, and residual claimant, the major organizational forms of a free enterprise system (classical capitalist firms, open corporations, and even closed corporations and partnerships) prevent forms of exploitation that are permitted once these roles are separated. Equity ownership is the real essence of private property in the means of production. Once a society abandons this form of ownership, it becomes vulnerable to these other forms of exploitation. The problem for socialism is that it is unable to countenance equity ownership of the means of production because the equity ownership is responsible for both substantial inequality of material condition and decentralized control of the economy. From a socialist point of view, inequality is a social vice of capitalist societies and decentralized control of the economy is responsible for the social irrationalities of the market. However, to be in a position to deal with these problems, a market socialist society must decompose equity ownership in such a way that new and distinctive opportunities for exploitation are created.

The Socialist Vision of the Good Society

The socialist credentials of the models proposed by Ellerman, Jay, and Estrin were called into question on the grounds that it is not clear whether ownership of the means of production in those models was truly social. In each case, there seems to be no major role for an institution (e.g., the state) responsible for and responsive to the interests of society as a whole. However, even if the socialist character of the structure of these economic systems could be vouched for, there remains the problem of realizing three crucial elements of the socialist vision of the good society: collective control of the rate and direction of economic growth, suppression of the social irrationalities of the market, and the achievement of relative equality of material condition. For the reasons indicated in the preceding two sections, the achievement of all of these aims is very problematic for each of these models. On the other hand, one of the main attractions of the worker control–state ownership model is that state ownership of society's capital is a way of realizing all of these crucial elements of the socialist vision of the good society, at least in theory. The contrast between the worker control–state ownership model and these other models on this point warrants some further elaboration and discussion.

In the worker control–state ownership model, the state controls the social surplus (as socialists call it). That is, the state receives the returns to capital and controls most new investment. The motivation for this is to control the rate and direction of economic growth. The state does not have these ownership rights in these other models. Even if the latter include some role for the state in planning new investment, it is hard to see how they could properly be said to control economic growth.[11] These systems are specified in such a way that the returns to capital go to individuals or to nonstate organizations, which means that the state would not have direct control over the financial resources used for new investment; equally important, these other organizations and/or individuals would have the financial muscle to thwart, in one way or another, any attempts to exert collective control over the economy that run contrary to their own interests. Both of these problems are averted if the returns to capital go directly to the state, as in the worker control–state ownership model.

Second, if the state controls the social surplus, this provides it with the financial resources to suppress or correct the various social irrationalities that would be caused by the unfettered operation of the market. By contrast, in all of the models discussed earlier in this chapter (with the possible exception of the pure state ownership model), the state does not have the financial resources to deal effectively with these problems. Like the state in a free enterprise system, it must rely on general tax revenues to address these problems. For this reason alone, it is not likely to do much better than states in free enterprise systems in dealing with these problems.

Finally, and perhaps most important, state ownership of capital in the worker control–state ownership model more or less automatically guarantees

relative equality of material condition among the citizens of a market socialist society. On the other hand, if the returns to capital went directly to the
cooperatives and thus their members, the fact that different firms have widely
different capital-to-labor ratios would mean that some workers would have
much higher incomes than others. To achieve some measure of equality of
material condition under these circumstances, society (in the guise of the
state) must find some way to pry loose some income from these wealthier
workers, or at least from their cooperatives. This is difficult to achieve in a
society in which the cooperatives control not just physical resources but also
financial resources. This gives them real independence from the state, and
they can presumably use those resources to influence state policies. Similar
problems arise in the Jay model with the quasi-equity owners and in the
Estrin model with its individual and collective stockholders receiving dividends from the holding companies.

If, however, the returns to capital went directly to the state and did so
more or less automatically (as they do in the worker control–state ownership
model), then the workers in the cooperatives would receive only the returns
to labor plus any residuals. The attractions of this arrangement from an egalitarian socialist perspective are considerable. In competitively efficient markets, pure profits (which is what the residuals represent) are vanishingly
small. In markets in transition, they are ephemeral, since the competitive
process causes them to evaporate. This means that, assuming a market socialist economy is tolerably efficient, interfirm variations in income would sometimes be noticeable in the short term but insignificant over the long haul. In
addition, for reasons explained in the second section of chapter 6, the distribution of income within the firm would be relatively egalitarian, at least in
comparison to free enterprise systems. In this way, the invisible hand of the
market and the visible hands of the cooperatives' compensation committees
would work to ensure, more or less automatically, a relatively egalitarian distribution of income in a market socialist society. Whatever inequalities remain
could be regarded as the price that must be paid to keep markets competitively efficient and the standard of living at a reasonable level.

The same point can be appreciated from another angle. Many socialists,
especially twentieth-century socialists, have maintained that one of the most
important vices of free enterprise systems is significant inequality of material
condition. Moreover, they believe that the problem cannot be corrected by
substantial redistribution through the state; indeed, that is one reason—perhaps the main reason—why they are socialists. They believe that reform in
this respect is futile either because the state represents the interests of the ruling class or because the fundamental interests of the ruling class serve as a
significant constraint on state action.[12] Public choice theorists have made the
case that once the state (in a free enterprise system) gets involved in wealth
or income redistribution, special interests (especially wealthy special interests) invariably hijack the process to serve their own ends (Wagner 1989).
These arguments taken together mean that the chances for significant redistribution of wealth or income in the direction of equality are, in point of fact,

very slim in a free enterprise system. This is why many egalitarians are radicals who want to replace a free enterprise system with a socialist economic system. But this means that egalitarian ends must be achieved more or less automatically and, to a large extent, outside of the political process. This is exactly what the worker control–state ownership model achieves, which is one of the main reasons why socialists do (or at least should) find it extremely attractive. This is part of the reason why disproportionate attention has been paid to this model in this book.

Despite these attractions from a socialist perspective, this type of economic system cannot realize the socialist vision of the good society. In point of fact, it cannot suppress the social irrationalities of the market. Although the state receives all of the returns to capital and thus has the financial muscle to deal with these problems, it is hopelessly compromised by the moral hazards it faces in trying to direct new investment to problems caused by the operation of the market. As a general matter, there is no way the state can reserve to itself the right to overturn the verdict of the market without opening itself up to the influence of those whose private agenda does not serve the public interest. This is not reducible to a matter of simple corruption that could be prevented by public-spiritedness among those state employees charged with decision making. Rather, it is a natural consequence of the multiple decision criteria used for investment decisions and important information asymmetries between the cooperatives and the state. The interaction of these two factors, mixed in with some opportunism on the part of the cooperatives or their agents, guarantees some distinctive forms of exploitation in the worker control–state ownership model.

To see how and why, notice that because the state is planning new investment and not just disbursing funds according to projected profitability, it must be using multiple decision criteria to make its investment decisions. Some of these criteria would be unrelated to the profitability of the investment (e.g., relieving unemployment in certain sectors). Moreover, there would inevitably be important informational asymmetries between cooperatives and the state about the former's abilities and intentions to meet the various criteria in which the state is interested. Does firm X really have the ability and intention to provide employment opportunities for the hard-core unemployed and to make a modest profit doing it? Can firm Y really develop the requisite expertise in pollution control technology and still break even with its new investment? The corresponding problems faced by banks who lend to firms in free enterprise systems are less serious in two respects: (1) their concerns are more narrowly focused, since all that they care about is profitability; and (2) capitalist organizations typically have an equity cushion to secure their loans, which serves not only that purpose but also as a bonding device to ensure that the firm's management and ultimate decision makers are being relatively honest about their projections for any new investment projects. By contrast, the workers put up no equity in the worker control–state ownership model, except perhaps their firm-specific assets, which would be lost if the firm went under or to be more exact, if the state *let* the firm go under.

Actually, the problem just described is not limited to state control over new investment in a market socialist system, though it is particularly serious in that area. The problem is pervasive in any market economy where the state has a potentially unlimited mandate to deal with the social irrationalities that fortuitously arise as a result of the operation of market forces or indeed any other uncontrolled or ill-understood social forces. In the last third of the twentieth century, societies with free enterprise systems have increasingly faced this problem as the state has nominally assumed greater responsibility for dealing with the misfortunes that befall its citizenry. However, there remains a presumption in favor of the verdict of the market that cannot be present in a market socialist system in which the state has significant ownership rights in society's capital and is charged with controlling most new investment in the public interest. In the face of ever-escalating demands on its resources, the state in a free enterprise system could credibly plead poverty long before its market socialist counterpart could. It is at least possible (though by no means certain) that the market socialist state will be able successfully to plead poverty only when the entire economy is bankrupt.

This brings us back to the topic of exploitation. Chapter 2 identifies the elimination of exploitation as one of the elements of the socialist vision of the good society. The account of exploitation developed in chapter 3 made it reasonably clear that the elimination of this phenomenon is a utopian dream that could never come to pass. Any market economy will suffer some exploitation, so the only question is, how much? Or, more precisely, how much in comparison to the alternatives? Could the worker control–state ownership model do better, at least, than a free enterprise system in minimizing the incidence of exploitative exchange? Chapters 5–7 argue that even this could not be achieved. It was argued that the worker control–state ownership model permits and encourages forms of exploitation that are precluded or discouraged in free enterprise systems. The first two sections of this chapter argue that other models (whether or not they are truly socialist) are also inferior to free enterprise systems, to greater or lesser degrees, on this score. Indeed, the discussion of chapter 5 suggests (though it does not prove outright) that a free enterprise system minimizes, in some absolute sense, the incidence of exploitative exchange because its characteristic organizational forms tend to minimize transactions costs. Whatever its absolute standing, however, chapters 6 and 7 and the first two sections of this chapter demonstrate that a free enterprise system is superior to the most plausible market socialist alternatives on the issue of exploitation. This answers the question asked at the end of chapter 7 about the larger significance of the main argument of chapters 6 and 7 as it pertains to the worker control–state ownership model. Though not all logically possible alternatives have been considered, it is doubtful whether there are very many other well-motivated versions of market socialism out there in logical space. If this is so, it is fair to say that substantial progress has been made in the capitalism/socialism dispute.

This progress can be made more secure by reassessing the significance of exploitation as it relates to the good society. Specifically, why is exploitation so important? Why can't the market socialist admit that the worker control–state ownership model is more exploitative than free enterprise systems but that the additional exploitation is a price worth paying? After all, this type of system could well satisfy other socialist goals, notably, relative equality of material condition; if inequality of material condition is responsible for as much evil in the world as many socialists seem to believe, this trade-off may appear to be reasonable.

There are two responses to this. One is that it is arguable that paying this price involves commitment to a society that is profoundly unjust. Recall from chapter 3 that what makes an exchange exploitative is that the exploited party is not getting the value of what he is giving up (i.e., the value of his contribution) and that he has no real alternative but to accept those terms of exchange. The first of these conditions involves a failure of reciprocity; there is a tradition in philosophy, going back at least to Aristotle that conceives of the lack of reciprocity as central to injustice.[13] So the short answer to the question about the importance of exploitation is that it is arguably a form of injustice; this means that if the worker control–state ownership model were to be realized, it would permit and encourage forms of injustice that either would not exist or would be minimized in a free enterprise system. If, as Rawls maintains, justice is the first virtue of social institutions (1971, 3), this is no small matter.

Some modern egalitarian socialists might be unimpressed by this argument from reciprocity, however. They believe that people's wealth or income should be relatively equal, in fact, as a matter of justice, which means that there is no compelling reason why people ought to be paid according to the value of their contributions. Indeed, if the account of the distribution of income in the worker control–state ownership model is accurate, why should exploitation, as it has been defined in this book, matter very much at all? If people end up with incomes that do not fall outside of an acceptable range, distributive justice has been assured. What difference does it make if some exploitation takes place along the way?

One answer to this question is that possibly it would not matter if, in fact, income were distributed in that way. However, this account of the distribution of income in the worker control–state ownership model completely abstracts from the effects of exploitation. Once those effects are taken into account, there is no guarantee that a relatively egalitarian income distribution would result. The myriad vulnerabilities to exploitation that afflict the worker control–state ownership model make it possible for some people to become much wealthier than others by exploiting the system, as it were. Especially in their relations with the state, cooperatives with unusually ruthless and opportunistic members or leaders would be able to expropriate considerable social wealth — much more than their more slow-witted or more honorable competitors. It is likely that the distribution of wealth and/or income in this society would track people's cleverness and penchant for opportunism even more closely than it does in free enterprise systems (and that is saying something). Because people differ considerably in both attributes, this system would be highly unlikely to assure an egalitarian outcome. It is also an unstable situation, since more honorable men and women would begin to feel like "chumps" as the opportunists went undetected and unpunished and, not coincidentally, as it became more and more difficult to survive according to the rules. Society might evolve into two classes, what the Poles have called "the unprotected" and "the unpunished." This seems to have been the pattern in centrally planned economies, where survival by the rules became, or perhaps always was, impossible. So there is no assurance that the worker control–state ownership model would realize distributive justice, even if the latter is best understood in terms of relative equality of material condition.

There is another reason why an egalitarian socialist cannot dismiss concerns about the exploitation that would take place in the worker control–state ownership model. Opportunism in the present context is defined as the violation of people's legitimate expectations concerning the performance of contractual obligations. Assuming the legitimacy of the basic system of property rights of this model (as the defender of the worker control–state ownership model must), proponents of this version of market socialism have no choice but to pronounce exploitative exchanges unjust or, at the very least, in violation of legitimate expectations. In other words, suppose (as proponents of the worker control–state ownership model believe) that society really ought to be the owner of all of its capital. If a cooperative systematically siphons value from the capital it controls into its members' pockets, it has violated legitimate expectations held by others in the society.

One final reason why proponents of market socialism cannot look benignly on the relatively widespread exploitation that would take place in the worker control–state ownership model is that paying people in accordance with the value of their contributions is a way of allowing them to control their own lives, at least in the interrelated spheres of production, consumption, and leisure. If the income that people receive bears little or no connection to what they contribute, it is difficult for them to exert control over their own lives at the intersection of these important areas. It is doubtful that a socialist could endorse a system in which this crucial component of self-determination was missing.[14] This is especially important in a regime of scarcity, that is, in a society in which people cannot have everything thing they want, or even everything it is reasonable for them to want. A regime of scarcity, of course, is what market socialism would face from now until as far into the future as it makes sense to look.

All of the models canvassed in this book are inferior to a free enterprise system as far as exploitation is concerned. However, some of the ones discussed in this chapter do not seem to be so bad, that is, so exploitative relative to free enterprise systems that they could not have counterbalancing virtues, especially the virtues associated with self-management. Justice may be the first virtue of social institutions, but it is not the only one. And perhaps (Rawls notwithstanding) it is not lexically prior to all the others. Instead, it may be first in some vaguer sense, which grants it pride of place but allows some trade-offs with other virtues. Perhaps one of these other models might prove superior, in some all-things-considered sense, to a free enterprise system.

A defense of one of these models, however, is arguably not a defense of a socialist economic system because it is not at all clear that these models are forms of social ownership of the means of production. Perhaps more importantly, a defense of this sort would require giving up on the socialist vision of the good society. That vision springs from a widely shared critique of capitalist society that has its roots in the nineteenth century and has persisted throughout most of the twentieth century. All the social virtues identified in chapter 2 are mirror images of social vices that socialists have attributed to the free enterprise system over the past century and a half. The promise of socialism is the promise of an economic system that eliminates these ills or reduces them to the status of mere social blemishes. The argument of this book has been that perhaps the best motivated version of market socialism from a socialist perspective would, in point of fact, be responsible for some of the vices (most notably exploitation) that have been attributed to the capitalist system. Indeed the only virtue of market socialism whose realization has not been called into question in this book is the virtual elimination of alienation in the workplace. If someone wants to defend one of the models identified in this chapter—or some hybrid of these models—and to mount that defense on the basis of some other conception of the good society, that may be a project with some prospects for success, but it requires one to give up on socialism, both as an economic system and as a vision of the good society. While this would not vindicate the free enterprise system as the economic system of the good society, it would bring the capitalism/socialism dispute to an end with a defeat for socialism and a clear, though limited, victory for capitalism.

Notes

Chapter 1

1. Whether or not one believes that free enterprise (capitalist) systems can in fact realize socialist goals and values is perhaps the decisive difference between socialists and social democrats.

2. For discussion of Yugoslavia, see Pejovich (1966), Milenkovitch (1971), Vanek (1977a), Estrin (1983), and Lydall (1984; 1989). For Mondragon, see Thomas and Logan (1982). For the kibbutz experience, see Leviatan (1991) and the references cited therein. The cases of Yugoslavia and Mondragon will be discussed in more detail in chapter 6.

3. For a fuller articulation of this position, see Buchanan (1982, 60–81). The criticisms that follow in the text are also due to Buchanan.

4. See, for example, Nozick (1974, 233).

5. For a useful historical discussion of utopian socialist thought, see Kolakowski (1978, 182–233).

6. Actually, it is easy to prove that the concept of a good society is not the same as the concept of an ideal society. A good society has an economic system. Any society with an economic system has lawyers (to interpret the rules of the system). No ideal society has lawyers. Therefore, no good society is an ideal society.

7. In principle, the condition in question could be a sufficient condition for a society to be a good society. However, it would be an impoverished theory that held that a society's having a certain type of economic system is sufficient for it to be a good society. On the face of it, it seems self-evident that a society could have the right type of economic system and still fail to be a good society for other reasons.

8. Unfortunately, a good deal of contemporary economics is a purely formal, mathematical enterprise. The economics that is relevant to this dispute must have a fairly substantial empirical component. Notice also that a full-blown economic theory (of prices, distribution, etc.) may not be necessary to substantiate some central claim or claims that a defender of one or the other type of system makes. All that may be required are some warranted causal claims connecting a type of economic system and its effects.

9. John Rawls says, "Justice is the first virtue of social institutions just as truth is the first virtue of systems of thought" (1971, 3). Though justice may be the first virtue of social institutions, it is certainly not the only one. All good societies are just, but the converse is highly doubtful; some contemporary liberals notwithstanding, there is more to the good society than satisfying the demands of justice.

10. This view derives from a certain normative conception of human nature, that is, what makes a life a good life for human beings. For discussions of this normative

263

element in Marx's writings about human nature, see Elster (1985, chap. 2.2), Wartenberg (1982, 77–78), Buchanan (1982, 18–19), Miller (1981, 324–27), Nasser (1975, 486–88), Gregor (1968, 377).

11. For some representative recent socialist criticisms of the free enterprise system, see Schweickart (1980), Horvat (1982), Nove (1983), Nielsen (1985), Miller (1989b), and Le Grand and Estrin (1989a). For a sample of criticisms of socialism, see Hayek (1944), Kolakowski (1974), Rutland (1985), Lavoie (1985; 1986), and Evers (1989).

12. This objection to John Roemer's account of exploitation under capitalism has been raised by Allen Buchanan (1985, 121–22). I have argued elsewhere that the problem that Buchanan calls attention to is legitimate but that Roemer's definition of exploitation can be repaired so as to avoid it (Arnold 1990, 126–28).

13. Because of the way the terms 'free enterprise system' and 'socialist economic system' have been defined, there might be some minor exceptions to this general principle. Suppose that a critic of free enterprise systems believes that widespread private ownership of the means of production is *malum in se*. Since a prohibition on this is part of the very definition of a socialist economic system, this critic of the free enterprise system is committed to the proposition that no socialist economic system has that problem. Being true by definition, it requires no proof.

14. In a similar vein, when proponents of a free enterprise system criticize existing socialist systems for the shortages, generalized poverty, and tyrannical political systems that they associate with those economic systems, they explicitly or tacitly hold out the prospect of escaping or avoiding these social problems by embracing a free enterprise system. This was one of the messages of Hayek (1944).

15. I have reconstructed and critically evaluated these arguments elsewhere (Arnold 1990, 193–201, 268–81).

16. See note 13.

17. This is especially true of socialists, both those opposed to the existing capitalist order in the West and those opposed to the bureaucratic socialism that characterized Eastern Europe. For some examples of the former, see Levine (1984), Schweickart (1980), and Miller (1989a). For an example of the latter, see Horvat (1982).

18. Exceptions are claims that display a logical relation between type-defining features and social virtues, for example, some libertarians' claims linking free enterprise systems to respect for basic human rights.

19. This paragraph touches on some important and difficult issues in the philosophy of social science, such as the correct understanding of ceteris paribus clauses and the role of background assumptions in social scientific explanation. For a nuanced discussion of these and related issues, see Kincaid (1990).

20. This view is so widespread among socialists, especially contemporary socialists, that documentation is scarcely needed. For representative views, see Nielsen (1985) and the articles in Le Grand and Estrin (1989a).

21. Indeed, it used to be thought to be the only task. Once the concepts had been clarified, it was time to clock out and head for the local tavern. Almost no analytic philosophers believe this anymore.

22. For a recent example, see DeJasay (1990, 9–10).

23. This tacitly assumes that the best society that one can reasonably hope for is not beset by widespread and pervasive alienation. While this assumption may or may not be a reasonable belief, it is certainly a reasonable hope.

24. As a point of logic and dialectics, this requires more than criticizing one's opponents' arguments, since their premises might be false and yet their conclusions true. It is surprising how many critics of free enterprise systems rest content with criticiz-

ing *arguments* offered by those who favor such systems. To criticize the free enterprise system, it is insufficient to discover deficiencies in the reasoning of, for example, Robert Nozick or Milton Friedman.

Chapter 2

1. The best representations of mainstream opinion are to be found in those enormous introductory economics textbooks that college students are forced to buy. The successive editions of Paul Samuelson's *Economics* provide a good chronicle of the changes in mainstream opinion among economists over the past two decades. An examination of the relevant sections of this text over a number of editions reveals that Samuelson's overall assessment of central planning has become increasingly less favorable over the years. Some truly embarrassing quotations on the Soviet economy from Samuelson and other economists are collected in Arnold Beichman's column in the *Washington Times* of December 18, 1989.

2. The consensus was not unanimous. The passage quoted from Heilbroner and Thurow has been retained in later editions of *The Economic Problem*. Heilbroner and Thurow, like many economists in the public eye, maintain a remarkable serenity and equanimity in the face of events that reveal their predictions and other public pronouncements to be contrary to the plainest facts. Events such as these would produce an intellectual, if not a personal, crisis for most individuals. The only historical parallel to this equanimity that I am aware of is the ancient Pyrrhonian skeptic's attitude of detachment (*ataraxia*) from the world of sensory experience, an attitude cultivated by an intensive and careful study of skeptical arguments.

3. See, for example, Wlodzimierz Brus's review essay in the *New Left Review* (Brus 1985).

4. See, for example, Brus and Laski (1989, 132–52) and the writings of Janos Kornai over the past four decades. The most comprehensive statement of Kornai's views can be found in Kornai (1992).

5. The best and most comprehensive discussion of the debate is to be found in Lavoie (1986), which explains why Mises's critics missed the simple point alluded to in the text. This book also contains the most complete citation of sources on the debate up to about 1985. For more recent discussions of the Mises-Hayek argument and the socialist calculation debate, see Rutland (1985, 24–48), Shapiro (1989), and Arnold (1989, 177–91; 1990, 246–63). Much of Nove (1983) restates and illustrates in considerable detail some of the general points first made by Mises and Hayek.

6. Lavoie has argued that some of this vital information takes the form of tacit knowledge, which by its very nature cannot be articulated and thus cannot be transmitted to the planners (1986, 103).

7. See the quotation from Heilbroner and Thurow. One can be reasonably sure that those who believed this had no detailed empirical knowledge about what life was like under such a system. What has changed in recent years is not the performance of centrally planned economies, which has always been dismal, but the perception of those systems among some segments of the elites in both the West and the East.

8. It is ironic that most formerly socialist countries now have a ministry of privatization instead of a ministry of socialization. Though statues of Mises have not yet been erected, many statues of Lenin and Marx have been toppled.

9. See, especially, Schweickart (1980, chap. 3) and Le Grand and Estrin (1989b, 4). This point is discussed in greater detail in the second subsection of the last section of this chapter.

10. There are some difficult and complex issues here in the philosophy of economics, notably, the usefulness of the Pareto concepts to assess the efficiency of economic systems. There are, however, grounds for serious skepticism about the possibility or meaningfulness of noncomparative efficiency judgments. See Buchanan (1985, chap. 2).

11. A question that lurks around the edges of this discussion is whether or not there could be some third alternative to central planning and the market. The only contemporary theorists of whom I am aware who advocate neither central planning nor markets are Michael Albert and Robin Hahnel. See Albert and Hahnel (1978; 1987; 1991). For penetrating criticisms of their model, see Prychitko (1988).

12. As was pointed out in chapter 1 (p. 7), the state in capitalist societies often limits the various rights, terms, and conditions associated with ownership of the means of production. However, as indicated, so long as residual rights of control are in private hands, ownership is private. This is not to deny that there will be borderline cases in which there is no determinate answer to the question of whether or not there is private ownership, but in general, there is a determinate answer to the question of whether residual rights of control are in private hands or not.

13. The qualifier about a fully functioning market economy is important. At least until recently, socialist thought has been notorious for its vagueness about the institutions for future socialist society. Because of this, the claim in the text has more analytical than historical reach. For example, syndicalism fits neither of the subsequent models discussed in the text; under syndicalism, entire industries are controlled (owned?) by those who work in them. However, syndicalism does not constitute a counterexample to the claim to which this note is appended, since as a matter of empirical fact, there could be no fully functioning market economy in which each industry is effectively constituted by one firm. If for no other reason, problems about monopoly pricing would soon produce institutional paralysis.

14. Nationalization is particularly attractive if all one really cares about is getting rid of capitalism. The simplest and most direct way to achieve that end is to seize state power and nationalize most enterprises. This thought must have occurred to Lenin, probably around the age of six.

15. What is true in principle may not be true in practice. Janos Kornai argues that there is an affinity between markets and private ownership on the one hand and central planning and state ownership on the other hand (Kornai 1992, 447–50, 497–500). The point at issue here, however, concerns what is theoretically possible.

16. The root of this idea can be found in Marx's later theory of the state. See Marx ([1852] 1963, 122; [1871] 1975, 329–30). For an illuminating discussion of Marx's theories of the state, see Aveneri (1968, 51–52).

17. I do not mean to suggest that all of these authors unanimously agree about all of the details that follow in the text. Rather, what all of these writers share, or seem to share, is a belief that the economic system should be changed so that some type of worker cooperative would be the main form of economic organization. Some of these authors are too vague in their descriptions for one to ascribe to them anything more definite than this. What follows is what I believe to be the best motivated type of market socialist economic system in which some of the more important details about property rights have been spelled out. The motivations for this type of system will be discussed, primarily in the next section. Chapter 8 discusses some other alternatives.

18. The account of the capital usage fee that follows in the text echoes Schweickart (1980, 52–53).

19. See note 16.

20. Three authors who favor market socialism but do not straightforwardly endorse state control of new investment are David Winter, Saul Estrin, and David Miller (Estrin and Winter 1989, 115–19; Estrin 1989, 183–91; Miller 1989a, 309–11). They see potential dangers to democracy and efficiency in this idea. However, their positive proposals do not make it clear whether they believe that new investment should be determined largely outside of the political process or not. This question is of considerable importance, since political control of society's economic destiny seems to be a common thread in nearly all nonanarchist socialist thought. The political control of society's economic destiny is discussed in greater detail in the next section, and alternative forms of market socialism are discussed in chapter 8.

21. Of course, there is some state planning of new investment in existing free enterprise systems under the guise of industrial policy, but no one seriously maintains that the state controls most new investment in, for example, Germany or Japan. In other words, there is a categorical difference between what passes for industrial policy in existing free enterprise systems and the kind of planning that market socialists envision for the system they favor. This will become clearer in the next section, which examines the motivations for investment planning in this type of market socialist system.

22. For ease of reference, the term 'market socialism' will be reserved for this family of types of economic systems from this point up until chapter 8, where some alternative forms of market socialism will be discussed.

23. An important caveat emptor: the reader should not infer that I endorse the arguments and explanations that follow in the text. To the extent that anything later in this book depends on accepting or rejecting any of them, I will state and defend my own views at the appropriate time. Also, to keep the length of this chapter within reasonable bounds, I shall attribute various views to Marx without much in the way of supporting arguments and documentation. These interpretive arguments and documentation can be found in Arnold (1990), chaps. 2 (alienation) and 3 (exploitation).

24. This account of alienated labor combines objective features (e.g., lack of worker control) and subjective features (e.g., various forms of dissatisfaction). For more on subjective versus objective alienation, especially as it has shaped research in sociology, see Seeman (1991) and the other articles in Oldenquist and Rosner (1991).

25. Some discussion of these problems is fairly common in the writings of most market socialists, not to mention standard economic textbooks. For a clear, concise statement from a market socialist perspective, see Estrin and Winter (1989, 107–15). For a more elaborate discussion (not in the context of the debate between capitalism and socialism), see Buchanan (1985, chap. 2).

26. For a sensitive discussion of the tension in market socialism between commitment to the market and commitment to certain end-states as part of the socialist vision of the good society, see Plant (1989). Not all socialists see the contrast between free enterprise systems and market socialism in this way. Some see it as a choice between the undemocratic procedures that are found in the former and the democratic procedures that would be found in the latter. I owe this observation to Justin Schwartz.

27. I have attempted a comprehensive discussion and critical evaluation of these reformulated arguments in Arnold (1990, chaps. 4 and 5). The reader is directed there for a critical discussion of these arguments. My purpose here is to represent without criticizing central elements of a socialist critique of free enterprise economic systems as a way of motivating the elements of market socialism identified in the last section. In addition, in what follows I will make no attempt to argue for my representation of Marx's argument as the correct interpretation of what he had in mind. I have argued for this interpretation in detail in Arnold (1990, chap. 3).

28. See Arnold (1990, chap. 3, esp. pp. 74–86) for an argument in support of this harsh judgment on the labor theory.

29. For a discussion of this point, see Becker (1986, 143).

30. This view, or something close to it, is advocated or discussed in Holmstrom (1977, 359); Elster (1985, 167); Miller (1981, 337); Reiman (1987, 4); DiQuattro (1984, 70–71); Young (1978, 441–44).

31. Writers such as Holmstrom (1977) and Reiman (1987) have maintained that this forcing is a logically independent evil (and, in some sense, more important than the failure of reciprocity). In other words, even if the capitalists were entitled to their profits, the unfreedom the worker is subjected to by being forced to work for the capitalist is independently objectionable. This view is worked out in detail by Justin Schwartz in an unpublished manuscript, "What's Wrong with Exploitation?" See also Brenkert (1985).

32. Roemer (1982a; 1982b) has a very different conception of exploitation that does not seem to be most naturally understood in terms of a failure of reciprocity. For a critical evaluation of Roemer's conception of exploitation and the related charge against capitalism, see Arnold (1990, chap. 5).

33. The literature on this is enormous. For some examples, see Nielsen (1985), Dworkin (1981a; 1981b), Griffin (1986), G. A. Cohen (1989), Sen (1987).

34. This latter view of the relationship between the state and the ruling class is argued for by Jon Elster (1988, 213–15).

35. It is on this point that socialists and social democrats have a fundamental difference of opinion. Unlike socialists, social democrats believe that significant redistribution by the state can take place in the context of a free enterprise system. The difference between socialists and social democrats on this point may be as much about the meaning of 'significant' as it is about the empirical question of how much of the right kind of redistribution the state can accomplish in a society with a free enterprise system.

36. This, of course, is the mirror image of one of the main social vices that has been attributed to state socialist economic systems, namely, their failure to meet people's basic material needs satisfactorily.

37. Two especially clear examples of this are Levine (1984) and Miller (1989a).

Chapter 3

1. For a comprehensive discussion and critical evaluation of the literature on this charge, see Arnold (1990, chaps. 3–5).

2. One notable exception is the theory of exploitation developed by Miller (1989a, chap. 7). His theory, like the one presented in this chapter, is a perfectly general account of exploitative exchange.

3. Cohen's argument does not make exactly this supposition. His claim is only that the capitalist is not a producer, but he seems to believe that this is sufficient for a failure of reciprocity. For a full discussion of this wrinkle in Cohen's argument, see Arnold (1990, 99).

4. The following is a very compressed statement of criticisms of Cohen and Schweickart that I have made in more detail elsewhere (Arnold 1990, 102–8); see also Arnold (1985).

5. The account of exploitation being developed here makes exploitation a property of transactions or exchanges. Though that is the dominant view in the literature on economic exploitation, it is not the only one. Over the past decade, John Roemer

has developed a theory of exploitation in which classes are the primary subjects and objects of exploitation (Roemer, 1982a; 1982b; 1985). Individuals are said to be exploited only derivatively insofar as they are members of the exploited class. I have discussed Roemer's views in detail elsewhere (Arnold 1990, chap. 5).

6. Notice that this distinction all but disappears in the case of the contribution of the laborer, if the labor theory of value were in fact true. According to the labor theory, value just *is* (socially necessary) labor.

7. There may be other forms of exploitation that take place in and through the economic system. For example, sexual harassment and some other forms of degradation in the workplace may be forms of exploitation. But however intimately they are tied up with the workings of the economic system, these forms of exploitation are not instances of economic exploitation, since they are not directly concerned with the distribution of economic value (wealth or income). For a discussion of how the workers might be noneconomically exploited in a capitalist system, see Arnold (1990, 112–15).

8. For an accessible discussion of ideal markets and perfect competition, see Buchanan (1985, chap. 2).

9. This conception of pure profits and entrepreneurship is due to the so-called Austrian economists (which these days include many Americans and other anglophones). For relatively recent and complete statements of this conception, see Kirzner (1973; 1979).

10. It is perhaps best to think of F-exchanges as those that take place within a somewhat narrow range of values, instead of at a particular value. F-exchanges are going to turn out to be a subset of the nonexploitative ones, and it would be implausible to say that what makes an exchange exploitative is that its terms differ only slightly from the terms of an exchange that is nonexploitative. For instance, one would not want to say that someone who paid $1,000 for something that was "really" worth only $999 was being exploited.

11. Though 'fair' seems to be the most natural term to describe these exchanges, the foregoing is not meant to be an analysis of the meaning of the terms 'fair' or 'fair exchange.' The choice of the term 'fair' is meant to be evocative only. The main substantive claim being advanced here is not about fairness but about the value of what someone has to offer in an exchange.

12. This claim presupposes one restriction and one simplifying assumption. The restriction is that 'well-being' is to be understood as referring to well-being insofar as it can be affected by exchangeable goods and services. Some elements of well-being cannot be secured by exchangeable goods and services, which just means that there is more to the good life than what the economic system can provide. This restriction is implicitly recognized in that the topic of this chapter is *economic* exploitation. The simplifying assumption is that given all the relevant factual information, individuals are the best judges of what enhances their own (material) well-being. In this context, this means that they are better judges than the most likely alternative judge, the state. Though this assumption does not hold in certain cases (which is why it is a simplifying assumption), it is difficult to see how one could deny it as a general principle and still favor the market as a way of organizing production.

13. For the sake of simplicity, this illustration abstracts from other determinants of the new equilibrium price, including the government's monetary, fiscal, and tax policies. These policies can affect the equilibrium price of a good or service in a variety of ways (e.g., through income effects). This simplification does not affect the general point, which is that whatever the determinants of the new equilibrium price, the lead-

ing-edge price of a market in transition at any given time is simply whatever price is closest to what will emerge as the new equilibrium price.

14. It is important to note that these so-called unfair exchanges need not be exploitative; unfair terms of exchange are a necessary but not a sufficient condition for exploitation. As the next section argues, if buyers have a "real alternative" to an unfair exchange, then they are not being exploited.

15. For more on the ethical and political implications of this conception of the role of pure profits in a market economy, see Arnold (1987c).

16. This account of the failure of reciprocity is similar to one of the conditions in David Miller's theory of exploitation (1989a, 186–89). One important difference is that for Miller, the benchmark equilibrium situation is defined not in terms of existing entitlements to resources and the like (as it is in the present account) but instead relative to a set of entitlements that are regarded as morally defensible on other grounds (p. 187). This may lead to a problem in identifying exploitative exchanges insofar as it is difficult to determine what exchange rates would emerge under the preferred set of entitlements. Another difference is that Miller's account does not countenance the contribution of the entrepreneur.

17. John Roemer (1985) has taken a similar position, though on different grounds.

18. Another possibility is that she does not know that she is giving up more than she is getting. There is some suggestion of this in Marx's claim that the wage contract helps to mystify the extraction of surplus value from the worker. Though this might be part of his explanation for the medium-term stability of capitalism, the principal Marxist explanation for why the workers put up with the alleged failure of reciprocity is that the workers are, in some manner, forced to work for the capitalists.

19. This account is officially agnostic about the question whether or not she is forced to work for the company. It does not really matter. Under the circumstances, she has no feasible alternative to working for the company; if she is getting less than the value of what she is contributing, then she is being exploited.

20. For criticisms of many extant alternative accounts of exploitative exchange, see Arnold (1990, chaps. 4 and 5). The main alternative account of exploitation in which exploitation is not a property of exchanges is Roemer's. For criticisms of Roemer, see Arnold (1990, chap. 5).

Chapter 4

1. As stipulated in chapter 2, for ease of exposition, the term 'market socialism' will be reserved for the type of economic system described and motivated there. Chapter 8 discusses some alternative forms of market socialism.

2. In some free enterprise systems (e.g., Germany), some members of the boards of directors are representatives of the workers, but these board members are not so numerous or powerful that they (or the workers whom they represent) have residual rights of control over the firm's assets. In other words, these firms are still essentially privately owned even if workers have some say at the highest levels. Although the system is called a social market economy (*Sozialmarktwirtschaft*), it is not a form of market socialism, as the term is used both in this book and, indeed, in most of the theoretical literature on socialism.

3. Indeed, one of the heroines of the Right, Margaret Thatcher, is revered for her privatization drives against the bureaucratic kulaks in Great Britain. There remains, however, an unresolved question about the role of the state in the right-wing conception of the good society. This is as it should be, since there is significant disagree-

ment on the Right about this question. A more complete defense of the free enterprise system would have to address this issue.

4. Elsewhere (Arnold 1987a; 1987d) I have argued in detail that cooperatives would have a strong tendency to degenerate into capitalist organizations. Gilboa (1991) shows that this argument is not plausible in the case of cooperatives comparable in size to the open corporation. The argument should be restricted to smaller cooperatives, which would be likely to degenerate into classical capitalist firms. A different argument would be needed to show that large cooperatives would evolve into open corporations.

5. For more on these Ulysses-and-the-sirens type problems, see Elster (1979).

6. Socialists are likely to object to this presumption as it applies to market socialism even before they hear the reasons for it. The first section of chapter 6 contains a thorough discussion and defense of this assumption.

7. It is worth pointing out that this book does not aim at a comprehensive evaluation of worker cooperatives. Cooperatives can take many different forms, especially as it pertains to the ownership of capital. Moreover, cooperatives can exist not only in market socialist systems but also in free enterprise systems and in systems that are neither socialist nor free enterprise. The focus of this book is narrow in the sense that it is concerned only with cooperatives as specified (and motivated) in chapter 2. The appropriateness of these restrictions is dictated by the larger framework within which this book is located, namely, the capitalism/socialism dispute.

8. This assumption about some stability in the environment is crucial to the evolutionary approach. In a rapidly changing environment, advantageous traits will not have the opportunity to take root and spread. This means that the evolutionary hypothesis must be restricted in scope or otherwise qualified to take account of factors that would disrupt the selection process. More qualifications and cautionary observations about the evolutionary strategy are added at the beginning of chapter 5.

9. An unstated assumption in this article is that the central contracting agent has ultimate decision-making authority. Although the authors do not provide it, it is easy enough to give a transactions cost explanation for joining these two roles. The basic idea is that separating them creates a potential for conflict of interest and associated inefficiencies that do not exist if they are joined.

10. Those who provide raw materials and semifinished products may have ongoing contractual relations that are difficult to distinguish from the relations that employees have with employers. For this reason, the firm-market boundary on the input side is sometimes blurred.

11. Opportunistic behaviors are necessarily deceptive and unanticipated. If it were widely known up front how much input would be withheld as a result of a person's opportunism, that could be factored into his remuneration. See also chapter 5, note 6.

12. The notion of a zone of acceptance comes from March and Simon (1958, 90). See also Williamson (1985, 218, 220). It is arguable that these residual rights of control (management rights), together with residual claimancy status (income rights), constitute the essence, in some important sense, of ownership. For an illuminating discussion of residual rights of control, see Grossman and Hart (1986).

13. See note 9.

14. Proponents of market socialism undoubtedly believe that the cooperative would be afflicted with much less shirking than the classical firm. The second section of chapter 6 explains why that is probably not true.

15. Since Simon's earlier writings (e.g., Simon 1961), the psychological picture of

these limitations and defects has been filled out in some detail. See Nisbett and Ross (1980) and Kahneman, Slovic, and Tversky (1982) for a more detailed and up-to-date picture of the relevant psychology.

16. Implicit in these different perspectives are, I believe, some important philosophical issues for normative economics—issues that warrant a fuller treatment than can be provided here.

17. This is closely related to what Milgrom and Roberts (1990) call "influence costs." Airplane hijackers usually do not bill the airlines for the expenses they incur in taking over a plane. Organizational hijackers almost always do.

18. What is at work in these examples are bounded rationality and uncertainty in the form of private information. The general problem, of which these examples are illustrations, is that complete, costlessly enforceable contracts governing every contingency cannot be written.

Chapter 5

1. This particular comparative claim will be made explicit and argued for in detail in the next section of this chapter.

2. It is not surprising that some of the critical treatments of transactions cost analysis have come from sociologists, especially sociologists of organizations. By inclination and training, they are disposed to see the hand of non-economic forces at work. See, for example, Perrow (1986, chaps. 6 and 7), Zald (1988), and Granovetter (1986). For a more sympathetic treatment of transactions cost analysis by a political scientist, see Moe (1984). This article is an excellent comprehensive summary of recent work in transactions cost analysis. Despite his sympathy for much of this work, Moe argues elsewhere (1989; 1990a; 1990b) that the explanatory principles invoked in transactions cost analysis have little application to political organizations. More on this in chapter 7.

3. For another good illustration, see Williamson's transactions cost explanation of the common promotion and pay policies ("internal labor markets," as the phenomenon is sometimes called) found in modern corporations (1975, 57–81).

4. As the term is defined here, in the open corporation most of the capital that the firm uses is owned or supplied by shareholders and thus does not take the form of debt. Of course, there are large corporations in free enterprise systems that do raise much of their capital through debt financing. The transactions cost advantages and disadvantages of debt versus equity financing in large corporations will be discussed at the end of the subsection on equity ownership in the third section of this chapter. See also Jensen and Meckling (1976).

5. Sometimes this type of organization is nominally owned by a family instead of an individual—as, for example, when all and only family members are on a board of directors of a corporation. Incorporation is often done for tax purposes, however. Whatever their legal status, these organizations are essentially classical capitalist firms since one person is in charge. They are to be distinguished from the closed corporation (the term comes from Fama and Jensen 1983b) in which a small number of people, who may or may not be related to the chief executive officer, have a real and direct equity stake in the firm and have some say over how it is managed. More on the closed corporation at the end of the next section.

6. Notice that shirking and other forms of opportunism are necessarily deceptive and unanticipated. If the behaviors in question (e.g., loafing on the job) are wholly anticipated, their value is reflected in the market price for the factor in question.

Everyone—including bosses—expects janitors, nightwatchmen, maintenance men, state highway workers, assistant deans, and so on to spend much of their time out of sight doing nothing productive. Although these people are loafing, they are not shirking. To shirk in jobs like these requires an unusual penchant for opportunism and a really strong antipathy toward productive labor.

7. This is true of the typical case, which is the object of the present investigation. One can imagine unusual circumstances under which other, more egalitarian monitoring arrangements would be superior. Putterman discusses some of these, but makes no claim that these circumstances are common (1984, 173–74).

8. This is not to be confused with ultimate decision-making authority. Someone may have ultimate decision-making authority without having any operational control, including residual rights of control. Indeed, this is precisely the situation of stockholders in the open corporation. They have ultimate decision-making authority in the sense that the firm's assets are managed in their interests. However, they cede residual rights of control—effective control—to management. More on ultimate decision-making authority in the classical capitalist firm shortly.

9. There are, of course, exceptions. Professional athletes under multi-year contracts who have had an especially good year do exactly this (pull a "holdup") when they threaten not to report to work or when they warn that they will "not be able to concentrate on the game" unless and until their contracts are renegotiated. Unlike other inputs, the central contracting agent does not have physical control over human labor or its owner.

10. Perhaps the most frequently cited article is this literature is Stephen Marglin's (1974) "What Do Bosses Do?" See also Karen Stone's (1974) "The Origins of Job Structures in the Steel Industry," and Charles Perrow's (1986) *Complex Organizations*, chaps. 7 and 8. For a general account of economic power that is consistent with transactions cost analysis on this point, see Bartlett (1989, chap. 7).

11. This contrasts with the standard Marxist explanation for this phenomenon, which presumes that the capitalist holds onto this power with white-knuckled fear lest the workers discover that they could carry on production just fine without him.

12. See note 4, this chapter. Also, the term 'equity owner' seems to have more than one meaning, depending on the context and who is using it. Sometimes, it just means 'residual claimant,' but in the law, the equity owner is also liable for the execution of debt. The problem is that economists, lawyers, and accountants have systematically different concerns, so they conceive of equity ownership in systematically different ways. The sentence to which this note is appended is a stipulative definition adopted for the purposes of this book.

13. Williamson was instrumental in changing the attitude of the U.S. Justice Department toward mergers and acquisitions. The previous policy saw attempts at vertical integration simply as attempts to amass market power with no efficiency advantages. The current policy recognizes that there can be transactions cost efficiencies in mergers and acquisitions. (See U.S. Department of Justice 1984, sec. 3.5.)

14. Notice that at the time of its breakup, AT&T, even in its long-distance operations, might have reached its size not because of any transactions cost efficiencies but instead because of its protected status as a monopoly. However (up to a point anyway), large size seems to have been an advantage in the ensuing struggle for survival. Its primary competitors are also quite large, which suggests (but does not prove) that there are transactions cost advantages to large size in this particular market.

15. Economies of scale are usually conceived of as production cost efficiencies instead of transactions cost efficiencies. However, as has been pointed out elsewhere

in this book, technology does not directly and uniquely determine an ownership structure. For this reason, it is most appropriate to treat economies of scale as a transactions cost efficiency.

16. These forms of opportunism are practiced at all levels in a bureaucratic hierarchy—whether in the public or the private sector—which is not to say that the problems are everywhere the same. In particular, it matters quite a bit who monitors the monitors (more on this in chapters 6 and 7). Nevertheless, the problem is ubiquitous, and because of imperfect monitoring, those who bear the wealth losses of these bureaucratic inefficiencies have nowhere else to go; they are, therefore, exploited. For an entrée into the relevant sociological literature, see Perrow (1986); for more specific discussions of the economic inefficiencies of hierarchy, see Williamson (1985, chap. 6), Milgrom and Roberts (1990) and Liebenstein (1987).

17. For a useful discussion of decision making and monitoring in true nonprofit organizations such as charities, cultural organizations, and churches, see Fama and Jensen (1983b, 318–20). Unlike the open corporation, these organizations are characterized by the absence of alienable claims on the residuals (however residuals are understood in such an organization) and the active involvement in decision making by people who donate money and time.

18. In practice, this type of organization is fraught with risks for the limited partner. For a discussion of some of these risks, see Wolfson (1985). The exact nature of these risks and how they are dealt with need not detain us here, since the concern of this section is the open corporation. Suffice it to say that limited partnerships are relatively uncommon and, not coincidentally, they are suited only to unusual economic microenvironments. They are the marsupials of the economic kingdom.

19. The term comes from Jensen and Meckling (1979). They argue that the pure rental firm is an impossibility because certain intangible capital (e.g., product design and engineering, distribution systems, good will) must be owned by the firm and so cannot be rented (1979, 476–78, 480–81). Perhaps, then, one should speak of the 'nearly pure rental firm,' though I shall not. Nevertheless, the points about to be made in the text must be slightly qualified or moderated to take into account the possibility that firms must own at least some of the capital that they use. The discussion of this subsection touches on some interesting questions in financial economics about the explanation of the ratio of debt to equity in the open corporation. The seminal article in this literature is another paper by Jensen and Meckling (1976). More on this issue shortly.

20. The organizational alternatives discussed in this and surrounding subsections seem exceedingly odd and counterintuitive in the abstract. However, they are worth discussing not only because of the comparative nature of the transactions cost efficiency claims being advanced on behalf of the distinctive features of the open corporation but also because some of these exotic organizational formations will be found on the wall of Plato's cave, market socialism. To anticipate chapter 6, under market socialism, the worker cooperative will turn out to have some of the features of the pure rental firm with the taxpayers as capital providers and workers as ultimate decisionmakers and residual claimants. Some of the discussion in chapters 6 and 7 details some of the ways in which the taxpayers can be exploited by the workers through this organizational structure.

21. Another reason debt is attractive, at least in the United States, is that it is subject to favorable tax treatment. This, of course, is a non-transactions-cost consideration in favor of debt financing.

22. They are also relatively rare. The average debt-equity ratio in nonfinancial

institutions in the United States in recent years has hovered below .8. Even in Japan, where firms are more highly leveraged, debt-equity ratios have been below 1.4 (*Economist*, August 10, 1991, p. 69).

23. See, e.g., Schweickart (1987a; 1987b). The theoretical foundations for this picture were laid by Berle and Means (1932). For an interesting collection of articles on Berle and Means and the accountability of corporate managers, see the June 1983 issue of the *Journal of Law & Economics*, especially the article by Demsetz (1983).

24. The information in this paragraph comes from personal communication with certified public accountants with experience in major public accounting firms.

25. For a fuller discussion of the ways in which boards can monitor management, see MacAvoy et al. (1983).

26. Demsetz and Lehn (1985) provide some empirical evidence of this point by examining how far ownership is concentrated in the five hundred largest corporations. They find, among other things, that the five largest ownership interests control, on average, 25 percent of the shares issued.

27. Another option is the proxy fight whereby dissident shareholders try to oust managers and boards they believe are incompetent. For a discussion of the relative merits of the takeover as compared to the proxy fight, see Williamson (1983, 361–65).

28. This organizational innovation was invented by Pierre DuPont at the DuPont Nemours Corporation and Alfred P. Sloan at General Motors. The definitive history of the development of the multidivisional corporation is Alfred D. Chandler's (1966) *Strategy and Structure*.

29. For references to additional and more elaborate critical discussions of these arguments, see chapter 3, notes 1 and 3–5.

30. For a clear and concise statement of this view, see Hayek (1979). For a more elaborate statement, see Hayek (1960). See also Rothbard (1972).

31. See chapter 3, note 13.

32. I hasten to emphasize the hypothetical nature of the claims made in this example. The current sorry state of education in the United States has led many thoughtful people to the conclude that teachers are getting far *more* than the value of their contributions and through the power of their unions and their monopoly on public financing of education, are leaving those who employ them with no real alternative but to pay inflated wages. As a general point, it is worth remarking that sometimes the reason that asset owners have nowhere else to go is that their assets are highly *overvalued* in comparison to what they would get from other uses or from other users of their assets.

33. What follows is highly speculative. Moreover, even if there is something to it, it is probably a good illustration of how transactions cost efficiencies may be only one factor in explaining the persistence of a phenomenon.

34. Over the past twenty-five years union power has declined in the industrialized West, in part because of the growth of the world economy; that growth has provided both consumers and employers with real alternatives and has resulted in a decline in exploitation by these unions.

35. See note 24.

36. The only other alternative is that the market is highly volatile, that is, prices are in a state of flux and are not heading toward a new equilibrium. Recall from chapter 3 that the value of something in such circumstances is undefined. It follows that no such exchange could be exploitative. This may have counterintuitive consequences in the case of an exchange that takes place at terms that are very far out of line with what occurs elsewhere in a volatile market. Perhaps the account of exploitation and the associated definition of value given in chapter 3 should be amended to take this

into account, though that is not obvious. This problem has no bearing on the issue at hand, however, since the systematically exploitative nature of the labor contract in a free enterprise system could not be established by appeal to this type of exchange.

37. Of course, another reason that workers might be facing about the same prospects everywhere is that the relevant labor markets are competitively efficient, and workers are, in fact, getting the value of their respective contributions (and thus are not exploited). Notice that if one confuses necessary with sufficient conditions, free enterprise systems would appear to be massively exploitative. Very often, workers have no real alternative, in the sense defined, to their current situation. And, very often, workers are not being paid the value of their contributions because the market for their labor is in transition, and they are not on its leading edge. If either or both of these conditions were a sufficient condition (and not merely a necessary condition) for exploitation, then exploitation of workers would indeed be rampant in existing free enterprise systems.

38. In the employment relation, members of these latter two groups often have nowhere else to go, precisely because they are receiving more than the value of their contributions!

Chapter 6

1. The economic literature on the Yugoslav system is voluminous. Information in this and subsequent paragraphs is based on Pejovich (1969), Milenkovitch (1971), Sirc (1979), Estrin and Bartlett (1982), Estrin (1983), Lydall (1989) and Kornai (1992, chap. 20).

2. For relevant discussions of Mondragon, see Thomas and Logan (1982), Thomas (1982), and especially Bradley and Gelb (1982).

3. It is important nevertheless to distinguish what people say they believe from what they actually do believe. As Hume points out, "Many eminent theologians . . . affirm that tho' the vulgar have no formal principles of infidelity, yet they are really infidels in their hearts, and have nothing like what we call a belief of the eternal duration of their souls. For let us consider on the one hand what divines have display'd with such eloquence concerning the importance of eternity. . . . And after this let us view on the other hand the prodigious security of men in this particular: I ask if these people really believe what . . . they pretend to affirm; and the answer is obviously in the negative" ([1739] 1978, 113–14).

4. Though the exact proportion of internally financed new investment cannot be known, it will doubtless be low for the following reason. If a cooperative pays out residuals to its workers, they get 100 percent of those funds. By contrast, if those funds are reinvested, the assets purchased with those funds become part of the firm's capital; effective ownership of those assets would then revert to the state. Sometimes, the new residuals they can earn from reinvestment will justify the decision to do it, but usually it will make more sense to take the money and run. Also, if the business opportunity they are looking at is sufficiently attractive, it is likely they can fund it through normal channels. Finally, the state would be reluctant to permit or encourage too much new investment to be beyond its purview, since that could easily frustrate its own plans. For more elaborate discussions of internal versus external financing of new investment, see Pejovich (1969; 1973), Furubotn and Pejovich (1970), and Bonin and Putterman (1987, 68–72).

5. For an entrée into the substantial empirical literature on this, see Deutsch (1985, chap. 15).

6. As was pointed out earlier, even if some of the workers in Mondragon are not getting the value of their contributions, they are nevertheless not exploited because they do have somewhere else to go, namely, to noncooperative firms elsewhere in the area.

7. The supposition that the unskilled workers are in the majority may not hold in all firms. Firms that sell professional services come to mind as possible exceptions, though they often have substantial supporting staff. However, most firms will have more unskilled (or less skilled) workers if only because the talents and training required of more highly skilled labor are relatively scarce.

8. See Robert Nozick's discussion of judgments of self-esteem (1974, 239–43). See also Frank (1985).

9. See the second and third sections of chapter 3 for a discussion of why marginalist thinking about value is the appropriate way to think about the economic value of someone's contribution.

10. This discussion abstracts from the racial, ethnic, regional, and sexual biases found in every culture. If those biases are factored in, one could imagine different coalitions forming, different distributions of income emerging, and different groups of people being exploited. I owe this point to Richard Arneson.

11. It used to be thought that this phenomenon could be explained solely by reference to the fact that cooperatives aim at maximizing net income per worker, rather than net income (as capitalist firms are assumed to do). This has sometimes been called the "Ward effect" (see Ward 1958). However, Jacques Drèze (1989) has constructed a model of a market economy consisting of labor-managed firms in which workers receive income shares in the firm; these income shares adjust in such a way that labor markets clear as readily in his model as they do in corresponding models of free enterprise systems. This allows him to prove that his model and a model in which all firms are profit maximizers (i.e., a model of a free enterprise system) are equivalent in equilibrium. Nevertheless, these results have no direct bearing on any of the claims in this book, since Drèze's model of the worker-managed enterprise abstracts from many of the details about organizational structure—as well as other nonorganizational factors—that are crucial to the discussion in this and subsequent sections.

12. Estrin's own proposal for market socialism, which differs from the one under consideration here, does not face these problems in such a stark form. His proposal will be considered in some detail in chapter 8.

13. It does not follow, however, that there would be less exploitation, all things considered, in the very small cooperative. As explained later in this section, there are opportunities for exploitation of the capital providers that more than offset whatever modest advantage very small cooperatives might have in monitoring workers.

14. One of the best discussions of the relationship between base and superstructure in Marx's thought is to be found in Cohen (1978, chaps. 8–10).

15. Actually, this assumption is overly optimistic on behalf of market socialism in two respects. First, as explained in the last section, cooperatives are less inclined to expand and contract in response to changes in the market. This means that it is possible that some transactions cost inefficiencies (and the opportunities for exploitation they represent) would persist in a market socialist system that would be eliminated in a free enterprise system. Second, in the next chapter, it is argued that mergers and acquisitions would be less frequent in a market socialist system than in a free enterprise system, which also implies that some transactions cost inefficiencies might persist that would otherwise be eliminated.

16. What this assumption means is that if the small cooperative has advantages, as

far as exploitation is concerned, over the large, open corporation (or vice versa), that will make no difference in any final overall assessment of the two types of systems. Similar considerations apply to comparisons between the classical capitalist firm and the large cooperative on the potential for exploitation. I believe that restricting the terms of comparison to the small cooperative versus the classical capitalist firm and the large cooperative versus the open corporation is not consequential in a final comparative evaluation of the two types of systems. However, the discussion that follows would be significantly more complicated if the small-to-medium-sized cooperative had to be compared to both the classical capitalist firm and the open corporation and if the large cooperative also had to be compared to both of these types of organizations.

17. This is one reason why it would not be a good idea for governments in former communist countries to insist on profit-sharing cooperatives in their current attempt to join the world market economy. Reports from Eastern Europe, the former Soviet Union, and China suggest that shirking has been and is pandemic under communism. To turn organizations around in these countries, someone is going to have to grapple with deeply entrenched habits and attitudes. To insist that this person share equally all the gains to be realized *if* he succeeds in these battles would be the height of folly.

18. See the discussion in the second section of chapter 5 of these roles in the classical capitalist firm. In what follows in the text, the assumption that one and the same person is monitor, central contracting agent, and director of the firm's product is not essential. Though it makes it easier to tell stories about what is likely happen, the main points of those stories remain unchanged if these roles are separated. Indeed, I suspect that separating these roles would create additional opportunities for exploitation, though I shall not press that point here.

19. Notice that once again, in the very small cooperative, these problems may effectively vanish. If everyone is involved in setting (relatively narrow) parameters for routine decision making and if everyone is involved in entrepreneurial decisions, then the opportunities for exploitation under discussion here may well be insignificant. This puts the very small cooperative on virtually the same footing as the very small classical capitalist firm in this respect.

20. To foreshadow some of the results of the second section of chapter 7, this exploitation is likely to go on longer in a market socialist system than in a free enterprise system because the state will be slower to pull the plug on losing operations than the market is in a free enterprise system.

21. Might not the firm offer him all of the entrepreneurial gains as an inducement to join the firm? Possibly, but that might well put the cooperative on the road to being a classical capitalist firm. For more on this, see Arnold (1987a; 1987d, section 2).

22. The main argument of Arnold (1987c) links entrepreneurial contribution to desert. In other words, entrepreneurs deserve the pure profits (positive or negative) that their firms earn because of their entrepreneurial contribution. It also explains why the fact that the successful entrepreneur does not deserve his special talents and abilities (if indeed that is a fact) does not attenuate his deserts. Independently of this observation, that argument is not fully consistent with the account of the entrepreneur's contribution developed in chapter 3 and the observation here about the significance of luck. It needs to be amended to take these points into account.

23. The points in this paragraph are explained in detail in any basic accounting textbook. See, for example, Kieso and Weygandt (1983, 524–27).

24. Because there are no tradable shares of equity ownership in the cooperative, assessing the quasi-rent value of firms would be very difficult, to say the least. This

creates real problems if the cooperatives are expected to pay the state a capital usage fee on this quasi-rent value. More on this in the second section of chapter 7.

25. Some of the points in the remainder of this section are based on Jensen and Meckling's (1979) discussion of the inefficiencies of the "pure rental firm" and the Yugoslav cooperative.

26. Both types of firms, of course, would want to prevent individual workers from that form of opportunism that consists in misusing equipment to make the job go easier, but the point in the text is about those forms of misuse, abuse, and failure to perform maintenance that improve the bottom line in the near term.

27. These methods of appropriating quasi-rents were thought up by two economists (Jensen and Meckling) and a philosopher (this author). It is worth point out that all three, especially the latter, are *rank amateurs* when it comes to these matters. In a market economy that has the structure of ownership rights under discussion, individuals of consummate cleverness and unparalleled rapacity (in other words, the real professionals) would crawl out from under their respective rocks and sell their services to the highest bidders. It is at least possible that a self-reinforcing process would get underway resulting in the virtual destruction of the economy. Though there is no way to predict this with moral certainty, what can be predicted with confidence is that these opportunities for exploitation would exist and would not go unnoticed.

28. One way to deal with all of these problems would be for the capital providers—the state—to have a direct hand in managing the firm or at least in choosing the managers. This, of course, is inconsistent with the fundamental right of worker self-management in the cooperative, which is why it has not been considered here. This possibility will be discussed in chapter 8, which systematically considers various alternatives to the form of market socialism under discussion here.

Chapter 7

1. In cooperatives of sufficient size, the workers' council might be so large that it would make sense for them to elect or appoint a smaller body, a kind of politburo, to hire and monitor management. This is the case in Mondragon (Thomas 1982, 135). In what follows, I ignore this possible complication and assume that the workers' council exercises the same functions that a board of directors does in the open corporation. As will become apparent, the interposition of another group between the workers and the monitors of management would not alter the general conclusions of this chapter in a way that is favorable to market socialism. At most, this two-tiered supervisory structure would create additional distinctive opportunities for exploitation in a market socialist system.

2. However, the problem of opportunistic on-the-job consumption may not go away; it may instead just go underground. Recent revelations indicate that communist dictators were outstanding practitioners of the art of inconspicuous consumption (subject to occasional indiscretions), an art that cooperative managers might revive and master.

3. For the evidence, see Estrin and Bartlett (1982, 86) and the references cited therein.

4. For a variety of reasons, it is also generally true that state officials are not well monitored by the public. This point is discussed in more detail in the next section.

5. This is not universally true. Individuals or institutions that own relatively large blocks of a company's stock have a more difficult time getting out with their quasi-rents more or less intact.

6. Clearly, in a free enterprise system, managers of target firms have a strong incentive to block acquisitions and sometimes mergers. One of the devices that has evolved over the years to neutralize that incentive is the "golden parachute." This is a severance payment to senior managers that they themselves can trigger by resigning after an unfriendly takeover. Of course, these can be misused. For a useful discussion, see Williamson (1985, 314–16). Imagine the cost of providing "golden parachutes" for all the ultimate decision makers in a large cooperative who might lose their jobs as a result of a merger or acquisition!

7. For more on the inefficiencies of hierarchy, see Leibenstein (1987) and Williamson (1985, chap. 6).

8. For a useful account of collective versus individual preferences and collective versus individual decision making in this context, see Schweickart (1980, 108) and the references he cites.

9. See Lavoie (1985) for a good discussion of these problems.

10. In free enterprise systems, the public accounting firm reports to the board of directors, which represents the interests of the equity owners, that is, the suppliers of capital. It is likely the state would hire public accounting firms in a market socialist system, or they might do the audits themselves, since it is their assets that are at risk.

11. Firms in existing free enterprise systems do have other ways of exploiting customers and taxpayers through the state, such as tariffs on imports, regulations that differentially harm competitors, and so on. These forms of exploitation are not discussed here for two reasons. First, they are not features of free enterprise systems per se but are artifacts of the political system of existing free enterprise systems. Generally, defenders of the free enterprise system favor abolishing forms of government intervention designed to allow firms to exploit their customers in these and myriad other ways. Second, even if tariffs and the like were endogenous to free enterprise systems, it is virtually certain that they would be endogenous to a market socialist systems as well. Indeed, because the economic and political systems are more intimately connected, problems of this sort are likely to be even worse in a market socialist system.

12. The assumption throughout this section is that the organizations that handle new investment (i.e., the banks) are state organizations. They could not be regular profit-making cooperatives because they must be answerable, in some fairly direct way, to political authorities if they are to implement whatever economic plans issue from the planning agencies and, ultimately, the political process. If they were regular cooperatives and their only criterion for making loans was profitability, planning would have been effectively abandoned. Given the assumption of planning, then, it is reasonable to assume that the actual dispensers of investments funds would be state organizations.

13. For a clear, accessible statement of this issue, see Gwartney and Wagner (1988, 11–17). For a useful introduction to public choice theory, see Wagner (1989).

14. The problems with this assumption are addressed in the so-called social choice literature. For overviews of this literature, see Coleman (1988) and Seabright (1989). In this book, I have avoided a discussion of the social choice and public choice literatures because both are relatively independent of the details of the organizational structure of public institutions, whereas the focus of this book has been on organizational structures. Though I cannot argue for it here, I believe that an application of the more theoretically secure areas of social choice and public choice would be very damaging to socialists' faith in the efficacy of political decision making.

15. See the subsection on debt financing in the open corporation in chapter 5 for a discussion of the transactions cost attributes of debt financing.

16. This seems to have been the case in the government bailout of the U.S. savings and loan industry. It has proven difficult to distinguish loans that went bad despite due diligence on the part of lenders from foreseeably bad risks, which in turn have been difficult to distinguish from outright fraud.

17. For surveys of that literature, see Furubotn and Pejovich (1972) and De Alessi (1980).

Chapter 8

1. Some terminological innovation is called for in this chapter, since different versions of market socialism will be identified and discussed. Let us call the version that has been the main subject of this book the *worker control–state ownership model*. I use the term 'model' because it is much less cumbersome than 'version of market socialism.' However, it is worth pointing out that the term 'model' is misleading because models in economics are typically formal, whereas the objects of discussion in this book are systems of property rights that are specified without the benefit—or hindrance—of formal machinery.

2. The reasons why those who occupy these two roles in a free enterprise system cannot regularly and systematically exploit laborers were discussed in the last section of chapter 5. A crucial part of that story is that, in general, there are adequately functioning labor markets. Notice that there are no corresponding capital markets in the worker control–state ownership model, since the state owns all the capital. Another important difference between labor assets in a free enterprise system and (nonhuman) capital assets in the worker control–state ownership model is that the value of labor assets (i.e., the value of human capital) cannot ordinarily be dissipated or sold off without the owner's knowledge.

3. A similar point is made by Putterman (1988b, 334). For a survey of portfolio theory, see Jensen (1972) or Fama (1976).

4. See the account of the amelioration of alienation in the final section of chapter 2 for the main reasons why socialists do and should favor self-management as a means to important elements of the socialist conception of the good society (i.e., social virtues).

5. Ellerman has a conceptual schema for thinking about ownership rights that systematically differs from the more conventional one employed in this book (1990, chap. 3). In accordance with his schema, he denies that the internal capital accounts represent equity ownership (p. 79); instead, he refers to them as internal debt. I have tried to ensure that the differences between his exposition and my exposition of his views are merely terminological.

6. Of course, state bureaucracies in any society may be thought of as economic organizations, since they produce exchangeable goods and services. However, the Ellerman model does not envision widespread state ownership (or other forms of state control) of the means of production.

7. Ellerman's model also allows for this type of financing, though he does not envision it as the predominant form (1990, 87); see also Vanek (1977a, chap. 11) and McCain (1977, 358–59). This system does not rule out—and, as a practical matter, may require—some worker ownership of shares in the firm. Outside investors may not be willing to invest in a firm in which the workers put up no capital and have no status as residual claimants (Putterman 1988a, 258; Estrin 1989, 181).

8. To be fair to Jay, he seems relatively unconcerned with establishing the social-ist credentials of his system, although he occasionally refers to it as a market socialist system. Instead, his main arguments are addressed to a British audience at the dawn of the Thatcher era. His proposal was intended to solve some problems with that par-ticular system at that time. Jay does not make a concerted effort to link his proposal to the larger socialist tradition. One of my purposes in the text is to show that those linkages are, in fact, quite weak.

9 To buttress his socialist credentials, Estrin might call attention to the fact that he favors a form of noncoercive investment planning called *indicative planning* (Estrin and Winter 1989, 115–17). Indicative planning involves the state as a provider of infor-mation and a coordinator of some investment plans for the cooperatives. In effect, it is a somewhat more ambitious version of what these days is called "industrial policy." However, the state's power to direct resources to particular projects or even sectors of the economy is no greater than the power of the state in free enterprise systems. (It "indicates" rather than "commands" the direction new investment should take.) This has led some observers to question whether or not this process really should be called "planning." For more on this problem, see Lutz (1969, 99) and Pejovich (1966, chap. 2).

10. For more on these opportunities, see the discussion of equity ownership in the second section of chapter 5. Of course, there are highly leveraged firms in free enter-prise systems, but for reasons explained in the second subsection of the second sec-tion of chapter 5, few firms approach the debt-equity ratios envisioned in Estrin's model. Moreover, highly leveraged enterprises often cede substantial decision-mak-ing authority to the debt holders, and the latter also receive a risk premium. Under these circumstances, the line between debt and equity becomes blurred, and the nom-inal debt holders begin to resemble equity owners.

11. As noted earlier (see note 9), Estrin favors indicative planning, but it is at least arguable that this more modest role for the state really involves giving up on the idea of collective control of the rate and direction of economic growth.

12. This follows from Marx's theories of the state. See Marx ([1852] 1963, 122; [1871] 1975, 329–30). See also Elster (1988, 213–15).

13. For a discussion of this see, for example, Barry (1979).

14. I owe this observation about the connection between payment in accordance with contribution and self-determination to James Rachels's discussion of desert (1978, 159).

References

Albert, Michael, and Robin Hahnel. 1978. *Unorthodox Marxism*. Boston: South End Press.

———. 1987. Socialist economics. *Socialist Review* 17:87–104.

———. 1991. *The political economy of participatory economics*. Princeton, N.J.: Princeton University Press.

Alchian, Armen. 1950. Uncertainty, evolution, and economic theory. *Journal of Political Economy* 58:211–21.

Alchain, Armen, and Harold Demsetz. 1972. Production, information costs, and economic organization. *American Economic Review* 62:777–95.

Arnold, N. Scott. 1985. Capitalists and the ethics of contribution. *Canadian Journal of Philosophy* 15:87–102.

———. 1987a. Further thoughts on the degeneration of market socialism: A reply to Schweickart. *Economics and Philosophy* 3:320–30.

———. 1987b. Final reply to Professor Schweickart. *Economics and Philosophy* 3:335–38.

———. 1987c. Why profits are deserved. *Ethics* 97:387–402.

———. 1987d. Marx and disequilibrium in market socialist relations of production. *Economics and Philosophy* 3:23–46.

———. 1989. Marx, central planning, and utopian socialism. *Social Philosophy & Policy* 6:160–99.

———. 1990. *Marx's radical critique of capitalist society*. New York: Oxford University Press.

Arrow, Kenneth. 1964. The role of securities in the optimal allocation of risk bearing. *Review of Economic Studies* 31:91–96.

Aveneri, Shlomo. 1968. *The social and political thought of Karl Marx*. Cambridge: Cambridge University Press.

Barry, Brian. 1979. Justice as reciprocity. In *Justice*, ed. Eugene Kamenka and Alice Erh-Soon Tay, 50–78. London: Edward Arnold.

Bartlett, Randall. 1989. *Economics and power: An inquiry into human relations and markets*. Cambridge: Cambridge University Press.

Barzel, Yoram. 1987. The entrepreneur's reward for self-policing. *Economic Inquiry* 25:103–16.

Becker, Gary. 1962. Theory of the allocation of time. *Economic Journal* 70:9–49.

Becker, Lawrence. 1986. *Reciprocity*. London: Routledge and Kegan Paul.

Berle, Adolph, and G. C. Means. 1932. *The modern corporation and private property*. New York: Macmillan.

Bonin, J.P., and Louis Putterman. 1987. *The economics of cooperation and the labor-man-*

aged economy. Fundamentals of pure and applied economics, vol. 14. London: Harwood Academic Press.

Bowles, Samuel, and Herbert Gintis. 1986. *Democracy and capitalism*. New York: Basic Books.

Bradley, Keith, and Alan Gelb. 1981. Motivation and control in the Mondragon experiment. *British Journal of Industrial Relations* 19:211–31.

———. 1982. The Mondragon cooperatives: Guidelines for a cooperative economy? In Jones and Svejnar (1982), 153–72.

Brenkert, George. 1985. Cohen on proletarian unfreedom. *Philosophy and Public Affairs* 14:91–98.

Brus, Wlodzimierz. 1985. Socialism: Feasible and viable? *New Left Review* 153:43–62.

Brus, Wlodzimierz, and Kazimierz Laski. 1989. *From Marx to the market*. Oxford: Clarendon Press.

Buchanan, Allen. 1982. *Marx and justice*. Totowa, N.J.: Rowman and Allenheld.

———. 1985. *Ethics, efficiency, and the market*. Totowa, N.J.: Rowman and Allenheld.

Chandler, Alfred P. 1966. *Strategy and structure*. New York: Doubleday.

Coase, Ronald. 1937. The nature of the firm. *Economica* n. s. 4:386–405. Reprinted in *Readings in price theory*, ed. G. S. Stigler and K. E. Boulding. Homewood, Ill.: Richard D. Irwin, 1952.

Cohen, G. A. 1978. *Karl Marx's theory of history: A defence*. Princeton: Princeton Unversity Press.

———. 1979. The labor theory of value and the concept of exploitation. *Philosophy and Public Affairs* 8:338–60. Reprinted in *Marx, justice, and history*, ed. Marshall Cohen, Thomas Nagel, and Thomas Scanlon, 135–58. Princeton: Princeton University Press, 1980.

———. 1983. The structure of proletarian unfreedom. *Philosophy and Public Affairs* 12:3–33.

———. 1989. On the currency of egalitarian justice. *Ethics* 99:906–44.

Cohen, Joshua. 1989. The economic basis of deliberative democracy. *Social Philosophy & Policy* 6:25-50.

Cohen, Joshua, and Joel Rogers. 1983. *On democracy*. New York: Penguin Books.

Coleman, Jules. 1988. Democracy and social choice. In *Markets, morals, and the law*, ed. Jules Coleman, 290–310. Cambridge: Cambridge University Press.

Dahl, Robert. 1985. *A preface to economic democracy*. Berkeley: University of California Press.

De Alessi, Louis. 1980. The economics of property rights: A review of the evidence. *Research in Law and Economics* 2:1–47.

DeJasay, Antony. 1990. *Market socialism: A scrutiny*. Occasional Paper no. 84. London: Institute for Economic Affairs.

Demsetz, Harold. 1983. The structure of ownership and the theory of the firm. *Journal of Law & Economics* 26:375–93.

———. 1988a. The control function of private wealth. In *Ownership, control, and the firm*, ed. Harold Demsetz, 1:229–35. Oxford: Basil Blackwell.

———. 1988b. Toward a theory of property rights. In *Ownership, control, and the firm*, ed. Harold Demsetz 1:104–16. Oxford: Basil Blackwell.

Demsetz, Harold, and Kenneth Lehn. 1985. The structure of corporate ownership: Causes and consequences. *Journal of Political Economy* 93:1155–77.

Deutsch, Morton. 1985. *Distributive justice: A social-psychological perspective*. New Haven: Yale University Press.

DiQuattro, Arthur. 1984. Value, class, and exploitation. *Social Theory and Practice* 10:55–80.

Drèze, Jacques. 1989. *Labour management, contracts, and capital markets: A general equilibrium approach*. New York: Basil Blackwell.

Dworkin, Ronald. 1981a. What is equality? Part 1: Equality of welfare. *Philosophy and Public Affairs* 10:185–246.

———. 1981b. What is equality? Part 2: Equality of resources. *Philosophy and Public Affairs* 10:283–345.

Ellerman, David. 1984. Workers' cooperatives: The question of legal structure. In *Worker cooperatives in America*, ed. Robert Jackall and Henry Levin, 257–74. Berkeley: University of California Press.

———. 1986. Horizon problems and property rights in labor managed firms. *Journal of Comparative Economics* 10:62–78.

———. 1990. *The democratic worker-owned firm*. London: Unwin and Hyman.

Elster, Jon. 1979. *Ulysses and the sirens*. Cambridge: Cambridge University Press.

———. 1985. *Making sense of Marx*. Cambridge: Cambridge University Press.

———. 1988. Marx, revolution, and rational choice. In *Rationality and revolution*, ed. Michael Taylor, 198–222. Cambridge: Cambridge University Press.

Estrin, Saul. 1983. *Self-management: Economic theory and Yugoslav practice*. Cambridge: Cambridge University Press.

———. 1989. Workers' co-operatives: Their merits and limitations. In Le Grand and Estrin (1989a), 165–92.

Estrin, Saul, and William Bartlett. 1982. The effects of enterprise self-management in Yugoslavia: An empirical study. In Jones and Svejnar (1982), 83–95.

Estrin, Saul, and David Winter. 1989. Planning in a market-socialist economy. In Le Grand and Estrin (1989a), 100–138.

Evers, Williamson. 1989. Liberty of the press under socialism. *Social Philosophy & Policy* 62:211–235.

Fama, Eugene. 1976. *Foundations of finance*. New York: Basic Books.

Fama, Eugene, and Michael Jensen. 1983a. Agency problems and residual claims. *Journal of Law & Economics* 26:327–48.

———. 1983b. Separation of ownership and control. *Journal of Law & Economics* 26:301–25.

Foulkes, Fred. 1981. How top nonunion companies manage employees. *Harvard Business Review* (October–November):90–96.

Frank, Robert. 1985. *Choosing the right pond: Human behavior and the quest for status*. New York: Oxford University Press.

Freeman, R. B., and J. Medoff. 1979. The two faces of unionism. *Public Interest* (Fall):69–93.

Furubotn, Erik, and Svetojar Pejovich. 1970. Property rights and the behavior of the firm in the socialist state: The example of Yugoslavia. *Zietschrift für Nationalokonomie* 30:431–54.

———. 1972. Property rights and economic theory: A survey. *Journal of Economic Literature* 10:1137–62.

Gilboa, David. 1991. Where have all the profits gone? Unpublished manuscript.

Gilson, Ronald, and Robert Mnookin. 1988. Coming of age in a corporate law firm: The economics of associate career patterns. *Stanford Law Review* 41:567–95.

Goodman, Nelson. 1965. *Fact, fiction, and forecast*. 2d edition. Indianapolis: Bobbs-Merrill.

Granovetter, Mark. 1986. Labor mobility, internal markets, and job matching. *Research in Social Stratification and Mobility* 5:3–39.

Gray, John. 1988. Against Cohen on proletarian unfreedom. *Social Philosophy & Policy* 6:77–112.

Gregor, A. James. 1968. Marxism and ethics: A methodological inquiry. *Philosophy and Phenomenological Research* 28:368–84.

Griffin, James. *Well-being*. Oxford: Clarendon Press.

Grossman, Sanford, and Oliver Hart. 1986. The costs and benefits of ownership: A theory of vertical and lateral integration. *Journal of Political Economy* 94:691–719.

Gwartney, James D., and Richard E. Wagner. 1988. Public choice and the conduct of representative government. In *Public choice and constitutional economics*, ed. James D. Gwartney and Richard E. Wagner, 3–28. Greenwich, CT: JAI Press with the Cato Institute.

Hayek, F. A. 1935. *Collectivist economic planning*. London: Routledge and Kegan Paul.

———. 1937. Economics and knowledge. *Economics* 4:33–54. Reprinted in Hayek (1949), 33–56.

———. 1944. *The road to serfdom*. London: Routledge and Kegan Paul.

———. 1945. The use of knowledge in society. *American Economic Review* 35:519–30. Reprinted in Hayek (1949), 77–91.

———. 1949. *Individualism and economic order*. London: Routledge and Kegan Paul.

———. 1960. *Prices and production*. London: Routledge and Kegan Paul.

———. 1979. *Unemployment and monetary policy: Government as generator of the "business cycle."* San Francisco: Cato Institute.

Heilbroner, Robert, and Lester Thurow. 1984. *The economic problem*, 7th ed. Englewood Cliffs, N.J.: Prentice-Hall.

Hirschman, Albert O. 1970. *Exit, voice and loyalty*. Cambridge: Harvard University Press.

Holmstrom, Bengt and Paul Milgrom. 1991. Multi-task principal-agent analyses: Incentive contracts, asset ownership, and job design. *Journal of Law, Economics and Organizations* 7:24–52.

Holmstrom, Nancy. 1977. Exploitation. *Canadian Journal of Philosophy* 7:353–69.

Honoré, A. M. 1961. Ownership. In *Oxford essays in jurisprudence*, ed. A. G. Guest. Oxford: Oxford University Press.

Horvat, Branko. 1982. *The political economy of socialism*. Armonk, N.Y.: M.E. Sharpe.

Hume, David. [1739] 1978. *A treatise of human nature*. Ed. L. A. Selby-Bigge. 2d edition. Annotated by P. H. Nidditch. London: Oxford University Press.

Jay, Peter. 1980. The workers' cooperative economy. In *The political economy of cooperation and participation*, ed. Alasdair Clayre, 9–45. Oxford: Oxford University Press.

Jensen, Michael C. 1972. Capital markets: Theory and evidence. *Bell Journal of Economics and Management Science* 3:357–98.

Jensen, Michael C., and William Meckling. 1976. Theory of the firm: Managerial behavior, agency costs, and ownership structure. *Journal of Financial Economics* 3:305–60.

———. 1979. Rights and production functions: An application to labor-managed firms and codetermination. *Journal of Business* 52:469–506.

Jones, Derek C., and Jan Svejnar, eds. 1982. *Participatory and self-managed firms*. Lexington, Mass.: Lexington Books, D. C. Heath.

Joskow, Paul and Richard Schmalensee. 1983. *Markets for power*. Cambridge: MIT Press.

Kahneman, Daniel, Paul Slovic, and Amos Tversky. 1982. *Judgment under uncertainty: Heuristics and biases*. Cambridge: Cambridge University Press.

Kieso, Donald, and Jerry J. Weygandt. 1983. *Intermediate accounting*, 4th ed. New York: John Wiley and Sons.

Kincaid, Harold. 1990. Defending laws in the social sciences. *Philosophy of the Social Sciences* 20:56–83.

Kirzner, Israel. 1973. *Competition and entrepreneurship*. Chicago: University of Chicago Press.

———. 1979. *Perception, opportunity and profit*. Chicago: University of Chicago Press.

Klein, Benjamin. 1991. Vertical integration as organizational ownership: The Fisher Body–General Motors relationship revisited. In *The nature of the firm*, ed. Oliver E. Williamson and Sidney G. Winter, 213–26. New York: Oxford.

Klein, Benjamin, Robert C. Crawford, and Armen Alchian. 1978. Vertical integration, appropriable rents, and the competitive contracting process. *Journal of Law & Economics* 21:297–326.

Kolakowski, Leszak. 1974. The myth of human self-identity: Unity of civil and political society in socialist thought. In *The socialist idea: A reappraisal*, ed. Leszak Kolakowski and Stuart Hampshire, 18–35. New York: Basic Books.

———. 1978. *Main currents of Marxism*, vol. 1. Oxford: Oxford University Press.

Kornai, Janos. 1992. *The socialist system*. Princeton: Princeton University Press.

Landes, D. S., ed. 1966. *The rise of capitalism*. New York: Macmillan.

Lange, Oskar. 1938. *On the economic theory of socialism*. Ed. B. E. Lippincott. Minneapolis: University of Minnesota Press.

Lavoie, Don. 1985. *National economic planning: What is left?* Washington, D.C.: The Cato Institute.

———. 1986. *Rivalry and central planning*. Cambridge: Cambridge University Press.

Le Grand, Julian, and Saul Estrin, eds. 1989a. *Market socialism*. Oxford: Clarendon Press.

———. 1989b. Market socialism. In Le Grand and Estrin (1989a), 1–24.

Leibenstein, Harvey. 1987. *Inside the firm: The inefficiencies of hierarchy*. Cambridge: Harvard University Press.

Leviatan, Uriel. 1991. Hierarchical differentiation and alienation. In Oldenquist and Rosner (1991), 159–78.

Levine, Andrew. 1984. *Arguing for socialism*. London: Routledge and Kegan Paul.

Lutz, Vera. 1969. *Central planning for the market economy: An analysis of the French experience*. London: Longman Green.

Lydall, Harold. 1984. *Yugoslav socialism: Theory and practice*. Oxford: Clarendon Press.

———. 1989. *Yugoslavia in crisis*. Oxford: Clarendon Press.

MacAvoy, Paul, Scott Cantor, Jim Dana, and Sara Peck. 1983. ALI proposals for increased control of the corporation by the board of directors: An economic analysis. In *Statement of the business roundtable of the American Law Institute's proposed principles of corporate governance and structure: Restatement and recommendations*. Philadelphia: American Law Institute.

McCain, Roger. 1977. On the optimal financial environment for worker cooperatives. *Zeitschrift für Nationalokonomie* 37:355–84.

Manne, Henry G. 1965. Mergers and the market for corporate control. *Journal of Political Economy* 73:110–20.

Manning, Bayless. 1977. *A concise textbook on legal capital*. Mineola, N.Y.: Foundation Press.

March, James G., and Herbert Simon. 1958. *Organizations*. New York: Wiley.

Marglin, Stephen. 1974. What do bosses do? The origins and functions of hierarchy in capitalist production. *Review of Radical Political Economy* 6:33–60.

Marx, Karl. 1848. *The communist manifesto*. In Karl Marx and Friedrich Engels, *Collected works*, vol. 6. London: Lawrence and Wishart.

———. [1852] 1963. *The Eighteenth Brumaire of Louis Bonaparte*. New York: Progress Publishers.

———. [1875] 1971. *Critique of the Gotha program*. Moscow: Progress Publishers.

———. [1871] 1975. *The civil war in France*. In Karl Marx and Friedrich Engels, *Collected works*, vol. 20. New York: International Publishers.

———. [1848] 1976. *The German ideology*. In Karl Marx and Friedrich Engels, *Collected works*, vol. 5. New York: International Publishers.

———. [1863] 1977. *Capital*, vol. 1. Moscow: Progress Publishers.

Milenkovitch, D. D. 1971. *Plan and market in Yugoslav economic thought*. New Haven: Yale University Press.

Milgrom, Paul, and John Roberts. 1990. Bargaining costs, influence costs, and the organization of economic activity. In *The foundations of political economy*, ed. J. Alt and K. Shepsle. Cambridge, MA: Harvard University Press.

Miller, David. 1989a. *Market, state, and community*. Oxford: Clarendon Press.

———. 1989b. Why markets? In Le Grand and Estrin (1989a), 25–49.

Miller, Richard. 1981. Marx and Aristotle: A kind of consequentialism. In *Marx and morality*, 323–52. *Canadian Journal of Philosophy*, suppl. vol. 7, ed. Kai Nielsen and Steven C. Patten, 323–52. Guelph, Ontario: Canadian Association for Publishing in Philosophy.

Mises, Ludwig von. 1919. Economic calculation in the socialist commonwealth. Reprinted in Hayek (1935), 87–130.

———. 1951. *Socialism*. New Haven: Yale University Press.

Moe, Terry. 1984. The new economics of organizations. *American Journal of Political Science* 28:739–77.

———. 1989. The politics of bureaucratic structure. In *Can the government govern?* ed. John E. Chubb and Paul E. Peterson, 267–329. Washington, D.C.: Brookings Institution.

———. 1990a. Political institutions: The neglected side of the story. *Journal of Law, Economics, and Organizations* 6:213–53.

———. 1990b. The politics of structural choice: Toward a theory of public bureaucracy. In *Industrial organization*, ed. Oliver E. Williamson, 116–53. Brookfield, Vt.: E. Elgar.

Mortenson, Dale T. 1978. Specific capital and labor turnover. *Bell Journal of Economics and Management Science* 9:572–86.

Nasser, Alan. 1975. Marx's ethical anthropology. *Philosophy and Phenomenological Research* 35:484–500.

Nielsen, Kai. 1985. *Equality and liberty: A defense of radical egalitarianism*. Totowa, N.J.: Rowman and Allenheld.

Nisbett, Richard E., and Lee Ross. 1980. *Human inference: Strategies and shortcomings of social judgment*. Century Psychology Series, Englewood Cliffs, N.J.: Prentice Hall.

Nove, Alec. 1983. *The economics of feasible socialism*. London: Allen and Unwin.

Nozick, Robert. 1974. *Anarchy, state, and utopia*. New York: Basic Books.

Oldenquist, Andrew, and Menachem Rosner, eds. 1991. *Alienation, community, and work*. Contributions in sociology, no. 96. Westport, Conn.: Greenwood.

Pejovich, Svetojar. 1966. *The market-planned economy of Yugoslavia.* Minneapolis: University of Minnesota Press.

———. 1969. The firm, monetary policy, and property rights in a planned economy. *Western Economic Journal* 7:193–200.

———. 1973. The banking system and the investment behavior of the Yugoslav firm. In *Plan and market: Economic reform in eastern Europe,* ed. Morris Bornstein, 285–311. New Haven: Yale University Press.

———. ed. 1978. *The codetermination movement in the West.* London: Heath Levington.

Perrow, Charles. 1986. *Complex organizations.* 3d ed. New York: Random House.

Pfeffer, Jeffrey, and Nancy Langton. 1988. Wage inequality and the organization of work: The case of academic departments. *Administrative Science Quarterly* 33:588–606.

Plant, Raymond. 1989. Socialism, markets, and end states. In Le Grand and Estrin (1989a), 50–77.

Prychitko, David L. 1988. Marxism and decentralized socialism. *Critical Review* 2:132–39.

Putterman, Louis. 1984. On some recent explanations of why capital hires labor. *Economic Inquiry* 22:171–87.

———. 1988a. The firm as an association versus the firm as a commodity: Efficiency, rights, and ownership. *Economics and Philosophy* 4:243–66.

———. 1988b. Marx and disequilibrium: Comment. *Economics and Philosophy* 4:333–36.

Rachels, James. 1978. What people deserve. In *Justice and economic distribution,* ed. John Arthur and William H. Shaw, 150–63. Englewood Cliffs, N.J.: Prentice Hall.

Rawls, John. 1971. *A theory of justice.* Cambridge: Harvard University Press.

Reid, J. D., and R. C. Faith. 1980. The union as its members' agent. CE 80-9-6. Fairfax, Va.: George Mason University, Center for Study of Public Choice.

Reiman, Jeffrey. 1987. Exploitation, force, and the moral assessment of capitalism: Thoughts on Roemer and Cohen. *Philosophy and Public Affairs* 16:3–41.

———. 1989. An alternative to "distributive Marxism": Further thoughts on Roemer, Cohen, and exploitation. In *Analyzing Marxism, Canadian Journal of Philosophy,* suppl. vol. 15, ed. Robert Ware and Kai Nielsen, 299–332. Calgary: University of Calgary Press.

Roemer, John. 1982a. *A general theory of exploitation and class.* Cambridge: Harvard University Press.

———. 1982b. Property relations vs. surplus value in Marxian exploitation. *Philosophy and Public Affairs* 11:281–314.

———. 1985. Should Marxists be interested in exploitation? *Philosophy and Public Affairs* 14:30–65.

———. 1988. *Free to lose.* Cambridge: Harvard University Press.

Rothbard, Murray. 1963. *For a new liberty.* New York: Macmillan.

———. 1972. *America's great depression.* Los Angeles: Nash Publishing Co.

Rutland, Peter. 1985. *The myth of the plan.* Lasalle, Ill.: Open Court.

Samuelson, Paul A. 1967. *Economics.* 7th ed. New York: McGraw Hill.

Schumpeter, Joseph A. 1942. *Capitalism, socialism, and democracy.* New York: Harper and Row.

———. 1961. *The theory of economic development.* Trans. Redver Opie. Harvard economic studies, vol. 44. Cambridge: Harvard University Press.

Schweickart, David. 1980. *Capitalism or worker control?* New York: Praeger.

——. 1987a. Market socialist capitalist roaders: A comment on Arnold. *Economics and Philosophy* 3:308–19.

——. 1987b. A reply to Arnold's reply. *Economics and Philosophy* 3:331–34.

Seabright, Paul. 1989. Social choice and social theories. *Philosophy and Public Affairs* 18:365–87.

Seeman, Melvin. 1991. Sentiments and structures: Strategies for research in alienation. In Oldenquist and Rosner (1991), 17–34.

Selucky, Radoslav. 1979. *Marxism, socialism, freedom.* New York: St. Martin's.

Sen, Amartya. 1987. Equality of what? In *Liberty, equality, and the law*, ed. Sterling M. McMurrin, 137–62. Salt Lake City: University of Utah Press.

Shapiro, Daniel. 1989. Reviving the socialist calculation debate: A defense of Hayek against Lange. *Social Philosophy & Policy* 6:139–59.

Simon, Herbert. 1961. *Administrative behavior.* 2d ed. New York: Macmillan.

——. 1978. Rationality as process and as product of thought. *American Economic Review* 68:1–16.

Sirc, Ljubo. 1979. *The Yugoslav economy under self-management.* New York: St. Martin's.

Stone, Karen. 1974. The orgins of job structures in the steel industry. *Review of Radical Political Economy* 6:61–97.

Stuckey, John. 1983. *Vertical integration and joint ventures in the aluminum industry.* Cambridge: Harvard University Press.

Thomas, Hendrik. 1982. The performance of the Mondragon cooperatives in Spain. In Jones and Svejnar (1982), 129–35.

Thomas, Hendrik, and C. Logan. 1982. *Mondragon: An economic analysis.* London: Allen and Unwin.

United States Department of Justice. 1984. *U.S. Department of Justice Merger Guidelines.* Washington, D.C.: U.S. Department of Justice.

Vanek, Jan. 1972. *The economics of workers' management: A Yugoslav case study.* London: Allen and Unwin.

Vanek, Jaroslav. 1970. *The general theory of labor-managed economies.* Ithaca, N.Y.: Cornell University Press.

——. 1977a. *The labor-managed economy.* Ithaca, N.Y.: Cornell University Press.

——. 1977b. The Yugoslav economy viewed through the theory of labor management. In Vanek (1977a).

Wagner, Richard E. 1989. *To promote the general welfare.* San Francisco: Pacific Research Institute.

Ward, Benjamin. 1958. The firm in Illyria: Market syndicalism. *American Economic Review* 48:566–89.

Wartenberg, Thomas. 1982. Species being and human nature in Marx. *Human Studies* 5:77–95.

Williamson, Oliver. 1975. *Markets and hierarchies: Analysis and antitrust implications.* New York: Free Press.

——. 1983. Organization form, residual claimants, and corporate control. *Journal of Law & Economics* 26:351–66.

——. 1985. *The economic institutions of capitalism.* New York: Free Press.

Winter, David. 1989. Market socialism and the reform of the capitalist economy. In Le Grand and Estrin (1989a), 139–64.

Wolfson, M. 1985. Empirical evidence of incentive problems and their mitigation in oil and gas tax shelter programs. In *Principals and agents: The structure of busi-*

ness, ed. J. Pratt and R. Zeckhauser, 101–25. Cambridge: Harvard Business School Press.

Young, Gary. 1978. Justice and capitalist production: Marx on bourgeois ideology. *Canadian Journal of Philosophy* 8:421–57.

Zald, M. 1988. Review essay: The new institutional economics. *American Journal of Sociology* 93:701–8.

Index

Accounting firms, 148, 160–61, 208, 219–20, 275n.24, 280n.10. *See also* Auditing

Acquisitions, of firms, 216, 277n.15, 280n.6. *See also* Firm-market boundary

Adverse selection, 114–16, 174, 193, 207, 231–32, 235. *See also* Moral hazard

Affected interests principle, 241–42

Albert, Michael, 266n.10

Alchian, Armen, 101–4, 106–8, 122–23

Alienability, right of, 135, 151, 246–47

Alienation, 28–29, 46, 244, 267n.24. *See also* Commodity fetishism
  absence of, in market socialism, 51–52, 56, 62, 63, 182, 261, 281n.4
  in free enterprise systems, 29, 50–51

Alternatives, 85–92, 277n.6. *See also* Exploitation
  lack of, under market socialism, 180
  no-real-alternatives condition, 86–89, 162

Arneson, Richard, 277n.10

Asset specificities, 116–21, 137–40, 169. *See also* Quasi-rents
  human, 158–61, 164

Assets, valuation of, 199–200
  exploitation through, 219–21

Auditing, 208
  of cooperatives, 219–21, 235
  of corporations, 148

Banks, under market socialism, 48, 54, 199, 222

Barzel, Yoram, 109–10, 133–35

Behavioral assumptions. *See* Opportunism; Rationality

Board of directors, 94–95, 98–99, 137, 141, 148–50, 208–12, 245
  monitoring of, 149, 275nn.25–27, 280n.10

Bondholders. *See* Debtholders

Boss, the, 98, 136

Brenkert, George, 85

Buchanan, Allen, 264n.12

Burden of proof. *See also* Economic systems
  of critics of economic systems, 19–21, 27–29
  of defenders of economic systems, 21

Bureaucracy. *See* Hierarchy; Organizations

Business cycle, 18, 41, 53, 156–57

Buyouts, leveraged. *See* Debt financing

Capital, human, 158–61, 164. *See also* Asset specificities; Unions

Capital providers, 98–99, 109, 134–36, 141–46, 207, 243. *See also* Classical capitalist firm; Cooperative; Corporation
  in Mondragon, 167–68

Capital requirements, large. *See* Corporation

Capital reserve fund, 47, 62, 63, 99, 175, 199, 202–3

Capital, social ownership of, 212–13. *See also* Capital usage fee
  forms of, 8–10, 44, 234–54
  in the worker control-state ownership model, 47–50, 175–76, 218–19, 260

Capital usage fee, 278–79n.24
  and exploitation, 218–21

Capital usage fee (*cont.*)
and new investment, 53, 97
and social ownership, 47–49, 53, 59,
62–63, 99, 175
Capitalism/socialism dispute, 1–5, 232–33
economic issues in, 15–16, 23–26,
231–33
philosophical issues in, 13, 16, 25–26,
59, 64
Capitalist economic system. *See* Free
enterprise system
Capitalization, of decisions, 135–36, 196
Central contracting agent, 98, 106,
108–9, 130–34, 271n.9. *See also*
Classical capitalist firm;
Cooperative
Central planning. *See* Planning
Ceteris paribus clauses, 110–11, 264n.19
Classical capitalist firm, 216, 249, 253,
278nn.18,21
capital provision in, 94, 98, 134–35,
200–201
central contracting agent in, 130–34, 194
defined, 94–95, 98, 127, 272n.5
director of the firm's product in,
133–34, 194
explanation of, 106–11, 126–36
monitoring in, 106–9, 122–23,
127–35, 188–92, 194
residual claimancy in, 98, 106,
108–10, 132–36, 196–97, 201
ultimate decision-making authority
in, 98, 135, 141–46, 201
Coase, Ronald, 101–2, 137
Cohen, G. A., 58–59, 67, 85, 268n.3
Commodity fetishism, 50, 56
absence of, in market socialism,
52–54, 62, 63
evils of, 53
Competition, 83, 122–24, 140. *See also*
Efficiency; Free enterprise system;
Markets
competitive process, 38–39, 73
perfect, 73–74
Contribution. *See also* Entrepreneur;
Exploitation; Inequality; Workers
of the capitalist and the worker,
57–58, 67–68, 70
distinguished from the value thereof,
69–70

economic value of, 70–74, 76–80,
87–88, 157, 176, 178, 184, 275n.32,
277n.9, 282n.14
Cooperative, worker, 99, 165–69,
253–54, 266n.17, 271n.7, 277n.11.
See also Equity ownership;
Investment; Market socialist
economic system; State; Workers
capital provision in, 198–203, 207,
211–13, 236–40, 243, 246–48,
279n.28
central contracting agent in, 193–95,
210–11
director of the firm's product in,
193–95, 210–11
equity ownership of, 234–46, 281n.7
expansion and contraction of,
181–84, 235, 250
as a form of social ownership, 9, 46,
63, 93–94, 175, 240–41
formation of new, 186, 222, 250–51,
253
managers in, 175–76, 193–98,
206–15, 278n.17
mandated under market socialism,
96
monitoring in, 187–96, 206–15,
235–36, 279n.1
residual claimancy in, 99, 175, 177,
181, 184–85, 191, 193, 201, 204,
207, 211–13, 234
self-management in, 46, 49, 51, 62,
63, 175, 236–38, 244, 260,
279n.28, 281n.4
stability and instability of, 236–37,
239, 271n.4
ultimate decision-making authority
in, 98–99, 167, 175–77, 181,
184–85, 189–91, 193, 201, 207,
212, 216, 247, 280n.6
valuation of assets in, 199–200, 202
workers' councils in, 165, 206–14,
245–47
Corporation, closed, 95, 125–26, 152.
See also Board of directors
Corporation, highly leveraged, 145–46
Corporation, multidivisional, 125,
151–52, 216
Corporation, open, 136–53, 196. *See
also* Free enterprise system

as a bulwark against exploitation,
138–40
capital providers in, 141–46, 272n.4
capital requirements of, 136–40,
146
defined, 94–95, 98–99, 125, 136–37
entrepreneurship in, 147
equity ownership in, 141–51, 185,
207, 212–14
liability to execution of debt, 143–46,
151
management in, 146–50, 215
monitoring in, 147–51, 230
residual claimancy in, 140–52, 185
ultimate decision-making authority
in, 95, 98–99, 141–46, 216
Councils, workers'. *See* Cooperative
Counterfactual conditionals, 122–23

Debt financing, 126, 239, 247–48,
252–53. *See also* Quasi-equity
ownership
in the open corporation, 145–46, 216,
230, 272n.4, 274n.21, 274–75n.22,
282n.10
Debt, liability to execution of, 135–36,
142–44, 153
as negative residuals, 144
Debtholders, 143, 212, 221, 238–39
contrasted with equity owners, 99
Decision control, 148–49, 152
Decision management, 149, 152
Decision-making authority. *See* Ultimate
decision-making authority
Demsetz, Harold, 106–9, 122–23, 149,
275n.26
Depreciation fund. *See* Capital reserve
fund
Desert, 67, 197–98, 224, 260, 278n.22,
282n.14. *See also* Reciprocity
Director of the firm's product, 98,
133–35. *See also* Classical capitalist
firm; Cooperative; Corporation;
Entrepreneur
Drèze, Jacques, 277n.11

Economic growth, state control of, 48,
53, 218, 241–42, 249, 255. *See also*
Investment
Economic issues in the capitalism/social-

ism dispute, 16, 23–26, 231–33,
263nn.1,8
Economic systems, 4–5, 22, 196–97,
232–33, 266nn.10–11. *See also* Free
enterprise system; Market socialist
economic system; Socialism
complete defense of, 29–30
criticisms of, 27–29, 31, 232,
264nn.11,14, 264–65n.24
differences between free enterprise
and market socialist, 93–97
and exploitation, 97, 99–100, 169–71,
173–75, 217
limited defense of, 23–24, 31, 38–42
stout defense of, 30–31
type-defining features of, 23–31, 93
well-motivated, 32, 232–33
Economics. *See* Capitalism/socialism
dispute
Efficiency, economic, 266n.10. *See also*
Exploitation; Free enterprise
system; Markets; Transactions cost
efficiencies and inefficiencies
connection with exploitation, 91–92
and evolution of organizations,
103–6, 110–11, 215
of hierarchies, 101–2, 131
presumption of, 105, 122
as a social virtue, 42–43
Ellerman, David, 236, 238–43,
281nn.5–7, 285nn.5–8
Empirical data
on bailouts, 222–23
on capital consumption, 204–5
on debt-equity ratios, 274–75n.22
on income differentials, 177–78
role and relevance of, 124, 167, 169
Employment relation, 126, 149,
154–56, 158, 163. *See also* Workers
Entrepreneur, 98, 162, 182–84, 246,
249, 253. *See also* Central contracting agent; Director of the firm's
product; Market mechanism;
Profits
in the classical capitalist firm, 109,
111, 133–35
contribution of, 76–77, 81–84
in the corporation, 141, 147
in market socialism, 186–87, 194–98,
211, 236, 239, 243–44

Equality of material condition, 13, 26,
     27, 59, 62, 242, 249, 254, 259. *See*
     also Inequality
   explanation for, in a market socialist
     system, 60–61, 63, 255–57
Equity ownership, 95, 141–46, 148, 191,
     201, 254. *See also* Corporation;
     Exploitation; Quasi-equity owner-
     ship
   of cooperatives, 234–46, 281n.7
   as a cushion for debtholders, 145,
     212, 221, 239, 248, 250, 252,
     257
   vs. debt financing, 145–46, 272n.4,
     274n.21, 274–75n.22, 282n.10
   defined, 98, 136, 273n.12
   in Mondragon, 167, 238–39
   transactions cost efficiencies of, 144,
     205, 212, 214
Estrin, Saul, 50–51, 61, 186, 250–53,
     267n.20, 277n.12, 282n.9
Evolution. *See* Organizational forms
Exchanges. *See also* Contribution;
     Markets
   fair, 74, 76–77, 79–82, 84, 88–90,
     265nn.10,11, 270n.14
   on the leading edge of markets in
     transition, 76–77, 83–84, 157
Exploitation, economic, 87, 90–92,
     134–35, 180, 258–60, 268nn.32,2,
     268–69n.5, 269n.12, 270nn.17,20.
     See also Alternatives; Employment
     relation; Expropriation hazards;
     Quasi-rents; Reciprocity
   abolition of, 59, 62, 63
   in the absence of alternative organiza-
     tional forms, 168, 217, 232–33
   in the absence of equity ownership,
     141–46, 201–5, 211–13, 223,
     253–54
   as the appropriation of quasi-rents,
     120–21, 127–28, 278–79n.24
   of capital providers, 144, 198–205,
     219–21, 279n.27
   of customers, 186, 250, 280n.11
   determinants of, 170–71, 259–60
   of equity owners by managers,
     146–47, 150, 230, 239, 244
   and the firm-market boundary,
     138–39

forcing, as a condition of, 85,
     268n.31, 270n.17
   in a free enterprise system, 183, 188,
     276n.37, 280n.11
   and full state ownership, 243–44
   general conditions for, 111–17,
     169–70, 174–75
   through holding companies, 252–53
   of managers, 195, 197, 210, 237, 239,
     243–44
   Marxist charge of, 17, 19, 20, 57–59,
     65–68, 85–86
   through organizational forms, 100,
     174–75, 231–33, 254, 277–78n.16
   of quasi-equity owners, 247–48
   of taxpayers, 202–4, 211–13, 228–31,
     244, 280n.11
   theories of, 65–66, 70, 84, 85–86,
     87–90
   of workers by managers, 194–96,
     213–14, 231–32, 237
   of workers in free enterprise systems,
     154–55, 162–64
   of and by workers in market
     socialism, 176–79, 181–83, 187–91,
     231, 235
Expropriation hazards, 124, 128,
     137–40, 161, 189, 216–17, 247
Externalities. *See* Social irrationalities

Firm-market boundary, 102, 140, 189,
     215–17, 277n.15
Forcing. *See* Exploitation
Franchise arrangement, 217
Free enterprise system, 17, 188, 212,
     236, 241–43, 248, 258–61,
     280n.11. *See also* Exploitation;
     Labor Markets; Markets
   defined, 5–7, 93–96, 264n.13, 270n.2
   efficiency of, 39, 41–43, 73, 186, 217
   inequality in, 59–61, 268n.35
   new investment in, 224, 229–33, 253
   organizations in, 97–99
Frequency (of transactions), 117–18
Fundamental transformation, 117–18,
     120–21, 158, 169

Good society, visions of the, 13–16, 49,
     91–92, 95, 261, 263n.9. *See also*
     Vices; Virtues

based on reasonable hopes, 14, 29,
91, 233, 263n.1, 264n.23
relationship between economic
systems and, 15–16, 27–32,
232–33, 264n.13
socialist, 26–27, 49, 63–64, 91, 94,
181, 237, 241–44, 249, 252–53,
256, 259, 267n.26, 281n.4
Good will, 200, 219–21

Hahnel, Robin, 266n.11
Hayek, F. A., 18, 31, 36–39, 264n.14
Heilbroner, Robert, 35, 265n.2
Hierarchy, 101–2, 127, 177, 254, 280n.7
efficiencies of, 130–32, 138
inefficiencies of, 140, 216
Holding companies, 250–53
Holmstrom, Nancy, 268n.31
Honoré, A. M., 43–44
Horizon. *See* Time horizon
Hume, David, 276n.3

Inequality, 47, 59, 60, 249–50, 252,
259–60. *See also* Equality of material condition
of workers' income under market
socialism, 176–81, 183–85
Injustice, distributive. *See also*
Redistribution
and exploitation, 19, 80, 90, 92
Innovation, 103
Input providers (suppliers), 98, 107,
108, 127, 130–31, 142, 271n.10
Integration, vertical, 102, 120, 137–38
Investment, state control of, 41, 48–49,
53–54, 62, 166, 176, 267nn.20,21.
See also Economic growth;
Organizations; Political officials
cooperative control of, 235, 238,
240–41, 276n.4
exploitation through, 222–25,
228–29, 257–58
mechanism of, 221–23, 280n.12
motivations for, 48, 53, 63, 218–19,
255
Irrationalities, social. *See* Social
irrationalities

Jay, Peter, 246–50, 282n.8
Jensen, Michael, 274n.19, 279nn.25,27

"Junk bonds," 145
Justice, theories of distributive, 16, 19,
26, 90, 157, 180, 259–61

Kornai, Janos, 266n.15

Labor markets, 243, 247. *See also*
Exploitation; Workers
in a free enterprise system, 6,
154–57, 162–64, 276n.37, 281n.2
in other systems, 10, 96, 181–86, 235,
243, 247
Labor theory of value, 57, 269n.6
Lange, Oskar, 39
Lavoie, Don, 265nn.5,6
Law of one majority, 245
Lawyers, disparaging remarks about,
79, 104, 121, 159–60, 170, 189,
223, 231, 263n.6
Leading edge, of markets in transition.
See Exchanges; Markets
Leasing, of capital goods, 142. *See also*
Rental
Lehn, Kenneth, 275n.26
Liability to execution of debt. *See* Debt
Limited liability, of corporations, 143,
151
Luck, 38, 109, 278n.22

Maintenance rules for capital goods,
235, 279n.26
and exploitation, 202
and social ownership, 47, 49, 62, 63,
99, 175, 198
Managers, 94–95, 98–99, 243–44,
247–48. *See also* Classical capitalist
firm; Cooperative; Corporation;
Entrepreneur; Exploitation;
Monitor(ing); Workers
Market mechanism (process), 38–41,
49, 53, 63, 73–75, 138, 157, 166
Market socialist economic system,
253–61, 267n.22, 270n.1. *See also*
Cooperative; Economic systems;
Exploitation; Socialism
differences between free enterprise
systems and, 93–94, 96, 99–100,
196–97, 217, 231–33
differences between Yugoslavia,
Mondragon and, 165–69

Market socialist economic system (*cont.*)
  equity ownership in, 234–38
  Estrin's model, 250–53, 282nn.9–11
  full state ownership model, 9, 243–45
  Jay's model, 246–50
  opportunism in, 172–75
  ownership rights in, 44–49, 198–200,
    212–14, 218–19, 233
  worker control-state ownership
    model, 46–49, 62–63, 99, 166–69,
    234–36, 245–46, 248, 253,
    255–60, 281nn.1,2
Markets, 266n.15. *See also* Exchanges;
    Prices
  chaotic, 78–79, 275–76n.36
  competitively efficient, 73–74, 76–79,
    80–84, 90, 157, 162, 256
  for cooperative shares, 237–38
  for corporate control, 150, 214
  costs of, 137–39
  efficiencies of, 40–42, 73
  vs. firms, 101–2
  ideal, 72–74, 80–81
  inefficiencies of, 41, 73
  labor. *See* Labor markets
  for managers, 209–10
  in a socialist system, 40–41, 46, 62,
    63, 166
  stagnant, 78, 79, 82–84, 87, 90,
    162–63, 253
  stagnant, in market socialism, 181–87,
    237
  stock. *See* Stock markets
  in transition, 76, 83–84, 90, 157, 162,
    269–70n.13, 276n.37
Marx, Karl, 17, 48, 50–53, 56–58, 60,
    263–64n.10, 266n.16
Meckling, William, 274n.19,
    279nn.25,27
Mergers, 216–17. *See also* Firm-market
    boundary
Milgrom, Paul, 272n.17
Miller, David, 55–56, 267n.20, 268n.2,
    270n.16
Mises, Ludwig von, 18, 31, 36–39
Mnookin, Robert, 104
Moe, Terry, 226–29, 272n.2
Mondragon, cooperatives in, 9, 129,
    167–69, 180, 191, 201, 230, 238–39
Monitor(ing), 273n.7, 274nn.16,17

  and the assumption of opportunism,
    172–75
  in the classical capitalist firm, 106–9,
    122–23, 127–35, 188–92, 194
  in the cooperative, 187–96, 206–15,
    235–36, 279n.1
  in the corporation, 146–51, 230
  defined, 98, 107–8, 129–30, 132–33
  of political organizations, 228
Moral hazard, 115–16, 120, 134, 148,
    232, 235, 239
  dynamics of, 173–74, 193
  in the small cooperative, 207
  of state control of new investment,
    222–24, 257

Nove, Alec, 35

Opportunism, 119–21, 231, 257, 259,
    272n.17, 279n.2. *See also* Shirking
  assumption of, 112, 170–75
  defined, 112–113, 172–73, 271n.11,
    272–73n.6
  and the need for monitoring, 107–8,
    127, 134, 147, 150, 230, 274n.16
  propensity for, 113–15, 129, 171–75
  by workers, 114, 128, 160, 187–88,
    191, 193, 205
Organizational forms, 33, 124–26, 168,
    188, 232–33, 254. *See also* Classical
    capitalist firm; Cooperative; Corpo-
    ration; Exploitation; Transactions
    cost efficiencies and inefficiencies
  and economic roles, 98
  evolutionary theory of, 102–6, 110,
    122–23, 140, 217, 271n.8, 272n.2
Organizations, non-profit, 274n.17
Organizations, public (state), 95, 251,
    281n.6
  differences between private and,
    225–26, 272n.2
  monitoring in, 228
  structural inefficiencies of, 225–30
Ownership. *See* Property rights

Partnerships, 125–26, 151
  residual claimancy in, 142, 152–53
  limited, 141–42, 274n.14
Planning, central, 10–11, 31, 44, 71,
    101, 254. *See also* Investment

problems of, 36–38, 260, 265nn.5–7
repudiation of, 34–36, 41,
    265nn.1,2,8
Planning, indicative, 282nn.9,11
Planning, of new investment. *See*
    Investment
Political officials, 225–29, 244–45
    monitoring of, 228, 279n.4
    role of, in investment decisions,
        221–23
    time horizons of, 213, 225
Portfolio problem. *See* Risk bearing
Power, 273n.13
    as an explanation for exploitation,
        155–56
    as an explanation for hierarchy, 131,
        273nn.10,11
    political, 225–26
Prices, 38, 46, 166, 269–70n.13. *See also*
    Exchanges; Markets
Production for exchange vs. production
    for use, 52
Profits, pure (entrepreneurial), 83, 141,
    256, 269n.9. *See also* Residuals
    and the entrepreneur's contribution,
        76–78, 197, 244, 270n.15, 278n.22
    and the market process, 38, 73–74,
        81, 151, 162–63
Property rights, 7, 11, 166–67, 232–33,
    241, 254, 266n.11. *See also*
    Cooperative; Free enterprise
    system; Market socialist economic
    system; Residuals
    full liberal ownership, 43–44, 46–47,
        94
    full state ownership, 9–11, 12, 18,
        44–46, 93–94, 95, 243–45,
        281n.6
    management and income rights, 44,
        46–49, 51, 59, 61, 62, 99
Public choice, theory of, 256, 280n.13
Pure rental firm. *See* Rental

Quasi-equity ownership, 246–50
Quasi-rents, 118–21, 169, 204,
    279nn.27,5. *See also* Asset specifici-
    ties; Exploitation
    of capital, 138–41, 160, 198, 213–14
    of firms, 200, 204–5, 212, 219–20,
        235, 253, 278–79n.24

of workers, 127, 154–59, 164,
    184–85, 213–14, 220

Rachels, James, 282n.14
Rationality, bounded, 111–12, 117, 121,
    169–70, 272n.18
Rawls, John, 263n.9
Reciprocity, failure of. *See also*
    Exploitation
    in the cooperative, 177–79
    in the employment relation, 154
    as a necessary condition for exploita-
        tion, 57–59, 66–70, 84–86, 88,
        259, 268n.3, 270n.16
Redistribution, 60, 65, 242, 256–57,
    268n.35. *See also* Injustice
Reiman, Jeffrey, 85–86, 268n.31
Rental
    of capital goods, 47, 142–44, 201–3
    pure rental firm, 142–44, 199,
        274nn.19,20, 279n.25
Residual claimants, 46, 51, 243, 244,
    250. *See also* Classical capitalist
    firm; Cooperative; Corporation;
    Partnerships
    conflict of interest with debtors, 143
    current vs. future, in the cooperative,
        211–12
Residual rights of control, 130–31,
    166–67, 266n.12, 272n.8
Residuals, 94–95, 134, 143–44, 185
    in a market socialist system, 60, 194,
        220, 230, 256
Risk bearing, 141, 145, 147–48, 152,
    236, 238, 247
Roberts, John, 272n.17
Roemer, John, 264n.12, 268n.32,
    268–69n.5

Schwartz, Justin, 268n.31
Schweickart, David, 67, 266n.18
Secession of units in cooperatives,
    216–17
Securities analysts, 150
Self-management. *See* Cooperative
Shareholders. *See* Equity ownership
Shirking, 170, 271n.14, 272–73n.6,
    278n.17. *See also* Monitor(ing);
    Opportunism
    by managers, 108, 134, 191, 195, 210

Shirking (*cont.*)
  and the need for monitoring, 51,
    106–8, 129, 147, 187, 193, 210, 236,
Simon, Herbert, 111
Social choice, theory of, 280nn.8,14
Social democracy, 7–8, 263n1, 268n.35
Social irrationalities, 157–58, 241–43,
    249, 258. *See also* Good society
  in free enterprise systems, 54–55,
    254
  and market socialism, 41, 62–63, 218,
    222, 229, 257
Socialism, economic system of, 7–11,
    233, 244–45, 254–55, 261,
    266n.13, 267n.20, 268n.36, 270n.2.
    See also Cooperative; Economic
    systems; Market socialist economic
    system
  Marxian, 8–11
  the meaning of, 4, 7–11, 26–27, 237,
    240–41, 248–50, 252, 282nn.8,9
  and private property rights, 44–46,
    236, 249
  wage labor in, 45
State, the, 270n.20. *See also* Cooperative;
    Exploitation; Investment; Market
    socialist economic system;
    Organizations; Property rights
  as capital provider, 44–48, 198–203,
    218–19
  as a representative of society, 48,
    212–13, 218, 244–45, 255
  responsible for correcting social irra-
    tionalities, 53–55, 257–58
State ownership of capital, 9, 44–46
Stock markets, 79, 95, 185, 207. *See also*
    Markets
  in Estrin's model, 251–52
  function of, 150–51, 182, 213–14
  in Jay's model, 246–49
Stockholders. *See* Equity ownership

Taxation, 61, 242
Taxpayers. *See* Exploitation
Team production. *See* Monitor(ing);
    Shirking
Thurow, Lester, 35, 265n.2
Time horizon, 168, 213, 244, 253
  of the classical capitalist, 108, 135–36,
    201

  in the cooperative, 201–5, 234–35,
    238–39, 247
Transactions cost efficiencies and ineffi-
    ciencies, 102–6, 161, 184, 188–89,
    273–74n.15. *See also* Classical capi-
    talist firm; Cooperative;
    Corporation; Equity ownership,
    Exploitation; Fundamental
    transformation; Hierarchy
  of corporations vs. classical capitalist
    firms, 140, 215
  as explanations, 104–6, 110, 122–25,
    273n.14, 275n.33
  of policies and procedures, 103–5,
    158–61, 272n.3
  of rentals, 142–44, 201–2
Transactions costs, of firms vs. markets,
    101–2
Transactions, features of. *See* Asset
    specificities; Frequency;
    Uncertainty
Type-defining features. *See* Economic
    systems

Ultimate decision-making authority, 95,
    98, 243, 244–45, 251, 271n.9,
    273n.8. *See also* Classical capitalist
    firm; Cooperative; Corporation
Uncertainty, 116–17, 183, 272n.18
  political, 225, 227
Unions, 158–59, 184–85, 243, 275n.34

Value, economic. *See* Contribution;
    Quasi-rents
Valuation of assets. *See* Assets
Vices, social, 13, 22, 25, 27–33, 64. *See
    also* Alienation; Commodity
    fetishism; Economic systems;
    Exploitation; Inequality; Social
    irrationalities
  of free enterprise systems, 18–21,
    27–29, 61–62, 96–97
  of socialist systems, 18, 31, 34–38,
    268n.36
Virtues, social, 13, 15, 23–25, 62, 64,
    260–61, 264n.18. *See also* Economic
    growth; Efficiency; Equality of
    material condition; Investment
  conceived as the absence of vices, 21,
    33

Williamson, Oliver, 111–12, 115,
    273n.13
Winter, David, 267n.20
Workers, 98, 99, 243. *See also*
    Cooperative; Employment relation;
    Markets
  exploitation of, in a free enterprise
    system, 153–64, 276n.37
  exploitation of and by, in market

socialism, 176–79, 181–83, 187–91,
    231, 235
  quasi-rents of, 127, 154–56, 158

Yugoslavia, cooperatives in, 9, 165–67,
    204–5, 222–23, 240

Zone of acceptance, 109, 130, 272n.12